UNITED NATIONS CONFERENCE ON TRADE AND DEVELOPMENT

TRADE AND DEVELOPMENT REPORT 2017

BEYOND AUSTERITY: TOWARDS A GLOBAL NEW DEAL

Report by the secretariat of the
United Nations Conference on Trade and Development

UNITED NATIONS
New York and Geneva, 2017

Note

Symbols of United Nations documents are composed of capital letters combined with figures. Mention of such a symbol indicates a reference to a United Nations document.

The designations employed and the presentation of the material in this publication do not imply the expression of any opinion whatsoever on the part of the Secretariat of the United Nations concerning the legal status of any country, territory, city or area, or of its authorities, or concerning the delimitation of its frontiers or boundaries.

Material in this publication may be freely quoted or reprinted, but acknowledgement is requested, together with a reference to the document number. A copy of the publication containing the quotation or reprint should be sent to the UNCTAD secretariat; e-mail: tdr@unctad.org.

UNCTAD/TDR/2017

UNITED NATIONS PUBLICATION

Sales No. E.17.II.D.5

ISBN 978-92-1-112913-7
eISBN 978-92-1-362245-2
ISSN 0255-4607

Foreword

In sharp contrast to the ambitions of the 2030 Agenda for Sustainable Development, the world economy remains unbalanced in ways that are not only exclusionary, but also destabilizing and dangerous for the political, social and environmental health of the planet. Even when economic growth has been possible, whether through a domestic consumption binge, a housing boom or exports, the gains have disproportionately accrued to the privileged few. At the same time, a combination of too much debt and too little demand at the global level has hampered sustained expansion of the world economy.

Austerity measures adopted in the wake of the global financial crisis nearly a decade ago have compounded this state of affairs. Such measures have hit the world's poorest communities the hardest, leading to further polarization and heightening people's anxieties about what the future might hold. Some political elites have been adamant that there is no alternative, which has proved fertile economic ground for xenophobic rhetoric, inward-looking policies and a beggar-thy-neighbour stance. Others have identified technology or trade as the culprits behind exclusionary hyperglobalization, but this too distracts from an obvious point: without significant, sustainable and coordinated efforts to revive global demand by increasing wages and government spending, the global economy will be condemned to continued sluggish growth, or worse.

The *Trade and Development Report 2017* argues that now is the ideal time to crowd in private investment with the help of a concerted fiscal push – a global new deal – to get the growth engines revving again, and at the same time help rebalance economies and societies that, after three decades of hyperglobalization, are seriously out of kilter. However, in today's world of mobile finance and liberalized economic policies, no country can do this on its own without risking capital flight, a currency collapse and the threat of a deflationary spiral. What is needed, therefore, is a globally coordinated strategy of expansion led by increased public expenditures, with all countries being offered the opportunity of benefiting from a simultaneous boost to their domestic and external markets.

The Sustainable Development Goals (SDGs) agreed to by all members of the United Nations two years ago provide the political impetus for this much-needed shift towards global macroeconomic policy coordination. The *Trade and Development Report 2017* calls for more exacting and encompassing policy measures to address global and national asymmetries in resource mobilization, technological know-how, market power and political influence caused by hyperglobalization that have generated exclusionary outcomes, and will perpetuate them if no action is taken.

This *Report* argues that, with the appropriate combination of resources, policies and reforms, the international community has the tools available to galvanize the requisite investment push needed to achieve the ambitions of the SDGs and promote sustainable and inclusive outcomes at both global and national levels.

Mukhisa Kituyi
Secretary-General of UNCTAD

Acknowledgements

The *Trade and Development Report 2017* was prepared by a team led by Richard Kozul-Wright, Director of the Division on Globalization and Development Strategies. The team members included Diana Barrowclough, Stephanie Blankenburg, David Bicchetti, Rachid Bouhia, Elissa Braunstein, C.P. Chandrasekhar, Shaun Ferguson, Padmashree Gehl Sampath, Jayati Ghosh, Ricardo Gottschalk, Alex Izurieta, Pierre Kohler, Jörg Mayer, Nicolas Maystre, Stephanie Seguino and Edgardo Torija Zane.

Research support and inputs were provided by Andrew Cornford, Francis Cripps, Ian Orton, Walter Park and Guy Standing. Reviewers included Gary Dymski, Xiaolan Fu, David Kucera, Richard McGahey, Irmgard Nübler and Steven Toms.

Statistical support was provided by Lyubov Chumakova and Juan Pizarro, with the assistance of UNCTAD's Development Statistics and Information Branch, headed by Steve MacFeely.

The manuscript was edited by Praveen Bhalla and Sue Littleford with the assistance of Vania Robelo, with production and layout by Petra Hoffmann. Cover design by Sylvie Sahuc and Mariana Alt.

Contents

Chapter I

CURRENT TRENDS AND CHALLENGES IN THE WORLD ECONOMY

Chapter II

INCLUSIVE GROWTH: ISSUES AT STAKE

List of figures

Figure

Figure

Box figure

List of tables

List of boxes

Explanatory notes

Classification by country or commodity group

The classification of countries in this *Report* has been adopted solely for the purposes of statistical or analytical convenience and does not necessarily imply any judgement concerning the stage of development of a particular country or area.

There is no established convention for the designation of "developing", "transition" and "developed" countries or areas in the United Nations system. This *Report* follows the classification as defined in the *UNCTAD Handbook of Statistics 2016* (United Nations publication, sales no. B.16.II.D.6) for these three major country groupings (see http://unctad.org/en/PublicationsLibrary/tdstat41_en.pdf).

For statistical purposes, regional groupings and classifications by commodity group used in this *Report* follow generally those employed in the *UNCTAD Handbook of Statistics 2016* unless otherwise stated. The data for China do not include those for Hong Kong Special Administrative Region (Hong Kong SAR), Macao Special Administrative Region (Macao SAR) and Taiwan Province of China.

The terms "country" / "economy" refer, as appropriate, also to territories or areas.

References to "Latin America" in the text or tables include the Caribbean countries unless otherwise indicated.

References to "sub-Saharan Africa" in the text or tables include South Africa unless otherwise indicated.

When used, abbreviations for country names are based on ISO Alpha-3 country codes (https://www.iso.org/iso-3166-country-codes.html).

Other notes

References in the text to *TDR* are to the *Trade and Development Report* (of a particular year). For example, *TDR 2016* refers to *Trade and Development Report, 2016* (United Nations publication, sales no. E.16.II.D.5).

References in the text to the United States are to the United States of America and those to the United Kingdom are to the United Kingdom of Great Britain and Northern Ireland.

The term "dollar" ($) refers to United States dollars, unless otherwise stated.

The term "billion" signifies 1,000 million.

The term "tons" refers to metric tons.

Annual rates of growth and change refer to compound rates.

Exports are valued FOB and imports CIF, unless otherwise specified.

Use of a dash (–) between dates representing years, e.g. 1988–1990, signifies the full period involved, including the initial and final years.

An oblique stroke (/) between two years, e.g. 2000/01, signifies a fiscal or crop year.

A dot (.) in a table indicates that the item is not applicable.

Two dots (..) in a table indicate that the data are not available, or are not separately reported.

A dash (-) or a zero (0) in a table indicates that the amount is nil or negligible.

Decimals and percentages do not necessarily add up to totals because of rounding.

Abbreviations

BCBS	Basel Committee on Banking Supervision
BEA	Bureau of Economic Analysis (United States Department of Commerce)
BEPS	base erosion and profit shifting
BIS	Bank for International Settlements
BOPS	Balance of Payments Statistics (IMF database)
CEO	chief executive officer
CFS	consolidated financial statement (also UNCTAD CFS database)
CIS	Commonwealth of Independent States
CPI	Consumer price index
EIG	Economic Innovation Group
EU	European Union
FDI	foreign direct investment
FSF	Financial Stability Forum
G20	Group of 20
G7	Group of Seven
GCC	Gulf Cooperation Council
GCIP	Global Consumption and Income Project
GDP	gross domestic product
GPM	Global Policy Model (of the United Nations)
GVC	global value chain
ICT	information and communication technology
IFR	International Federation of Robotics
IFS	International Financial Statistics (IMF database)
ILO	International Labour Office (or Organization)
IMF	International Monetary Fund
INEGI	National Institute of Statistics and Geography (Spanish abbreviation for Instituto Nacional de Estadística y Geografía, México)
IPR	intellectual property right
IT	information technology
LAC	Latin America and the Caribbean
M&A	merger and acquisition
MNC	multinational corporation
NIE	newly industrializing economy
OECD	Organisation for Economic Co-operation and Development
OPEC	Organization of the Petroleum Exporting Countries
PFI	private finance initiative
PIAAC	Programme for the International Assessment of Adult Competencies
PPP	purchasing power parity
R&D	research and development
ROA	return on assets
SDG	Sustainable Development Goal
SOE	State-owned enterprise
TRIPS	Trade-Related Aspects of Intellectual Property Rights (WTO Agreement)
UBI	universal basic income
UN DESA	United Nations Department of Economic and Social Affairs
UNIDO	United Nations Industrial Development Organization
WTO	World Trade Organization

OVERVIEW

Fifty years ago, at New York's Riverside Church, Martin Luther King made a passionate plea for a more equal, more just, more peaceful and more dignified world. Calling for "a radical revolution of values", King concluded, "We must rapidly begin ... the shift from a thing-oriented society to a person-oriented society. When machines and computers, profit motives and property rights are considered more important than people, the giant triplets of racism, extreme materialism and militarism are incapable of being conquered".

There is a contemporary ring to King's call for a more inclusive agenda. The "giant triplets" that he warned about are resurfacing, accompanied by a retreat into resentful nationalism and xenophobic comfort zones. The gaps between the rich, the middle class and the poor have almost certainly widened since King's time. And across much of the world, the drive to achieve full employment with strong welfare provision was thrown into reverse gear decades ago, as governments effectively reinvented themselves as "enablers" rather than "providers".

Ten years after the gales of financial destruction originating in Wall Street swept across the heartland of America and beyond, the world economy remains marooned in a state of sub-standard growth, while the social and economic inequities exposed by the crisis show few signs of moderating. Governments have closed down the most egregious loopholes and toxic instruments exposed by the crisis; but however good their intentions, the reality is that few who caused the crash have been held accountable for their actions, and little has been done to tackle its root causes.

As "hyperglobalization" with the help of the very visible hand of the State has recovered its poise, business as usual has set in; the push for "light touch" regulation is under way yet again, and austerity has become the preferred response to "excessively" high levels of public debt. Meanwhile robots, rents and intellectual property rights are taking precedence over the livelihoods of people and their aspirations. History, it seems, has a troubling knack of repeating itself.

Unlike the textbook world of pure competition, hyperglobalization has led to a considerable concentration of economic power and wealth in the hands of a remarkably small number of people. This need not necessarily be antithetical to growth. But if history is any guide, it tends to generate political tensions that clash with wider public and social interests. Indeed, more clear-headed supporters of "the market", since Adam Smith, have warned of the political dangers that can follow the concentration of economic wealth. It is therefore hardly surprising to find a popular backlash against a system that is perceived to have become unduly biased in favour of a handful of large corporations, financial institutions and wealthy individuals.

The real threat now is to the underlying trust, cohesion and sense of justice that markets depend upon in order to function effectively. No social or economic order is safe if it fails to ensure a fair distribution of its benefits in good times and the costs in bad times.

Insisting that "there is no alternative" is yesterday's political slogan. People everywhere desire much the same thing: a decent job, a secure home, a safe environment, a better future for their children and a government that listens and responds to their concerns; in truth, they want a different deal from that offered by hyperglobalization. The 2030 Agenda for Sustainable Development, codified in a series of goals, targets and indicators, points in that direction. What is still needed is a supportive policy narrative and bold political leadership; there are hopeful signs that some of the discarded strategies and solutions that helped re-build the global economy after the Second World War are receiving a much welcomed twenty-first century makeover and are attracting a new generation determined to build a better world.

This time around, any new deal will need to "lift all boats" in both developing and developed countries and face up to the challenge that many of the imbalances inhibiting sustainable and inclusive growth are global in nature. Prosperity for all cannot be delivered by austerity-minded politicians, rent-seeking corporations and speculative bankers. What is urgently needed now is a global new deal.

The global economy: Ten years on

It is ten years since the world economy discovered the dangers of hyperglobalization. The sudden stop in interbank lending in August 2007, along with heightened counterparty risk, caused serious jitters in financial markets, plunged several financial institutions into an insolvency spiral and lit the fuse on a Great Recession. Most of these countries are yet to return to a sustainable growth trajectory.

Although the United States acted quickly to stem the financial collapse that came one year later, the subsequent recovery has been sluggish by historical standards, and unbalanced between the middle class and the wealthy, between Wall Street and Main Street, and between urban metropoles and smaller towns and rural communities. The crisis in Europe was more pronounced and has proved more obdurate, particularly in some peripheral economies where the resulting economic turmoil has had devastating social consequences. The rise in unemployment, in particular, has proved difficult to contain or reverse. A principal reason is that most developed countries, to varying degrees, retreated prematurely from the initial expansionary fiscal response to the crisis, relying instead on monetary policy. This helped banks and financial firms to stabilize and return to profit-making, but it was less successful in boosting consumer spending and investment. In response, policymakers have been nudging interest rates into negative territory in an unprecedented attempt to push banks to lend. Even so, a strong recovery has remained elusive.

Despite buoyant financial markets and signs of a cyclical bounce-back in Western Europe and Japan towards the end of the year, global economic growth in 2016 was well below the levels recorded in the run-up to the crisis. In the United States, signs of a slowdown towards the end of 2016 continued into 2017, with gross domestic product (GDP) growing at a rate of 1.4 per cent in the first quarter, while real wage growth remained sluggish despite falling unemployment, as reflected in a significant deceleration in household spending. Growth across the euro zone has varied significantly, being stronger in some of the smaller and poorer countries in the first half of 2017, but subdued in the core countries. The good news is that unemployment has, on average, dropped to single-digit levels (with some notable exceptions such as in Greece and Spain), although the quality of new employment is a concern.

The United Kingdom's economy remained unexpectedly buoyant in the second half of 2016, following the Brexit vote, as a result of a fall in the value of the pound sterling, which boosted exports and increased household spending, propelled by higher consumer borrowing and rising house prices. But the subsequent deceleration (down to 0.2 per cent GDP growth in the first quarter of 2017) may persist due to new political uncertainties generated by a hung parliament as the Government negotiates a Brexit deal. In Japan, the recent recovery is, in reality, an uptick from a prolonged period of low growth, largely driven by exports following a correction to the long-standing overvaluation of its currency.

The absence of a robust recovery in developed countries and renewed volatility of global capital flows have constrained economic growth in developing countries, albeit with considerable regional and country-level variation. In general, the rapid recovery from the initial financial shock of 2008 has given way to a persistent slowdown since 2011. Growth in the world's two most populous economies − China and India − remains relatively buoyant, but the pace is slower than before the crisis and faces some serious downside risks. The start of 2017 has seen other larger emerging economies move out of recession, but with little likelihood of growth at the rates registered in the first decade of the new millennium.

Two factors have been exercising a major influence on growth. The first is that oil and commodity prices, while emerging from their recent troughs, are still well below the highs witnessed during the boom years. This has dampened recovery in the commodity-exporting countries. Second, with developed economies abnegating responsibility for a coordinated expansionary push, austerity has become the default macroeconomic policy position in many emerging economies facing fiscal imbalances and mounting debt levels. This could worsen if an exit of foreign capital necessitates a cutback in imports in order to reduce trade and current account deficits that become harder to finance. Not surprisingly, anxious policymakers across the South, who are increasingly aware that they have limited control over some of the key elements of their economic future, are closely tracking the United States Federal Reserve's interest rate policy, the actions of commodity traders and the predatory practices of hedge funds.

The Latin America and Caribbean region is expected to register positive growth this year, but only just, following two years of contraction in 2015 and 2016 when GDP fell by 0.3 per cent and 0.8 per cent respectively. The average growth rate for the South American economies as a group is projected to be 0.6 per cent, but higher for the Caribbean, at 2.6 per cent. Commodity prices and political developments in Argentina and Brazil, which together account for over half of the region's output, will have a significant bearing on regional growth prospects. Growth in Mexico has flattened at a low but stable rate; however inflationary pressures, fiscal consolidation and uncertain policies of the Trump Administration have added downside risks to its growth this year.

Growth in the Asia-Pacific region remains robust, albeit lower than the recent historical trend, rising from 4.9 per cent in 2016 to an estimated 5 per cent in 2017. Much will depend on the performance of its two largest economies. How China manages the explosion of domestic debt since 2009 will be of great significance in this regard. China's estimated debt-to-GDP ratio is 249 per cent, compared with 248 per cent in the United States and 279 per cent in the euro zone. As the Chinese Government introduces measures to contain its rising debt, domestic demand could be squeezed, with adverse consequences for the rest of the region. India's growth performance depends to a large extent on reforms to its banking sector, which is burdened with large volumes of stressed and non-performing assets, and there are already signs of a reduction in the pace of credit creation. Since debt-financed private investment and consumption have been important drivers of growth in India, the easing of the credit boom is likely to slow GDP growth. In addition, the informal sector, which still accounts for at least one third of the country's GDP and more than four fifths of employment, was badly affected by the Government's "demonetization" move in November 2016, and it may be further affected by the roll-out of the Goods and Services Tax from July 2017. Thus, even if the current levels of growth in both China and India are sustained, it is unlikely that these countries will serve as growth poles for the global economy in the near future.

Meanwhile, lower oil prices and the end of the commodity boom, especially since 2014, have adversely affected the African region (parts of which suffered a drought), with regional growth falling from 3.0 per cent in 2015 to 1.5 per cent in 2016. Only East Africa appeared to buck this trend with average growth in 2016 remaining above 5 per cent. This masks significant differences in the growth performance of individual countries in 2016, from above 7 per cent in Côte d'Ivoire and Ethiopia, to 1.1 per cent in Morocco and 0.3 per cent in South Africa. Indeed, South Africa fell into a "technical recession" as GDP declined in two consecutive quarters, by 0.3 per cent in the fourth quarter of 2016 and by 0.7 per cent in the first quarter of 2017. This was due to the poor performance of manufacturing and trade, though there were marked improvements in agriculture and mining. Nigeria saw its GDP contract by 1.5 per cent, while in Equatorial Guinea it fell by about 7 per cent. The recent predicament of many of these economies is the result of their continued failure to achieve growth through diversification; most of the countries remain heavily dependent on one or very few commodities.

Where will global demand come from?

Against a backdrop of policy unreliability and capricious expectations, boom and bust is likely to continue as the default growth pattern in many countries. There may be fleeting moments of more widespread optimism, but inclusive growth across the global economy will remain an elusive goal in the absence of sustained international efforts to manage a coordinated expansion.

There is much uncertainty as to where the stimulus for a more robust recovery could come from. In the past, the United States economy functioned as the principal driver of global demand, importing from the rest of the world and running large current account deficits. With the United States dollar serving as the world's reserve currency, there were sufficient capital inflows to finance not only those deficits, but also the large outflows of capital from the country. In the process, there emerged a mutually convenient relationship between the United States and the rest of the world.

That changed dramatically after the global financial crisis. Following a fall in the United States deficit after 2008, its net stimulus has stabilized at well below the pre-crisis level. Since 2013, other developed economies have posted growing current account surpluses, implying that, as a group, they no longer provide a net demand stimulus to the world economy. Meanwhile, developing and transition economies, as a group, ran surpluses until 2014, which turned into deficits thereafter. However, these deficits were much smaller in absolute size, and not nearly enough to counter the impact of the declining net demand from the developed economies.

China's current account surplus, which until 2010 was the largest in the world, has since been declining, albeit erratically. Germany has taken over running the largest surpluses, which have even increased recently. However, unlike the Chinese expansion, which during the boom fostered growth in a range of other developing countries by drawing them into value chains for exporting products to the more advanced countries, the German expansion has not had similar positive impacts in most developing countries. The resulting adverse effect on the global economy has been compounded by a wider trend in the euro zone, where austerity policies have augmented the region's current account surplus, exporting the euro zone's deflation and unemployment to the rest of the world.

Finding quick and effective ways to recycle and reduce those surpluses is a singularly critical challenge for the international economic community, a challenge that will prove difficult to tackle as long as austerity remains the dominant macroeconomic mood in a hyperglobalized world. Since 2010, the majority of advanced economies have opted for "medium" to "severe" austerity, and even the countries that have considerable fiscal room for manoeuvre have resisted robust expansion. Until recently, some major emerging market economies were exceptions to this trend; but evidence suggests that they too are now curbing expenditure with a view to fiscal consolidation.

Significant long-term investments that enable expansion in lower income countries could be one means of reviving demand globally. It is, therefore, encouraging that Germany has recently announced its intention to launch a Marshall Plan for Africa. However, neither the scale nor the intent appears to match the original model that helped to rebuild post-war Europe. By contrast, China's "One Belt, One Road" initiative seems more ambitious. If implemented as planned, the investments involved will be huge: an estimated $900 billion. However, so far, much of the project is on the drawing board, and the pace of implementation as well as its impact will depend on how China manages its domestic imbalances, and on the mode of financing the proposed investments in participating countries.

Testing times for trade and capital flows

Ever since the United States Federal Reserve began to suggest it might taper its quantitative easing policies, capital flows have been volatile. Since the second quarter of 2014, net capital flows to developing and transition economies turned negative. This could have extremely adverse consequences, as discussed in last year's *Trade and Development Report*. So far, the Federal Reserve has been ultra-cautious in nudging rates higher (just 50 basis points in the first half of 2017). Nevertheless, capital flight threatens even the stronger emerging economies. For example, China experienced sudden and large capital outflows that caused its foreign exchange reserves to fall from $4.1 trillion in June 2014 to $3.3 trillion in June 2016, and to a further $3.1 trillion by end October 2016. To stem this tide of outflows, the Government imposed some capital controls in November 2016, which had a stabilizing effect. That this could happen in a country that had been the favoured destination for global capital for decades, and still has the largest holdings of foreign exchange reserves in the world, suggests that no country is immune to the potentially destabilizing effects of mobile capital flows.

World trade is likely to pick up this year from its very sluggish performance in 2016, but there are doubts about the sustainability of the export surge from emerging markets that underlies this improvement. Given weak worldwide demand, global trade is unlikely to serve as a broad stimulus for growth, other than for particular countries that benefit from special circumstances. Moreover, hopes of an imminent breakthrough in multilateral trade negotiations, with a strong development orientation are fading.

Commodity prices, which increased last year and at the beginning of 2017, provided some boost to commodity-exporting developing countries. However, they are already easing off, and remain significantly below their average in the first decade of the millennium. Crude oil prices have been particularly volatile since early 2017, but in a generally downward direction, and are stuck at well below the $50 mark despite tensions in West Asia. There are also signs of a rise in oil inventories in the United States as shale makes a comeback (in the context of earlier price increases and technology-driven cost reductions), which will further dampen oil prices over the medium term. Prices of metals have similarly registered declines recently due to weakening demand in the United States.

* * * *

In today's challenging and unpredictable global environment, efforts to build inclusive economies and societies will need to accelerate. Ending austerity and harnessing finance to serve society once again, rather than the other way around, are the most urgent challenges. Reinvigorating the multilateral trading system as a global public good with renewed momentum and relevance is also essential for achieving the Sustainable Development Goals. But as long as organized business faces little pushback across several key sectors, increased market concentration and the spread of rent-extracting behaviour will continue apace. This will exacerbate inequalities that have been rising over the past three decades of hyperglobalization, and technological changes may worsen the situation if they hamper job creation, adding to a growing sense of anxiety. As good jobs become scarce, they are also more stringently rationed, and reinforce patterns of social discrimination, particularly along gender lines, but also affecting other disadvantaged groups. Correcting these imbalances requires systematic and concerted action at the national and international levels. Indeed, there is a pressing need for a global new deal.

Follow the money: The financial origins of inequality and instability

The world economy shifted abruptly after the early 1980s following an extensive deregulation of markets − particularly financial and currency markets − in rich and poor countries alike, and a steady attrition of the public sphere. An additional contributory factor was the idolizing of profit-making, not only across all aspects of economic life, but also in the social, cultural and political realms. The resulting withdrawal of public oversight and management of the economy included the curtailment, and sometimes even the elimination, of measures previously adopted by States to manage their integration into the global economy; "open for business" signs were enthusiastically hung up across the global economy.

Hyperglobalization found an eager group of technocratic cheerleaders to acclaim the creative and calming properties of competitive markets and profit-maximizing agents. But on the ground, it was financial interests that led the charge. Under hyperglobalization, finance was not only able to bend the real economy to its speculative endeavours; it also became increasingly absorbed in interacting with itself. As a result, banks became bigger and more diversified and, along with a range of other financial institutions, invented a myriad of financial assets on which to speculate. This combination of leverage and financial innovation turned toxic in 2007, leading eventually to panic and meltdown a year later.

Since 2009, there have been efforts to temper the excesses of the financial sector with sundry government commissions, some legislative discipline on bank behaviour, heightened monitoring and calls for self-restraint, as well as the occasional fine for the most blatant displays of fraudulent behaviour. But the underlying macrofinancial structures have remained broadly intact. Despite the trillions of central bank dollars directed at the sector, the promised broad-based recovery has failed to materialize in most countries. Above all, there has been almost no effort to tackle the connections between inequality and instability that have marked the rise of unregulated finance.

Although financialization started in the early 1980s in many developed countries, various indicators show its marked acceleration in all countries from the early 1990s. In most developed countries, total banking sector assets have more than doubled since then, to over 200 per cent of GDP in many European countries and the United States, and to over 400 per cent of GDP in Japan. On a rough calculation, this makes banking a one hundred trillion dollar sector. The picture for developing and transition economies is different only in degree, with banking sector assets peaking at over 200 per cent of GDP in countries such as Chile, China and South Africa.

Increasing financial openness led to a rapid build-up of international positions by these ever-larger financial players, exposing individual countries to forces beyond the control of national policymakers, thereby intensifying financial vulnerability and heightening systemic risk. At the time of the 2008 financial crisis, the combined weight of banks' external assets and liabilities ranged from 100 per cent of GDP in Brazil, China and Turkey to more than 250 per cent of GDP in Chile and South Africa. In most developed countries, this indicator hovered between 300 per cent and 600 per cent of GDP. Such an environment reflected the expansion of cross-border capital flows and foreign exchange trading that vastly exceeded the requirements of trading in goods and services. It also led to greater banking concentration, with the total assets of the top five banks representing up to four times the GDP in some developed countries, and up to 130 per cent of GDP in some large developing countries.

Financialization was given a further boost by the capture of regulatory and policy agendas, particularly in the most important financial centres. Faith in the efficiency of the market contributed to the political momentum for aligning public sector spending and services more closely with those of private investors. This opened the door for the privatization of health care, higher education and pensions, and in the process, in many countries it burdened households with rising debts. As their status and political clout rose, financiers promoted a culture of entitlement that switched from justifying to celebrating extravagant remuneration and rent extraction.

As Keynes recognized from his experience in the run-up to the Great Depression of the early 1930s, the tendency towards a widening income gap due to the free play of market forces, combined with the higher savings propensity of the wealthier classes, has its limits in insufficient aggregate demand (underconsumption) and excessive financial gambling that favours short-term speculative and rent-seeking activities over long-term productive investment. Also, as envisioned later by Minsky, while these conditions can lead to periods of prosperity and (apparent) tranquillity, an accelerating pace of financial innovation encourages even more reckless investment decisions. The result is an increasingly polarized and fragile global economic system, with stability feeding instability and instability leading to vulnerability and shocks.

This unfettered development of financial markets encouraged the extension of credit to poorer households, temporarily compensating for the stagnation and (relative) decline of labour incomes that accompanied the competitive pressures released by hyperglobalization. Consequently, the level of consumption stabilized or even increased in many countries, but only because it was fuelled by rising household debt. At the same time, large financial and industrial conglomerates used their growing profits (derived, in part, from exploiting cross-border wage and corporate tax rate differentials) to borrow and speculate. Unsustainable debt-led growth in some countries and export-led successes in others led to widening global imbalances, adding new layers of vulnerability and risk to an inherently polarized and unstable system. Financial crises thus became more frequent and widespread. Many emerging market economies were the early victims, but these were warm-ups for the bigger showdown to come.

Two of the dominant socioeconomic trends of recent decades have been the massive explosion in public and private debt, and the rise of super-elites, loosely defined as the top one per cent. These trends are associated with the financialization of the economy and the widening ownership gap of financial assets, particularly short-term financial instruments. As such, inequality is hard-wired into the workings of hyperglobalization. Since the late 1970s, the gap between the top 10 per cent of income earners and the bottom 40 per cent widened in the run-up to 4 out of 5 observed financial crises, but also in 2 out of 3 post-crisis countries. While the run-up to a crisis is driven by "the great escape" of top incomes especially favoured by financial developments, the aftermath often results from stagnating or falling incomes at the bottom. When crises occur, macrofinancial dislocations, one-sided reliance on financial sector bailouts and monetary policy, with a consequent protracted weakness of aggregate demand and employment, tend to worsen income distribution and exacerbate tendencies towards instability.

Furthermore, as observed following major crisis episodes, such as the Asian crisis in 1997–1998 and the global financial crisis in 2008–2009, in the absence of international coordination, most countries will tend to pursue austerity policies in an often failed attempt to induce investors to return to their pre-crisis modus operandi. Thus, while profits accrue to top income earners during financial booms, during the crises that follow, the burdens are almost always borne by public sectors and transmitted to domestic economies; the hardest hit are the most vulnerable sectors, while large financial and industrial conglomerates tend to be first on the financial life boats.

Revenge of the rentiers

Since the start of the hyperglobalization era, finance has tended to generate huge private rewards absurdly disproportionate to its social returns. Less attention has been given to the ways in which non-financial corporations have also become adept at using rent-seeking strategies to bolster their profits and emerge as a pervasive source of rising inequality.

Rents may be broadly defined as income derived solely from the ownership and control of assets or from a dominant market position, rather than from innovative entrepreneurial activity or the productive deployment of a scarce resource. These are being captured by large corporations through a number of non-financial mechanisms, such as the systematic use of intellectual property rights (IPRs) to deter rivals. Others have been acquired through the predation of the public sector, including large-scale privatizations – which merely shift resources from taxpayers to corporate managers and shareholders – and the handout of subsidies to large corporations, often without tangible results in terms of improved economic efficiencies or income generation. Yet others have involved near fraudulent behaviour, including tax evasion and avoidance, and extensive market manipulation by the managers of leading corporations for their own enrichment.

Given the multiplicity of rent-seeking schemes and lax corporate reporting requirements globally, it is difficult to measure the size of corporate rents. One way of approximating their magnitude is by estimating, by sector, surplus or "excess" corporate profits that deviate from "typical" profits. On this measure, surplus profits have risen markedly over the past two decades, from 4 per cent of total profits in 1995–2000 to 23 per cent in 2009–2015. For the top 100 firms, this share increased from 16 to 40 per cent.

The data point to growing market power as a major driver of rent-seeking. A rising concentration trend, particularly in developed-country markets, has been observed with increasing alarm. Moreover, the contagion is spreading. On several measures – market capitalization, firms' revenues and their (physical and other) assets – concentration is rising across the world economy, but in particular the top 100 firms. Market concentration and rent extraction can feed off one another, resulting in a "winner-takes-most competition" that has become a visible part of the corporate environment, at least in some developed economies. The resulting intra-firm differences have contributed to growing inequality. In 2015, the average market capitalization of the top 100 firms was a staggering 7,000 times that of the average for the bottom 2,000 firms, whereas in 1995 it was just 31 times higher.

Significantly, while these firms were amassing ever greater control of markets, their employment share was not rising proportionately. On one measure, market concentration for the top 100 firms rose fourfold in terms of market capitalization, but less than doubled in terms of employment. This lends further support to the view that hyperglobalization promotes "profits without prosperity", and that asymmetric market power is a strong contributory factor to rising income inequality.

Intense lobbying by the patent community has been a major force driving the consolidation of market power, along with regulatory capture by large corporations. As a result, the scope and life of patents, for example, have been expanded considerably, and patent protection has been extended to new activities that were not previously considered areas of technological innovation, such as finance and business methods. Patents are being granted for "innovations" in finance, e-commerce and marketing methods that are not tied to any particular technological product or process, but involve data and information processing in purely electronic form. This not only fosters greater concentration, but also restricts access to data and knowledge. Such a strategic, rather than productive, use of IPRs to boost excess profits by keeping rivals at bay has become a core rent-seeking strategy.

Multinational corporations' excessive use of patent protection for defensive purposes also directly affects innovation dynamics in major emerging economies such as Brazil, China and India. Sharp increases in United States affiliates' sales over the past two decades in relatively high-technology goods (e.g. information and communication technologies, chemicals and pharmaceuticals) in these three countries have generally been closely associated with their strongly expanding patent protection.

In addition, mounting evidence suggests that other non-financial rent-seeking strategies, such as tax evasion and avoidance, public sector gouging (of both assets and subsidies) and rampant market manipulation to boost compensation schemes for companies' top management, are being adopted by firms not only in the more advanced economies, but also, increasingly, in developing economies.

Reining in endemic rentierism, and the inequalities it generates, requires fixing the power imbalances that allow such behaviour to flourish. This will not be easy, but it is indispensable if the objective of truly inclusive and sustainable growth is to be realized. A good start would be to recognize that both knowledge and competition are first and foremost global public goods, and that their manipulation for private profit should be effectively regulated.

Rage against the machine

Hyperglobalization has ridden a series of technological waves that have compressed time and distance. These have lent an air of inevitability to the growth and distribution patterns that have emerged primarily from political and policy decisions, and have also shaped the policy response to growing worries about people being "left behind", with a singular emphasis on boosting education and training.

In reality, the rise and spread of new technologies and the associated breakdown of existing ways of life have been a recurring source of policy debate and design since at least the Industrial Revolution, if not earlier. And if history is any guide, over time the benefits of new technologies can outweigh the costs. Past technological breakthroughs, such as the steam engine, electricity, the automobile and the assembly line, were disruptive, and resulted in substantial job losses and declining incomes for some sectors and sections of society, but only in the short run. These adverse effects were more than offset in the long term when the fruits of innovation spread from one sector to another, and were eventually harvested across the economy as workers moved to new and better-paying jobs.

Still, the digital revolution (in particular the rapid march of robot technology) is making people more anxious. On some accounts, because robots are exponentially getting smarter, more dexterous and cheaper, they are threatening to upend the world of work. With an ever-smaller number of highly skilled people required for their operation, large-scale job displacement and wage erosion are already seen to be hollowing out the middle class in the more advanced economies and halting its rise in emerging economies. The worry is that the 2030 Agenda's commitment to inclusive economies is being technologically subverted before it even gets off the ground.

While there may be cause for such concerns, in hard economic terms, these technological changes cannot explain current labour market woes. This is not to deny the potentially employment-threatening effects of digital technologies in the future; rather, to point out that their real novelty lies less in their wider scope, faster speed or greater dexterity than in their emergence at a time of subdued macroeconomic dynamism in the more advanced economies and stalled structural transformation in many developing economies. This has tended to hold back the investment needed to properly absorb the new technologies and to create new sectors that can provide improved employment opportunities for displaced workers.

Industrial robots can affect employment and income distribution through various channels, but in one way or another their spread involves firms weighing the potential savings on labour costs against the cost of investment in the new capital equipment. This means that job displacement by robots is economically more feasible in relatively skill-intensive and well-paying manufacturing, such as the automotive and electronics sectors, than in relatively labour-intensive and low-paying sectors, such as apparel production. Many existing studies overestimate the potential adverse employment and income effects of robots, because they neglect to note that what is technically feasible is not always also economically profitable. Indeed, the countries currently most exposed to automation through industrial robots are those with a large manufacturing sector that is dominated by industries which offer relatively well-paying jobs, such as automotives and electronics. By contrast, robotization has had a relatively small direct effect in most developing countries so far, and this is unlikely to change in the foreseeable future, given their lack of diversification and technological upgrading.

Despite the hype surrounding the potential of robot-based automation, the use of industrial robots remains small, with an estimated total of only 1.6 million units in 2015. However, their use has increased rapidly since 2010, and is estimated to exceed 2.5 million units by 2019. The vast majority of operational industrial robots are located in developed countries, with Germany, Japan and the United States, combined accounting for 43 per cent of the total. Robot density (the number of industrial robots per employee in manufacturing) is the highest in developed countries and former developing countries that are now at mature stages of industrialization, such as the Republic of Korea. The recent annual increase in robot deployment has been the most rapid in developing countries, but this is mainly due to China, which has a large manufacturing sector.

The distributional effects of robotics are likely to be diverse and will depend on various factors, including a country's stage in structural transformation, its position in the international division of labour, demographic developments, and its economic and social policies. But there are already signs that industrial robots are increasing the tendency towards concentration of manufacturing activities in a small group of countries. This concentration tends to harm inclusiveness at the international level, and given the sluggish global demand, poses significant challenges for developing countries to achieve structural transformation towards well-paying jobs in manufacturing. In this sense, robotics could make it more difficult for countries to pursue economic development on the basis of traditional industrialization strategies and achieve the goals of the 2030 Agenda for Sustainable Development.

Indeed, some of the adverse employment and income effects of robotization may well be felt in countries that do not use robots. This is because robotization can boost companies' international cost competitiveness, thereby spurring exports from the home countries at the expense of other countries, as the latter will be forced to bear at least part of the adverse distributional consequences from robot-based automation through reduced output and employment opportunities. Further, developing countries' employment and income opportunities in these sectors may be adversely affected by the reshoring of manufacturing activities and jobs back to developed countries. It is true that, so far, there is relatively little evidence for such reshoring, and where it has occurred, it has fallen short of the expected positive employment effects in developed countries. Such reshoring has mostly been accompanied by capital investment, such as in robots, and the little job creation that has occurred has been concentrated in high-skilled activities. This means that jobs that "return" with reshored production will not be the same as those that left.

Some have suggested that slowing down automation by taxing robots would give an economy more time to adjust, while also providing fiscal revenues to finance adjustment. But such a tax may hamper the most beneficial uses of robots: those where workers and robots are complementary, and those that could lead to the creation of digitization-based new products and new jobs. Others have suggested promoting a more even distribution of the benefits from increased robot use, based on the fear that robots will take over tasks with higher productivity and pay compared to the average tasks that continue to be performed by workers. If unchecked, the distributional effects from robotics would increase the share of income going to the owners of robots and of the intellectual property they incorporate, thereby exacerbating existing inequalities.

Digitization could also create new development opportunities. The development of collaborative robots could eventually be particularly beneficial for small enterprises, as they can be set up easily without the need for special system integrators, and they can rapidly adapt to new processes and production-run requirements. Combining robots and three-dimensional printing could create additional new possibilities for small manufacturing enterprises to overcome size limitations in production and conduct business on a much larger scale; if local demand grows in tandem, participation in global value chains may become less a matter of necessity and more one of strategic choice. At the same time, digitization may lead to a fragmentation of the global provision and international trade of services, with a good deal of uncertainty as to whether digitally-based services would provide greater or less employment, income and productivity gains as compared to traditional manufacturing activities.

From a development perspective, the key question is whether the greater use of robots reduces the effectiveness of industrialization as a development strategy. This will depend on a number of factors, including who owns and controls robot technologies, possible first mover advantages from the use of robots, and in which manufacturing sectors their impact is likely to be the most pronounced. In all these respects, what will play a decisive role is the effective design and implementation of digital industrial policies, and ensuring that countries have the requisite policy space to implement them.

Harnessing the potential of the digital revolution so that it accelerates productivity growth and feeds a more equitable and more sustainable global economic expansion is undoubtedly required for achieving the goals of the 2030 Agenda. Ultimately, whatever the current impacts from the digital revolution, the final outcomes for employment and inclusiveness will be shaped by policy choices, regulatory acumen and social norms.

Gender and the scramble for bad jobs

For most people, finding a "good job" is the route to a better life, and providing such jobs is key to creating an inclusive economy. Good jobs are associated with decent work; and they tend to be in the formal sector, where earnings are higher, job ladders accessible and working conditions better regulated. In a development context, these jobs are more likely to be located in the industrial than in the agricultural or services sectors.

For half the world's population, finding a good job encounters the barrier of gender discrimination. The call for making hyperglobalization more inclusive has therefore, rightly, acquired a strong female voice. But there is much more to this challenge than increasing the participation of women in markets and boardrooms.

And even adding a gender dimension to financial inclusion, entrepreneurship or trade facilitation offers, at best, a limited path to a more inclusive economy. The institutions and social norms underlying gender inequality tend to be reproduced in labour markets. In the workplace, most women experience discrimination and segmentation – practices that cannot be delinked from the wider pressures of hyperglobalization.

In particular, the prevailing global policy environment, combined with the forces of technology and structural change, has limited the availability of jobs, particularly "good jobs", relative to labour supply. And the scarcity of good jobs has intensified both job rationing by gender and the exclusion of women from better work opportunities, even as women's employment participation has increased and that of men has declined overall.

Against the backdrop of boom and bust cycles, austerity and mobile capital, there is a danger that greater gender equality in employment can become gender conflictual, with women's employment rates rising (which they are in most countries of the world), and men's employment rates falling. This is an almost invisible phenomenon that is not widely discussed, and although its strongest manifestations are in the more advanced economies, it is now a troubling feature of job markets worldwide, barring some cases of declining women's labour participation in major economies such as China and India.

The hollowing out of traditional factory jobs and manufacturing communities has been a very visible feature of growing inequality in developed countries, and is taking a particularly heavy toll on middle-aged working class men. But the number of industrial sector jobs is also declining in many developing countries that are facing premature deindustrialization and stalled industrialization, and the negative impact is much larger on women's industrial employment than on men's. In developing countries, the share of industrial employment in men's total employment declined by an average of 7.5 per cent between 1991 and 2014, compared with a 39 per cent average decline for women. Moreover, as industrial production becomes more capital-intensive, women tend to lose jobs in this sector, even after controlling for education, thus challenging the argument that women lose these jobs because of differences in skills. With the increase in capital intensity and automation, it seems unlikely that a technological revolution in the South will improve gender equality.

Ultimately, an increase in employment opportunities in the industrial sector should offer a gender inclusive alternative, but one that will require a sustainable expansion in demand for industrial goods. For developing countries, higher net exports of manufactures improve industrial job prospects for women, provided that public policies provide a certain amount of protection against imports; hence less trade liberalization seems to be good for women workers. Expansive fiscal policies also contribute to inclusion by increasing labour demand in ways that lower job competition between women and men (it increases women's industrial employment without compromising men's access); thus austerity may be particularly bad for women.

Simply increasing economic growth, and hoping for a trickle-down effect on gender equality has not delivered; it has had a limited impact on women's relative access to good jobs. What is more worrying for gender equality is that increasing women's labour force participation without supportive demand-side policies and structures to productively absorb these new market entrants worsens gender segregation in labour markets and encourages the crowding of women into low-value-added, informal service sector activities.

Does gender segregation in labour markets (or occupational hoarding by gender) have a negative impact on labour overall, as reflected in the wage share of income? In general, class dynamics appear to be gender cooperative in the sense that what is good for women workers is also good for labour overall, including men. Controlling for other factors, there is evidence that the decline of women's relative access to industrial sector work has been associated with a decline in labour's share of income in developing countries since the early 1990s. However, at the same time, when good jobs are scarce, higher labour force participation by women constrains wage growth, potentially setting in motion a low-wage growth path characterized by increasing economic insecurity and gender conflict, since women's labour participation appears to adversely affect men's employment prospects.

Given the employment challenges associated with structural and technological change, and women's primary responsibility for both paid and unpaid care work, transforming unpaid and paid care activities into decent work should become an integral part of strategies aimed at building more inclusive economies.

A way forward: Towards a global new deal

At present, too many people in too many places are integrated into a world economy that delivers inequitable and unjust outcomes. Economic and financial crises, like that of 2008–2009, are only the more visible manifestations of a world economy that has become increasingly unbalanced in ways that are not only exclusionary, but also destabilizing and dangerous for the political, social and environmental health of the planet. Even when a country has been able to grow, whether through a domestic consumption binge, a housing boom or exports, the gains have disproportionately accrued to the privileged few. At the same time, a combination of too much debt and too little demand at the global level has hampered expansion. The subsequent turn to austerity in response to the bust has hit some of the poorest communities hardest, leading to further polarization and heightening people's anxieties about what the future might hold. Meanwhile political elites have been adamant that there is no alternative. All this has proved fertile economic ground for xenophobic rhetoric, inward-looking policies and a beggar-thy-neighbour stance.

Identifying technology or trade as the villains of these developments distracts from an obvious point: without significant, sustainable and coordinated efforts to revive global demand by increasing wages and government spending, the global economy will be condemned to continued sluggish growth, or worse. Now is the ideal time to crowd in private investment with the help of a concerted fiscal push to get the growth engines revving again, and at the same time help rebalance economies and societies that, after three decades of hyperglobalization, are seriously out of kilter. However, in today's world of mobile finance and liberalized economic borders, no country can do this on its own without risking capital flight, a currency collapse and the threat of a deflationary spiral. What is needed, therefore, is a globally coordinated strategy of expansion led by increased public expenditures, with all countries being offered the opportunity of benefiting from a simultaneous boost to their domestic and external markets.

Moving away from hyperglobalization to inclusive economies is not a matter of simply making markets work better, whether by enhancing human capital, filling information gaps, smartening incentives, extending credit to poor people, or providing stronger protection to consumers. Rather, it requires a more exacting and encompassing agenda that addresses the global and national asymmetries in resource mobilization, technological know-how, market power and political influence caused by hyperglobalization, which generate and perpetuate exclusionary outcomes.

In many ways, the current conjuncture is propitious for such a transformative agenda. The established order is under attack from both ends of the ideological spectrum, and its legitimacy is being called into question by the wider public. The Sustainable Development Goals agreed to by all members of the United Nations provide the political impetus for change. The aim should now be to harness this moment of consensus to ensure an appropriate combination of resources, policies and reforms needed to galvanize the requisite investment push and promote inclusive outcomes at both global and national levels.

Despite all the talk of its increasing irrelevance and imminent demise, the nation State still remains the basic unit of legitimacy and leadership in today's interdependent world, and to which citizens ultimately turn for economic security, social justice and political loyalty. But no less than in the past, achieving prosperity for all should involve paying close attention to the biases, asymmetries and deficits in global governance that can stymie inclusive and sustainable outcomes. Effective internationalism continues to rest on responsible nationalism, and finding the right balance remains at the heart of any meaningful multilateral agenda.

With this in mind, there needs to be widespread support for a global new deal. The original New Deal, launched in the United States in the 1930s and replicated elsewhere in the industrialized world, particularly after the end of the Second World War, established a new development path that focused on three broad strategic components: recovery, regulation and redistribution. While these components involved specific policy goals tailored to particular economic and political circumstances, they made job creation, the expansion of fiscal space and the taming of finance a common route to success along this new path.

Building a new deal today could draw on those same components; and, as before, States require the space to tailor proactive fiscal and other public policies to boost investment and raise living standards, supported by regulatory and redistributive strategies that tackle the triple challenges of large inequalities, demographic pressures and environmental problems. However, the specific challenges of inequality and insecurity in the twenty-first century will not be tackled by countries trying to insulate themselves from global economic forces, but rather by elevating, where appropriate, some of the elements of Roosevelt's New Deal to a global level consistent with today's interdependent world.

Elements to consider include:

- **Ending austerity** – This is a basic prerequisite for building sustainable and inclusive economies. It involves using fiscal policy to manage demand conditions, and making full employment a central policy goal. Monetary expansion should also be used differently, so as to finance public investments which add to inclusive and sustainable outcomes. As part of a general expansion of government spending that covers physical and social infrastructure, the state can act as an "employer of last resort"; specific public employment schemes can be very effective in job creation, especially in low-income countries, where much of the workforce is in informal and self-employed activities. Both public infrastructure investments and employment schemes are important for reducing regional imbalances that have arisen in developed and developing countries.

- **Enhancing public investment with a strong caring dimension** – This would include major public works programmes for mitigating and adapting to climate change and promoting the technological opportunities offered by the Paris Climate Agreement, as well as addressing problems of pollution and degradation of nature more generally. It also means dealing with demographic and social changes that erode local communities and extended families by making formal public provision of child care and elderly care a necessity. In both respects, public investments should be designed to enable and attract more private investment, including SMEs and in more participatory ownership forms such as cooperatives.

- **Raising government revenue** – This is key to financing a global new deal. A greater reliance on progressive taxes, including on property and other forms of rent income, could help address income inequalities. Reversing the decline in corporate tax rates should also be considered but this may be less important than tackling tax exemptions and loopholes and the corporate abuse of subsidies, including those used to attract or retain foreign investment.

- **Establishing a new global financial register** – Clamping down on the use of tax havens by firms and high-wealth individuals will require legislative action at both national and international levels. Interim efforts in this direction could include a global financial register, recording the owners of financial assets throughout the world.

- **A stronger voice for organized labour** – Wages need to rise in line with productivity. This is best achieved by giving a strong voice to organized labour. At the same time, job insecurity also needs to be corrected through appropriate legislative action (including on informal work contracts) and active labour market measures. More innovative supplementary income support schemes could be considered for achieving a fairer income distribution, such as a social fund that could be capitalized through shares issued by the largest corporations and financial institutions.

- **Taming financial capital** – Crowding in private investment requires taming financial institutions to make them serve the broader social good. In addition to appropriate regulation of the financial sector, it is important to tackle private banking behemoths, including through international oversight and regulation, as well as to address the highly concentrated market for credit rating and the cosy relationship between rating agencies and the shadow banking institutions that have allowed "toxic" financial products to flourish.

- **Significantly increasing multilateral financial resources** – This should include meeting ODA targets, but also ensuring better capitalized multilateral and regional development banks. In addition, the institutional gap in sovereign debt restructuring needs to be filled at the multilateral level.

- **Reining in corporate rentierism** – Measures aimed at curtailing restrictive business practices need to be strengthened considerably if corporate rentierism is to be reined in. The 2013 OECD BEPS initiative is a start, but a more inclusive international mechanism for the regulation of restrictive business practices will be needed. Earlier attempts in the United Nations, dating back to the 1980s, would be a good place to begin. Meanwhile, stricter enforcement of existing national disclosure and reporting requirements for large corporations would be useful. A global competition observatory could facilitate the task of systematic information gathering on the large variety of existing regulatory frameworks, as a first step towards coordinated international best practice guidelines and policies, and to monitor global market concentration trends and patterns. Competition policy more generally should be designed with an explicit distributional objective.

- **Respecting policy space** – Meaningful reform of the many restrictive investment and intellectual property policies enshrined in thousands of bilateral – and the growing number of regional – trade and investment agreements, will be impossible without a fundamental overhaul of the current international investment regime. This should begin with rethinking its current narrow purpose of protecting foreign investors in favour of a more balanced approach that takes the interests of all stakeholders on board and recognizes the right to regulate at the national level. The international investment dispute settlement and arbitration system needs to be fixed, and if necessary, replaced by a more centralized system with proper appeal procedures and grounding in international law. An Advisory Centre on International Investment Law could help developing country governments navigate disputes with multinational corporations on more egalitarian terms.

In 1947, drawing on the values of the original New Deal, the international community sought to rebalance a world economy shattered by depression and war: the International Monetary Fund (IMF) opened its doors to business, the World Bank provided its first restructuring loan, the General Agreement on Tariffs and Trade (GATT) concluded its first multilateral trade deal, George Marshall launched the most successful development cooperation project in modern history, and the United Nations opened its first regional office and convened its first major conference (on trade and employment). Seven decades later, an equally ambitious effort is needed to tackle the inequities of hyperglobalization in order to build inclusive and sustainable economies. ∎

CURRENT TRENDS AND CHALLENGES IN THE WORLD ECONOMY

A. The world economy: Performance and prospects

Despite renewed optimism about the prospects for a broad-based global recovery, global growth is unlikely to rise much beyond the average rate of 2.5 per cent recorded in the five-year period 2011–2016; the forecast for the world economy in 2017 is 2.6 per cent, not much higher than in 2016 (2.2 per cent) and the same as in 2015 (table 1.1). The pick-up in performance can be attributed largely to the turn-around in some larger developing countries that were experiencing recession, and in the group as a whole (from 3.6 in 2016 to 4.2 per cent in 2017). But with growth in Japan, United States, and the core euro zone economies stuck at a low level and clear signs of a slowdown in the United Kingdom, the global environment will – unless there is a significant, and coordinated, break with fiscal caution and austerity in these economies – continue to hamper growth prospects across the developing world.

1. Ten years on

There is no disagreement about when and where the Great Recession started. In July 2007, with housing prices in the United States already on a downward tilt, the securities-trading company turned investment bank Bear Stearns revealed that two of its hedge-fund operations had run out of money. The subsequent sudden stop in interbank lending in August, along with heightened stress around other short-term money market instruments, sent financial markets into palpitations and several financial institutions exposed to mortgage-backed assets into cardiac arrest, to which Bear Sterns itself, along with Northern Rock, a bank in the United Kingdom, would shortly succumb.

It would take another year for the full effects of heightened financial stress to be felt; but crucially the warning signs went largely ignored by markets

and policymakers alike. The International Monetary Fund did indicate concerns about market turmoil in its *World Economic Outlook* (IMF, 2007: xi), but this was judged to be a temporary threat to otherwise "sound fundamentals". Inflationary pressures in emerging economies and further fiscal consolidation in advanced economies purportedly remained the big policy challenges, with global growth for 2008 predicted to slow, "but remain at a buoyant pace".

That prognosis proved highly optimistic and the world economy, beginning in its most advanced regions, suffered a financial meltdown following the collapse of Lehmann Brothers and fell into recession in 2008 and 2009. Nearly a decade later, despite buoyant financial markets and recent signs of a cyclical bounce-back, global growth remains well below the levels recorded in the run-up to the crisis and continues to depend, to an unhealthy extent, on rising levels of debt. Inadequate demand, weak investment and declining productivity growth in many countries further constrain the growth potential.

The United States acted quickly to stem the financial collapse in 2008 but the subsequent recovery has been sluggish by historical standards and unbalanced in the distribution of gains between the middle-class and the wealthy and between finance and industry. The crisis in Europe was more pronounced and has proved more obdurate. A principal reason is that having been forced by the severity of the crisis to opt for a strong fiscal stimulus, most developed countries retreated from their expansionary fiscal stance and relied instead on monetary policy instruments, in the form of quantitative easing and low interest rates, including negative policy rates in recent years. While the withdrawal of the fiscal stimulus affected growth adversely, the monetary policies that helped banks and financial firms to stabilize and return to

TABLE 1.1 World output growth: Annual percentage change 1991–2017[a]

Country or area	1991–2000	2001–2008	2008	2009	2010	2011	2012	2013	2014	2015	2016	2017[b]
World	**2.9**	**3.2**	**1.5**	**−2.1**	**4.1**	**2.8**	**2.2**	**2.3**	**2.6**	**2.6**	**2.2**	**2.6**
Developed countries	**2.6**	**2.2**	**0.0**	**−3.7**	**2.6**	**1.5**	**1.1**	**1.2**	**1.8**	**2.2**	**1.7**	**1.9**
of which:												
Japan	1.3	1.2	−1.1	−5.4	4.2	−0.1	1.5	2.0	0.3	1.2	1.0	1.2
United States	3.6	2.5	−0.3	−2.8	2.5	1.6	2.2	1.7	2.4	2.6	1.6	2.1
European Union (EU-28)	2.2	2.2	0.4	−4.4	2.2	1.7	−0.4	0.3	1.7	2.3	1.9	1.9
of which:												
Euro zone	2.1	1.9	0.4	−4.5	2.1	1.6	−0.9	−0.3	1.2	2.1	1.7	1.8
France	2.0	1.8	0.2	−2.9	2.0	2.1	0.2	0.6	0.6	1.3	1.2	1.4
Germany	1.7	1.3	1.1	−5.6	4.1	3.7	0.5	0.5	1.6	1.7	1.9	1.9
Italy	1.6	1.0	−1.1	−5.5	1.7	0.6	−2.8	−1.7	0.1	0.8	0.9	1.0
United Kingdom	2.6	2.5	−0.6	−4.3	1.9	1.5	1.3	1.9	3.1	2.2	1.8	1.5
EU Member States after 2004	2.0	4.9	3.7	−3.4	2.0	3.1	0.5	1.2	2.9	3.6	2.9	3.2
Transition economies	**−4.9**	**7.1**	**5.4**	**−6.6**	**4.7**	**4.7**	**3.3**	**2.0**	**0.9**	**−2.2**	**0.4**	**1.8**
of which:												
Russian Federation	−4.7	6.8	5.2	−7.8	4.5	4.3	3.5	1.3	0.7	−2.8	−0.2	1.5
Developing countries	**4.8**	**6.2**	**5.3**	**2.4**	**7.8**	**5.9**	**4.9**	**4.8**	**4.4**	**3.8**	**3.6**	**4.2**
Africa	2.6	5.7	5.4	3.0	5.2	1.2	5.7	2.4	3.7	3.0	1.5	2.7
North Africa, excl. the Sudan and South Sudan	2.8	5.0	6.3	2.8	4.1	−6.6	10.2	−3.7	1.2	2.9	2.1	3.2
Sub-Saharan Africa, excl. South Africa	2.7	6.8	6.0	5.4	6.8	4.9	4.8	5.8	5.8	3.8	1.7	3.2
South Africa	2.1	4.4	3.2	−1.5	3.0	3.3	2.2	2.3	1.6	1.3	0.3	0.5
Latin America and the Caribbean	3.1	3.9	3.9	−1.8	6.0	4.4	3.0	2.8	1.0	−0.3	−0.8	1.2
Caribbean	2.3	5.1	2.6	−0.9	3.1	2.2	2.2	2.9	2.8	3.9	1.7	2.6
Central America, excl. Mexico	4.4	4.6	3.8	−0.7	3.7	5.4	4.8	3.6	3.8	4.3	3.7	4.0
Mexico	3.1	2.7	1.4	−4.7	5.2	3.9	4.0	1.4	2.2	2.6	2.3	1.9
South America	3.1	4.2	5.0	−0.8	6.6	4.7	2.6	3.3	0.2	−1.8	−2.5	0.6
of which:												
Brazil	2.8	3.7	5.1	−0.1	7.5	3.9	1.9	3.0	0.1	−3.8	−3.6	0.1
Asia	6.2	7.3	5.8	3.9	8.8	7.1	5.5	5.8	5.6	5.2	5.1	5.2
East Asia	8.2	8.4	7.0	6.1	9.7	7.8	6.2	6.4	6.2	5.5	5.5	5.6
of which:												
China	10.6	10.9	9.7	9.4	10.6	9.5	7.9	7.8	7.3	6.9	6.7	6.7
South Asia	4.9	6.9	4.9	4.4	9.1	5.5	3.2	4.9	6.4	6.1	6.5	6.3
of which:												
India	6.0	7.6	6.2	5.0	11.0	6.1	4.9	6.3	7.0	7.2	7.0	6.7
South-East Asia	5.0	5.6	4.2	1.6	8.0	4.8	5.8	5.0	4.4	4.4	4.5	4.7
West Asia	4.0	5.8	4.1	−2.0	6.1	8.4	5.0	5.2	3.4	3.7	2.2	2.7
Oceania	2.6	2.7	0.7	1.3	5.6	1.9	1.9	3.2	4.7	4.4	2.0	2.6

Source: UNCTAD secretariat calculations, based on United Nations Department of Economic and Social Affairs (UN DESA), *National Accounts Main Aggregates* database, and *World Economic Situation and Prospects: Update as of mid-2017*; ECLAC, 2017; *OECD.Stat*, available at: http://stats.oecd.org/ (accessed 17 July 2017); IMF, 2017; Economist Intelligence Unit, *EIU CountryData* database; JP Morgan, *Global Data Watch*; and national sources.

a Calculations for country aggregates are based on gross domestic product at constant 2005 dollars.
b Forecasts.

profit have been less successful in boosting consumer spending and investment.

As long as debt was being incurred largely to save the financial sector there were no objections to large-scale public borrowing. But once that was done, the traditional hostility of finance against government deficits and public debt resurfaced, on the (often hidden) assumption that increased taxation of high earnings and profits to finance larger state expenditures was not possible. The retreat from proactive fiscal policy was further justified on the grounds that a high public debt-to-GDP (gross domestic product) ratio would generate stagflationary pressures.

Despite the massive infusion of liquidity by central banks, lending to firms and households did not resume as expected. In response, policymakers have nudged interest rates into negative territory, in an unprecedented attempt to push banks into lending rather than holding interest-bearing deposits with the central bank.[1] The difficulty, until recently, was that households and firms seemed to be wary about borrowing more, as they were still not sure that the bad times were behind them. Banks, too, remained cautious about increasing their exposure to indebted households. This could partly explain the thirst for government bonds that has driven their yields to negative territory as well. On the other hand, as countries

BOX 1.1   Austerity: The new normal

In the search for signs of a return to growth of the magnitude seen before the 2008 crisis, one factor that is often ignored is the role of procyclical fiscal policies in prolonging the recession. After a short period immediately following the crisis, when almost all countries opted for fiscal stimuli that ensured a rebound from the depths of the crisis, most governments have adopted a conservative fiscal stance. Austerity, and therefore low growth, is the new normal. An assessment of trends in a geographically dispersed, economically diverse and illustrative set of 19 countries suggests that barring five (Brazil, China, Germany, India and South Africa), all others have been holding down government spending over the six years ending 2016.

The exercise reported here tests for the presence of austerity by first projecting what annual general government spending (excluding on interest payments) in the post-2007 period would have been if the pre-crisis trend in spending persisted, and then comparing the forecast figures with actual spending. Projections are made by extrapolating the trend increase in real spending excluding interest payments (deflated by the consumer price index) over a period ending in the fourth quarter of 2007. Periods from which the trend rate is estimated vary because of the availability of data, with the longest period taken for calculating the trend rate of growth of spending stretching from the first quarter of 1996 to the last quarter of 2007. The intensity of austerity is captured by calculating the cumulative or total excess of projected spending over actual spending across the six years 2011–2016, and expressing it as a ratio of actual spending in 2016.

In countries with no austerity the ratio would equal zero (if actual spending is on trend) or turn negative (because actual spending is above projected levels, and the excess of the latter over the former is a negative number). For the rest, for purposes of capturing the intensity of austerity, countries for which the ratio is positive but below 0.5 (or a cumulative shortfall of 50 per cent of 2016 spending over 2011–2016) are considered as reflecting *limited austerity*; those with ratios in the range of 0.5 to 1 as reflecting medium levels of austerity; those with ratios in the range above 1 but going up to 2 as reflecting significant austerity; and those with ratios above 2 as reflecting severe austerity. Two countries out of the selected 19 (Greece and Hungary) are subject to severe austerity, whereas Austria, France, Poland and the United States are only subject to limited austerity. Eight (Argentina, Bulgaria, Czechia, Italy, Netherlands, Portugal, Spain and the United Kingdom) are distributed in the medium and significant austerity categories.

No austerity (figures ≤ 0)	Brazil, China, Germany, India, South Africa
Limited austerity (figures > 0 but ≤ 0.5)	Austria, France, Poland, United States
Medium austerity (figures > 0.5 but ≤ 1)	Argentina, Bulgaria, Netherlands
Significant austerity (figures > 1 but ≤ 2)	Czechia, Italy, Portugal, Spain, United Kingdom
Severe austerity (figures > 2)	Greece, Hungary

What emerges, therefore, is that many countries in this sample are wedded to austerity. Interestingly, in the selected sample, emerging market economies dominate the 'no austerity' group. In the case of some of these (Brazil and South Africa, for example), high spending was a result of the commodities boom, which lasted until 2014 and increased revenues and outlays. With the boom having ended, countries are now choosing to rein in expenditures. Since spending cuts following the end of the boom occur with a lag, the countries concerned have recorded relatively high levels of spending when compared to their pre-crisis trend rate of growth. But there are signs in 2016 that spending is being curtailed by governments in these countries as well. In others, such as China and India, governments seem to have reduced spending less from the immediate post-crisis stimulus levels. The difficulty, however, is that in China this spending has been financed by large-scale borrowing, especially by provincial governments, making it harder to sustain. Finally, in the case of Germany, despite the absence of fiscal austerity as defined here, saving exceeds investment, so that the country is contributing inadequately to global demand even while exporting its way to growth.

have gone in for interest-rate cuts and reduced capital inflows, the effective depreciation of currencies has been significant vis-à-vis the United States dollar, but only marginal vis-à-vis one another, diminishing the chances of an export boom.

With fiscal expansion off the table and monetary policy inadequate, the new normal has been sluggish growth. In fact, austerity seems to characterize the fiscal position in most developed countries (box 1.1), as real government spending has fallen short of what it would have been if the trend increase in government expenditure prior to the crisis had been sustained.

By early 2017, optimism about the prospects of a break with the past seem to have made a guarded return, based on better employment figures and/or an uptrend in otherwise volatile quarterly growth figures. The IMF (2017) raised its forecast for global growth to 3.5 per cent for 2017[2] and the World Trade Organization (WTO, 2017) anticipated a return to a more robust international trading environment; the media quickly echoed this optimism as an antidote to the string of bad news stories over the previous 12 months. A pick-up in growth and a steady drop in unemployment in Western Europe, in particular, have been heralded as indicating a fresh start for the region and beyond. Signs of a recovery in Japan in the fourth quarter of 2016 also continued into the first quarter of 2017, albeit from a low level.

Other economic signals, however, carry more mixed messages. The economy of the United States performed indifferently in the first quarter of 2017, growing at an annualised rate of just 1.4 per cent, while real wage growth remains sluggish and inflation well below the Federal Reserve's target despite falling unemployment. The United Kingdom, which was among the fastest-growing G7[3] economies in recent years, has also begun to show signs of a Brexit backlash with growth in the first quarter of 2017 at just 0.2 per cent.

The situation in developing economies is, if anything, even more difficult to gauge, with considerable regional and country-level variation. The rapid recovery from the initial financial shock of 2008 has given way to a persistent slowdown in growth. The rate of output growth for the group declined continuously from 7.8 per cent in 2010 to 3.6 per cent in 2016, and is currently projected to rise to 4.2 per cent in 2017. Growth in the world's two most populous economies, China and India, remains relatively buoyant, but is still at a slower pace than before the crisis and with serious downside risks. The start of 2017 also saw some of the other larger emerging economies move out of the recessionary conditions of the previous year, but with little chance of growth returning to rates registered in the first decade of the new millennium.

Two factors play a role here. The first is the fact that, while oil and commodity prices are up from their recent troughs, they are still well below the highs they experienced during the boom years, which dampens the recovery in commodity-exporting countries. Second, fiscal tightening and/or enforced austerity continue to constrain domestic demand and growth in many countries. Indeed, with advanced economies abnegating responsibility for a coordinated expansionary push, austerity has become the default macroeconomic policy position in many emerging economies. This is certainly true of those facing fiscal imbalances and mounting debt levels, but is also relevant in other countries pressured by foreign, especially financial, investors (see box 1.1). If capital flight necessitates a cutback in imports in order to reduce the trade and current account deficits on the balance of payments, matters could deteriorate further. Not surprisingly, anxious policymakers across the South are focusing their attention on the actions of the United States Federal Reserve, on the decisions of commodity traders and on the predatory practices of hedge funds, with a growing realization that they have limited control over some of the key components of their economic future.

In the absence of sustained international efforts to manage a coordinated expansion across the global economy, boom and bust, against a backdrop of austerity, is likely to remain the dominant growth pattern. Despite some moments of guarded optimism, stable and inclusive economies will remain elusive.

2. Where will global demand come from?

There is much uncertainty about the possible sources of the stimulus for a more robust recovery. In the past, the economy of the United States functioned as the principal driver of global demand, drawing imports from the rest of the world and running large current account deficits. Its status as the home of the world's reserve currency allowed it to finance these deficits with capital inflows, which were even adequate to finance large outflows of capital from the country. In the process, a mutually convenient relationship emerged between the United States and the rest of the world, which "financed" domestic expansion in the United States by providing capital flows that triggered credit-financed private investment and consumption booms. That expansion then had positive effects on growth in the rest of the global economy, since it was accompanied by rising imports into the United States. While major exporting nations like China, Germany and, to a lesser extent, Japan, were the chief beneficiaries of this, expansionary impulses did spread to other countries and regions, albeit to varying degrees.

But this mode of global growth could not be sustained, since it created macroeconomic imbalances that were

**FIGURE 1.1 Current account balance,
global and by region, 2008–2017**

(Billions of current dollars)

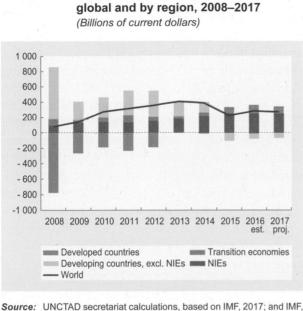

Source: UNCTAD secretariat calculations, based on IMF, 2017; and IMF,
Balance of Payments Statistics database.
Note: NIEs = Hong Kong (China), Republic of Korea, Singapore and
Taiwan Province of China.

**FIGURE 1.2 Current account balance,
selected country groups, 2008–2017**

(Billions of current dollars)

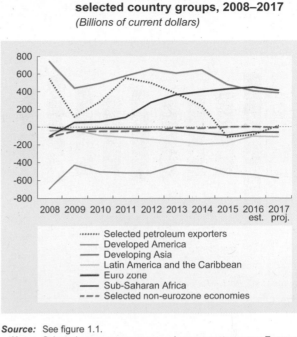

Source: See figure 1.1.
Note: Selected non-euro zone economies are non-euro zone European
Union Member States after 2004 and South-East Europe.
Selected petroleum exporters are developing and transition
economies with the following criteria: average 2013–2015 share
of country fuels (Standard International Trade Classification
(SITC) 3) export in the total country export (SITC 0–9) > 50 per
cent and average 2013–2015 share of country fuels (SITC 3)
export in the total world fuels (SITC 3) export > 0.1 per cent. This
group overlaps with others.

bound to hit limits at some point, and possibly erupt in crises, as they did in 2001 and again more severely in 2008–2009. A better and more preferable route to global growth would be to enable and allow domestic expansion within countries. That would require international coordination, which has been lacking in the recent past. This is unfortunate, because since the global financial crisis, the net stimulus of the economy of the United States to the rest of the world has been shrinking. And in the absence of other demand stimuli the global economy cannot escape its "new normal".

As figure 1.1 shows, the developed economies as a group ran a huge current account deficit of more than $700 billion in 2008. This shrank dramatically the following year, and thereafter, especially since 2013, many advanced economies have posted growing current account surpluses, implying that, as a group, they no longer provide a net demand stimulus to the world economy. Meanwhile developing economies, as a group, ran surpluses until 2014, which have since turned to deficits. However, these deficits were much smaller in absolute size and so could not counteract the impact of the declining net demand from the advanced economies.

Figure 1.2 provides the regional division of these current account balances over this period. Several significant features emerge: a rise and then equally

sharp decline in the surpluses of the petroleum exporters, driven by swings in oil prices; a decline, increase and then decline again for emerging and developing Asia; a decline in the North American deficit followed by only a marginal increase after 2014; and most strikingly of all, a very significant increase in the surpluses of the euro zone.

While these regional aggregates are instructive, it is clear that they are driven by a few large countries. Figure 1.3 provides data on the three most significant: China, Germany and the United States. The deficit of the United States fell after 2008 and since then the net stimulus coming from that economy has been stagnant or falling. The Chinese current account surpluses have been much more variable and since 2015 on a clearly declining path. The exception is Germany, which since 2010 has been running the largest surpluses of any economy in the world – and furthermore, these surpluses have been increasing recently. Unlike the Chinese expansion, which during the boom created more growth in a range of other developing countries by drawing them into value chains for export to the advanced countries, the German expansion has not

**FIGURE 1.3 Current account balance,
major economies, 2008–2016**
(Billions of current dollars)

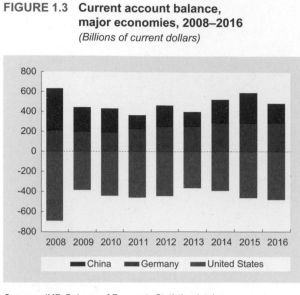

Source: IMF, *Balance of Payments Statistics* database.

had similar positive effects for most developing countries. Moreover, the adverse influence this has on the global economy has been compounded by a wider euro zone trend, whereby austerity policies and slower wage growth in the peripheral economies have added to the region's current account surplus, in an implicit effort to export the euro zone's deflation and unemployment to the rest of the world.

Finding quick and effective ways to recycle surpluses is a singularly critical challenge for the international economic community. Germany, which now has the largest current account surplus both in absolute and relative (share of GDP) terms, has recently announced its intention to launch a Marshall Plan for Africa, though neither the scale nor the intent appear to have much in common with the original model that helped to rebuild post-war Europe. The "One Belt, One Road" project in China offers much greater ambition. If implemented as planned, the investments involved in the project are huge – an estimated $900 billion.[4] As of now, however, much of the project is still on the drawing board; and both the scale and the pace of implementation may depend on how the domestic imbalances in China are managed.

3. Implications for global trade

Given the generalized weakness of demand, global trade does not promise to serve as a stimulus for growth for any group of economies. It is true that after significant slowdowns in 2015 and 2016, global

trade showed some signs of recovery in early 2017, but thus far the upturn is modest and the strength and longevity of the revival are open to question. The trade recovery was led by a marked rebound in merchandise imports into emerging Asia and a weaker expansion of imports into the United States and Latin America in late 2016 and early 2017. In Europe, though trade (both imports and exports) stalled in late 2015–early 2016, it recovered to roughly the same growth as experienced since early 2013. This contrasts with imports into Africa and West Asia, which recorded a cumulative decline of more than 20 per cent in real terms since late 2015. Incorporating the expected recovery, the annual growth figure for total merchandise trade in volume in 2017 is expected to be above 3 per cent – a definite improvement when compared with the previous four years, even if from a low base.

This forecast assumes that no major deterioration in trading relationships occur in the near future. During the first half of 2017, the likelihood of a major trade policy change, primarily in the United States, that would adversely affect global demand had diminished. The United States Administration announced plans to renegotiate and update the North American Free Trade Agreement rather than withdraw completely from it. It also diluted criticism of trade and exchange rate policies of China. But more recently, promises of enhanced tariff protection for the steel industry in the United States, which could trigger retaliatory measures on the part of other countries, have led to increased uncertainty.

Global merchandise trade recovered from the troughs of late 2015 to early 2016, according to monthly data available until May 2017 (figure 1.4). Nevertheless, the prognosis for 2017 is not so bright. On average, import and export volumes grew by only 1.9 per cent in 2016 (table 1.2), significantly lower than the average annual rate of 7.2 per cent recorded during the pre-crisis period 2003–2007. As anticipated in *TDR 2016*, this growth rate was below that of global output for the third consecutive year, a feature that otherwise in the last two decades has been observed only in periods of major crises. Further, in the advanced economies, import volumes during the first five months of 2017 were only 6.3 per cent above their level in 2008.

The growth of exports from the developed countries was either low or negative in 2016, because of feeble demand from key developing countries.

Major exporters of commodities in Africa, Latin America and West Asia, affected by declining and low commodity prices since 2014, experienced a significant decline in imports. While import growth remained positive in the rest of developing Asia, some recently released soft indicators on trade suggest that this could peter out. For example, recently declining freight rates suggest that trade between Asia and developed markets may have peaked.[5] These trends suggest that any sustained recovery in merchandise trade would have to wait for a revival of global demand.

Global services trade was also sluggish in 2016. World services exports measured in current United States dollars remained under $5 trillion, recording an annual growth rate of just 0.4 per cent.[6] Developing countries and transition economies recorded the second of two consecutive years of decline, with services exports falling by 1.1 per cent and 0.9 per cent respectively in 2016. Exports of services from least developed countries recorded a 3.6 per cent decline, with travel receipts (which account for almost half of total services) declining by 3.4 per cent. Meanwhile, in developed economies, exports of services grew by a meagre 1 per cent, largely driven by the robust growth of 6.9 per cent in Japan.

This subdued expansion at the global level was the outcome of contrary trends across the main categories of exports of services. On the one hand, transport (which accounts for roughly one fifth of total trade in services) shrank by 4.3 per cent, influenced also by declining transportation costs. Exports of financial services (almost 9 per cent of trade in services) also registered a decline of 3.9 per cent. This partly reflected falls for the second consecutive year in Europe and the United States, the two main providers of financial services abroad. On the other hand, export of travel services (about one quarter of global trade in services) expanded by 1.8 per cent, because of continued expansion mainly in Japan and to a lesser extent in Latin America and the Caribbean. Telecommunications, computer and information services – one of the fastest-growing components of trade in services in recent years that now account for about one tenth of total exports in services – grew by 4.5 per cent.

Volume figures for the two largest components of trade in services – which provide quantity data and thus avoid concerns related to valuation issues – offer additional insight on trends in the trade in services.

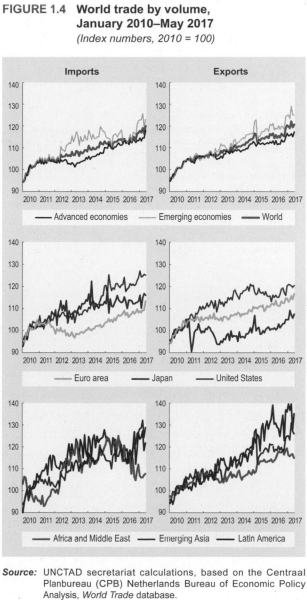

FIGURE 1.4 **World trade by volume, January 2010–May 2017**
(Index numbers, 2010 = 100)

Source: UNCTAD secretariat calculations, based on the Centraal Planbureau (CPB) Netherlands Bureau of Economic Policy Analysis, *World Trade* database.

Note: Country groupings are those used by the CPB Netherlands Bureau of Economic Policy Analysis, *World Trade* database.

World seaborne trade volumes grew 2.6 per cent in 2016, up from 1.8 per cent in 2015. Although positive, this growth rate is short of the historical average of 3 per cent recorded over the past four decades. In China, import demand was the main driver, with the country's import volumes rising by 6.7 per cent in 2016. However, subdued expansion in the import demand of other countries – especially commodity-exporting and oil-exporting developing economies – limited overall growth. Even so, developing countries continued to fuel international seaborne trade both in terms of imports and exports, accounting for 59 per cent of goods loaded and 64 per cent of goods unloaded (UNCTAD, 2017).

TABLE 1.2   **Export and import volumes of goods, selected regions and countries:**
            Annual percentage change 2013–2016

Country or area	Volume of exports				Volume of imports			
	2013	2014	2015	2016	2013	2014	2015	2016
World	**3.1**	**2.0**	**1.4**	**1.7**	**2.3**	**2.5**	**1.9**	**2.1**
Developed countries	**2.1**	**1.7**	**2.1**	**1.0**	**0.0**	**2.8**	**3.3**	**2.7**
of which:								
Japan	−1.5	0.6	−1.0	0.3	0.3	0.6	−2.8	−0.3
United States	2.6	3.3	−1.1	−0.2	0.8	4.7	3.7	3.6
European Union	1.9	1.6	3.3	1.1	−1.0	3.2	4.1	2.8
Transition economies	**2.0**	**0.5**	**1.0**	**−1.6**	**−0.4**	**−7.9**	**−19.9**	**7.3**
Developing countries	**4.4**	**2.5**	**0.6**	**2.8**	**5.5**	**2.7**	**1.1**	**1.1**
Africa	−1.6	−2.0	0.6	2.9	6.8	3.6	0.7	−4.6
of which:								
Sub-Saharan Africa	2.8	1.9	0.7	−0.3	7.5	4.3	−0.3	−6.6
Latin America and the Caribbean	2.4	2.3	3.2	2.3	3.8	0.0	−2.0	−4.2
East Asia	6.7	4.9	−0.6	0.6	7.0	3.4	−1.1	2.2
of which:								
China	8.5	5.6	−0.9	0.0	9.1	2.9	−1.8	3.1
South Asia	0.0	1.1	−1.4	18.1	−0.4	4.7	7.4	8.9
of which:								
India	8.5	3.5	−2.1	6.7	−0.3	3.2	10.1	7.3
South-East Asia	5.0	3.7	3.7	3.9	4.2	2.4	5.7	4.4
West Asia	3.7	−3.2	−0.6	3.5	6.7	2.2	3.1	−2.4

Source: UNCTAD secretariat calculations, based on *UNCTADstat.*

International tourist arrivals grew 3.9 per cent in 2016, its lowest rate since 2009. Figures varied across regions with Africa registering the highest increase (8.3 per cent) on the back of a strong rebound in sub-Saharan Africa (10.7 per cent), followed by developing Asia (7.4 per cent) and Latin America and the Caribbean (5.5 per cent). Meanwhile, tourist arrivals in developed economies grew 4.9 per cent. In transition economies, performances were rather mixed, but overall negative owing to a decline of 8.6 per cent in the Russian Federation. During the first four months of 2017, the situation improved with 6 per cent growth year on year, suggesting a rising trend in this sector. Momentum remained in destinations that registered robust positive figures in previous years, while arrivals rose in regions that had displayed a sluggish trend (UNWTO, 2017).

4. Commodity price trends

One much-cited tendency in global markets in recent months is the reversal of the commodity price decline that began after the end of the boom in 2011. The index of prices for all commodities is projected to rise by 14.4 per cent in 2017, based on a comparison of the average of the price index over January to June 2017 and the average over January to December 2016 (table 1.3). The rebound in the prices of petroleum

products plays an important role here. However, there is considerable uncertainty on whether that rebound will be sustained. Crude oil prices have registered gains, but remain below the $50 mark despite tensions in West Asia and OPEC (Organization of the Petroleum Exporting Countries) efforts to curb supply. There is also news of a rise of oil inventories in the United States, as shale makes a comeback in the context of a gradual price increase and technologically driven cost-reduction. This seems to be pushing prices down once again. Thus, the OPEC Reference Basket touched $45.21 per barrel in June 2017, representing a decline of over $7 from the previous peak recorded in January 2017. Metals prices also registered recent declines because of a fall in demand from China and the United States, among other importers. So, while most commodities did recover from the downturn experienced after the end of the commodity price boom, the rebound appears to be losing momentum.

In real terms, commodity prices globally are at the levels of the late 1980s, albeit with major variations in the dynamics of the different groups. In particular, agricultural commodities are at one of their lowest levels since 2002. Few commodities are currently doing better than in the 1980s in terms of price levels, among which are oil and the precious metals, including gold, silver and platinum.

TABLE 1.3 World primary commodity prices, 2008–2017

(Percentage change over previous year, unless otherwise indicated)

Commodity groups	2008	2009	2010	2011	2012	2013	2014	2015	2016	2017[a]
All commodities[b]	**33.4**	**−30.8**	**24.6**	**27.8**	**−3.5**	**−4.2**	**−8.0**	**−34.3**	**−8.7**	**14.4**
Non-fuel commodities[c]	**21.7**	**−17.3**	**28.1**	**18.8**	**−12.7**	**−6.9**	**−8.0**	**−17.1**	**1.7**	**9.8**
Non-fuel commodities (in SDRs)[c]	**17.6**	**15.0**	**29.4**	**14.8**	**−10.1**	**−6.2**	**−8.0**	**−10.0**	**2.4**	**12.0**
All food	**32.9**	**−8.8**	**10.9**	**23.1**	**−6.5**	**−9.6**	**−1.1**	**−13.8**	**2.5**	**1.0**
Food and tropical beverages	**32.4**	**−1.2**	**10.3**	**22.8**	**−9.7**	**−9.2**	**2.4**	**−10.9**	**0.6**	**1.0**
Tropical beverages	20.5	4.0	15.9	26.7	−20.4	−19.8	21.1	−5.1	−4.8	0.6
Coffee	15.4	−6.9	27.3	42.9	−25.7	−23.6	29.9	−19.7	2.1	3.3
Cocoa	32.2	11.9	8.5	−4.9	−19.7	2.0	25.6	2.3	−7.7	−29.5
Tea	27.2	16.5	−1.0	11.4	0.8	−23.9	−10.4	43.1	−15.6	28.9
Food	36.7	−2.8	8.4	21.4	−5.6	−5.8	−2.8	−12.9	2.6	1.1
Sugar	26.9	41.8	17.3	22.2	−17.1	−17.9	−3.9	−21.0	34.4	−3.0
Beef	2.6	−1.2	27.5	20.0	2.6	−2.3	22.1	−10.5	−11.1	7.6
Maize	34.0	−24.4	13.2	50.1	2.6	−12.1	−22.2	−14.7	−4.1	−2.9
Wheat	27.5	−31.4	3.3	35.1	−0.1	−1.9	−6.1	−23.1	−15.5	4.8
Rice	110.7	−15.8	−11.5	5.9	5.1	−10.6	−17.8	−10.9	2.2	0.0
Bananas	24.6	0.7	3.7	10.8	0.9	−5.9	0.6	2.9	4.8	5.1
Vegetable oilseeds and oils	**34.0**	**−22.6**	**12.2**	**23.8**	**0.5**	**−10.3**	**−8.2**	**−20.4**	**7.3**	**1.1**
Soybeans	36.1	−16.6	3.1	20.2	9.4	−7.9	−9.7	−20.6	3.9	−0.8
Agricultural raw materials	**8.7**	**−16.4**	**41.7**	**23.9**	**−20.3**	**−9.5**	**−12.7**	**−13.3**	**−0.7**	**10.0**
Hides and skins	−11.3	−30.0	60.5	14.0	1.4	13.9	16.5	−20.6	−18.8	3.6
Cotton	12.8	−12.2	65.3	47.5	−41.8	1.5	−8.8	−14.7	5.4	15.6
Tobacco	8.3	18.0	1.8	3.8	−3.9	6.3	9.1	−1.7	−2.3	0.5
Rubber	16.9	−27.0	90.3	32.0	−30.5	−16.7	−30.0	−20.3	5.3	40.0
Tropical logs	39.3	−20.6	1.8	13.5	−7.1	2.6	0.4	−16.5	−0.3	−2.2
Minerals, ores and metals[d]	**16.3**	**−26.9**	**45.4**	**12.3**	**−16.2**	**−2.4**	**−14.1**	**−23.1**	**1.7**	**23.1**
Aluminium	−2.5	−35.3	30.5	10.4	−15.8	−8.6	1.1	−10.9	−4.2	18.0
Phosphate rock	387.2	−64.8	1.1	50.3	0.5	−20.3	−25.6	6.5	−5.8	−13.1
Iron ore	26.8	−48.7	82.4	15.0	−23.4	5.3	−28.4	−42.4	4.6	27.7
Tin	27.3	−26.7	50.4	28.0	−19.2	5.7	−1.8	−26.6	9.4	13.7
Copper	−2.3	−26.3	47.0	17.1	−9.9	−7.8	−6.4	−19.8	−11.6	18.4
Nickel	−43.3	−30.6	48.9	5.0	−23.4	−14.3	12.3	−29.8	−18.9	1.7
Lead	−19.0	−17.7	25.0	11.8	−14.2	3.9	−2.2	−14.8	4.7	18.9
Zinc	−42.2	−11.7	30.5	1.5	−11.2	−1.9	13.2	−10.6	8.2	28.7
Precious metals	**23.5**	**7.8**	**27.4**	**30.8**	**3.6**	**−15.8**	**−11.0**	**−9.8**	**7.2**	**−0.7**
Gold	25.1	11.6	26.1	27.8	6.4	−15.4	−10.3	−8.4	7.6	−0.8
Fuel commodities	**38.7**	**−38.9**	**22.6**	**31.4**	**−0.9**	**−1.1**	**−7.5**	**−43.8**	**−17.7**	**22.0**
Crude petroleum[e]	36.4	−36.3	28.0	31.4	1.0	−0.9	−7.5	−47.2	−15.7	19.5
Memo item:										
Manufactures[f]	**4.9**	**−5.6**	**3.0**	**8.9**	**−1.7**	**3.6**	**−1.5**	**−9.8**	**−1.9**	..

Source: UNCTAD secretariat calculations, based on UNCTAD, *Commodity Price Statistics Online*; and United Nations Statistics Division (UNSD), *Monthly Bulletin of Statistics*, various issues.

Note: In current dollars unless otherwise specified.
    a   Percentage change between the average for the period January to June 2017 and the average for 2016.
    b   Including fuel commodities and precious metals. Average 2013–2015 weights are used for aggregation.
    c   Excluding fuel commodities and precious metals. SDRs = special drawing rights.
    d   Excluding precious metals.
    e   Average of Brent, Dubai and West Texas Intermediate, equally weighted.
    f   Unit value of exports of manufactured goods of developed countries.

What needs to be noted (figure 1.5) is that while the commodity price cycles for the major groups of commodities were more or less similar, the post-2011 end to the boom varied across commodity groups. Energy prices were stable during 2011–2014 and then declined, while prices of other commodities have declined continuously after 2011. In the case of fuel oil, the price reduction after 2014 was so sudden and sharp because previous price trends themselves affected supply by making unused locations and technologies viable, adding supply factors to the impact of fluctuations in demand. The duration of the price decline was the longest in the case of minerals, ores and metals, for which the rebound in prices was also the strongest.

FIGURE 1.5   Monthly commodity price indices by commodity group, January 2002– June 2017

(Index numbers, 2002 = 100)

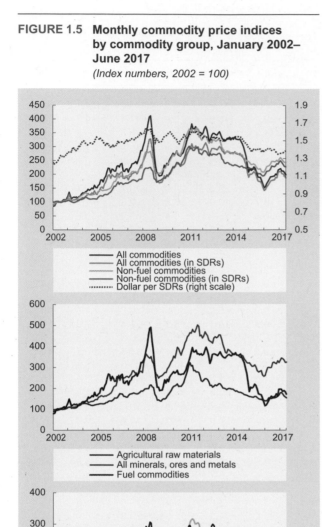

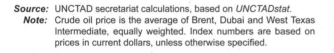

Source: UNCTAD secretariat calculations, based on *UNCTADstat*.
Note: Crude oil price is the average of Brent, Dubai and West Texas Intermediate, equally weighted. Index numbers are based on prices in current dollars, unless otherwise specified.

5.   Capital flows

The landscape with respect to capital flows has changed significantly in recent years. After the surge in capital flows during the easy money years of the pre-crisis period between 2003 and 2007, flows to developing countries collapsed in the midst of the crisis, when international investors booked profits in emerging market economies and transferred funds to

FIGURE 1.6   Net private capital flow by regions, 2007–2017

(Billions of current dollars)

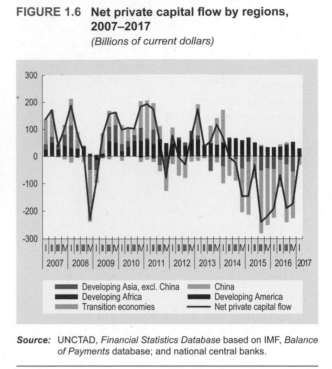

Source: UNCTAD, *Financial Statistics Database* based on IMF, *Balance of Payments* database; and national central banks.

cover losses incurred at home. But as governments and central banks in the developed world chose to opt for large-scale liquidity infusion at near-zero interest rates, the flow of capital to many developing countries revived, with certain periods when flows surged.

However, ever since the United States Federal Reserve began to speak of the possibility of tapering off its quantitative easing policies, capital flows have once again become volatile, beginning with the "taper tantrum" of 2013. As figure 1.6 shows, net capital flows to developing and transition economies have been negative since the second quarter of 2014, with the adverse consequences discussed in *TDR 2016*.

In most of the so-called emerging markets, capital outflows consist largely of the outflow of portfolio investment from debt and equity markets. Volatile portfolio capital flows were evident in China as well, with the period of positive net inflows from mid-2011 ending in the last quarter of 2014. Thereafter there were net outflows of portfolio capital from China, which went from $8.1 billion in the first quarter of 2015 to $40.9 billion in the first quarter of 2016. Chinese Government intervention in the form of limited capital controls caused net inflows to turn positive once again. While some have attributed the overall capital outflow from China over this period partly to a substantial increase in Chinese foreign direct investment (FDI) abroad, especially from the second half of 2015, there was additionally the impact of a pronounced decline of FDI into China from 2013.

Other developing regions were also affected by declining net inflows or rising net outflows of capital. The only exception is Africa, where the relatively stable positive capital flows have largely been driven by FDI. Overall, the trend towards negative net capital flows continues to pose a core challenge for developing and transition economies, particularly in view of the expected return to a "normal" monetary and interest-rate policy in the United States. Although there was a sharp fall in net capital outflow to $3.8 billion into developing countries as a group in the first quarter of 2017, it does not follow that they will experience net inflows in the near future, as the exchange rate policies of China and further tightening of capital controls have played a major role in this result. Other regions (developing America and Africa) that have enjoyed positive inflows in recent years are experiencing declining inflows.

A feature of capital flows is the continuing importance of external debt. Total external debt stocks of developing countries and economies in transition are estimated to have reached $7.1 trillion in 2016, an overall increase of 80 per cent since 2009, representing an average annual growth rate of 8.8 per cent over the period. Even though external debt-to-GDP ratios remain relatively low by recent historical standards, rising from 21 per cent in 2009 to 26.3 per cent by 2016, debt service burdens have risen sharply over 2015 and 2016. For all developing countries, the ratio of external debt service to GDP rose from 9.1 per cent in 2009 to 13.1 per cent in 2015, and was 12.3 per cent in 2016. This increase in debt service burdens has hit the most vulnerable developing countries the hardest, including commodity exporters, countries dealing with large refugee inflows, and small island developing states. Further signs of trouble on the horizon include the growing share of short- relative to long-term debt in total external debt stocks (up from 21 per cent in 2009 to 27 per cent in 2016); as well as a significant slowdown in the growth of international reserves, which grew by only 4 per cent between 2009 and 2016, compared to 24 per cent between 2000 and 2008.

Aggregate debt, domestic and external in emerging market economies, especially private sector non-financial debt, has been of particular concern for some time. This now stands at over 140 per cent of combined GDP, with credit to the Chinese private non-financial sector having risen from 114 per cent to 211 per cent between the fourth quarters of 2008 and 2016.

B. Regional growth trends

1. Developed countries

Within the overall scenario of depressed demand, the performance of individual economies and the factors influencing that performance have not necessarily been similar. The recent slowdown in the United States reflects a significant slowdown in household spending, at a time when the return to fiscal conservatism has set limits on government expenditure. Growth of personal consumption expenditure in the first quarter of 2017 was at its lowest since 2009, standing at an annual 1.1 per cent, or well below the 3.5 per cent rate in the previous quarter and 1.6 per cent and 2.3 per cent respectively in the corresponding quarters of 2016 and 2015. The persistence of the Great Recession was widely seen as being partly the result of a decline in credit-financed spending by households that were already overburdened with large debts at a time when the value of their housing equity and other assets had fallen. This means that balance sheet effects could continue to hold back growth (see box 1.2).

This prospect of persistently low growth in the United States is reinforced by waning expectations of a shift from a monetary to a fiscal stimulus generated by the new United States Administration. While the Trump Administration has promised a tax-cut stimulus, there is no concrete plan to ensure that this does not result in a substantial widening of the fiscal deficit, and so it is likely to face obstacles in implementation. Meanwhile, there is no evidence yet of a significant step up in infrastructure spending, which too is likely to run up against a fiscal constraint.

As table 1.1 makes clear, the euro zone recovery came much later than in the United States, lagging behind by several years, with growth staying well below the peak reached in the immediate post-crisis

BOX 1.2 Debt and recovery: The experience of the United States

In the United States, one expected consequence that followed the adoption of an easy money regime is inflation in financial asset values. Reflecting this tendency, the New York Stock Exchange composite index registered a trend increase from its early 2009 trough to reach levels higher than where it stood at its peak in mid-2007. The effect this has had on aggregate wealth increase was greater than that due to increased housing equity resulting from house price increases and new acquisition of houses. As figure 1.B2.1 shows, the contribution that financial assets made to the net worth of households and non-profit institutions was much higher than the contribution of non-financial assets in recent years. But there are two reasons why this did not generate a strong wealth effect, in the form of increased private borrowing to finance consumption and investment. First, consumers and banks were still unsure whether the financial turnaround would last and would not be followed by a return to crisis. Second, since wealth accumulation was predominantly in the form of capital gains in financial markets, it has mainly occurred among the already rich, increasing inequality but not spurring demand.

FIGURE 1.B2.1   **Contribution to growth to net worth of households and non-profit organizations in the United States, second quarter 1990–first quarter of 2017**
(Percentage points)

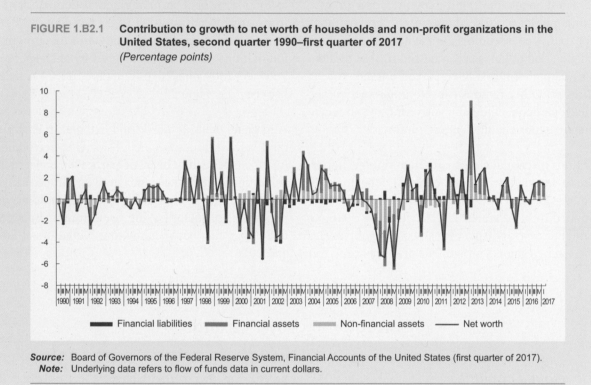

Source: Board of Governors of the Federal Reserve System, Financial Accounts of the United States (first quarter of 2017).
Note: Underlying data refers to flow of funds data in current dollars.

However, the large infusion of liquidity and zero or negative interest rates charged by the Federal Reserve have put considerable pressure on banks to lend, to some effect. As figure 1.B2.2 indicates, the process of deleveraging that had begun in the third quarter of 2008 was reversed in the second quarter of 2013, at a time when total household debt was still 54 per cent above its 2003 level, when the global liquidity surge began. Around half of the loans taken on after this recent return to borrowing on the part of households are mortgage loans, with salutary effects on the housing market. House prices bottomed out in mid-2009 and were flat until mid-2013, after which they have been rising. A consequence of this rise in price of both housing and financial asset prices is that the ratio of the net worth of households and non-profits to personal disposable income has gone up from its post-crisis low in early 2009, and especially after mid-2011.

recovery. This is largely because of tight fiscal policy in the core countries and significant to severe austerity in the periphery, with economic and social stress levels remaining high. Unemployment has fallen only moderately, from a high of 12 per cent in 2013 to 10 per cent in 2016, and is still well above the pre-crisis level. Moreover, earnings have not risen, as workers have to make do with lower-quality work and reduced working hours. Annual real wage growth between 2008 and 2015 was below 1 per cent with the

FIGURE 1.B2.2   **Total household debt balance and its composition**
(Trillions of dollars)

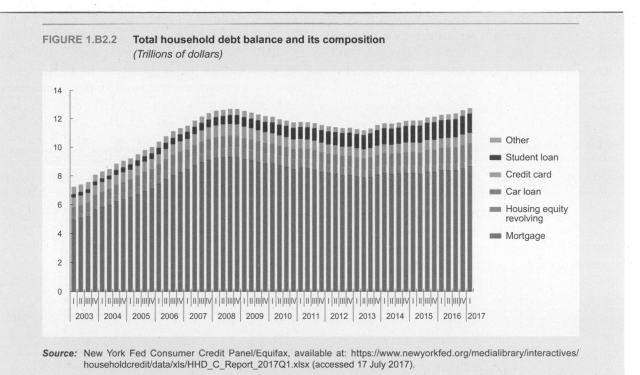

Source: New York Fed Consumer Credit Panel/Equifax, available at: https://www.newyorkfed.org/medialibrary/interactives/householdcredit/data/xls/HHD_C_Report_2017Q1.xlsx (accessed 17 July 2017).

Significantly, the composition of the stock of household debt has been changing. In mid-2013 mortgage loans accounted for 70 per cent of outstanding household debt, but they contributed only 50 per cent of the increase in household debt between then and the first quarter of 2017 (figure 1.B2.3). On the other hand, car loans and student loans (which were respectively 7.3 per cent and 8.9 per cent of the debt stock in the second quarter of 2013) contributed 22.5 and 22.3 per cent of the increment in debt up to the first quarter of 2017. In other words, close to 45 per cent of the increase in credit in the period when banks have been "forced" to lend was on account of car loans (which increased by 66 per cent over this period) and student loans (which more than doubled).

This shift in the composition of debt may have had an adverse impact on output growth. The rising magnitude of student debt leads those who hold these loans to defer entry into mortgage agreements and postpone home-ownership, thereby reducing the demand for mortgage loans. Hence, the growth-inducing effect of this round of increased household borrowing is likely to be lower than it would have been if such education was publicly funded. Moreover, it is now becoming clear that car loans were provided to many who did not have the ability to meet the debt service commitments involved. The situation with student loans is worse. The percentage of loan balances going into "serious delinquency" has been hovering around a 10 per cent annual rate since 2012.

FIGURE 1.B2.3   **Composition of stock of and increment in household debt**
(Percentage)

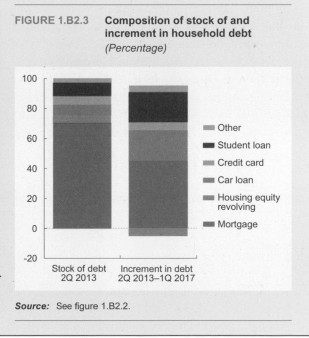

Source: See figure 1.B2.2.

exceptions of Estonia, Latvia and Slovakia, and wages have actually contracted in several member countries.

Some good news is that growth in the peripheral countries of the euro zone badly hit by the crisis, has overtaken that in the three biggest economies in the zone: Germany, followed by France and Italy. As a result, overall growth in the zone is expected to pick up this year, providing the basis for wider growth optimism in some circles. But this should be tempered by the recognition that even with Germany recording its best sustained growth performance for quite some time, the core of the zone (and the European Union) continues to exhibit weak average growth.

It is in this light that optimistic perceptions of an imminent and strong recovery in Europe should be assessed. A series of factors underpin this optimism. After peaking in 2013, the euro area unemployment rate fell as noted above. Household financial indicators and surveys of consumer confidence have shown a steady improvement over the same period. As unemployment drops and confidence grows, household consumption has supported the ongoing recovery. In addition, the combination of low inflation and interest rates has contributed to a steady depreciation of the real effective exchange rate of the euro since 2014. Improved external competitiveness has translated into strong export growth across the region between 2014 and 2017. Finally, business confidence, manufacturing activity and investment indicators are all in positive territory.

However, several challenges remain. First, despite the current upturn, aggregate euro area GDP by the first quarter of 2017 was still barely 3.1 per cent above its level in 2008. Indeed, aggregate domestic demand has failed to recover, as euro area spending remains below pre-crisis levels. Sustained fiscal consolidation combined with high unemployment rates account for these developments. In addition, aggregate investment in the euro area shows a declining trend over the last decade, decreasing from 23.1 per cent of GDP in 2007 to 20.1 per cent in 2016. The ensuing reliance on external demand to sustain the recovery, as discussed earlier, imposes significant strains on the rest of the global economy. It is worth recognizing that this weak economic performance helps to account for the recent political uncertainty observed in the region.

Second, there is the divergent character of the recovery. This can be observed through the evolution of several indicators in the euro core area and the periphery. In the case of GDP per capita, while Germany has enjoyed a 9.7 per cent increase with respect to its pre-crisis levels, the picture is different in the periphery. GDP per capita remains well below the 2008 levels for countries such as Greece, Portugal and Spain. This is also true for Italy, and even the second largest economy of the bloc, France, has barely managed to recover. Over this period, French GDP per capita has increased only 0.7 per cent. Labour markets present a similar picture. While unemployment in Germany has dropped to 3.8 per cent in the second quarter of 2017, this indicator remains stubbornly high for the countries that were hit harder by the crisis. Broad unemployment and youth unemployment are 22.6 and 46.6 per cent in Greece; 11.8 per cent and 38.7 per cent, respectively, for Italy; 9.9 and 24.3 per cent in Portugal; and 18.2 per cent and 40.8 per cent for Spain. In the meantime, consumer price indices (CPI) tell a related story of divergent economic performance. Headline CPI for the entire euro area has been getting closer to the 2 per cent inflation target set by the European Central Bank over the first months of 2017. But this has been influenced by the increase in the CPI indicator for Germany since the beginning of 2016. Inflationary pressures in Germany contrast with low inflation elsewhere: increases in CPI in Greece, Italy, Portugal and Spain remain stuck below 1 per cent because of weak domestic demand and unutilized productive capacity.

A third challenge, as noted earlier, is the impact of the current European growth path on the rest of the world. Pre-crisis growth was based on the expansion of intra-European trade and financial imbalances. Since the crisis, the reduction of domestic demand and competitive real exchange rates, underpinned by wage deflation and a weak euro, have allowed Europe to export these imbalances to the rest of the world. Current account balances, by definition, must even out on a global scale, so from the perspective of developing countries this is especially troubling.

The economy of the United Kingdom remained buoyant in the second half of 2016 following the Brexit vote. This was largely thanks to strong household spending on the back of rising housing prices and a return to the debt market, though the decline in the value of the sterling also provided a boost to exports. However, currency depreciation is also driving inflation because of the increased cost of imports. As the benefits of lower oil and commodity prices disappear, this problem can intensify. Real wages, which had fallen 8 per cent since the 2008 crisis, have shown some signs of recovering but only slowly, rising by 2.1 per cent in the three months to March 2017. However, the start of Brexit negotiations which only began in June 2017 have been marked by a good deal of political uncertainty which seems likely to stymie the economic recovery over the near term. Growth in the first quarter of 2017 slowed to 0.2 per cent quarter-on-quarter with the United Kingdom performing worse than most European economies.

The new uncertainties generated by a hung parliament that needs to negotiate the Brexit deal may constrain growth even more.

The economy of Japan has now expanded, albeit it weakly, for six consecutive quarters, which is the longest run of growth in more than a decade, with a growth rate of 1.2 per cent expected this year. However, this growth has been largely driven by exports, and not by domestic demand, especially private consumption, which the Japanese Government has tried hard to stimulate. Part of the reason for the increase in exports is the correction of the long-term overvaluation of the currency, with its value falling from ¥101 to the dollar in late September 2016 to about ¥117 to the dollar at the end of December 2016. Exports, which had been shrinking for many months preceding December 2016, have since recorded positive changes (relative to the corresponding month of the previous year) until April and are being seen as the main stimulus to growth. But with the world economy still sluggish, this does not give grounds for much optimism. Meanwhile, the yen has shown signs of once again appreciating vis-à-vis the dollar, touching around ¥110 to the dollar in early June.

The failure of domestic demand to pick up is related to rather unusual trends in the Japanese labour market. An ageing population has ensured that despite many decades of stagnation or low growth, the unemployment rate in Japan, at 2.8 per cent, is at a 20-year low. Still, a significant part of the workforce is in temporary or part-time occupations with no security of employment. As a result, the tight labour market has not resulted in any upward pressure on wages, with both nominal and real wages being stagnant. This partly explains why the government's push to increase consumption, spur demand and inflate the economy has, so far, proved only partially successful.

2. Transition economies

After two years of a regional economic downturn caused by a considerable terms-of-trade shock, the economic performance of transition economies in the Commonwealth of Independent States (CIS) finally started to improve in the last quarter of 2016 and the beginning of 2017. A barely positive growth of GDP in 2016 is likely to strengthen moderately in 2017 on the back of a slight increase in global commodity prices from their recent trough, and a modest recovery in the Russian Federation. Given weak global demand, slow growth of international trade, and, in particular, the uncertain future direction of international commodity prices, the prospects for a more dynamic growth of the CIS economies, which are characterized by high commodity dependence and low economic diversification, are not too bright.

The Russian economy's return to growth in 2017 because of the recovery of energy prices will have a positive effect on other CIS economies, which are heavily reliant on remittances and import demand from the leading economy of the region. However, the recent currency devaluations in most of these economies will not translate into much stronger export performance because of their limited manufacturing capacities and the low price elasticity of their main exports. Policy space in several countries will continue to be limited, because of the adoption of IMF programmes, the lingering effects of the recent financial crisis, and the dollarization of their economies. In the medium term, however, the potential influence of China through its "One Belt, One Road" initiative, promises to diminish serious infrastructure and financial bottlenecks of the countries in the region and create conditions for higher economic growth.

In contrast to the CIS countries, the performance of the transition economies in South-East Europe is noticeably better, and is likely to remain so. GDP growth of 2.7 per cent in 2016 is likely to accelerate further and surpass 3 per cent in 2017. The improvement in economic conditions of the European Union, which consumes between 50 per cent and 80 per cent of the total exports of the South-East European economies, coupled with more abundant FDI, increase in remittances from the European Union and growth of tourism receipts, has translated into strengthening of real incomes and domestic demand.

3. Developing countries

(a) Latin America: The costs of dependence

Latin America is among the regions that have been significantly affected by the policy-driven persistence of the Great Recession, with sluggish trade growth and a weak and much-delayed recovery. Short-term assessments point to a minor recovery in 2017 in the economies of Latin America and the Caribbean (LAC), after two years of contraction in 2015 and 2016 when GDP fell by 0.3 per cent and

0.8 per cent respectively. Underlying this is a fall in investment. Aggregate investment rates have fallen from 21.3 per cent in 2013 to 18.4 per cent in 2016. Growth in the region is projected to exceed 1 per cent in 2017, which is a small improvement when seen in the context of the negative growth of the previous two years. To recall, between 2004 and 2010, LAC countries as a group recorded relatively high rates of growth in all years except 2009, when the region, like the rest of the world, suffered the consequences of the financial crisis in Europe and the United States.

However, average performance indicators tend to obscure the heterogeneity that characterizes Latin America, with countries at different points of the economic cycle in 2017. In the case of Mexico, low oil prices and uncertainty regarding United States trade policy are expected to cause a further deceleration in growth to 1.9 per cent in 2017. The situation is more complex in South America. Countries that have been able to cope with the commodity downturn with a degree of success, such as Chile, Colombia and the Plurinational State of Bolivia, are expected to pick up again in 2017. Other oil exporters, such as the Bolivarian Republic of Venezuela and Ecuador, are expected to continue with low growth. Brazil, the largest economy of the region, is projected to stabilize after two years of economic contraction, albeit achieving a rate of growth of just 0.1 per cent. In general, Central American and Caribbean economies have been able to outperform commodity exporters in South America.

As discussed in various *TDR*s since 2003, the relatively long period of high growth in Latin America and the subsequent bust was closely connected to commodity price movements and related capital flows.

In many countries, commodity exports have a significance far beyond being drivers of foreign exchange earnings. In the case of Mexico, for example, net oil exports accounted for only 0.7 per cent of GDP in 2014, but they amounted to 30 per cent of fiscal revenues. This makes the impact of a decline in oil revenues far more significant than the importance of those export revenues to the country's GDP. Overall, the fiscal position of many countries in the region improved because of the gains from increases in the volume as well as the terms of trade. On the other hand, when the boom ended, public revenue growth was adversely affected, undermining the ability of Latin American governments to finance the many

social protection and redistribution schemes they had put in place, which had helped to reduce poverty and inequality. Between 2002 and 2014, general government social spending across the region rose from 15.2 per cent to 19.5 per cent of GDP (ECLAC, 2017). Although central government spending remained broadly stable after the commodity shock, amounting to 20.5 per cent of GDP in 2016, the fiscal deficit in South America increased from 2 per cent in 2013 to 3.9 per cent in 2016. This willingness to increase borrowing (from a low base) has softened the impact of the commodity bust, but the effects of the latter are visible.

The recent reversal of commodity price trends has led to the expectation that the recession in many LAC countries has now bottomed out. Average GDP growth rate in 2017 for the South American economies as a group is projected to be 0.6 per cent. Even this low but positive growth estimate is encouraging, inasmuch as it comes in the wake of two years of contraction in South America. The subregion contracted 1.8 per cent in 2015 and 2.5 per cent in 2016.

In Mexico, inflation triggered by currency depreciation resulting from a trade slowdown has prompted the Mexican Central Bank to implement contractionary monetary policy measures, while the government is in the midst of a multi-year fiscal consolidation plan. According to the OECD's index of industrial production, production is slightly down in the first quarter of 2017, after an essentially flat year in 2016 (growth of −0.1 per cent). Exports fell 1.9 per cent in 2016 despite the export advantages that exchange rate depreciation is supposed to bring. The merchandise trade balance in Mexico has been negative every year since 1997, despite its sizeable merchandise trade surplus with the United States (which was equivalent to 10.7 per cent of the GDP of Mexico in 2015).

Matters are better for the Central American economies, in which growth (excluding Mexico) had decelerated from 4.3 per cent in 2015 to 3.7 per cent in 2016. Because of resilient domestic demand, this deceleration appears to have been halted, with the growth rate forecast for 2017 placed at 4 per cent. For the Caribbean, average growth is forecast at a respectable 2.6 per cent in 2017, when compared with a contraction of 1.7 per cent in 2016.

Another factor often referred to when examining the influences on economic expansion in the LAC region is the movement of capital into and out of countries, which – through its direct impact on investment, and indirect impact mediated by the levels of liquidity and credit and by exchange rates and export volumes – can affect growth. However, from an examination of trends in the biggest six LAC countries during this century it appears that only two (Brazil and Mexico) benefited substantially from the post-2003 surge in cross-border flows. Even in their case, such flows were very volatile and the period since mid-2014 has seen a collapse in capital inflows. This compounded the problems created by the end of the commodity boom, by depressing domestic investment and consumption as well.

In sum, while growth is low in much of the LAC region, it seems to have hit a floor from which some economies at least seem to be rebounding. The problem is that a strong recovery seems to be dependent on a significant turnaround in export prices and volumes, which, given trends elsewhere in the world economy, especially in China, seems unlikely in the near future. In addition, there is considerable uncertainty with respect to the trade policies that the current United States Administration would adopt, which could have significant implications for growth in the region.

(b) African growth engine back in second gear

Beginning in 2014, lower global oil prices and the end of the commodity boom have affected the African continent (parts of which also suffered a drought) extremely adversely, with growth in the region falling from 3 per cent in 2015 to 1.5 per cent in 2016, and projected to rise to 2.7 per cent in 2017. This masks significant differences in the growth performance of individual countries in 2016, from above 7 per cent in Côte d'Ivoire and Ethiopia, to 1.1 per cent in Morocco and 0.3 per cent in South Africa. In addition, Nigeria saw GDP contracting by 1.5 per cent, while Equatorial Guinea recorded a fall of around 7 per cent.

In the case of many of these economies, their recent predicament is the result of a long-term failure to ensure growth through diversification, and in most case overdependence on one or a very few commodities. An extreme case is Nigeria, one of the largest economies of the African region, where the oil and gas sector accounts for a little more than a third of its GDP and more than 90 per cent of export earnings. The oil price decline dampened demand through its direct effects and indirect effects on government revenues and expenditures, and so was clearly responsible

for economic contraction in Nigeria. The recovery in early 2017 is still halting at best. On the other hand, the absence of adequate economic diversification and the consequent dependence on imports has meant that current account deficits have widened, leading to currency depreciation and domestic inflation. So the structure of the Nigerian economy has made it a victim of stagflation driven by current global circumstances. Other economies affected by recent oil price movements include Democratic Republic of the Congo; Equatorial Guinea, where oil accounts for 90 per cent of GDP and is almost the only export earner; and Libya, which derives 95 per cent of its export revenues from oil.

Given the overall high level of commodity-export dependence in African economies, the generalized decline and subsequent low level of commodity prices noted earlier has generated similar outcomes in many other economies. Needless to say, the extent and duration of the price change varied. Non-fuel commodity prices rose 1.7 per cent in 2016 relative to 2015 levels, partly due to the slow recovery in metal and mineral prices, as the deceleration of growth in China led to falls in demand. China accounts for 9 per cent of African merchandise exports and primary commodities account for about 92 per cent of African exports to China. As a result, countries with all kinds of commodity dependence have been affected adversely.

Meanwhile, South Africa fell into a "technical recession", two consecutive quarters of negative GDP growth, with a drop of 0.3 per cent in the fourth quarter of 2016, followed by a drop of 0.7 per cent in the first quarter of 2017[7]. This contraction was due to the poor performance of manufacturing and trade, so much so that despite marked production improvements in agriculture and mining, the contraction of the former two sectors could not be neutralized. Clearly internal demand constraints have also played a role here.

All in all, Africa has been hit badly in the current global environment, even though East Africa, led by Ethiopia, Kenya, Rwanda and United Republic of Tanzania, managed to record respectable growth in 2016.

(c) Can high growth return to developing Asia?

Asia continues to be the most dynamic region in the world economy, with robust domestic demand in the region's largest economies helping to keep GDP growth on a reasonable even keel. Growth in the region, though modest relative to the recent historical trend, is an estimated 5.1 per cent in 2016 and projected to be 5.2 per cent for 2017. The corresponding figures for the two most populated and fastest-growing countries in the region were 6.7 per cent in 2016 and estimated to stay the same in 2017 for China; and 7 per cent and 6.7 per cent for India.[8] The issue in the region, therefore, is not the rate of growth relative to the rest of the world, but rather whether the future is going to see a return to the much higher rates of growth of the past or approach lower levels. In fact, the slowdown in China, which has become a major source of global demand, gives some cause for concern. There are reasons to worry about other countries in the region too, particularly because the contribution of investment to overall growth has also waned, especially in countries such as Indonesia, Malaysia and Thailand.

The export-led growth strategy of some of the countries in the region is coming under severe strain amid the continuing weakness in external demand, volatile capital flows and tightening of global financial conditions. The economies of South-East Asia are unlikely to see a return to the growth rates enjoyed before the global crisis any time soon. Exports continued to remain low for cyclical and structural reasons; despite a partial recovery in 2016, they dipped far below what was observed in the years following the 2008 crisis until 2012 for most countries of the region. In addition to industrial exports, the region has also experienced trade losses among net commodity exporters (e.g. Indonesia) to some extent. Imports, having contracted during the first half of 2016, recovered in the latter half of 2016 in many countries of the region such as China, India, Indonesia and Thailand. Growth in a number of countries in South Asia, including Bangladesh and Pakistan, appears to have benefited in recent years from new opportunities linked to the "One Belt, One Road" initiative in China.

The gradual slowdown of China is expected to continue as it moves ahead with rebalancing its economy, towards domestic markets. However, the explosion of domestic debt since the crisis is proving a major challenge to sustained growth. According to comparable data from the Bank for International Settlements, the debt-to-GDP ratio of China stands at 249 per cent as compared with 248 per cent in the United States and 279 per cent in the euro zone. Despite this debt build-up, which calls for deleveraging, every time there are signs of a slowdown the only instrument

in the hands of the Chinese Government seems to be to expand credit. Fears of a hard landing resulted in a ¥6.2 trillion increase in debt in the first three months of 2017.[9]

The Indian banking sector, too, which since 2003 has expanded credit to the retail sector (involving personal loans of various kinds, especially those for housing investments and car purchases) and to the corporate sector (including for infrastructure projects), is now burdened with large volumes of stressed and non-performing assets. Data for all banks (public and private), relating to December 2016, point to a 59.3 per cent increase over the previous 12 months, taking it to 9.3 per cent of their advances, compared with a non-performing assets (NPAs) to advances ratio of 3.5 per cent at the end of 2012.[10]

Rising NPAs are making banks much more cautious in their lending practices with signs of a reduction in the pace of credit creation. Since debt-financed private investment and consumption was an important driver of growth in India, it is more than likely that the easing of the credit boom would slow GDP growth as well. Thus, the dependence on debt makes the boom in China and India difficult to sustain and raises the possibility that when the downturn occurs in these countries, deleveraging will accelerate the fall and make recovery difficult. Expecting these countries to continue to serve as the growth poles that would fuel a global recovery is clearly unwarranted.

(d) West Asia

In 2016 GDP growth in West Asia weakened further, dropping to 2.2 per cent, down from 3.7 per cent in 2015 as a result of the fall in oil prices, oil production cuts mandated by OPEC, and fiscal austerity. Reductions in oil production will continue to keep GDP growth in 2017 to around 2.7 per cent, well below pre-crisis levels.

The weak recovery in oil prices after the collapse hurts most the oil exporters, and among them those characterized by extreme dependence on energy for national income, exports and revenues, like the Gulf Cooperation Council countries (GCC – Bahrain, Kuwait, Oman, Qatar, Saudi Arabia and United Arab Emirates). The windfall from the oil price boom of the 2000s resulted in large fiscal and current account surpluses that enabled these countries to rapidly accumulate assets and expand their Sovereign Wealth Funds. For instance, prior to the 2014 oil price fall, in

2013, the regional average fiscal surplus was 9.2 per cent of GDP. However, between 2014 and the end of 2016, regional budget surpluses have given way to a deficit averaging 10.4 per cent of GDP; while current account surpluses gave way to deficits averaging 3.3 per cent of GDP.

Over 2015–2016, economic performance in the subregion has been dominated by the terms-of-trade shock delivered by the collapse in oil prices that started in June 2014 and the subsequent policy responses to the shock. Reacting to the terms-of-trade shock, governments drew down reserves and sold Sovereign Wealth Fund assets, resorted to large-scale external borrowing ($38.9 billion in 2016 alone), adopted domestic fiscal austerity involving spending cuts, placed controls on the public sector wage bill and reduced subsidies. With oil prices not expected to return to budgetary breakeven levels, fiscal deficits and financing needs are expected to remain large in GCC countries over the short to medium term.

The strong growth of Turkey since 2000 has doubled its per capita GDP and propelled it to the status of an upper-middle income country, with the seventeenth-largest economy in the world. However, since 2015, Turkey has not been able to sustain this performance. In 2016, GDP growth rate decelerated to 3 per cent, down from 5.8 per cent in 2015 but is projected to pick up to around 4 per cent in 2017. Unemployment in 2016 rose to 10.9 per cent, up from 9.1 per cent in 2011. A sharp decline in tourism revenue, the rise in global oil prices and the depreciation of the lira have contributed to a more difficult economic environment. The Iranian economy has, by contrast, been experiencing a revival, with growth of 4.7 per cent in 2016 and an estimated 5.1 per cent in 2017 (as compared with 0.4 per cent in 2015), thanks largely to a sharp increase in oil production after the lifting of sanctions, and the effects of this on household incomes, consumption and domestic investment. Inflation in the Islamic Republic of Iran, which was high during the sanction years, fell to single-digit levels, and is currently around 9 per cent per year. Like other oil-exporting countries, the immediate economic prospects of the Islamic Republic of Iran depend on the trend in oil prices, as oil accounts for around 60 per cent of exports.

C. The way forward

Whether a country has been able to grow largely based on the domestic market or has relied on exports as the driver of growth, global conditions are not conducive for a return to more widespread buoyancy. Talk of technology or trade as the disruptive villains in this narrative distracts from an obvious point: unless significant and sustainable efforts are made to revive global demand through wage growth in a coordinated way, the global economy will be condemned to prolonged stagnation with intermittent pick-ups and recurrent downturns.

In a world of mobile finance and liberalized economic borders, no country can attempt a significant fiscal expansion alone without risking capital flight, a currency collapse and a crisis. On the other hand, closing borders to preclude that outcome is unwelcome and difficult because of the large volume of legacy foreign capital that has accumulated within the borders of many countries. Any sign of imposition of stringent capital controls would trigger large-scale capital flight with the same consequences. What is needed therefore is a globally coordinated strategy of expansion led by state expenditures, with intervention that guarantees some policy space to allow all countries the opportunity of benefiting from the expansion of their domestic and external markets. As of now the sentiment seems to be different, with nationalist rhetoric, protectionist arguments and a beggar-thy-neighbour outlook dominating economic discourse. Growing inequalities feed this xenophobic turn, which provides a convenient "other" to blame for everybody's problems.

Clearly, viable and equitable growth in this context will require a fiscal stimulus, along with other elements of a regulatory and redistributive framework, that must be coordinated across countries. ■

Notes

1 This possibility was anticipated by Michał Kalecki, 1971 [1943]: 4–5.

2 The IMF figure is based on PPP exchange rates, equivalent to 2.9 per cent using market exchange rates.

3 Group of Seven: Canada, France, Germany, Italy, Japan, the United Kingdom and the United States.

4 Estimate by Fitch Ratings quoted in Peter Wells and Don Weinland, "Fitch warns on expected returns from One Belt, One Road", *Financial Times*, 26 January 2017, available at: https://www.ft.com/content/c67b0c05-8f3f-3ba5-8219-e957a90646d1 (accessed 8 May 2017).

5 The average cost of shipping a 40-foot container from China to northern Europe rose from about $400 in March last year to above $2,000 in October. By May, it had fallen back to about $1,700. See Jonathan Wheatley, "Has the global trade revival run out of puff?", *Financial Times*, 30 May 2017, available at: https://www.ft.com/content/d94e8898-412d-11e7-9d56-25f963e998b2 (accessed 17 July 2017).

6 Data on trade in services described in this paragraph come from *UNCTADstat* and correspond to the concepts and definitions of the IMF (2009), *Balance of Payments and International Investment Position Manual*, sixth edition.

7 Statistics South Africa (2017), *Gross Domestic Product, First Quarter 2017*, available at: http://www.statssa.gov.za/publications/P0441/P04411stQuarter2017.pdf (accessed 17 July 2017).

8 China is reported to have grown at an annual rate of 6.9 per cent in the first two quarters of 2017, and India has reported a fall in growth to 6.2 per cent in the first quarter.

9 Gabriel Wildau and Don Weinland, "China debt load reaches record high as risk to economy mounts", *Financial Times*, 24 April 2016, available at: https://www.ft.com/content/acd3f2fc-084a-11e6-876d-b823056b209b?mhq5j=e1 (accessed 14 July 2017).

10 Data compiled by Care Ratings and reported in George Mathew, "Bad loan crisis continues: 56.4 per cent rise in NPAs of banks", *The Indian Express*, 20 February 2017, available at: http://indianexpress.com/article/business/banking-and-finance/bad-loan-crisis-continues-56-4-per-cent-rise-in-npas-of-banks-rbi-4533685/ (accessed 17 July 2017).

References

ECLAC (2017). *Social Panorama of Latin America 2016*. Santiago de Chile, United Nations Economic Commission for Latin America and the Caribbean.

IMF (2007). *World Economic Outlook: Globalization and Inequality*, October. Washington, DC, International Monetary Fund.

IMF (2017). *World Economic Outlook: Gaining Momentum?* April. Washington, DC, International Monetary Fund.

Kalecki M (1971 [1943]). Political aspects of full employment. In: Kalecki M, *Selected Essays on the Dynamics of a Capitalist Economy: 1933–1970*. Cambridge, Cambridge University Press: 138–145.

UNCTAD (2017). *Review of Maritime Transport 2017*. United Nations publication. New York and Geneva (forthcoming).

UNCTAD (*TDR 2016*). Trade and Development Report, 2016: Structural transformation for inclusive and sustained growth. United Nations publication. Sales No. E.16.II.D.5. New York and Geneva.

WTO (2017). Annual Report 2017. World Trade Organization, Geneva.

UNWTO (2017). *World Tourism Barometer and Statistical Annex*, volume 15(3), July. Madrid, World Tourism Organization.

INCLUSIVE GROWTH: ISSUES AT STAKE

II

A. An age of anxiety

Anxiety is fast becoming a new *zeitgeist* of the twenty-first century global economy. While the sources of anxiety among those disillusioned with globalization are well known, if not fully understood, recent events have raised considerable alarm amongst its proponents. Any sign of rising trade protection, or talk of currency wars or stricter controls on migration, have been interpreted as the start of a dangerous race to roll back the open global economic order built over the previous seven decades. Some are even warning of a return to the kind of economic and political chaos witnessed during the interwar years.

There are, undoubtedly, reasons to worry about the current health of the global economy, and about emerging threats to rising living standards, political stability and environmental sustainability. Questions over the strength and effectiveness of multilateral institutions designed to help manage the challenges of an interdependent world order are also of concern. However, much of the current discussion assumes that these institutions were immaculately conceived at the end of the Second World War, and that, subsequently, they have overseen a steady march towards a level global playing field of open and competitive markets and broadly shared prosperity. The reality is more punctuated and nuanced.

The three decades or so after the Second World War ushered in multilateral rules and structures to prevent "beggar-thy-neighbour" policies, restrain volatile capital flows and extend international cooperation. But there was still enough space for national governments to undertake proactive public policies in support of full employment and extended welfare provision in the North, and resource mobilization and industrialization in the South. This balancing act was built around a political consensus (and related compromises) aimed at avoiding a repeat of the

international economic disintegration of the 1930s, and the waste, wretchedness and war that followed. That consensus required the leading economies (and their corporations) to accept some constraints on their ability to dominate international markets and to move capital freely from location to location, whilst giving a privileged role to the dollar as a means of stabilizing foreign exchange markets. But it also supported high rates of aggregate capital formation along with wages that rose broadly in line with productivity in the developed countries. These generated strong global aggregate demand, leading to a rapid rise in international trade. Nevertheless, this remained only a *partial globalization*, in that the rules and structures were designed primarily by and for developed rather than developing countries, and was concerned more with openness to trade than to financial flows or transfers of technology.

These arrangements buckled under a series of distributional pressures and economic shocks in the 1970s, giving way to *hyperglobalization* from the early 1980s. It was characterized by an extensive deregulation of markets – particularly financial and currency markets – in rich and poor countries alike, the attrition of the public realm, and the extension of profit-making opportunities to ever-widening spheres of not only economic, but also social, cultural and political life. The associated withdrawal of public oversight and management of the economy included the curtailment, and sometimes even the elimination, of policy measures previously used by States to manage their integration into the global economy. This was based on the belief that the unregulated forces of supply and demand were best suited to this task.

New patterns and players in international trade emerged along with a surge in international capital flows and significant shifts in the international division of labour. East Asia's strong growth trajectory established under partial globalization continued, and spread to China. Rapid growth in China from the late 1990s, along with the loosening of monetary and credit policy in the North, which was required to keep hyperglobalization running after the dotcom crisis, triggered a period of robust growth and poverty reduction across the developing world in the first decade of the new millennium. However, progress with respect to structural transformation, employment and distributional outcomes has been uneven, and in some cases it has even experienced a reversal (*TDR 2016*).

Hyperglobalization has also been accompanied by a radical break in the governance of the post-war international framework, whereby "bodies once designed to foster sovereignty are now recast to curtail it" (Mazower, 2012: 421). Meanwhile, there has been a proliferation of more informal cross-border governance arrangements built around corporate networks and public-private partnerships. Developing countries are typically expected to commit to a level of obligations much closer to those of developed countries, and across a range of areas extending well beyond tariffs and related border restrictions. Expansionary monetary policies have become the principal instrument of macroeconomic management, even as tight fiscal policies have constrained expansion. And the goal of financial stability has taken a back seat to the promotion of "financialization", enabling financial markets, financial motives, financial institutions and financial elites to assume the upper hand in the operation of the economy and its governing institutions, at both the national and international levels. Together these pressures have steadily eroded the checks and balances that had previously helped channel market forces into the creative and productive activities needed for long-term growth. Capital formation has stagnated, speculative investments (by banks, businesses and households) have proliferated, and rising levels of private debt have replaced rising wages as the binding agent in increasingly insecure and fragile socio-economic structures.

Even as many economists were anticipating a prolonged period of economic stability and income convergence, hyperglobalization entered its own *dämmerung* with the financial crisis of 2008–2009, causing deep and long-lasting damage in the developed economies and a delayed, but now evident, slowdown in developing economies. As discussed in chapter V of this *Report*, the crisis was linked to

FIGURE 2.1 GDP recovery in the United States after three crises: 1929, 1980 and 2008–2009
(Percentage change)

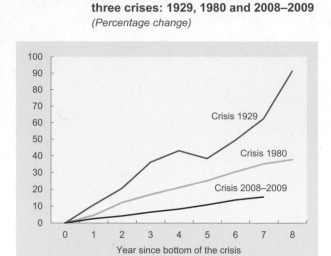
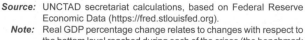

Source: UNCTAD secretariat calculations, based on Federal Reserve Economic Data (https://fred.stlouisfed.org).
Note: Real GDP percentage change relates to changes with respect to the bottom level reached during each of the crises (the benchmark years being 1933, 1982 and 2009 respectively).

rising economic inequalities both as a cause and an effect, and those inequalities were further accentuated by the policies adopted after the crisis. This trend has become a growing concern for policymakers seeking to promote hyperglobalization to an increasingly sceptical public.

Global economic ties have broken down before, most notably at the end of the 1920s and during the 1970s. In both instances, volatile financial flows were the catalyst, but policy choices in the leading economies determined the response. However, unlike these previous episodes, the 2008–2009 financial crisis has not yet elicited a deep-seated reform agenda aimed at establishing a new growth path (figure 2.1). Rather, the global economy has spluttered along a familiar policy route towards "a new normal", wherein "global growth has become too low, for too long benefiting too few" (Lagarde, 2016). In this context, the abiding neoliberal refrain that "there is no alternative" has not only compounded a growing sense of popular frustration; it has also begun to erode the trust between citizens and their political representatives.

To prevent this new normal from becoming seriously disruptive and disorderly, attention has turned to making hyperglobalization "work for all". It is acknowledged that some individuals, communities, and even countries, lack the information, incentives or ingenuity required to grasp the opportunities offered by today's borderless and knowledge-intensive world. Since these are essentially viewed as matters of omission rather than commission, the resulting policy challenge is defined less in terms of changing the rules of the game than ensuring that all the players are properly equipped to participate.

This view misses a crucial point, that most of those who have experienced absolute or relative declines in economic well-being have not been excluded from the processes of hyperglobalization; rather, they have been integrated into such processes, often deeply so, even as they have been excluded from the benefits, and have typically borne the bulk of its costs (Meek, 2017). They have participated in more flexible labour markets that offer precarious and insecure jobs, often at lower wages, while large rootless corporations have enjoyed booming profits; they have had to deal with the consequences of fiscal austerity in the form of reduced public services and social protection, while high-wealth individuals have hidden away their runaway earnings in exotic locations; they have struggled under mounting debts as their underlying assets have been buffeted by distant financial forces; and they have watched as the managers of those same forces have been bailed out, even as their own communities have been left to sink into decay and despair.

This simultaneity of inclusion and exclusion leaves hopeful phrases such as "work for all" and "inclusive growth" open to misrepresentation. Many of its champions simply take it as a given that technological progress and the spread of market forces impart an inevitability to hyperglobalization, such

that policymakers are reduced to finding the most market-friendly ways of compensating "the losers" and extending a helping hand to those "left behind".

In reality, the economic and political consequences of the interdependence of nations, the rise and spread of new technologies and the breakdown of existing ways of life have been a recurring source of policy debate and design since at least the French Revolution, if not earlier (Stedman Jones, 2004). Hyperglobalization is not an independent and immutable economic force over which governments have no control. Rather, it has resulted from a set of politically constructed rules, norms, practices and policies that shape the ways in which countries, their firms and their citizens interact with their counterparts elsewhere in the global economy. And as social and economic gaps widen, within and across countries, it is hardly surprising that trust in the rules of the game (and in those administering them) to deliver fair and inclusive outcomes is breaking down, with further damaging consequences.

What is perhaps more surprising is the resilience of those rules, despite the consequences. In particular the institutions, policies and regulatory norms relating to financial markets, corporate governance, wage bargaining and macroeconomic management, have persisted without much change despite repeated shocks and crises. As noted in chapter I of this *Report*, a decade after the global financial crisis began to unfold, many of the economic and social imbalances that preceded it persist, and may even have increased; and austerity has remained the default policy response to a variety of economic troubles.

B. A more measured debate? Estimating trends in inequality and exclusion

There is now a greater willingness to acknowledge that inequality may be an obstacle to growth, that it can pose a serious political threat to more open societies, and that current levels of inequality are morally unacceptable. However, the challenge of forging a more inclusive agenda is compounded by difficulties in measuring the problem. In recent years, poverty has been the metric of choice, particularly in the international community, in part because it seems to be relatively easy to measure, and it speaks to a tangible challenge. However, beyond some basic indicators of extreme deprivation, measuring poverty has never

been straightforward; it is subject to changing social attitudes and political sentiments (Reddy and Lahoti, 2016). Moreover, poverty data quickly become embroiled in a whole range of contentious issues that divide supporters and critics of hyperglobalization; for example, is it "the market" or the Chinese State that deserves the most applause for lifting more than a billion people out of extreme poverty?

The United Nations Sustainable Development Goals (SDGs), with their related targets and indicators, offer a comprehensive monitoring framework for policymakers concerned with fostering inclusive development.[1] Goal 10 of the SDGs calls for reducing inequalities based not only on income, but also on age, sex, disability, race, ethnicity, origin, religion and economic or other criteria, both within a country and among countries. And because income inequality is strongly linked to other measures of social well-being, it continues to provide an obvious departure point for tackling the wider inclusiveness challenge (Wilkinson and Pickett, 2009).

Measuring inequality, however, has its own long and contested history. Part of the difficulty is that *economic* sources of inequality are many and complex, and they are often connected to forms of *categorical* inequality that arise out of multiple social and cultural identities (Galbraith, 2016). The class and gender aspects of this relationship are examined in chapter IV. The measuring difficulties are compounded by an increasingly interdependent world, where, clearly, there is a need for some internationally comparable income- and/or consumption-related measures of inequality that will allow comparison across countries and over time. Not surprisingly, considerable lacunae in the data persist, and efforts to fill the gaps are perforce largely assumption-driven. The results are sensitive not only to what is being measured and how, but also to various other factors such as country selection and weighting, the time periods covered and the exchange rates used for making local data internationally comparable.[2]

There are also issues relating to measuring incomes or consumption within countries. While household surveys, earnings data and tax records are commonly used in developed economies to generate income inequality data, different series can generate divergent trends. To give some indication of the problems involved, Atkinson (2015) has recorded the variations in individual earnings dispersion and household inequality since the 1950s for the United Kingdom and the United States of America, which demonstrate some clear disparities between two countries that are often portrayed as sharing a common history of inequality trends. But since such data for developing countries tend to be less extensive, replicating these series for many of these countries would be almost impossible.

It is true that in recent years, researchers have been exploiting new data sources and devising new inequality measures (Atkinson, 2015; Picketty, 2014; Milanovic, 2016; Palma, 2011; Cobham et al., 2015; Galbraith, 2016; Lahoti et al., 2016). Piketty and

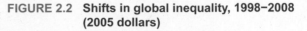

FIGURE 2.2 Shifts in global inequality, 1998−2008 (2005 dollars)

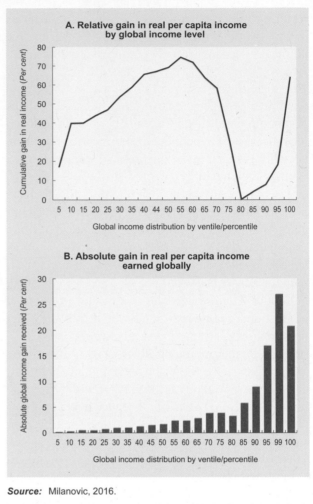

Source: Milanovic, 2016.

his colleagues, in particular, have made significant strides in tracking the income (and more recently wealth) of the top 1 per cent of income earners, albeit concentrating largely on the developed world. Chapter V of this *Report* uses the relatively new Palma ratio in its discussion of the links between income inequality and economic crises. This is the ratio of the share in gross national income (GNI) of the top 10 per cent of income earners to that of the bottom 40 per cent in any given country, and is well-suited to capturing polarization trends, assuming, as the empirical evidence broadly suggests, that the share of the "homogeneous middle" of income earners (i.e. those receiving between 90 and 50 per cent of GNI) has been relatively stable in most countries. However, while the index draws attention to polarization, it does not capture the material insecurity of the middle classes that has been widely observed in many developed countries. Chapter IV of this *Report* uses the more familiar measure of the labour share of national income to assess the impact of gender inequality in labour markets on the functional distribution of income. This is of significance because, as women's participation in the labour force increases – a nearly universal phenomenon in both developed and developing countries in the era of hyperglobalization – household incomes rise because of additional workers, and not because of rising wages.

Although statistical challenges persist at the national level, bold attempts have been made to construct a comprehensive measure of global inequality, combining inequality both within and across countries,

and its evolution over time. This has given rise to Milanovic's elephant chart (figure 2.2A) based on relative gains in real per capita income across income ventiles of the global population between 1988 and 2008, which reveals an emerging middle class in the South, the hollowing out of the traditional middle class in developed economies and an absconding global elite. But as Milanovic (2016) also notes, the absolute gains in real per capita income may be the more telling statistic (figure 2.2B). Inevitably, judging which of these measures – absolute or relative – best reflect the inequality challenge is an issue that continues to divide analysts and policymakers.

C. Explaining inequality and exclusion: Trade, technology and jobs

It may seem incongruous to talk about inclusive growth without first identifying possible causes of exclusion from the benefits of growth. However, much of the recent discussion about making globalization more inclusive does precisely that.[3] As a result, even as inequality has emerged as a primary political concern, the international community has lacked a convincing narrative linking distributional issues to the challenges of growth and development; instead, it has been focusing on the failure of national policymakers to adapt to the borderless forces of economic progress (*Economist*, 2016; Emmott, 2017).

The current discussion continues a debate that began in the early 1990s, on whether it is increased North-South trade or technological change that is the principal source of economic disruption in the developed economies. The details of earlier debates have been discussed in previous Reports (*TDRs 1995; 1997; 2012*). Suffice it to note here that the reluctance on the part of conventional economists to attribute significant economic damage to trade shocks[4] is due to the assumptions common to most theoretical trade models and simulation exercises based on the computable general equilibrium (CGE) model of fully employed resources and competitive markets (Kohler and Storm, 2016). This leaves technological change as the default explanation for labour market disruption, a line of argument that has been readily extended from the problems of unemployment in the early 1990s to rising inequality today.[5] The impact of technological change is usually traced to relative price movements, the factor content of production and elasticities of substitution, with a bias

towards new technologies (particularly information and communication technologies, or ICTs) that give skilled labour a wage premium over unskilled labour, thereby skewing income distribution. This argument (examined further in chapter III) seems to offer a more palatable explanation than trade shocks, given the ubiquitous reach of technological change and its reported growth impulses (traditionally measured through the large residual in growth accounting exercises). It also lends itself to an easy policy agenda that targets education as the surest way to achieve more inclusive growth.

The IMF (2017) has recently extended the technological change argument to explain falling wage shares in the North. It argues that technological progress, as reflected in the steep decline in the relative price of investment goods, has disproportionately encouraged firms to replace labour with capital, especially in more routine-based occupations. This argument assumes that changes in capital intensity result only from changing relative prices of capital and labour. It ignores the effects of the pattern of demand and the resulting product mix, which can make capital intensities of individual industries less significant in driving overall capital intensity. Overall, this focus on technology as the chief determinant of profit and wage shares downplays the impact of the power of the financial sector, reflected in that sector's much higher share of profits (driven principally by capital gains) as well as its higher share in gross domestic product (GDP) compared with those of the manufacturing sector – features that have persisted even after the 2008 crisis.

The "trade versus technology" discussion has served to highlight the critical role of employment in fostering inclusive economies, particularly given that a growing number of households are increasingly worried that the kind of stable, well-paid jobs needed to secure a middle-class lifestyle have already been hollowed out in the developed economies, and are also increasingly out of reach for an aspiring middle class in many emerging economies (OECD and World Bank, 2016). However, the evidence linking greater inequality to either trade or technology remains inconclusive, in part because the scale of changes in both these areas over the past two decades does not directly match the pattern of job destruction in the manufacturing sector (Schmitt et al., 2013). This is particularly so given recent evidence of falling productivity growth, and the heavy skewing of rewards in favour of those at the very top of the income ladder. Moreover, rising inequality also reflects growing wage differentials amongst those with the same or similar educational credentials (Mishel, 2011). These discrepancies have led to more hybrid accounts of rising inequality, which incorporate institutional changes in labour markets, changes in macroeconomic policies and changing interactions between trade and finance. The IMF (2007), for example, has argued that it was a mixture of technological progress and financial openness that turbo-charged the income premium for highly skilled and professional workers (including those in finance) as the most potent source of inequality. It also found that foreign direct investment (FDI) was a significant source of both faster growth and rising inequality, as it increasingly intertwined with trade and technology through global value chains.[6] On some assessments, the resulting reconfiguration of the international division of labour around these chains has helped narrow income gaps across countries (Baldwin, 2016), but on others, it is part of a "hollowing out" of the middle class in developed economies (Temin, 2017) and a "middle-income trap" in some developing economies (*TDR 2016*; Felipe et al., 2014), with ambiguous effects on gender inequality (see chapter IV). In any case, as noted in *TDR 2012*, what are seen as purely technology-driven distributional effects may well be related to shifts in macroeconomic policy, as well as to international wage competition that has been at least partly driven by trade and by changes in corporate behaviour resulting from domestic deregulation and financial globalization.

Another approach to making hyperglobalization work for all has seen the inclusiveness challenge as essentially about overcoming marginalization. The prediction that poverty could be alleviated by simply reducing the role of the State in the economy and by opening up to global market forces, which was expected to trigger rapid income gains, some of which would "trickle down" to the poorest segments of society, has not come to pass. Some research reported that the growth dividend from globalization was spread equally across all income cohorts, with little evidence that targeted policies made much of a difference (Dollar and Kray, 2001). But other research found that lower income cohorts were often further marginalized as growth picked up, thus requiring targeted, "pro-poor" growth policies (Kakwani et al., 2000). Subsequently, there has been a convergence of sorts on the view that stimulating growth serves to reduce absolute poverty, while targeted measures can raise the relative standing of the poor (Bourguignon, 2015). As a result, the World Bank introduced its Poverty Reduction Strategy Papers, which added (market-based) provision of primary education and health care to its traditional adjustment packages (UNCTAD, 2002), placing greater emphasis on the importance of human capital and sound economic governance (including the effective provision of public goods) as part of a more inclusive growth agenda (Commission on Growth and Development, 2008).[7] Widespread calls for increasing women's participation in paid activities, especially entrepreneurship, as a path to higher growth echo these perspectives. More recently, the World Economic Forum (WEF, 2017) has adopted a similar approach in response to the challenges of the so-called Fourth Industrial Revolution. It advocates a set of institutional and policy measures that moves beyond economic growth to focus on "people and living standards" through an emphasis on education, training and protection for non-standard work practices.

By contrast, the classical development literature on the interplay between growth, structural change and income distribution, directly addressed exclusionary pressures in the process of development. Kuznets (1955) described a trade-off between growth and inequality over the course of structural transformation: industrialization and urbanization would first generate rising inequality before levelling off and giving way to greater equality in a post-industrial context, as demographic, technological and other exclusionary pressures waned and political power became more evenly distributed. The dual-economy model of Arthur Lewis (1955) addressed the trade-off between growth and inequality by rejecting the assumptions that resources are always fully employed and that markets are perfectly competitive and clear automatically, thereby opening distributional outcomes to bargaining. Others argued that "polarization" is a permanent feature of market forces due to their strong cumulative tendencies (Myrdal, 1970), the first-mover advantages that could accrue from economies of scale and their lock-in through growing market concentration, which play out both within and between countries. Prebisch (1950) showed how structural and technological gaps across countries could, through unequal terms of trade, perpetuate underdevelopment in the South while reinforcing prosperity in the North. Hymer (1971) identified

similar stratification tendencies linked to the evolution of the multinational corporation, whereby the international division of labour would come to mirror the hierarchical vertical division of labour within the firm. As a result, global poverty was seen as a consequence of both diverging incomes between rich and poor countries, and the capture of State policy and resources by a small elite within developing countries (Myrdal, 1970), but not as an inevitability. A strong role was assigned to proactive policies, at both the national and international levels, to promote greater equality as a catalyst for development (see, for example, Myrdal, 1970: 64; UNCTAD, 1964).[8]

D. Beyond the trade-versus-technology debate: Power and politics

Clearly, institutional arrangements and policy choices have a determining influence over distributional outcomes, given the conflicting interests and unequal bargaining power in both developed economies (Levy and Temin, 2007; Jaumotte and Osorio Buitron, 2015; Stiglitz, 2015; Atkinson, 2015) and developing economies (Cornia and Martorano, 2012; Milanovic, 2016). This role of relative power means that economic polarization within and across countries and along various axes (wage earners and profit earners, skilled and unskilled workers, creditors and debtors, and financial and industrial interests) cannot be adequately addressed through a singular focus on either trade or technological change (*TDRs 1997*; *2012*). In particular, the impact of such changes cannot be isolated from the macroeconomic and institutional settings in which different groups voice their claims and bargain over the outcomes. This *Report* argues further, that the workings of the global economy and of individual national economies are closely tied to the cumulative sources of market power augmented through specific policy measures, including those that have helped to boost profits at the expense of wages. This has given rise to unstable growth regimes, driven by rising levels of debt, and it reinforces the point that hyperglobalization has become intimately connected to the financialization of economic activity and to concomitant increases in income inequality within and across economies.

Since the financial crisis of 2008–2009, researchers have paid growing attention to these links between polarization and instability, in part because inequality is increasingly considered a factor that contributed

to that crisis (Stiglitz, 2012; Stockhammer, 2015). Thomas Piketty's *Capital* has become the leading opus in this emerging canon, and, despite its methodological shortcomings (Galbraith, 2014; Rowthorn, 2014; O'Sullivan, 2015), it has refocused the inequality debate from the bottom of the income ladder (extreme poverty) to the top 1 per cent. This, in turn, has drawn attention to systemic economic causes of rising inequality. Moreover, by bringing wealth back into the discussion, Piketty has revived Adam Smith's political economy aphorism (borrowed from Thomas Hobbes) that wealth is power, and – by implication – that an increasingly unequal distribution of wealth is likely to skew political power, and with it, policy design in favour of those at the top of the income ladder.[9]

The issue of economic power – its distribution, dynamics, uses and implications – is an underlying and occasionally explicit theme of this *Report*. The continued power of finance to influence and benefit from national policies and regulations, as well as international structures and rules, has been discussed extensively in previous *TDRs* under the rubric of finance-led globalization. This has contributed to a climate of wage repression, which in turn affects patterns of consumption and investment. The resulting debt overhangs generate stagnationary or recessionary conditions. However, these cannot be redressed by equivalent public spending because of the continued focus on fiscal austerity. Such a focus itself is a reflection of the continued power of finance in influencing public policy choices. Asymmetric power structures (as expressed in relational inequalities such as those relating to gender discrimination) can segment labour and other markets, and thereby affect macroeconomic processes, as discussed in chapter IV. The nature of technological change (e.g. the advance of more automated production systems) and its impact tend to be seen as an external wave that impacts economies and societies in ways they cannot control, as discussed further in chapter III. However, as that chapter suggests, both the nature of that change and its implications are affected by policies and processes within economies, which in turn are driven by power dynamics within and between countries. Finally, corporate power in general − both sheer market power and the ability to gain from different kinds of rent − plays a significant role in influencing economic policies and in shaping macroeconomic patterns and distributional outcomes, as discussed in chapter VI.

E. Markets and inclusiveness

Since the global financial crisis of 2008−2009, making hyperglobalization more inclusive has become the new mantra in policy circles at both the national and international levels, and it has assumed even greater urgency following a series of unexpected political shocks in 2016. Partly because that crisis exposed the myth of efficient and self-correcting markets, policymakers have become more open to addressing "market failures" and to contemplating more radical measures to mitigate the self-destructive proclivity of some markets (Wolf, 2016). However, much of the inclusiveness agenda, particularly when extended to developing countries, has sought a revival of policies and efforts to boost markets at a local level.

As noted earlier, disappointment with structural adjustment programmes gave rise to a post-Washington Consensus agenda that aimed to include the poor more directly in market-driven wealth-creating processes. Talk of a more "inclusive capitalism" certainly helped to loosen the policy discussion somewhat, but it also reconsidered the poor in developing countries as fledgling entrepreneurs. This resuscitation of the entrepreneur as a catalytic figure in the development process tapped into a strand of the neoliberal project rooted in the Austrian economic tradition (Easterly, 2014).[10]

One of the first to allude to this inclusive entrepreneurial capitalism was Peruvian economist Hernando de Soto (1986), who saw the poor as "entrepreneurs in waiting", frustrated by indifferent bureaucrats and excessive regulations. He suggested that, if these regulations could somehow be dismantled and property rights strengthened, poverty and unemployment would quickly disappear. This claim was backed by Muhammad Yunus, the United States-trained Bangladeshi economist who subsequently received the Nobel Peace Prize along with the iconic Grameen Bank that he founded in 1983. Yunus focused more on the financial constraint on entrepreneurship, claiming that the poor (and particularly poor women) needed only a tiny loan (microcredit) to enable them to establish or expand informal microenterprises − or self-employment ventures − in order to escape poverty.

With the help of international aid agencies and philanthropic organizations, and the appeal of the gender equality arguments that characterized most of these approaches, the idea of poverty alleviation as a micro-motivational challenge quickly gained wider traction. Microcredit was promoted, along with a host of related "bottom-up" ideas designed to more effectively include the poor in creating and managing their own solutions to poverty and social exclusion. "Inclusive capitalism" was espoused through the promotion of concepts such as social entrepreneurship and social enterprises (Borzaga and Defourny, 2001), social capital (Woolcock and Narayan, 2000), the "bottom of the pyramid" notion (Prahalad and Hart, 2002), inclusive value chains (OECD and World Bank, 2015), financial inclusion (World Bank, 2014), and, more recently, new ICT-driven innovations applied to local financial operations, also known as "digital financial inclusion" (Klapper and Singer, 2014).

The simplicity of these innovations has helped expand the scale and scope of the "inclusive capitalism" idea, but with surprisingly little attention to analytical rigour or careful empirical assessment. The resort to a gender narrative in defence of such an approach is examined in greater detail in chapter IV of this *TDR*. But the original idea of individual entrepreneurship via microcredit, in particular, has been found to contain a number of fundamental flaws and it has a sub-standard track record in terms of poverty reduction. This has led to its re-evaluation or abandonment by many institutions and countries (Bateman, 2010; Roodman, 2011; Bateman et al., forthcoming; Bateman and Maclean, 2017).

Specifically, the *types* of businesses established by individual entrepreneurs with the help of microcredit are generally not the sort that boost employment creation – indeed they are more often than not employment displacing – nor do they create a sustainable and equitable local development trajectory based on productive diversification (Reinert, 2007; Sustainable Livelihoods Foundation, 2016). There is a similarly weak record on advancing gender equality or women's economic empowerment (Chant, 2016; Kabeer, 2005). Indeed, there is much evidence to suggest that intermediating scarce financial resources into these activities through microcredit institutions in preference to other types of scaled up activities and enterprises actually *blocks* the development process in the longer run (Bateman, 2010; Bateman and Chang, 2012; Chang, 2010: 157–167). Instead, as argued in *TDR 2016*, productive entrepreneurship in the global South involves the creation of a core of interconnected, formal small and medium-sized enterprises (SMEs) and larger enterprises capable of promoting industrial upgrading and structural transformation. Creating large numbers of new informal microenterprises might look good for the various individuals and programmes that promote individual entrepreneurship as an immediate escape from poverty or as a means to women's empowerment, but the long-term impact on the ground is one of permanently locking in poor communities to only the most unproductive, low-paying, temporary and self-exploitative business practices.[11] However, microcredit's serious failings were largely overlooked thanks to its inclusion into a wider microfinance paradigm, which also included other areas such as micro-savings, micro-insurance and micro-leasing.

This essentially microeconomic perspective on inclusive globalization appears to have found ready supporters in aid agencies, philanthropic organizations and non-governmental organizations (NGOs) (Haering, 2017). However, it fails to address the more systemic causes of exclusion stemming from the unstable and polarizing nature of deregulated markets. In particular, it ignores the new sources of insecurity and inequality that have emerged around market concentration and rent extraction.

F. Rents and rentiers

Two big trends characterize the era of hyperglobalization: a massive explosion in public and private debt, and the rise of super-elites loosely defined as the top 1 per cent of income earners. These trends are associated with the widening gap in ownership of financial assets, particularly short-term financial instruments, and the related growth of financial activities that, as James Tobin (1984) noted long ago, "generate high private rewards disproportionate to their social productivity". This is a world where rent extraction has become a much more pervasive source of income inequality.

The role of rents has a long and contested intellectual history. Some view rents as a hangover from feudal times, reflecting little more than legalized theft that bankrolls a new leisure class; others see them as the catalyst driving technological progress through a process of creative destruction, or as the deserved rewards for unique talents or abilities that enrich our cultures. However, both the classical and neoclassical traditions agree that when rentiers (i.e. those living on largely fixed incomes derived from legal ownership as well as from institutional and political control of physical and financial assets) gain the upper hand over entrepreneurs operating on the basis of expected profit from innovative and risk-taking real investment, the outcome will be "unproductive", "distortionary" and static. Rentiers' competition for a higher share of a given pie will prevail over entrepreneurial initiatives to grow the pie. As Stiglitz (2015: 141) points out, rent-seeking means "getting an income not as a reward for creating wealth but by grabbing a larger share of the wealth that would have been produced anyway", thereby relating the discussion of rising inequality to a range of strategies that in one way or another seek to game the system rather than helping to develop it.

Much of this discussion has focused on the financial sector. Keynes famously anticipated "the euthanasia of the rentier" which he described as "the cumulative oppressive power of the capitalist to exploit the scarcity-value of capital", a power which he viewed as "functionless". Keynes optimistically assumed that a monetary policy of low long-term interest rates, in combination with a gradual socialization of investment, would create a large enough capital stock to make rental (fixed) income from capital non-viable. However, more recent discourse has identified a new generation of rentiers emerging from the financial sector. In a seminal study of the savings and loan crisis in the United States, Akerlof and Roemer (1993) described how "looting" could be used to extract value, and could also become a more generalized strategy of market manipulation, including through the deliberate bankrupting of a company by its senior management to maximize their private gain. Black (2005) and Galbraith (2014) suggest that fraud was at the heart of the 2008 financial crisis, and was enabled by deregulated markets. More generally, firms employing predatory strategies "can quickly come to dominate markets, using their apparent financial success to attract capital, boost market valuation, and expand through mergers and acquisitions" (Galbraith, 2015: 160). At the same time, there is mounting evidence that firms in developed economies, but also in some emerging economies, are diverting profits away from reinvestment into dividend payments, share buy-backs and acquisitions in order to raise share prices and reward senior management (Lazonick, 2016; *TDR 2016*).

Various attempts have been made to gauge the size of rentier incomes in recent years. Defining these as profits realized by firms engaged primarily in financial intermediation plus interest income realized by all non-financial, non-government resident institutional units, Power et al. (2003), for example, found a rising trend in many countries of the Organisation for Economic Co-operation and Development (OECD) beginning in the late 1970s. However, their analysis stops in 2000. Seccareccia and Lavoie (2016) provide a longer trend for the Canada and the United States, albeit using a slightly narrower definition of the rentier class (drawn from Keynes) as owners of low-risk

financial assets. They find a particularly sharp rise in rentier incomes from the late 1970s, followed by a sharp drop in the late 1990s, and subsequently fluctuating around a positive trend through to the 2008 financial crisis. From a more microeconomic perspective, Phillipon and Resheff (2009) show that a significant proportion of the dramatic rise of relative wages in the financial sector in the United States from the mid-1980s is attributable to rents, rather than to education, occupational attributes or ability. This may also help explain the failure of regulators to keep tabs on the fraud that became inherent in that sector during this period. Wider distributional consequences of rentier strategies have surfaced since the 2008–2009 financial crisis through the socialization of losses, largely paid for by the bottom 90 per cent of the population, and with a particularly heavy burden carried by the lowest income segments. In so doing, this has compounded the privatization of earlier profits.

However, less attention has been given to the ways in which non-financial corporations have become adept at using rent-seeking strategies to bolster their profits. Indeed, financial incomes constitute only one part of rents in this broad definition. A significant proportion of rents has also accrued through monopolies or quasi-monopolies created by intellectual property rights (IPRs), while still others can be described as "political rents" derived from the ability to influence particular aspects and details of government policies in ways that disproportionately favour certain players. Recent evidence of rising market concentration across several sectors, both at the national and international levels, has revived interest in the links between market power, rent-seeking and income inequality. Market concentration and rent extraction can feed off one another, resulting in a "winner-takes-most competition" that has become a visible part of the corporate environment, at least in some developed economies. This makes intra-firm differences an increasingly important component of the rising inequality story (Bloom, 2017). These issues are explored in greater depth in chapter VI of this *TDR*.

G. From inclusive (hyper) globalization to a global new deal

This year's *TDR* examines three evident sources of exclusion: (i) the automation of production, in particular robotization, and the threat of this causing a "hollowing out" of the human workforce; (ii) the segmentation of labour markets, in particular in terms of the gender dimension, which threatens to engender a "race to the bottom"; and (iii) corporate strategies to concentrate control over markets, particularly by non-financial corporations, combined with growing "rent extraction". Each presents its own distinct challenges to policymakers, in both developed and developing countries, who seek more inclusive outcomes. However, they are all interconnected through the deregulation of markets and a tighter control of assets, along with asymmetries in market power as a potent source of growing inequality.

From all this, it is clear that moving away from hyperglobalization to inclusive economies cannot be a matter of simply boosting human capital, filling information gaps, honing incentives, ensuring better provision of public goods – particularly education – extending credit to the poor and providing stronger protection to consumers. Rather, it demands a more exacting and encompassing agenda, which addresses the global and national asymmetries in resource mobilization, technological know-how, market power and political influence that are associated with hyperglobalization, and which generate and perpetuate exclusionary outcomes.

Such an approach would bolster the SDG agenda of tackling income inequality, both within and across countries, with a strong narrative around which effective policy measures could be designed, combined and implemented. This *Report* suggests that the elements for such a narrative can be gleaned from UNCTAD's founding mandate of 1964 (section I, para. 1) for "a better and more effective system of international economic cooperation, whereby the division of the world into areas of poverty and plenty may be banished and prosperity achieved for all". This was based on the recognition that "economic and social progress should go together. If privilege, extremes of wealth and poverty, and social injustice persist, then the goal of development is lost".

A good deal has changed since 1964, in terms of the human and productive capacities accumulated in developing countries, the insertion of these countries into the global economy, the kinds of economic vulnerabilities they face and the policy space they can use to help climb the development ladder. However, as before, effective internationalism continues to rest on responsible nationalism, and finding the right balance remains at the heart of any meaningful multilateral agenda. Today, no less than 50 years ago, achieving prosperity for all in an interdependent world must still involve paying close attention to the biases, asymmetries and deficits in global governance that can stymie inclusive and sustainable outcomes.

With this in mind, a possible narrative around which an alternative inclusiveness agenda might be fashioned is a "global new deal" (UNCTAD, 2011). The original New Deal, launched in the United States in the 1930s and replicated elsewhere in the industrialized world, particularly after the end of the Second World War, established a new development path with three broad strategic components: recovery, redistribution and regulation. While these components gave rise to specific policy goals tailored to particular economic and political circumstances, they made the taming of finance a common route to success along this new path. Franklin D. Roosevelt, in his 1944 address to the United States Congress, belatedly added another ambitious set of economic rights as a final component to achieving a secure and prosperous post-war United States. These included: the right to a useful and remunerative job, the right to economic security at all stages of life, the right to fair competition, the right to a decent home, adequate medical care, good health and a good education.

Roosevelt's administration also pursued a very different kind of international cooperation agenda, particularly towards Latin America, which eventually informed, albeit in a diluted manner, the negotiations that led to the establishment of the Bretton Woods system (Helleiner, 2014). That system initially promoted New Deal ambitions through a combination of guaranteed policy space for national governments and strengthened international cooperation to correct the kinds of market failures that had generated interwar instability: in particular, destabilizing currency fluctuations, a shortage of international liquidity and volatile capital flows. However, the multilateral rules and regulations were incomplete and lacked a more inclusive dimension, giving way to a partial and technocratic multilateralism largely tailored to the competitive advantage and corporate interests of the developed economies (*TDR 2014*).

The shift from partial globalization to hyperglobalization has failed to bring about a more stable, secure and inclusive international order; and the lead role, ceded to unregulated financial markets, appears to be particularly ill-suited to delivering the SDGs. Just how an agenda built around recovery, regulation, redistribution and rights takes shape will depend, again, on local circumstances, and policymakers will need to ensure that they have the requisite policy space. However, the specific challenges of inequality and insecurity in the twenty-first century will not be tackled by countries trying to insulate themselves from global economic forces, but rather by elevating the elements of the original New Deal to a global level consistent with today's interdependent world. Some possible elements of that agenda are discussed in the final chapter of this *Report*. ■

Notes

1   A good deal of related statistical work is already under way, including for measuring specific indicators of inclusive growth (Anand et al., 2016) and inclusive development (WEF, 2017).

2   The widespread use of PPP exchange rates as the appropriate deflator for comparison purposes, for example, is not without serious problems (see Pogge and Reddy, 2002; Ghosh, 2008 and 2013; Reddy and Lahoti, 2016).

3   No doubt, this is partly a reflection of the dominance of conventional economic thinking, which has long held that for improving the welfare of people, distributional issues are a distraction from the principal task of increasing the size of the economic pie. The traditional, neoclassical theory of income distribution, as well as its more recent human capital variant, assumes that factors of production earn exactly what they contribute at the margin, and are subject to the laws of supply and demand. For a review and critique, see Folbre, 2016.

4   There is little hesitation, by contrast, in attributing very large gains to trade openness. For a recent example, see Hufbauer and Lu, 2017; and a critique by Baker, 2017.

5   Autor et al. (2015) suggest, at least for the United States, that the impacts of trade and technology differ across sectors and at different times, and that in the 1990s and 2000s, trade at least matched technology as a potential source of disruption (see also Wood, 2017).

6   These links are picked up again in IMF, 2017.

7   The early neoclassicists, including Marshall and Pigou, for example, were concerned that the labour classes were failing to save enough to enable them to survive periods of unemployment and to provide for their old age. This was regarded as "irrational behaviour", with a lack of foresight or self-control (Peart, 2000). Education was seen as the cure, and, once obtained, there would be no further need for government intervention. The lingering influence of such thinking can still be found in much of the literature on human capital.

8   Recent research supports the notion of a two-way causation between equality and growth (see, for example, Ostry et al., 2014; Cingano, 2014), although the results are contested (for a review, see Kolev and Niehues, 2016).

9   Smith (1776) was clear that this was not an automatic connection, stating that "Wealth, as Mr. Hobbes says, is power. But the person who either acquires, or succeeds to a great fortune, does not necessarily acquire or succeed to any political power, either civil or military. His fortune may, perhaps, afford him the means of acquiring both, but the mere possession of that fortune does not necessarily convey to him either." On predatory politics in practice, see Hacker and Pierson, 2010; and Galbraith, 2008.

10   For the evolution and limitations of the entrepreneurship narrative, see Nightingale and Coad, 2013; and Naude, 2013.

11   In fact, these and other flaws in the individual entrepreneurship component of the "inclusive capitalism" narrative have been long known to social anthropologists and labour economists (see, for example, Breman, 2003; Davis, 2006; Standing, 2016; see also UNCTAD, 2015: 97–98).

References

Akerlof GA and Roemer PM (1993). Looting: The economic underworld of bankruptcy for profit. Brookings Papers on Economic Activity No. 2, Brookings Institution, Washington, DC.

Atkinson AB (2015). *Inequality: What can de Done?* Cambridge, MA, Harvard University Press.

Anand R, Mishra S and Peiris SJ (2016). Inclusive growth: Measurement and determinants. Working Paper No. 13/135, International Monetary Fund, Washington, DC.

Autor DH, Dorn D and Hanson GH (2015). Untangling trade and technology: Evidence from local labour markets. *The Economic Journal*, 125 (584): 621–646.

Baker D (2017). The trade deniers. CEPR Beat the Press (blog), 15 May. Centre for Economic and Policy Research, Washington, DC.

Baldwin R (2016). *The Great Convergence: Information Technology and the New Globalization.* Cambridge, MA, Harvard University Press.

Bateman M (2010). *Why Doesn't Microfinance Work? The Destructive Rise of Local Neoliberalism.* London, Zed Books.

Bateman M and Chang H-J (2012). Microfinance and the illusion of development: From hubris to nemesis in thirty years. *World Economic Review*, 1: 13–36.

Bateman M and Maclean K, eds. (2017). *Seduced and Betrayed: Exposing the Contemporary Microfinance Phenomenon.* Albuquerque, NM, University of New Mexico Press.

Bateman M, Kozul-Wright R and Blankenburg S, eds. (forthcoming). *The Rise and Fall of Global Microcredit: Development, Debt and Disillusion.* London, Routledge.

Black WK (2005). The Best Way to Rob a Bank is to Own One: How Corporate Executives and Politicians Looted the S&L Industry. Austin, TX, University of Texas Press.

Bloom N (2017). Corporations in the age of inequality. *Harvard Business Review.* Available at: https://hbr.org/cover-story/2017/03/corporations-in-the-age-of-inequality.

Borzaga C and Defourney J (2001). *The Emergence of Social Enterprise.* London, Routledge.

Bourguignon F (2015). *The Globalization of Inequality.* Princeton University Press, Princeton, NJ.

Breman J (2003). The Labouring Poor in India: Patterns of Exploitation, Subordination and Exclusion. Oxford, Oxford University Press.

Chang H-J (2010). *23 Things They Don't Tell You About Capitalism.* New York, NY, Bloomsbury Press.

Chant S (2016). Women, girls and world poverty: Empowerment, equality or essentialism? *International Development Planning Review*, 38(1): 1–24.

Cingano F (2014). Trends in income inequality and its impact on economic growth. Social, Employment and Migration Working Papers No. 163, OECD Publishing, Paris.

Cobham A, Schlogl L and Sumner A (2015). Inequality and the tails: The Palma Proposition and Ratio revisited. Working Paper No. 143. United Nations, Department of Economics and Social Affairs (UN DESA), New York, NY.

Cornia A and Martorano B (2012). Development policies and income inequality in selected developing regions, 1980–2010. Discussion Papers No. 210, UNCTAD, Geneva.

Davis M (2006). *Planet of Slums.* London, Verso.

De Soto H (1986). *El Otro Sendero: La Revolución Informal.* Lima, Editorial El Barranco.

Dollar D and Kraay A (2001). Growth is good for the poor. Policy Research Department Working Paper No. 2587, World Bank, Washington, DC.

Easterly W (2014). *The Tyranny of Experts: Economists, Dictators, and Forgotten Rights of the Poor.* New York, NY, Basic Books.

Economist (2016). Why they are wrong. 1 October.

Emmot B (2017). Literary life: It is time for a new liberal lexicon. *Financial Times.* 15 March.

Felipe J, Kumar U and Galope R (2014). Middle-income transitions: Trap or myth? Working Paper Series No. 421, Asian Development Bank, Manila.

Folbre N (2016). Just deserts? Earnings inequality and bargaining power in the U.S. economy. Working Paper No. 2016-10, Washington Centre for Equitable Growth, Washington, DC.

Galbraith JK (2008). T*he Predator State: How Conservatives Abandoned the Free Market and Why Liberals Should Too.* New York, NY, Free Press.

Galbraith JK (2014). *The End of Normal: The Great Crisis and the Future of Growth.* New York, NY, Simon and Schuster.

Galbraith JK (2016). *Inequality: What Everyone Needs to Know.* Oxford, Oxford University Press.

Ghosh J (2008). Growth, macroeconomic policies and structural change. Discussion Paper, United Nations Research Institute for Social Development (UNRISD), Geneva.

Ghosh J (2013). Country income shares in PPP. Triple Crisis blog – Global Perspectives on Finance, Development and Environment. Available at: http://triplecrisis.com/country-income-shares-in-ppp/ (accessed on 12 May 2017).

Hacker JS and Pierson P (2010). *Winner-take-all Politics: How Washington Made the Rich Richer -- and Turned its Back on the Middle Class.* New York, NY, Simon and Schuster.

Haering N (2017). How India became Bill Gates' guinea pig: A conspiracy as recounted by the main actors. *Norbert Häring - Money and More Blog*, 21 February. Available at: http://norberthaering.de/en/32-english/news/784-gates-india-demonetization.

Helleiner E (2014). *Forgotten Foundations of Bretton Woods: International Development and the Making of the Postwar Order*. Ithaca, NY, Cornell University Press.

Hymer S (1971). The multinational corporation and the law of uneven development. In: Bhagwati JN, ed. *Economics and World Order: From the 1970's to the 1990's*. New York, NY, Macmillan: 113−140.

Hufbauer G and Lu Z (2017). The payoff to America from globalization: A fresh look with a focus on the costs to workers. Policy Brief No. 17–16, Peterson Institute for International Economics (PIIE), Washington, DC.

IMF (2007*). World Economic Outlook: Globalization and Inequality.* October, International Monetary Fund, Washington, DC.

IMF (2017). *World Economic Outlook: Gaining Momentum.* April, International Monetary Fund, Washington, DC.

Jaumotte F and Osorio Buitron C (2015). Inequality and labour market institutions. Staff Discussion Note No. 15/14, International Monetary Fund, Washington, DC.

Kabeer N (2005). Is microfinance a "magic bullet" for women's empowerment? Analysis of findings from South Asia. *Economic and Political Weekly*, 40(44–45): 4709–4718.

Kakwani N, Prakash B, and Son H (2000). Growth, inequality, and poverty: An introduction. *Asian Development Review*, 18(2): 1−21.

Klapper L and Singer D (2014). The opportunities of digitizing payments. World Bank, Washington, DC.

Kohler P and Storm S (2016). CETA without blinders: How cutting 'trade costs and more' will cause unemployment, inequality and welfare losses. Working Paper No. 16-03, Global Development and Environment Institute (GDAE), Tufts University, Medford, MA.

Kolev G and Niehues J., (2016). The Inequality-Growth Relationship: An Empirical Reassessment. IW, Köln. Available at: https://www.iwkoeln.de/studien/iw-reports/beitrag/galina-kolev-judith-niehues-the-inequality-growth-relationship-273596.

Kuznets S (1955). Economic growth and income inequality. *The American Economic Review,* 45(1): 1−28.

Lagarde C (2016). Boosting growth and adjusting to change. Remarks by Christine Lagarde, Managing Director of the IMF, at Northwestern University, 28 September. Available at: https://www.imf.org/en/News/Articles/2016/09/27/AM16-SP09282016-Boosting-Growth-Adjusting-to-Change.

Lazonick W (2014). Profits without prosperity. *Harvard Business Review*, September. Available at: https://hbr.org/2014/09/profits-without-prosperity.

Levy F and Temin P (2007). Institutions and inequality in 20th century America. Working Paper No. 13106, National Bureau of Economic Research, Cambridge, MA.

Lewis A (1955). *The Theory of Economic Growth*. Homewood, IL, Richard D. Irwin.

Mazower M (2012). *Governing the World: The History of an Idea, 1815 to the Present*. New York, NY, Penguin Books.

Meek J (2017). Sommerdale to Skarbimiertz. *London Review of Books*, 39(8), 20 April: 3–15.

Mishel L (2011). Education is not the cure for high unemployment or for income inequality. Briefing Paper No. 286, Economic Policy Institute, Washington, DC.

Milanovic B (2016). *Global Inequality: A New Approach for the Age of Globalization*. Cambridge, MA, Harvard University Press.

Myrdal G (1970). *The Challenge of World Poverty: A World Anti-Poverty Programme in Outline*. Harmondsworth, Penguin Books.

Naude W (2013). Entrepreneurship and economic development: Theory, evidence and policy. IZA Discussion Paper No. 7507, Institute for the Study of Labour, Bonn.

Nightingale P and Coad A (2013). Muppets and gazelles: Political and methodological biases in entrepreneurship research. *Industrial and Corporate Change*, 23(1): 113−143.

O'Sullivan MA (2015). A confusion of capital in the United States. In: Hudson P, Tribe K, eds. *The Contradictions of Capital in the Twenty-First Century: The Piketty Opportunity.* Newcastle-upon-Tyne, Agenda Publishing: 131–161.

OECD and World Bank (2015). Inclusive global value chains: Policy options in trade and complementary areas for GVC Integration by small and medium enterprises and low-income developing countries. Organisation for Economic Co-operation and Development and World Bank, Paris and Washington, DC.

OECD and World Bank (2016). The squeezed middle-class in OECD and emerging countries: Myth and reality. Issues Paper, Organisation for Economic Co-operation and Development and World Bank, Paris.

Ostry JD, Berg A and Tsangarides CG (2014). Redistribution, inequality, and growth. Staff Discussion Note No. 14/02, International Monetary Fund, Washington, DC.

Peart SJ (2000). Irrationality and intertemporal choice in early neo-classical thought. *Canadian Journal of Economics,* 33 (1): 175−189.

Palma G (2011). Homogeneous middles vs heterogenous tails, and the end of the inverted-U: The share of the rich is what it's all about. *Development and Change*, 42(1): 77−153.

Phillipon T and Resheff A (2009). Wages and human capital in the U.S. financial industry: 1909-2006. Working Paper No. 14644, National Bureau of Economic Research, Cambridge, MA.

Picketty T (2014). *Capital in the Twenty-First Century*. Cambridge, MA, Harvard University Press,

Pogge T and Reddy SG (2002). How not to count the poor. Barnard College, New York, NY. Available at: https://ssrn.com/abstract=893159 or http://dx.doi.org/10.2139/ssrn.893159.

Power D, Epstein G and Abrena M (2003). Trends in the rentier income share in OECD countries, 1960−2000. Working Papers No. 58a, Political Economy Research Institute (PERI), University of Massachusetts, Amherst, MA.

Prahalad CK and Hart SL (2002). The fortune at the bottom of the pyramid. *Strategy and Business* (26): 1–14.

Prebisch R (1950). *The Economic Development of Latin America and its Principal Problems*. United Nations publication. Sales No. 1950.II.G.2. Lake Success, NY.

Reddy S and Lahoti R (2016). $1.90 a day: What does it say? *New Left Review 97*, January-February.

Reinert ES (2007). *How Rich Countries Got Rich ... and Why Poor Countries Stay Poor*. New York, NY, Public Affairs.

Roodman D (2011). Due diligence: An impertinent inquiry into microfinance. Center for Global Development, Washington, DC.

Rowthorn R (2014). A note on Piketty's Capital in the Twenty-first Century. *Cambridge Journal of Economics*, 38(5): 1275–1284.

Schmitt J, Shierholz H and Mishel L (2013). Don't blame the robots: Assessing the job polarization explanation of growing wage inequality. Working Paper, Economic Policy Institute (EPI)-Center for Economic Policy Research (CEPR), Washington, DC.

Seccareccia M and Lavoie M (2016). Income distribution, rentiers, and their role in a capitalist economy: A Keynes–Pasinetti perspective. *International Journal of Political Economy*, 45(3): 200–223.

Smith A (1776). *An Inquiry into the Nature and Causes of the Wealth of Nations*. London, Strahan and Cadell.

Standing G (2016). *The Corruption of Capitalism: Why Rentiers Thrive and Work Does Not Pay*. London, Biteback Publishing Ltd.

Stedman Jones G (2004). *An End to Poverty? A Historical Debate*. London, Profile Books.

Stiglitz JE (2012). *The Price of Inequality: How Today's Divided Society Endangers Our Future*. New York, NY, W.W. Norton and Co.

Stiglitz JE (2015). Inequality and economic growth. *Political Quarterly*, 86(S1): 134–155.

Stockhammer E (2015). Rising inequality as a cause of the present crisis. *Cambridge Journal of Economics*, 39(3): 935–958

Sustainable Livelihoods Foundation (2016). South Africa's informal economy: Research findings from nine townships. Cape Town.

Temin P (2017). *The Vanishing Middle Class: Prejudice and Power in a Dual Economy*. Cambridge, MA, MIT Press.

Tobin J (1984). On the efficiency of the financial system. *Lloyds Bank Review*, 153: 1–15.

UNCTAD (1964). *Towards a New Trade Policy for Development: Report by the Secretary-General of the United Nations Conference on Trade and Development*. United Nations publication. New York and Geneva.

UNCTAD (2002). *Economic Development in Africa Report 2002: From Adjustment to Poverty Reduction – What is New?* United Nations publication. Sales No. E.02.II.D.18. New York and Geneva.

UNCTAD (2011). *Report of the Secretary-General of UNCTAD to UNCTAD XIII: Development-led Globalization: Towards Sustainable and inclusive Development Paths*. United Nations publication. New York and Geneva.

UNCTAD (2015). *Least Developed Countries Report: Transforming Rural Economies*. United Nations publication. Sales No. E.15.II.D.7. New York and Geneva.

UNCTAD (*TDR 1995*). *Trade and Development Report, 1995*. United Nation publication. Sales No. E.95. II.D.16. New York and Geneva.

UNCTAD (*TDR 1997*). *Trade and Development Report, 1997: Globalization, Distribution and Growth*. United Nations publication. Sales No. E.97.II.D.8. New York and Geneva.

UNCTAD (*TDR 2012*). *Trade and Development Report, 2012: Policies for Inclusive and Balanced Growth*. United Nations publication. Sales No. E.12.II.D.6. New York and Geneva.

UNCTAD (*TDR 2014*). *Trade and Development Report, 2014: Global Governance and Policy Space for Development*. United Nations publication. E.14. II.D.4. New York and Geneva.

UNCTAD (*TDR 2016*). *Trade and Development Report, 2016: Structural Transformation for Inclusive and Sustained Growth*. United Nations publication. Sales No.E.16.II.D.5. New York and Geneva.

Wilkinson R and Pickett K (2009). *The Spirit Level: Why Equality is Better for Everyone*. London, Penguin Books.

Wolf M (2016). Capitalism and democracy: The strain is showing. *Financial Times*. 30 August.

Wood A (2017). How globalisation affected manufacturing around the world. *Vox* (CEPR's Policy Portal), 18 March.

Woolcock M and Narayan D (2000). Social capital: Implications for development theory, research, and policy. *World Bank Research Observer*, 15(2): 225–249.

World Bank (2014). *Global Financial Development Report 2014: Financial Inclusion*. Washington, DC, World Bank.

WEF (2017). *The Inclusive Growth and Development Report, 2017*. World Economic Forum, Geneva.

ROBOTS, INDUSTRIALIZATION AND INCLUSIVE GROWTH

III

A. Introduction

Employment opportunities, and the income they generate, are a major determinant of inclusive growth. Economists, policymakers and the general public have long accepted that technological change greatly affects employment opportunities. Historically, it has offered novel ways of producing and consuming goods and services, created new profitable areas of economic activity, and underpinned rising living standards. In the process it freed humans from physically demanding, repetitive or dangerous work. However, the creative side of new technologies often has disruptive consequences for the existing practices and structures of economic life, including the outright destruction of companies, markets and jobs, with no guarantee that the gains from the new processes will fully compensate for the losses. Over time, the distributional consequences of new technologies depend on the scope of subsequent job opportunities and the pace at which they materialize. In large part this is because new technologies do not arrive as a *deus ex machina* but are embodied in (and disseminated by) capital equipment, institutional routines and human capabilities, and their impact is, therefore, conditioned by macroeconomic circumstances and policy responses.

Much of the discussion about making hyperglobalization more inclusive emphasizes investment in knowledge and skills as the way to harness human talent to the new opportunities associated with digital technologies (IMF, 2017). In this chapter, it is argued that the issue is more complex and that, in addition to investment in education, the overall framework of macroeconomic and sectoral policies remains crucial to ensuring the expansion of viable employment opportunities at different skill levels.

Economic history certainly suggests that technological breakthroughs, such as the steam engine,

electricity, the motor car and the assembly line, have been disruptive and result, in the short run, in substantial job losses and declining incomes for some sectors and sections of society. But it also shows that these adverse effects are more than offset in the long term when the fruits of innovation gradually spread from one sector to another and are eventually harvested across the economy when workers move to new, more technology-intensive and better-paid jobs (Mokyr et al., 2015). However, whether this history offers a useful guide for the effects of digitization is open to question (Galbraith, 2014; Gordon, 2016).

The newest technological wave builds around the generation, processing and dissemination of information. Although the computer launched this new wave, it is advances in the integrated circuit that have given it revolutionary impetus. Subsequent technological developments emerging from sizeable advances in computing power, increasingly sophisticated audio-visual products and artificial intelligence (AI) include the spread of Big Data, the Internet of Things and online sharing platforms. The combination of these different information and communication technologies (ICTs) makes up the digital revolution. Like previous technological revolutions, its impact is felt across most areas of social and economic life, including in employment opportunities. Part of this revolution concerns the potential of new technologies to boost automation and transform production processes. The rapid march of robot technology, in particular, simultaneously captures the imagination of entrepreneurs and policymakers and adds to a deepening sense of anxiety among much of the public.

The goals of the 2030 Agenda for Sustainable Development undoubtedly require harnessing the potential of the digital revolution, such that it accelerates productivity growth and feeds a more rapid and more sustainable global economic expansion. But if productivity growth is achieved on the back of automation that causes job displacement and wage erosion, it would compromise this Agenda, which aims to achieve inclusiveness through the creation of more and better jobs.

Most observers who believe in the transformative potential of digitization acknowledge that productivity growth has faltered in recent years, but argue that most productivity gains associated with digitization lie ahead, that any adverse effects from automation will be short-lived, and that increases in labour incomes and well-being will eventually be widespread (e.g. Brynjolfsson and McAfee, 2014). Seen from the perspective of long-term Schumpeterian waves, the current situation marks the stage of job destruction, related to process innovation, which will be followed by product innovation and ensuing job creation (Nübler, 2016; Perez, 2016). Others are more pessimistic. They hold that the digital revolution is much more disruptive than previous technology waves, because advances in artificial intelligence and robotics increasingly enable the substitution of cognitive, instead of just manual, tasks and this is occurring at an increasingly faster pace. Because of the greater scope of occupational applications of robots and the faster speed of their diffusion, the economy may not have sufficient time to adapt and compensate for job displacement by creating new and better jobs (e.g. Ford, 2015). A plethora of studies and media reports paint an alarming picture of technology destroying more jobs than it creates over time, with some anticipating a jobless future.[1]

Another concern relates to distributional impacts of the "digital storm" (Galbraith, 2014). Many activities that have already become digitized continue to generate an income stream which, as the required employment has dropped precipitously, flows to a small number of people at the top of the digital food chain, often in highly confined geographical regions. On some accounts, the next generation of automated machines will be much more durable and will probably require only a small number of highly skilled workers for their operation, rather than the large numbers of workers at any skill level that complemented earlier technological breakthroughs. As a result, most workers will be unable to move to better-paid jobs by upskilling, but will compete for a shrinking number of similar jobs or move to occupations with lower pay (e.g. Autor, 2015). Hence, the main risk of digitization may not be joblessness, but a future

where productivity growth only benefits the owners of robots and the intellectual property embodied in them, as well as a few highly skilled workers whose problem-solving adaptive and creative competencies complement artificial intelligence, while others are forced into precarious employment and "automated inequality".

However, the outcome of technological change is not an autonomous process; it is shaped by economic incentives and policies. The deployment of robots may be seen, at least in some countries, as responding to declining working-age populations. And its labour-saving outcomes have to be seen in the context of the policy turn to austerity and the drive towards lower labour costs that began in the 1980s (*TDR 2010*).

Taking this broader perspective, aggregate employment and income impacts from technology are largely determined by macroeconomic and regulatory forces. Appropriately expansionary macroeconomic policies can mitigate, if not prevent, any adverse employment and income effects from technological advances. However, such policies are currently missing (chapter I of this *Report*). This means that the novelty of the digital revolution lies not only in its greater scope and faster speed alone, but also in its occurrence at a time of subdued macroeconomic dynamism in the developed economies and stalled structural transformation in many developing economies, which tend to hold back the investment needed for the new technology to create new sectors and absorb displaced workers.

A major area of interest has been specifically the greater reliance on robotics in production, with much of the current debate focused on developed countries (e.g. Frey and Osborne, 2013; Acemoglu and Restrepo, 2017), and where the perceived threat to jobs has been heightened by concerns about the offshoring of production activities to developing countries. Obviously, the use of robots is part of a wider process of automation that affects production processes in both developed and developing countries. However, industrial robots differ from conventional capital equipment in that they are (i) automatically controlled (i.e. they operate on their own); (ii) multipurpose (i.e. they are reprogrammable and are capable of doing different kinds of tasks rather than repeating the same task); and (iii) operational on several axes (i.e. they have significant dexterity, as per ISO 8373).[2] These characteristics also make industrial robots different from other forms of automation, such as Computer Numerical Control systems that have allowed for the automation of machine tools since the 1960s but are designed to perform very specific tasks and, even if digitally controlled, lack the flexibility and dexterity of industrial robots. These characteristics and differences have attracted particular attention because of the dramatic changes that they are presumed to bring about, even though more traditional forms of automation, such as the simple mechanization of heavy-duty work, continue to affect production processes over and above those involving robotics. Indeed, this chapter argues that robotization is likely to have a comparatively small effect on such processes in many developing countries, where mechanization continues to be the predominant form of automation.

This chapter takes a development perspective, in which the most important question is whether the greater use of robots reduces the effectiveness of industrialization as a development strategy.[3] This will be the case if robot-based automation makes industrialization more difficult or causes it to yield substantially less manufacturing employment than in the past.[4] The chapter addresses this question within a broader discussion of whether the use of industrial robots can be expected to radically change the types of jobs that will be available in the future, how, where and by whom they will be done, and what impact this would have on possibilities for inclusive growth, in terms of declining income inequality both between and within countries.

Within the field of robotization in general, the main motivation for the focus on industrial robots is that industrialization, as discussed in *TDR 2016*, has traditionally been recognized as the main driver of economic prosperity.[5] It is also related to the emphasis in Goal 9 of the 2030 Agenda for Sustainable Development on the link between technological innovation and industrialization on the one hand and industrialization and sustainable development on the other.[6]

This chapter is organized as follows. Section B discusses the task-based approach to automation. It argues that robots affect industrialization particularly through the displacement of routine tasks that are more prevalent in manufacturing than in agriculture or services. It also argues that displacement by robots is economically more feasible in relatively skill-intensive manufacturing, such as the automotive and electronics sectors, than in relatively labour-intensive sectors, such as apparel. Most existing studies overestimate the potential adverse employment and income effects of robots, because they neglect to take account of that what is technically feasible is not always also economically profitable. Indeed, the countries currently most exposed to automation through industrial robots are those with a large manufacturing sector, which has a concentration of relatively well-paying activities, such as in the automotive and electronics sectors.

Section C provides cross-country evidence on the evolution of the share of manufacturing in countries' total value added and employment, as well as cross-country and cross-sectoral evidence on robot use. It argues that robots may further the tendency towards a concentration of manufacturing output and employment in a small number of economies, and that they may make upgrading towards more skill-intensive manufacturing more difficult. As such, robots would hamper inclusiveness at the international level. It also shows that countries at more mature stages of industrialization are currently most exposed to robot-based job displacement, as they have the highest intensity of routine tasks for which automation is economically feasible.

Section D argues that country-specific distributional effects from robotics are diverse and depend on a country's stage in structural transformation, its position in the international division of labour, demographic developments, and its economic and social policies. It also argues that some of the adverse employment and income effects that robots could create may well occur in countries that do not use robots. This is because robots boost companies' international cost competitiveness, which may in turn spur exports and thereby make other countries bear at least part of the adverse distributional consequences from robot-based automation through reduced output and employment opportunities. Section E summarizes the main findings and offers some policy conclusions that are further detailed in chapter VII of this *Report*.

B. Distributional effects of technological change

This section addresses the distributional effects of robot-based technological change. The task-based approach to automation is discussed first, followed by an analysis of the impacts of the automation of routine tasks on the production structure of an economy.

1. Automation and routine tasks

Technology can affect employment and income distribution through various channels but, in one way or another, the spread of automation involves firms weighing up the potential savings on labour costs against the cost of investment in the new capital equipment. In the process of automating the production process, the composition of the workforce will also change. The skill-biased technological change framework argues that there is no displacement of labour by capital-embodied technological change. Instead, technology is assumed to complement highly skilled workers and provide them with better employment opportunities, as well as a skill premium on their earnings compared to those of low-skilled workers (Acemoglu and Autor, 2011). Such a skill premium is said to be part of the "race between education and technology" (Goldin and Katz, 2008). This increases gaps in relative wages between skill groups in periods when the skill demands of new technology outrun the skill supply, and decreases such gaps when workers' education catches up with technological advances.

More recently, consensus has shifted towards a labour-displacing view of technological change (Acemoglu and Autor, 2011). A task-based approach has been developed, which hypothesizes that a job is composed of different tasks and that new technology does not always favour better-skilled workers but often complements workers in certain tasks of their job, while substituting for them in others (Autor et al., 2003).[7]

This approach distinguishes between manual, routine and abstract tasks. While many occupations involve a combination of tasks and different manual and routine tasks have been mechanized for centuries, the suggestion is that new technologies, including robots, predominantly substitute labour in *routine* tasks, which are those that can be clearly defined and follow pre-specified patterns, so that they can be coded and translated into the software. Robots have greater difficulty in substituting for more abstract tasks, such as creative, problem-solving and complex coordination tasks, as well as other non-routine tasks, such as those requiring physical dexterity or flexible interpersonal communication, as are often found in the services sector. This means that – from a technical point of view – workers doing routine tasks are most at risk of robot-based automation. It also means that the current wave of automation has increased displacement risks because it is characterized by machines that are technically capable of performing an increasingly wider range of such tasks.

One way of operationalizing the task-based approach and determining the technical feasibility of automation is the calculation of a routine-task intensity index, which links routine tasks to occupations that workers perform on their jobs (Autor and Dorn, 2013; IMF, 2017).[8] This calculation assumes that the task intensity of an occupation is fixed across economic sectors, across countries and over time. The resulting index indicates that routine-based tasks dominate in occupations that are typical for manufacturing, and are mostly performed by medium-skilled workers. The prevalence of routine tasks in manufacturing also indicates that an economy's structural composition is an important determinant of the effect of robot use on inclusiveness.[9]

However, a substitution of labour by capital, including in the form of robots, that is technically feasible will occur only if it also provides economic benefits. The economic profitability of labour-capital substitution has most likely increased in recent years and has probably been concentrated in the substitution of capital for labour engaged in routine tasks. This is because evidence suggests that technological progress has reduced the global price of capital goods relative to that of consumer goods by some 25 per cent between 1975 and 2012 (e.g. Karabarbounis and Neiman, 2014). Most of this decline stems from the size of transistors shrinking so rapidly that every one to two years twice as many of them can be fitted onto a computer chip, reducing the cost of digital computing power embodied in capital goods in the process.[10] The cost of robot-based automation may have further declined because of improved performance of robotics systems, combined with reduced cost of systems engineering (such as programming and installation) and of peripheral equipment (such as sensors, displays and safety structures).

This economic perspective suggests that the cost of automation must be compared with the cost of labour in routine tasks. The latter cost is crucially determined by labour compensation, which, as with the prevalence of routine tasks, tends to vary across different economic sectors, as further discussed in section B.2.[11]

2. Robots and sectoral structure

The observation that both the technical and the economic feasibility of automation vary across productive sectors implies that the distributional impact of robot use depends on an economy's structural composition. Accordingly, distributional changes from robots can be analysed in a framework emphasizing changes in economies' structural composition, that is, the changing distribution of output and employment across productive sectors.

An economy's structural composition itself largely depends on two factors. The first is its stage of structural transformation from a largely agrarian to an industrial and eventually services-based economy. Technology may trigger this evolution, with technologically more dynamic sectors enabling production at reduced cost per unit of production. If the resulting increase in productivity in these sectors translates at least partly into a decline in prices, demand for their output, as well as that from other sectors, increases and sets in motion a virtuous circle of growing demand, employment and income. Technologically induced labour-productivity growth makes higher-productivity sectors expand and draw workers away from the other sectors, increasing the economy's aggregate productivity and the number of better-remunerated jobs in the process. This virtuous circle will also tend to facilitate product innovation and create new employment and income opportunities that compensate for any employment lost in the lower-productivity sectors. It is this positive feedback mechanism between manufacturing activities on the one hand and well-paying jobs and thriving innovation on the other that makes maintaining sizeable manufacturing activities a policy objective even for developed countries.

Second, an economy's structural composition is affected by its position in the international division of labour. This position affects distribution not only through sector-specific demand effects, but also through intersectoral changes in the terms of trade.

Depending on the structure of global demand, an increase in the volume of global demand, or a shift in relative goods prices, will favour output and employment in some of the economy's sectors more than in others. These impacts from the global economy will affect the domestic dynamics of structural transformation and, hence, changes in the country's pattern of income distribution. A rise in external demand concentrated in manufactures or a change in relative goods prices in favour of manufactures will give an extra boost to higher-productivity activities and technological progress, so that forces from external demand and technology feed on each other.

The critical question is how robots might affect structural change. A sectoral breakdown of manufacturing with respect to the technological and economic feasibility of routine-task automation indicates significant dispersion across manufacturing sectors in terms of both these categories, as shown in figure 3.1. The routine-task intensity index used here is based on an OECD survey that asked workers about the intensity of tasks in their daily work that can be clearly identified as "routine" and follow predefined patterns, so

FIGURE 3.1 Proximate relationship between technical and economic feasibility of routine-task automation, by manufacturing sector

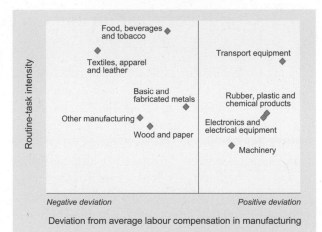

Source: UNCTAD secretariat calculations, based on Marcolin et al., 2016; and the Conference Board, *International Labour Compensation Comparisons* database.

Note: The axes have no scaling to underline the proximate nature of the relationship shown in the figure. All data are for a sample of 20 countries (see text note 12 for details) and refer to the latest available year. The routine task intensity index refers to 2011–2012. Labour compensation reflects sector-specific medians for the period 2008–2014. Calculating labour compensation on the basis of means instead of medians or on data for 2014 instead of 2008–2014 averages, or using larger country samples for labour compensation results in only marginal variation in the cross-sectoral relationship shown in the figure.

that from a technical point of view they can be codified and automated. This index can then be mapped into manufacturing sectors, following Marcolin et al. (2016).[12] While figure 3.1 assumes that a sector's content of routine tasks is fixed across countries, it underlines that exposure to routine-task automation varies significantly across manufacturing sectors.[13] As structural transformation generally involves a shift from lower-wage sectors, such as apparel, towards better-paid sectors, such as the automotive and electronics sectors, and the significance of routine tasks varies across these sectors, exposure to routine-task automation also changes over the course of development.

The estimates in figure 3.1 suggest that the three manufacturing sectors with the greatest intensity in routine tasks are food, beverages and tobacco; textiles, apparel and leather; and transport equipment. This means that the technical feasibility of automating workers' routine tasks appears largest in these three sectors. By contrast, the economic feasibility of routine-task automation (expressed in terms of relative unit labour costs) appears to be greatest in transport equipment, followed by rubber, plastic and chemical products; the electrical and electronics sector; and machinery. The economic feasibility of such automation appears lowest in the textiles,

apparel and leather sectors. This suggests that the automotive sector has the greatest potential for robot use, as it combines high technical and high economic feasibility of routine-task automation. In general, as firms probably respond more to economic feasibility, robot-based automation is likely to be concentrated in those manufacturing sectors that are on the right-hand side of the figure. Acting according to technical feasibility would instead mean concentrating robots in those manufacturing sectors that are towards the top of the figure.

The schematic evidence in figure 3.1 could also be interpreted as indicating that ongoing declines in the cost of digital automation will lead to gradual but continued automation of workers' tasks. This would be reflected by increases in routine-task automation in sectors on the left of the figure, thereby reducing the routine tasks performed by workers and labour compensation. However, even if the cost of such automation continues to decline, labour compensation cannot be continuously reduced in the aggregate over a prolonged period. Reduced worker incomes reduce consumption demand and therefore affect the inducement to invest. So, by reducing the effective average cost of labour, automation discourages the investment that would bring in further automation and eventually brings automation to a halt.

C. Industrialization and the international division of labour

The previous section indicated that robot-based automation affects the structural composition of an economy's manufacturing sector. Further, the extent to which robot use impacts the inclusiveness of growth and development also depends on whether manufacturing remains the driver of economic catch-up, and on whether that is determined by the share of manufacturing in output or in employment, given that robots will tend to produce a given level of output at lower levels of employment.

Focusing on the international dimension, this section assesses whether manufacturing activity and employment in recent years have been spread broadly across the world economy or concentrated in a small set of countries. This discussion supplements the historical analysis of *TDR 2016* that provides evidence for premature deindustrialization or stalled industrialization in some developing countries, and that also

concluded that the relative size of the manufacturing sector continues to be of crucial importance to an economy's catch-up potential.[14] In this context, country- and sector-specific evidence on the deployment of industrial robots is used to examine whether it has occurred primarily in those countries that have successfully industrialized over the past two decades, or elsewhere. This allows for an assessment of whether robot use tends to enhance past trends in terms of where manufacturing activities are located, or rather work towards reversing such trends.

1. Salient features of recent industrialization experiences

Output data measured in current prices show that the world as a whole slightly deindustrialized over the past two decades, mainly as a result of declines

TABLE 3.1 Manufacturing value added, selected economies and groups, 2005 and 2014 shares and 1995–2014 changes

(1)	(2)	(3)	(4)	(5)	(6)	(7)	(8)	(9)	(10)	(11)
	Current prices						Constant prices (2005)			
	Share in total value added			Share in total goods value added			Share in total value added		Share in total goods value added	
	2005	2014	Change 1995–2014 (Percentage points)	2005	2014	Change 1995–2014 (Percentage points)	2014 (Per cent)	Change 1995–2014 (Percentage points)	2014 (Per cent)	Change 1995–2014 (Percentage points)
	(Per cent)			(Per cent)						
World	16.9	16.5	-3.2	52.8	48.5	-9.3	17.9	1.7	55.9	6.8
Developed economies	15.6	14.1	-5.2	58.7	56.3	-6.4	15.2	-0.3	61.1	6.7
Germany	22.4	22.6	-0.1	74.4	73.0	5.9	23.4	1.8	77.4	11.7
Japan	19.9	19.0	-3.2	67.9	68.0	4.2	21.4	2.7	72.5	12.1
United States	13.2	12.3	-4.8	58.2	56.4	-10.3	12.7	-0.0	59.9	7.4
Developing economies	21.1	20.2	-1.2	43.6	43.2	-2.9	23.5	4.7	51.1	12.9
Africa	11.7	10.4	-4.4	23.3	21.3	-9.5	11.6	-1.1	27.2	2.5
Latin America and the Caribbean	17.2	13.5	-4.2	42.7	36.4	-12.1	15.4	-2.2	41.4	-1.8
Mexico	17.3	17.7	-1.9	41.2	43.1	-3.4	16.7	-0.1	43.8	4.3
Asia	24.0	23.2	-1.3	46.9	47.0	-0.4	27.1	6.7	55.6	16.9
China	32.3	28.3	-6.1	54.7	54.0	2.4	34.9	5.7	62.9	15.4
NIEs	25.7	25.3	0.2	73.2	74.6	9.9	29.9	8.6	80.6	20.5
Republic of Korea	28.3	30.3	2.5	69.6	74.7	13.4	32.7	10.7	77.5	22.5
Taiwan Province of China	30.5	30.0	1.0	83.1	80.9	9.0	38.2	12.4	92.6	23.9
Oceania	9.7	8.6	-1.0	25.9	18.4	-6.6	8.4	-1.0	20.7	-5.1
Developing economies, excl. China	18.1	15.7	-3.9	39.7	35.8	-9.1	18.4	1.4	44.1	8.0
Developing economies, excl. NIEs	20.4	19.8		40.3	41.2	-1.8	22.6	4.2	48.0	12.3
Transition economies	18.2	15.3	-5.9	40.9	36.1	-7.1	16.7	-0.6	41.5	2.5

Memo item:	Share in world manufacturing value added (Per cent)						Share in world manufacturing value added (Per cent)			
Developed economies	68.2	49.7	-27.0				55.9	-18.9		
Developing economies	29.6	47.4	26.0				42.0	18.8		
Developing economies, excl. China	19.9	23.4	6.3				22.8	5.0		
Developing economies, excl. NIEs	24.6	42.5	25.4				35.7	16.3		
Transition economies	2.2	2.8	1.0				2.1	0.1		

Source: UNCTAD secretariat calculations, based on United Nations, Department of Economic and Social Affairs (UN DESA), *National Accounts Main Aggregates* database; and Groningen Growth and Development Centre, *GGDC 10-Sector Database*.

Note: Group data are weighted averages. Manufacturing share for China in 1995 adjusted using the *GGDC 10-Sector Database*. NIEs = newly industrializing economies, including Hong Kong (China), Republic of Korea, Singapore and Taiwan Province of China.

in developed countries and transition economies (table 3.1). For developing countries as a group, the share of manufacturing in total value added fell only marginally and stayed within the long-term average range of 20 per cent to 23 per cent (see also Haraguchi, 2014). As noted in *TDR 2016*, developing countries as a whole have seen their share of global industrial (and manufacturing) output rise steadily since 1980. Between 1995 and 2014, developing countries raised their share in world manufacturing value added by more than 25 percentage points (from 21 per cent to 47 per cent, at current prices), of which

almost 20 points are accounted for by China.[15] This increase occurred despite a decline of manufacturing in the total value added of China, which nevertheless continued to exceed the developing country average. Indeed, if both China and the newly industrializing economies (NIEs) of Asia (which on some classifications, such as those used by the International Monetary Fund (IMF) and the United Nations Industrial Development Organization (UNIDO), are considered "advanced economies" or "industrialized economies") are excluded, the share of other developing economies in global manufacturing value added in current prices rose by only 3.6 percentage points (and just 1.6 percentage points in constant terms) over this period. As noted in *TDR 2016*, the attraction of building a robust manufacturing sector comes not only from its potential to generate productivity and income growth but from the fact that such gains can spread out across the economy through production, investment, knowledge and income linkages. It is therefore of some significance that so much of the increase in manufacturing activity was concentrated in China.

Each of sub-Saharan Africa and Latin America and the Caribbean registered significant declines in their already lower-than-average share of manufacturing in total value added. While manufacturing activities in these two groups of countries increased in absolute terms (*TDR 2016*), the decline in manufacturing shares and, hence, deindustrialization in these regions, as well as in developing Oceania, transition economies and developed countries (and most notably in the United States), was accompanied by an increase in the share of output from agricultural and mining activities. This is reflected in the sizeable declines in the share of manufacturing in total goods output in these country groups (table 3.1, column 7).

These deindustrialization tendencies were, in some countries, partly due to relative price developments between manufacturing and other economic sectors, and in particular the decline in the global price of labour-intensive manufacturing, relative to both skill-intensive manufactures and primary commodities (e.g. Fu et al., 2012). In developing Asia, changes in the manufacturing share were strongly positive at constant prices, particularly in China where the substantial fall in the relative price of manufactures was associated with a large increase in the share of manufacturing in total goods output (table 3.1, column 11). Within Latin America, deindustrialization in Mexico was relatively less pronounced than for other countries in the region, and manufacturing shares showed little change when measured in constant prices.[16]

However, stalled industrialization in many developing countries and premature deindustrialization in others, reflect more a combination of unfavourable macroeconomic and institutional conditions, weakening production linkages within and across sectors, insufficient economies of scale, unfavourable integration into global markets and other more structural factors (*TDR 2016*). In general, across developing countries, manufacturing became more concentrated in the larger and richer economies (*TDR 2016*; see also Haraguchi et al., 2017; and Wood, 2017), mostly in Asia.[17] This was largely because of differences in productivity growth: while average productivity in Asia (and especially in East Asia) rose steadily in the 1980s and climbed sharply in the 1990s and 2000s, in both Africa and Latin America it remained essentially flat (*TDR 2016*: figure 3.3). The differences in productivity performance were most marked with respect to manufacturing, which collapsed in the early 1980s in Africa and remained stagnant thereafter, while in Latin America it was more volatile over this period but with no overall gain.

Productivity growth from technological change should make increases in the share of manufacturing in total employment significantly less pronounced than that in output, because of more rapid labour-displacing technological change in manufacturing than in non-manufacturing activities. This tendency can be observed for the world as a whole, given that the employment share of manufacturing slightly declined between 1995 and 2014 (table 3.2), while over the same period that of output measured in constant prices somewhat increased.[18] It can also be observed for transition economies whose sizeable decline in the manufactured employment share significantly exceeded that of their output share, measured in constant prices.

But this is most evident for developed countries.[19] Between 1995 and 2014, these countries' share of manufacturing in total employment fell by more than five percentage points, with that in the United States falling below 9 per cent (table 3.2). Japan experienced an even larger decline than the United States, though its manufactured employment share remained significantly larger than that of the United States. By contrast, Germany recorded a decline in its manufactured employment share between 1995 and 2014 equivalent to only about half that experienced by developed countries taken as a group. Perhaps even more remarkably, Germany experienced an increase in that share between 2005 and 2014.

For developing countries taken as a group, the share of manufacturing in total employment slightly increased between 1995 and 2014 (table 3.2). Once again, manufacturing employment was increasingly concentrated in larger and richer developing countries, though less so than manufacturing output (see also Haraguchi, 2014); and once again China accounted for most of the increase.

TABLE 3.2 Share of manufacturing in total employment, selected economies and groups, 2005 and 2014 shares and 1995–2014 changes

	2005	2014	Change 1995–2014
	(Per cent)		*(Percentage points)*
World	13.4	13.3	-0.6
Developed economies	14.8	13.0	-5.1
Germany	19.4	19.8	-2.7
Japan	16.9	14.2	-6.3
United States	10.4	8.8	-5.1
Developing economies	13.0	13.3	0.8
Africa	6.3	6.9	1.0
Latin America and the Caribbean	13.0	13.0	-1.2
Mexico	16.6	15.6	-2.1
Asia	14.2	14.7	1.3
China	16.4	18.2	2.8
NIEs	19.9	18.3	-5.4
Republic of Korea	18.5	16.6	-7.0
Taiwan Province of China	27.5	27.4	1.2
Developing economies, excl. China	11.3	11.1	0.2
Developing economies, excl. NIEs	12.9	13.2	0.9
Transition economies	15.9	14.3	-4.3

Source: UNCTAD secretariat calculations, based on Haraguchi et al., 2017; and Wood, 2017.

Note: Data are partly estimated. Group data are weighted averages. The sample used for this table includes 148 economies, of which 33 developed, 99 developing economies and 16 transition economies.

For both Africa and developing countries in Latin America and the Caribbean, the evidence for deindustrialization is stronger for output (table 3.1) than for employment (table 3.2). Africa even registered an increase of manufacturing in total employment, albeit from comparatively low levels and on the basis of a greater extent of estimation of the data (see also Wood, 2017). This is in line with recent evidence that the reallocation of African labour from the primary to the manufacturing sector has been accompanied by a decline of labour productivity in manufacturing (Diao et al., 2017), suggesting very low technological dynamism in African manufacturing.

Evidence in tables 3.1 and 3.2 also indicates that the declines of manufacturing shares of both output and employment that many countries have experienced (giving rise to concerns about widespread premature deindustrialization) have been associated with the increasing concentration of manufacturing activities in a few developing countries. Historical evidence shows that attaining a share of manufacturing above

18 per cent of total employment has been critically important for sustained economic development, and that a high share of manufacturing employment is a significantly better predictor of eventual prosperity than is achieving a high share of manufacturing output (Felipe et al., 2015). This threshold has been attained not only by the developed economies but also by developing economies in Asia, such as China and the now industrialized economies of East Asia, particularly the Republic of Korea and Taiwan Province of China. Once these few successful economies reach a mature stage of industrialization and move to services, the other developing countries may industrialize more easily. Hence, developing manufacturing production and especially attaining a high share of manufacturing in total employment will be as relevant and important for these "follower" countries as it has been for others in the process of economic development.

The question is how robotics affects these developments. If robot use becomes concentrated in those countries where manufacturing also has come to be concentrated, associated improvements in labour productivity and international competitiveness would allow them to prevent a decline, or even achieve an increase, in their own manufacturing activities.[20] As a result, other countries will find it more difficult to move along the traditional path of industrialization. In such countries, the creation of manufacturing employment will tend to be limited to those sectors where robot use has remained constrained either for technical or for economic reasons.

2. Robot deployment: Cross-country and cross-sectoral evidence[21]

The previous section indicated that whether robots will facilitate economic catch-up based on industrialization, or make it more difficult, depends on which countries use robots and in which manufacturing sectors. This section focuses on where robots are used, while box 3.1 discusses where robots are produced and the related benefits reaped.

Despite the hype surrounding the potential of robot-based automation, currently the use of industrial robots globally remains quite small, only around 1.6 million in 2015 as indicated in table 3.3. However, it has increased rapidly since 2010 (figure 3.2), and it is estimated that by 2019 over 2.5 million industrial robots will be at work (IFR, 2016a). Developed

BOX 3.1   The distribution of benefits from robot production

A key element in the distribution of gains from technological change is the return provided to those controlling the knowledge and the machines in which it is embodied. In the case of robot-based automation, the countries and firms that produce robots and those that own the intellectual property embodied in them will benefit from robotics more than other countries and firms. This brings up the key issues of the geographical location of robot production and the extent to which the intellectual property in robots and the associated profits belong to firms in developed or developing countries.

No comprehensive data on the production of industrial robots are available either at the country or firm level. The IFR (2016a) reports country-specific production data only for China, Germany, Japan and Republic of Korea. These four countries accounted for about 83 per cent of the global production of industrial robots in 2015. With 138,160 units, Japan alone still accounted for over half of global production in 2015, even though its share declined from about 61 per cent in 2010 to about 54 per cent in 2015 (see the table in this box). The Republic of Korea followed with a share of about 12 per cent, and China and Germany, each having around an 8 per cent share in 2015. While all the industrial robots produced in China appear to be used within China, Germany and Japan exported more than three quarters of their production in 2015. In the same year, the Republic of Korea exported about one fifth of its production, but imported more than twice as many units. Germany also imported slightly more industrial robots than it exported in 2015, while imports to Japan amounted to less than 1 per cent of the country's production in 2015.

Production of industrial robots, world and selected countries, 2010–2015

	2010	2011	2012	2013	2014	2015
	Number of units ('000)					
World	120.6	166.0	159.3	178.1	220.6	253.7
	(Percentage shares)					
China	n.a.	n.a.	n.a.	5.3	7.2	8.0
Germany	9.8	11.4	11.6	11.1	9.4	7.8
Japan	61.3	59.1	59.8	53.6	54.8	54.4
Republic of Korea	14.2	12.8	10.0	8.9	12.2	12.6
Other countries	14.7	16.7	18.6	21.0	16.4	17.1

Source: UNCTAD secretariat calculations, based on IFR, 2016a.

Firm-level data for 2016 confirm the continued significance of Japan in the global production of industrial robots.[a] Three of the top four (accounting for 73 per cent of these four companies' production) and five of the top ten (62 per cent) globally leading robot-producing firms are Japanese. These firm-level data also indicate that Switzerland and the United States are likely to account for the bulk of the 18 per cent of the country-specific production data for 2015 which are not disaggregated by the IFR (2016a).

However, neither country- nor firm-specific data fully reveal where the economic benefits of robot production actually occur, because most robot suppliers produce in several countries. Moreover, a specific supplier may actually be owned by another firm from another country, such as the German robot maker KUKA, which is among the world's biggest robot suppliers and which was purchased by the Chinese company Midea in 2016 (IFR, 2016a: 164–165).

But most importantly, these data do not indicate where innovation takes place and, thus, innovation benefits are reaped. Data on robotics clusters – geographically proximate groups of interconnected companies and institutions active in robotics – indicate that in 2015 at least 72 per cent of them were located in developed countries, and that the United States alone accounted for 40 per cent of the geographical location of robotics clusters (Keisner et al., 2015). The only developing countries identified among the world's main geographical locations of robotics clusters in that year were China and the Republic of Korea, accounting for 5 per cent and 3 per cent, respectively, but with rapidly increasing importance. The vast majority of patent applications in robotics also come from the developed countries with, however, a significantly faster increase in the Republic of Korea since the early 2000s and China more recently. At the sectoral level, automotive and electronics companies file most of the patents related to robotics (Keisner et al., 2015).

Data indicating a strong increase in patent filings from China could suggest that robotics reduces the technology gap between developed and developing countries and that an increasing share of the benefits from innovation in robotics accrues to some developing countries. However, governments often encourage innovation through the provision of financial support that is contingent on patent filing, so patent filings may not always have a close link with significant innovation but rather be a means employed by firms to benefit from such financial support. For example, there is a perception that, as in several other countries that offer such incentives, only a small part of all patents filed in China can be classified as "invention" patents, and that Chinese firms actually file patents to receive cash bonuses, subsidies or lower corporate income taxes from the government.[b] Should such a quality gap actually exist, it may nonetheless be closing, given the substantial spending on education and research by China (see, for example, Kozul-Wright and Poon, 2017).

---

[a]   Abdul Montaqim, "Top 14 industrial robot companies and how many robots they have around the world", Robotics and Automation News, available at: https://roboticsandautomationnews.com/tag/top-10-robotics-companies-in-the-world/ (accessed 16 May 2017).

[b]   For this view see, for example, Margit Molnar, "Making the most of innovation in China", oecdecoscope, 10 April 2017, available at: https://oecdecoscope.wordpress.com/2017/04/10/making-the-most-of-innovation-in-china/.

TABLE 3.3   Industrial robots: Estimated annual installation and accumulated stock, selected economies and groups, 2010–2015[a]

	Annual installation						Stock of operational robots	Change in stock of operational robots
	2010	2011	2012	2013	2014	2015	2015	2010–2015
	('000 of units)							(Per cent)
World	120.6	166.0	159.3	178.1	220.6	253.7	1 631.7	54.1
	(Percentage shares)							
Developed economies	56.6	56.4	58.9	52.0	46.3	45.2	58.7	15.3
France	1.7	1.8	1.9	1.2	1.3	1.2	2.0	-6.8
Germany	11.7	11.8	11.0	10.3	9.1	7.9	11.2	23.3
Italy	3.7	3.1	2.8	2.6	2.8	2.6	3.8	-1.8
Japan	18.2	16.8	18.0	14.1	13.3	13.8	17.6	-6.9
United Kingdom	0.7	0.9	1.8	1.4	0.9	0.6	1.1	29.2
United States	11.9[b]	12.4	14.1	13.3	11.9	10.8	14.4[b]	42.4[b]
Developing economies	41.0	39.2	37.7	44.8	50.1	52.9	39.1	185.7
Africa	0.2	0.2	0.2	0.4	0.2	0.1	0.3	84.3
Latin America and the Caribbean	1.4[b]	2.3	2.5	2.5	1.9	2.8	2.0[b]	162.2[b]
Mexico	0.7[b]	1.2	1.3	1.5	1.1	2.2	1.2[b]	234.7[b]
Asia	39.4	36.7	34.9	42.0	48.0	49.9	36.8	188.2
China	12.4	13.6	14.4	20.5	25.9	27.0	15.7	390.5
NIEs	22.9	18.5	15.1	15.9	14.9	19.0	16.7	106.1
Republic of Korea	19.5	15.4	12.2	12.0	11.2	15.1	12.9	108.2
Taiwan Province of China	2.7	2.2	2.1	3.1	3.1	2.8	3.0	83.0
Developing economies, excl. China	28.6	25.6	23.2	24.3	24.2	25.9	23.3	123.0
Developing economies, excl. NIEs	17.9	20.1	22.0	28.1	34.6	33.2	22.4	300.7
Transition economies	0.2	0.2	0.3	0.4	0.2	0.1	0.2	172.9
Other economies	2.2	4.2	3.1	2.8	3.4	1.8	2.0	n.a.

Source: See figure 3.2.
  a The IFR calculates the operational stock of robots by accumulating annual deployments and assuming that robots operate 12 years and are immediately withdrawn after 12 years, except for those countries, such as Japan, that undertake robot stock surveys or have their own calculation of operational stock and where these country-specific data are used.
  b Estimations based on data reported as an aggregate until 2010 by the IFR database for North America (Canada, Mexico and the United States) and disaggregated annual data provided by the IFR through private exchange.

countries accounted for 60 per cent of the stock in 2015, with just the three countries – Germany, Japan and the United States – making up 43 per cent.[22] However, table 3.3 shows that their shares in annual deployment have been falling over time, particularly in Japan. By contrast, the recent increase in industrial robot deployment has been the most rapid in developing countries, but this too has been heavily concentrated and is mostly due to China.

Between 2010 and 2015 the stock of industrial robots in China quadrupled, with the increase almost four times that of the Republic of Korea. By 2015, the share in the global stock of industrial robots held by China exceeded that in Germany and the United States while remaining slightly short of the share of Japan. As a result, just three Asian countries – China, Japan and Republic of Korea – accounted for 46 per

FIGURE 3.2   Industrial robots: Global annual installation and annual growth of estimated global stocks, 1993–2015

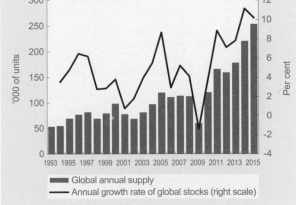

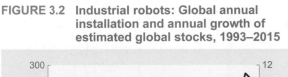

Source: UNCTAD secretariat calculations, based on the IFR database.

cent of the estimated global stock of industrial robots in 2015. All developing countries excluding China and the Asian NIEs (which, as already mentioned, on some classifications, such as those used by the IMF and UNIDO, are considered "advanced economies" or "industrialized economies") accounted for less than 7 per cent of the global stock. In Latin America and the Caribbean, Mexico alone accounts for the bulk of the region's industrial robot deployment, having registered a very large increase in the stock of industrial robots over the past few years. There are hardly any robots in Africa.

The use of industrial robots is also heavily concentrated in just five sectors: the automotive industry that accounted for 40 per cent to 45 per cent of annual deployment between 2010 and 2015, followed by computers and electronic equipment (about 15 per cent), electrical equipment, appliances and components (5 per cent to 10 per cent), closely followed by the group of rubber, plastic and chemical products, and by machinery (figure 3.3).

Given the evidence in table 3.3 and figure 3.3, it is not surprising to see the heavy concentration in a few countries of robot use in specific industrial sectors. This may be illustrated for the automotive industry

FIGURE 3.4 Industrial robots in the automotive industry: Annual installation, world and selected countries, 2010–2015

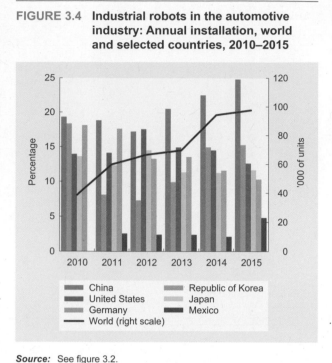

Source: See figure 3.2.

where, in the context of the already rapid increase in robot deployment in this sector as a whole between 2010 and 2015, the share of China in annual deployment steadily increased to reach almost 25 per cent in 2015 (figure 3.4). The remaining share was distributed among Germany, Japan, Mexico, the Republic of Korea and the United States.

The large absolute size of the manufacturing sector in China is in part responsible for this country's large share in the global stock of industrial robots. However, robot density (the number of industrial robots in manufacturing per manufacturing employee) is the highest in developed countries and developing countries at mature stages of industrialization (figure 3.5). The other developing countries with the highest recorded robot density, are Thailand, which ranks twenty-fifth, Mexico, which ranks twenty-seventh, Malaysia, which ranks thirty-first and China, which ranks thirty-fifth.[23] Given the sectoral concentration of robot deployment, it is not surprising that robot density in the automotive industry is larger than in total industry for all economies for which data are available (IFR, 2016a). Yet, it is interesting to note that this difference for developing countries is on average considerably larger than that for developed countries. This indicates that the sectoral concentration of robot density is particularly high in developing countries.

FIGURE 3.3 Industrial robots: Global annual installation, by manufacturing sector, 2010–2015

(Percentage of total robots in manufacturing)

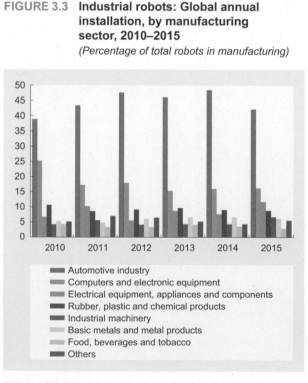

Source: See figure 3.2.

FIGURE 3.5 **Estimated robot density in manufacturing, 2014**

(Units of industrial robots per 10,000 employees)

Source: UNCTAD secretariat calculations, based on the IFR database; and Wood, 2017.

Note: The figure shows data for all those 70 economies for which data are available.

FIGURE 3.6 **Proximate relationship between technical and economic feasibility of routine-task automation, and estimated stock of industrial robots, by manufacturing sector**

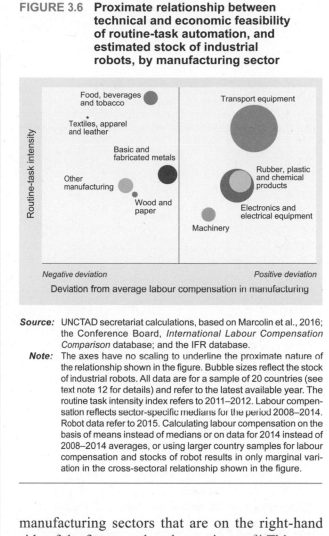

Source: UNCTAD secretariat calculations, based on Marcolin et al., 2016; the Conference Board, *International Labour Compensation Comparison* database; and the IFR database.

Note: The axes have no scaling to underline the proximate nature of the relationship shown in the figure. Bubble sizes reflect the stock of industrial robots. All data are for a sample of 20 countries (see text note 12 for details) and refer to the latest available year. The routine task intensity index refers to 2011–2012. Labour compensation reflects sector-specific medians for the period 2008–2014. Robot data refer to 2015. Calculating labour compensation on the basis of means instead of medians or on data for 2014 instead of 2008–2014 averages, or using larger country samples for labour compensation and stocks of robot results in only marginal variation in the cross-sectoral relationship shown in the figure.

To examine how actual robot deployment has navigated the trade-off between technical and economic feasibility, robot deployment can be added into figure 3.1. Doing so (figure 3.6) shows that robot deployment has been concentrated in those manufacturing sectors that are on the right-hand side of the figure, rather than at its top.[24] This suggests that economic factors are more important for robot deployment than the technical possibilities of automating workers' tasks. However, both technical and economic feasibility appear to be important: the bubble with the largest size, transport equipment, is also the topmost of the four sectors on the right-hand side of the figure; and the bubble sizes increase along the upper right quadrant, as routine-task intensity and unit labour costs both increase.

The figure also suggests that robot deployment has remained very limited in those manufacturing sectors where labour compensation is low, even if these sectors have high values on the routine-task intensity index. Robot deployment in the textiles, apparel and leather sector has been lowest among all manufacturing sectors even though this sector ranks second in terms of the technical feasibility of automating workers' routine tasks. It should be noted, however, that reduced robot adoption may also be related to technology issues of automation unrelated to workers'

FIGURE 3.7 Proximate current vulnerability to robot-based automation in manufacturing, selected economies

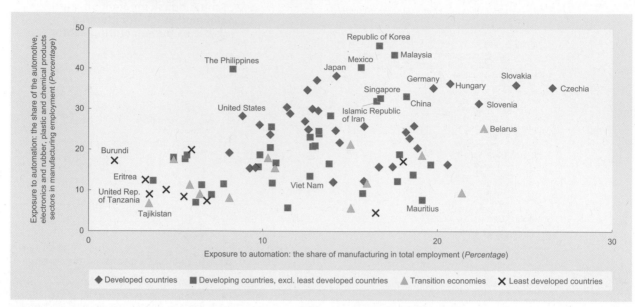

Source: UNCTAD secretariat calculations, based on Wood, 2017; and UNIDO, *Industrial Statistics* database.
Note: The horizontal axis reflects the share of manufacturing in total employment in 2014. The vertical axis reflects the share of the automotive sector, of the electronics sector and of the rubber, plastic and chemical products sector in manufacturing employment as an average for the period 2010–2014 over the years for which data are available. The sample includes all 91 economies for which data are available.

tasks, such as the pliability of fabrics in the apparel sector and the need to insert small flexible parts into tightly packed consumer electronics (Kucera, 2017).

Consideration of economic, in addition to technical, feasibility also bears on the gender impact of workplace automation. Studies only looking at technical feasibility (e.g. World Economic Forum, 2016; World Bank, 2016) find that the number of job losses is broadly the same for women and men. Yet, women are comparatively more affected because their participation in the labour force is lower, and because they are more likely to be rationed out of emerging jobs in areas that are complementary to robot use, for reasons elaborated in the next chapter. However, taking account of economic feasibility and low robot deployment in light manufacturing, such as apparel, where female employment tends to be concentrated, the gender impact of workplace automation may be reversed. A study for the United States, for example, found job displacement effects for both men and women, but the adverse effects for men were about 1.5–2 times larger than those for women (Acemoglu and Restrepo, 2017).

The concentration of robots in the automotive and electronics sectors, shown in figure 3.6, suggests that robot-based automation has, for now, largely left unaffected the initial stage of industrialization and establishment of labour-intensive manufacturing activities based on traditional labour-cost advantages, while it might well complicate subsequent industrial upgrading. Indeed, on current technological and economic indicators, developed countries and developing countries other than least developed countries (LDCs) would seem to be exposed to robot-based automation in manufacturing to a larger extent than LDCs (figure 3.7).

It should be noted that this evidence only refers to exposure to robot-based automation and does not take account of the risks to employment from other forms of automation. But it suggests that robot-based automation per se does not invalidate the traditional role of industrialization as a development strategy for lower income countries. Yet, the greater difficulty in attaining sectoral upgrading may limit the scope for industrialization to low-wage and less dynamic (in terms of productivity growth) manufacturing sectors. This could seriously stifle these countries' economic catch-up and leave them with stagnant productivity and per capita income growth.

At the same time, however, countries specialized in lower-wage labour-intensive manufacturing may benefit from favourable terms of trade effects. This will be the case if the concentration of robots in higher-wage skill-intensive manufactured goods translates at least partly into a global decline in the prices of such goods and reverses the trend decline in the global price of labour-intensive manufacturing relative to both skill-intensive manufactures and primary commodities that occurred over the past two decades.

3. Robots and reshoring

Robot use in low-wage labour-intensive manufacturing has remained low. Even so, developing countries' employment and income opportunities in these sectors may be adversely affected by the reshoring of manufacturing activities and jobs to developed countries. This would reduce the ability of developing countries to benefit from the special economic advantage that manufacturing confers in terms of economic catch-up.[25]

One element of this special economic advantage of manufacturing is its superior potential for the division of labour. This potential has, for example, been the basis for global value chains and the offshoring of certain labour-intensive manufacturing tasks from higher-wage to lower-wage economies. In developed countries, offshoring has enabled a shift in output from less productive to more productive manufacturing activities. And it has allowed some developing countries to move from low-productivity agricultural to higher-productivity and often labour-intensive manufacturing activities.[26] However, there is significant variation in the employment effects of offshoring in manufacturing across developed countries. Analysis of input–output data for the period 1995–2008 indicates sizeable losses of manufacturing employment from manufacturing value chains for the United States, as well as Japan, while the number of such jobs remained stable in Germany (Timmer et al., 2015).[27]

Adverse employment effects from offshoring combined with indications of an erosion of developing countries' labour-cost advantage may have triggered some reshoring of manufacturing activities to developed countries.[28] However, there is only fragmented and anecdotal evidence of the significance of reshoring.[29] Survey results and responses to firm-level questionnaires that aim to provide broader and more systematic evidence indicate that offshoring continues, but also that some reshoring

has occurred at a slow pace and across all industrial sectors, albeit at different intensities and for different motives (Fratocchi et al., 2015; Cohen et al., 2016; Stentoft et al., 2016). Moreover, an important part of new manufacturing activities in the United States relates to offshoring by European and Asian firms in relatively advanced manufacturing sectors, rather than to a reshoring by firms in the United States of labour-intensive manufacturing from developing countries (Cohen et al., 2016). Shifting production sites among these developed countries may have been facilitated by the greater compatibility of technology platforms.

Evidence also shows that where reshoring to developed countries has occurred, it has fallen short of expected employment effects. Reshoring has mostly been accompanied by capital investment, such as in robots, with the little job creation that has occurred concentrated in high-skilled activities (De Backer et al., 2016). This means that jobs that "return" with reshored production will not be the same as those that have left.

Indeed, reshoring is likely to be more about manufacturing output rather than employment, given the positive relationship between manufacturing output growth and productivity growth.[30] Evidence for the United States in the period 1991–2007, for example, indicates that firms in sectors where manufactured output declined and that experienced greater exposure to import competition from China also saw a decline in both their patent output and research and development (R&D) expenditure (Autor et al., 2016). This finding may raise concerns that production offshoring stifles innovation and, thus, reduces productivity growth in manufacturing.[31] An additional argument that links manufacturing output and innovation concerns the advantages of locating production geographically close to product design, as manufacturing competence is integral to innovation (Pisano and Shih, 2012).[32]

Given that design and innovation activities have not been offshored, this reassessment would recommend reshoring production because shorter supply chains would stimulate innovation and product development. Such a motivation would not only trigger reshoring but also the relocation of production activities to areas where firms expect that links between production and R&D, and its positive impact on innovation, can be best encouraged. Recognition of such links between manufacturing output, innovation and technology growth led to the creation of the National Network for Manufacturing Innovation in the United States, which was formally established in 2014 and is now known as Manufacturing USA. The initiative's main aim is "to support industry in establishing the ecosystems or industrial commons that will better enable innovators to develop the specific manufacturing technologies, processes, and capabilities needed to advance promising early stage technological inventions that can be scaled-up and commercialized by U.S. manufacturers" (Executive Office of the President of the United States, 2016: vii). But it also aims at encouraging manufacturers to locate production facilities in the United States (e.g. Hart et al., 2012). All this suggests that reshoring depends on factors that go significantly beyond simple labour-cost comparisons, which have driven offshoring decisions. This also suggests that developed countries may increasingly use robots to facilitate the reshoring of manufacturing production with a view to stimulating further technological progress, including in terms of product innovation.

This would most likely have adverse effects on the inclusiveness of growth at the international level.

One reason why the pace of reshoring has, nevertheless, remained slow may be tepid investment and sluggish aggregate demand in developed countries more generally. Moreover, these countries lack the supplier networks that some developing countries have built to complement assembly activities. And while labour-cost differentials remain a factor in firms' decisions of where to locate production, especially of goods with a high labour content, demand factors such as the size and growth of local markets are becoming increasingly important determinants. Accordingly, many companies that once moved production to, say, China, are now staying there for access to growing local demand. This suggests that the production of labour-intensive manufactures destined for rapidly growing markets in large developing countries with domestic production linkages is unlikely to be reshored.

D. Productivity and inclusiveness at national level

This section examines the relationship between robot use on the one hand and productivity, output, employment and wages in manufacturing on the other hand, within national economies.

Robot deployment has been associated with productivity growth (figure 3.8).[33] This positive association can be observed both for countries with relatively large robot density – such as Germany, Japan, Republic of Korea and the United States – and for economies with more modest robot density but rapidly increasing robot stocks – such as China and Taiwan Province of China.

Cross-country evidence for the same period suggests a positive relationship between increased robot use and an increased share of manufacturing in total value added. This relationship holds in particular for those economies where robot density is comparatively large (figure 3.9A). The evidence for any such relationship in economies with comparatively small robot density is somewhat less clear (figure 3.9B). But it is worth noting that many countries where industrial robot use is low also experienced deindustrialization in terms of a shrinking share of manufacturing in total value added. Figure 3.9 supports the finding in the

previous section that robot use tends to foster the concentration of manufacturing activity in a small number of countries.

Cross-country evidence for the same sample points to a slight negative relationship between changes in robot use and changes in the share of manufacturing in total employment (figure 3.10). Given the evidence on a positive relationship between robot use and labour productivity, and considering that the very purpose of using robots is to automate certain tasks, this finding is not surprising in itself.

Rather, it is interesting to note that some countries where robot density is large, including Germany and the Republic of Korea, as well as countries where the accumulation of robots has been rapid, such as China, experienced an increase, or only a small decline, in the share of manufacturing in total employment. China and Germany also experienced an increase in the absolute number of manufacturing jobs, while the Republic of Korea recorded a small decline (figure 3.11). While there appears to be little systematic relationship between changes in robot use in manufacturing and changes in real wages in manufacturing across the group of economies for which

FIGURE 3.8 **Robot use and labour productivity in manufacturing in selected economies: Change between 2005 and 2014**

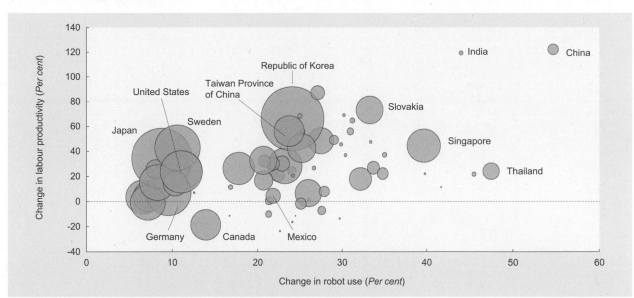

Source: UNCTAD secretariat calculations, based on the IFR database; and Wood, 2017.
Note: Change in robot use reflects the percentage change in the ratio of the average annual robot installation and the average robot stock over the period 2005 and 2014. Change in labour productivity reflects the percentage change in labour productivity in manufacturing between 2005 and 2014. The size of the bubbles reflects robot density in 2014. The chart includes the 64 economies for which data are available.

FIGURE 3.9 **Robot use and manufacturing output share in selected economies: Change between 2005 and 2014**

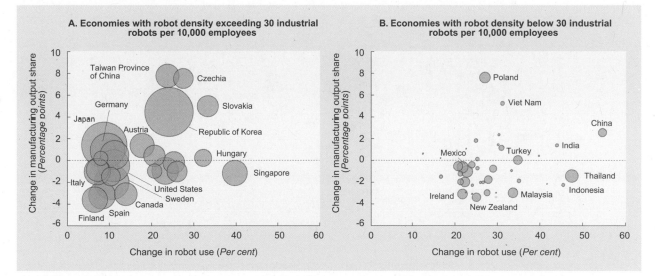

Source: See figure 3.8.
Note: Change in robot use reflects the percentage change in the ratio of the average annual robot installation and the average robot stock over the period 2005 and 2014. Change in manufacturing output share reflects the percentage point change in the share of manufacturing in total value added between 2005 and 2014. The size of the bubbles reflects robot density in 2014. The figures include the 64 economies for which data are available, of which 24 economies in figure 3.9A and 40 economies in figure 3.9B.

data are available, increased robot use was associated with real wage growth in all economies except Mexico, Portugal and Singapore which recorded small declines (figure 3.12). Growth of both real wages and robot use was particularly large in China (at roughly 150 per cent and 55 per cent, respectively).[34]

FIGURE 3.10 **Robot use and manufacturing employment share in selected economies: Changes between 2005 and 2014**

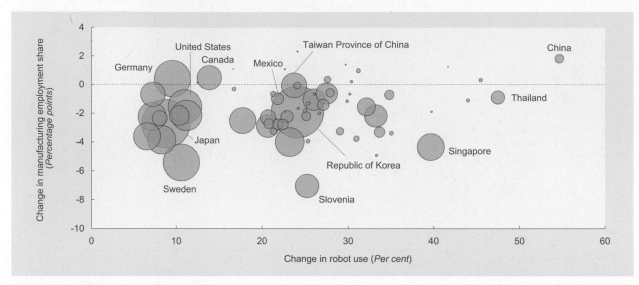

Source: See figure 3.8.
Note: The size of the bubbles reflects robot density in 2014. Change in robot use reflects the percentage change in the ratio of the average annual robot installation and the average robot stock over the period 2005 and 2014. Change in manufacturing employment share reflects the percentage point change in the share of manufacturing in total employment between 2005 and 2014. The figure includes the 64 economies for which data are available.

FIGURE 3.11 **Robot use and manufacturing employment in selected economies: Changes between 2005 and 2014**

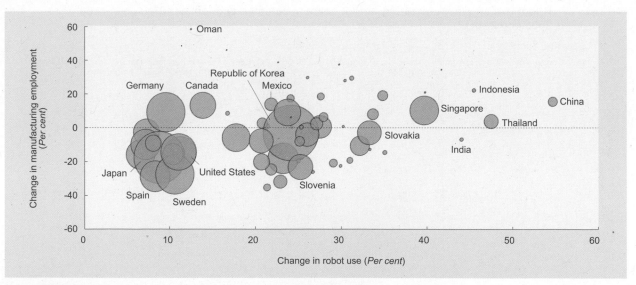

Source: See figure 3.8.
Note: The size of the bubbles reflects robot density in 2014. Change in robot use reflects the percentage change in the ratio of the average annual robot installation and the average robot stock over the period 2005 and 2014. Change in manufacturing employment reflects the percentage change in manufacturing employment between 2005 and 2014. The figure includes the 64 economies for which data are available.

This indicates that the impact of robot-based automation on manufacturing employment has varied greatly across countries. It clearly depends on country-specific conditions, including institutional arrangements (such as workers' bargaining power), macroeconomic conditions and processes, and country-specific robotics initiatives (as illustrated for China in box 3.2).

Economic policies greatly affect the impact of automation on aggregate demand. If productivity gains

FIGURE 3.12 Robot use and manufacturing wages in selected economies: Changes between 2005 and 2014

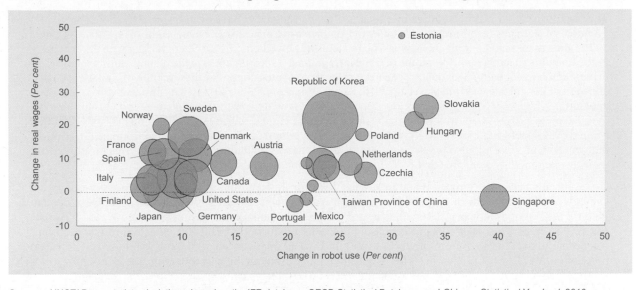

Source: UNCTAD secretariat calculations, based on the IFR database; OECD Statistical Database; and *Chinese Statistical Yearbook 2016*.
Note: The size of the bubbles reflects robot density in 2014. Change in robot use reflects the percentage change in the ratio of the average annual robot installation and the average robot stock over the period 2005 and 2014. Change in manufacturing wages reflects the percentage change in real manufacturing wages between 2005 and 2014. The figure includes the 28 economies for which data are available except China, which is an outlier along both axes and whose inclusion would blur the picture.

are shared and real wages grow in line with productivity growth, automation will tend to boost private consumption, aggregate demand and ultimately total employment. Obviously, in such cases an important role is played by macroeconomic policies that operate to sustain effective demand, employment and standards of living within a country.

Even if that is not the case, for some countries, employment could remain stable or even increase if the additional supply that results from automation-based productivity growth is absorbed through increased demand from exports. This would mean that any adverse employment and income effects of automation are transferred to other countries through trade. Germany and Mexico provide examples of this type, where an export-oriented strategy appears to have partially avoided the adverse effects of robot use on domestic employment.

In the case of Germany, the sizeable increase in robot density in the automotive sector from an already high base was associated with strong expansion of output and productivity and accompanied by a sizeable but somewhat smaller expansion of employment and real wages (table 3.4). This combined to produce a reduction in unit labour costs by about 10 per cent between 2007 and 2015. The favourable effect of automation on employment was facilitated by rapid

increase in the sector's exports, which helped to increase the trade surplus of Germany in this sector alone to more than 4 per cent of GDP in 2015. While the other highly automated manufacturing sectors – such as rubber and plastic products, pharmaceuticals and metals products – showed slightly less impressive growth, all of them contributed positively to the sizeable trade surplus of Germany.

Mexico is another interesting example, as the country combines significant automation in the automotive sector (accounting for 20 per cent share of manufacturing employment in 2015), more modest automation in electronics (about 12 per cent of manufacturing employment), and virtually no robot use in textiles and apparel (9 per cent of manufacturing employment). It is noteworthy that the sectors where automation increased most between 2011 and 2015 were also those with the largest output gains (table 3.4).[35] In the automotive sector excluding parts, for example, robot density increased from 121 robots per 10,000 employees in 2011 to 513 robots per 10,000 employees in 2015, with this sector's output growth vastly exceeding that of the manufacturing sector as a whole. A similar but smaller expansion was evident for the electronics sector, industrial machinery, and rubber and plastic products. The increased use of robots in Mexico has also been associated with expanding employment. As in

---

BOX 3.2   National robot strategy: The case of China

The "Made in China 2025" initiative by China is often considered to have been inspired by the "Industry 4.0 Strategy" of Germany (e.g. European Chamber of Commerce in China, 2017). Launched in 2015, "Made in China 2025" aims to turn its economy into a world manufacturing powerhouse by 2049, coinciding with the centenary of the founding of the People's Republic of China.[a] Its guiding principles are to make manufacturing innovation-driven, emphasize quality over quantity, achieve green development, optimize the structure of Chinese industry, and nurture human talent (Wübbeke et al., 2016; Kozul-Wright and Poon, 2017). In its thirteenth Five-Year Plan, adopted in March 2016, the Chinese Government sets out how to deepen the implementation of this strategy over the period 2016–2020. In support of the manufacturing targets, the government set up the CNY20 billion Modern Manufacturing Industry Investment Fund, CNY6 billion of which are allocated from the government budget (OECD, 2017). It also relies on private sector initiatives, including by calling on firms to self-declare their own technology standards and participate in international standards setting.

Given its emphasis on digitization and modernization of manufacturing, robots play an essential role in the strategy of China in terms of both their increased use and enhanced domestic production. The Development Plan for the Robotics Industry 2016–2020, issued in April 2016, aims at increasing robot density to 150 robots per 10,000 employees, as well as at increasing domestic production to 100,000 industrial robots per year.[b] According to data for 2015 from the IFR (2016a), this would imply a tripling in both robot use and domestic production. While robot use has been led by the automotive sector in the past few years, the electronics sector is envisaged to drive increased robot use in the next two or three years.[c]

The objective of guiding manufacturing away from labour-intensive and low value added activities to a set of manufacturing activities of a more capital-, high-skill- and knowledge-intensive nature is related to rising wage costs in these traditional export industries (Wei et al., 2016; *TDR 2010*, chap. II). Hence, manufacturers in China may feel pressured on the one hand by the labour-cost advantage of less-developed countries with far smaller domestic markets and, on the other hand, by the advanced economies that themselves have formulated initiatives supporting further development of their manufacturing sectors through robotization.[d]

However, while the greater use of robots in manufacturing production can compensate for the shrinking labour force and keep wage increases under control, with a view to smoothing the shift towards a new growth strategy, such rebalancing will also need to ensure the availability of a digitally skilled labour force and to prevent any balance-of-payments problems that could arise from expanding imports of machinery and technology-intensive intermediate inputs in the face of declining export revenues. From this perspective, attaining the policy targets of the Made in China 2025 initiative related to human capital and the domestic production of robots, as well as other high-end machinery, appears to be critical.[e]

---

[a] The "Made in China 2025" initiative is paired with the "Internet Plus" initiative, launched in July 2015, whose objective is to integrate mobile Internet, cloud computing, Big Data and the Internet of Things with modern manufacturing, to enhance the development of a wide array of services activities, and to increase the presence of domestic Internet-based companies in international markets. For further discussion, see the initiatives' websites, available at: http://english.gov.cn/2016special/madeinchina2025/ and http://english.gov.cn/2016special/internetplus/ as well as, for example, Wübbeke et al., 2016; and European Chamber of Commerce in China, 2017.

[b] See: http://english.gov.cn/state_council/ministries/2016/04/27/content_281475336534830.htm.

[c] See Direct China Chamber of Commerce, China industrial robot industry report and forecast 2016–2019, 15 July 2016; available at: https://www.dccchina.org/2016/07/china-industrial-robot-industry-report-and-forecast-2016-2019/.

[d] For this argumentation see, for example, Xinhua, " 'Made in China 2025' plan unveiled to boost manufacturing", 19 May 2015; available at: http://news.xinhuanet.com/english/2015-05/19/c_134252230.htm.

[e] The significant progress in innovation made by China in these areas is documented in, for example, Wübbeke et al., 2016; and, with a focus on robots, WIPO, 2015.

Germany, much of this was due to increased exports, as automotive and electronics exports from Mexico increased rapidly, while its exports of textiles and apparel declined between 2011 and 2015 (table 3.4).

As expected, unit labour costs declined faster on average in activities relying more on robotic automation than in industries with low robot density. As a result, such automation mostly rewarded capital and contributed to the downward trend in labour income share in Mexico, which declined by about 10 percentage points during the period 1995–2014 (ILO and OECD, 2015). Moreover, real wages in the highly automated automotive sector dropped by 1.6 per cent between 2011 and 2015, while real wages expanded by 1.5 per cent in manufacturing as a whole (table 3.4). This experience suggests that the overall distributional impact of robots may well be adverse.

TABLE 3.4   Germany and Mexico: Sectoral robot use and developments in output, employment, wages and trade, selected years

Country and sector	Robot density (Unit of robots per 10,000 employees)		Expansion of robot use	Change in output	Change in output per employee	Change in employ-ment	Change in real wages per employee	Change in unit labour costs	Change in exports	Change in trade surplus (or deficit)	Trade surplus (or trade deficit) (Percentage shares of GDP)	
	Initial period	Final period									Initial period	Final period
				(Per cent)								
Germany												
Total Manufacturing	**181.6**	**209.3**	**9.8**	**5.1**	**1.7**	**3.3**	**5.1**	**3.4**	**1.0**	**-9.2**	**11.3**	**10.7**
Food, beverages and tobacco	46.4	72.4	11.1	-1.5	-5.5	4.2	4.4	10.5	24.8	-34.8	-0.2	-0.2
Textiles, apparel and allied products	9.3	16.7	13.0	-11.4	2.1	-13.2	9.2	7.0	-5.7	53.1	-0.3	-0.2
Wood products except furniture	212.7	62.6	4.2	-3.4	-4.5	-7.7	0.3	5.0	-20.9	-90.2	0.0	0.0
Pharmaceuticals and cosmetics	54.6	168.7	14.2	13.7	1.4	12.1	6.2	4.7	32.8	71.4	0.6	1.0
Rubber and plastics products	143.4	400.6	13.0	6.8	0.2	6.6	3.4	3.2	-4.1	-28.8	0.8	0.6
Basic metals	96.1	87.3	8.1	-8.0	-8.2	0.2	1.7	10.8	-25.9	-26.4	-0.4	-0.3
Metal products, except machinery and equipment	63.4	129.3	13.3	0.7	-2.7	3.5	2.5	5.3	-18.7	-31.9	0.6	0.4
Machinery and equipment	29.5	75.2	13.0	-6.0	-15.2	10.9	3.2	21.8	-4.4	-9.8	3.5	3.3
Electrical/electronics	92.9	97.8	9.6	23.2	19.2	3.3	4.6	-12.3	-10.2	-153.3	0.4	-0.2
Motor vehicles, trailers and semi-trailers	944.7	1067.2	9.7	22.7	17.1	4.8	4.8	-10.6	8.1	7.1	3.8	4.3
Other transport equipment	61.1	53.3	8.7	39.1	23.2	12.9	18.2	-4.0	51.3	155.2	0.3	0.7
Mexico												
Total Manufacturing	**6.0**	**41.1**	**40.3**	**12.5**	**2.1**	**10.2**	**1.5**	**-0.7**	**26.2**	**-48.1**	**-1.8**	**-0.7**
Food, beverages and tobacco	0.1	2.8	39.3	6.8	4.6	2.1	2.7	-1.8	22.0	280.6	0.1	0.5
Textiles, apparel and allied products	0.0	0.0	n.a.	7.2	10.3	-2.8	3.1	-6.5	4.0	79.0	-0.2	-0.3
Wood products including furniture	0.0	1.1	87.5	7.8	3.9	3.7	3.1	-0.7	55.8	74.4	0.2	0.3
Paper and paper products	0.0	1.5	83.3	6.7	9.4	-2.5	4.3	-4.7	23.6	6.2	-0.3	-0.3
Pharmaceuticals and cosmetics	0.1	6.5	30.9	-3.5	1.1	-4.5	-7.1	-8.1	11.7	21.5	-0.2	-0.3
Rubber and plastic products	9.5	68.4	38.7	16.7	8.0	7.9	5.1	-2.7	28.4	18.1	-1.3	-1.5
Basic metals	1.2	16.4	41.9	11.0	0.8	10.1	4.4	3.5	-30.7	-74.6	0.3	0.1
Metal products, except machinery and equipment	1.4	5.7	41.5	11.7	9.7	1.8	1.7	-7.3	1.6	45.9	-0.7	-1.1
Machinery and equipment	4.1	39.1	33.3	7.5	-8.9	18.0	0.2	10.0	28.2	35.6	-1.1	-1.5
Electrical/electronics	0.5	8.5	34.1	19.3	14.2	4.5	3.2	-9.6	15.0	96.7	0.2	0.4
Automotive	29.5	153.5	41.5	42.7	-1.3	44.6	-1.6	-0.3	43.8	54.5	2.9	4.6
Motor vehicles, engines and bodies	121.4	513.1	39.8	39.9	4.2	34.3	n.a	n.a.	41.7	45.8	3.0	4.5
Automotive parts	15.6	103.5	42.7	46.3	0.1	46.1	n.a	n.a.	49.4	-288.3	-0.1	0.1
Other vehicles	16.5	12.4	20.7	86.8	21.7	53.5	n.a	n.a.	129.6	380.4	0.1	0.3

Source: UNCTAD secretariat calculations, based on National Institute of Statistics and Geography (INEGI), the Conference Board, and the IFR database.

Note: The time period depends on data availability and is 2007–2015 for Germany, and 2011–2015 for Mexico. Expansion of automation reflects the percentage change in the ratio of the average annual robot installation and the average robot stock over the sample period. Country-specific sectoral disaggregation depends on data availability. Robot data for wood and wood products in Germany include furniture. Sectoral breakdowns of wage and unit-labour cost data for Mexico are not fully comparable to those of the other data for Mexico: in particular, real wage and unit-labour costs data for "pharmaceuticals and cosmetics" refer to all chemical products and those for "automotive" refer to "transport equipment" and therefore also include "other vehicles". Trade data for aggregate manufacturing refer only to those sectors that are defined as manufacturing in trade statistics and therefore draw on fewer sectors than the other data regarding total manufacturing.

E. Conclusions

Despite substantial cross-country variation in the employment and income effects of robots, most existing studies overestimate the potential adverse effects. Job displacements are likely to occur only gradually, as what is technically feasible is not automatically economically feasible. Among jobs with identical displacement risk in technical terms, those at higher wage levels are exposed more to robot-based displacement for economic reasons. Such jobs are prevalent in more skill-intensive manufacturing sectors and in economies at a relatively mature stage of industrialization, rather than in labour-intensive manufacturing sectors and countries at an early stage of industrialization. And just as in past technological waves, digitization may create new products and sectors with new employment and income opportunities, even though there is little evidence that would point to digital technologies having already created large numbers of new jobs (e.g. Berger and Frey, 2016).

The creation of new employment and income opportunities that could compensate for adverse aggregate effects from robots, including by boosting employment where robots and workers are complementary, would be greatly facilitated by stable but expansionary global economic conditions, and by expansionary domestic macroeconomic policies. The associated policy shifts, which could drive sustained productive investment and support broad-based global income growth, are discussed in chapter VII of this *Report*. The continued absence of such shifts will tend to depress investment growth and hamper the unfolding of the job creation potential of the digital revolution. As a result, robotics will tend to further hold back aggregate demand growth by shifting employment away from technologically dynamic sectors, depressing productivity and real wage growth in relatively stagnant activities and "refuge sectors", and thereby reducing inclusiveness.

While much of the aggregate effect of robots remains uncertain and determined by macroeconomic forces, robot use does affect what jobs are available and where and by whom they will be done. Robots displace routine tasks that are usually done by workers on the middle rungs of the pay scale. The country-specific patterns of robot use indicate that industrial robots are sharpening the tendency towards concentration of manufacturing activities in a small group of countries. This concentration tends to harm inclusiveness at the international level and, given current global demand conditions, poses significant challenges for developing countries to achieve structural transformation towards well-paying jobs in manufacturing. In this sense, robotics could make it more difficult to pursue economic development on the basis of traditional industrialization strategies and achieve the 2030 Agenda for Sustainable Development.

Effects on inclusiveness at the national level depend on a range of country-specific conditions. These include a country's stage of industrialization and its position in the international division of labour. Sector-specific patterns of robot use indicate that engaging in the early stages of industrialization has largely remained unaffected at present, also because there is little evidence for reshoring of labour-intensive manufacturing tasks back to developed countries. It must be borne in mind, however, that robots are just one form of automation and that the early stages of industrialization may be exposed to job displacement through more traditional forms of automation, such as mechanization.

Another determinant is how countries use robots themselves, including with a view to avoiding what sometimes has been called the "middle-income trap" (*TDR 2016*). Robots can support the international competitiveness of firms that face rising labour compensation (such as from a shrinking labour force), uphold a large share of manufacturing in total output and facilitate structural transformation. However, this may result in a trade-off between creating large numbers of jobs with relatively little pay in labour-intensive sectors where robot-based automation is not (yet) economically feasible and fewer jobs with relatively higher pay for workers whose skills are complementary to robots.

Whether this dilemma can be avoided brings to the fore the impact of country-specific macroeconomic and trade policies as the third element that affects inclusiveness at the national level. Robot deployment in export-oriented manufacturing and compensating for potential adverse employment effects by increasing the scale of output appears to have helped some countries, such as Germany and Mexico, to smooth out adverse effects from robot use on inclusiveness. However, such a strategy also exports the negative employment and income effects to countries that import those goods.

To the extent that robot-based automation does actually reduce the number of manufacturing jobs globally, at least in the short run, countries that wish to maintain or build manufacturing employment will tend to compete in a shrinking global pool of manufacturing jobs. While great uncertainty remains as to how long that "short run" may last, the mere risk of protracted adverse effects on employment and inequality provides enough reason to consider how to minimize them. A more effective and sustainable strategy would emphasize the role of domestic macroeconomic policies, including public expenditure on activities (such as social spending) that improve the quality of life of citizens and generate large multiplier effects on output and employment, using the surpluses generated by increased productivity in the more dynamic sectors. This would be facilitated by coordination across countries, both developed and developing, to prevent beggar-thy-neighbour strategies from distorting such efforts.

Some have suggested that slowing down automation by taxing robots would give the economy more time to adjust and provide fiscal revenues to finance adjustment.[36] While this may well be the case, a robot tax presumes the possibility of avoiding tax havens where robots could be deployed tax-free. It also presumes the possibility of clearly separating what is produced by a worker from what is produced by a robot and the establishment of a fictitious income that a robot gets paid as a reference salary. Moreover, a robot tax may hamper the most beneficial uses of robots, i.e. those where workers and robots are complementary and those that could lead to the creation of digitization-based new products and new jobs.

Others have suggested a number of policies to promote a more even distribution of the benefits from increased robot use, based on the fear that robots will take over tasks with higher productivity and pay compared to the average tasks that will continue to be done by workers. If unchecked, these distributional effects from robotics would increase the share of income going to the owners of robots and the intellectual property that they incorporate, thereby exacerbating existing inequalities. Options to address these concerns include (i) raising wages through collective bargaining such that workers gain a higher share from productivity growth, and linking wage growth in technologically stagnant sectors to that in dynamic sectors in order to pull up aggregate investment and productivity growth; (ii) schemes where employee earnings depend on

the firm's profitability so that a substantial part of citizens' income would come from capital ownership rather than from working (e.g. Freeman, 2015); (iii) increased use of inheritance and wealth taxes that would even out access to capital;[37] and (iv) the introduction of a universal basic income (or basic dividend), as discussed in chapter VII of this *Report*, part of whose rationale is based on the argument that the digital revolution requires a rethinking of welfare systems that have been built around labour and stable jobs in manufacturing.

Of particular importance for developing countries at early stages of development might be building a dense network of intra-sectoral and cross-sectoral linkages and complementarities (*TDR 2016*, chapter VI). This could further stem the risk of reshoring, even as the cost of owning and operating robots further declines and the scope of economically feasible automation gradually broadens, to also affect traditional, labour-intensive sectors. Doing so requires enhanced public investment in logistics and telecommunications infrastructure, as well as in supportive technological and innovation systems. Also needed are reliable supply networks that provide production inputs of the right quality at the right place and at the right time. Moreover, enhanced regional trade integration among developing countries could help them attain a market size that is sufficiently large for even affiliates of transnational corporations to forgo reshoring and maintain production in these countries. Developing countries could further reduce disruptions from automation by redesigning education systems to create the managerial and labour skills needed to operate new technologies and widely diffuse the benefits of their use, as well as to complement them.

Digitization could also open up new development opportunities. The development of collaborative robots, which do not replace human work but work alongside and increase the productivity of human labour, remains in its infancy. But so-called "cobots" could eventually be particularly beneficial for small enterprises, as they can be easily set up and do not require special system integrators and they can rapidly adapt to new processes and production run requirements. Combining robots and three-dimensional printing could create further new possibilities for small manufacturing enterprises to overcome size limits in production and to conduct business – both cross-border and national – on a much larger scale. The ensuing greater importance of final demand for locational decisions regarding the production of manufactures could significantly reduce the role of global value chains for goods. As a result, the production of manufactures could become less global and more regional. Future developments in robotics that would allow robots to be used profitably for small-scale production could eventually cause unit production cost variations among countries to become smaller than international transport and communications costs, making large-scale international merchandise trade less attractive and creating significant opportunities for localized manufacturing activities, including in developing countries.

At the same time, digitization may lead to a fragmentation of the global provision and international trade of services (see, for example, UNCTAD, 2014). While this could open up entirely new avenues for developing countries' development strategies, it is yet unclear whether digital-based services could actually provide similar employment, income and productivity gains as manufacturing has traditionally done.[38]

This discussion shows that disruptive technologies always bring a mix of benefits and risks. But whatever the impacts, the final outcomes for employment and inclusiveness are shaped by policies. ■

Notes

1 See, for example, Frey and Osborne, 2013; Galbraith, 2014; Ford, 2015; Chang et al., 2016; World Bank, 2016; McKinsey Global Institute, 2017.

2 For a definition of robots and robotic devices operating in both industrial and non-industrial environments, see https://www.iso.org/obp/ui/#iso:std:iso:8373:ed-2:v1:en.

3 For discussion of digital development in agriculture and services, see United Nations, 2016.

4 For some initial discussion of this issue, see also UNCTAD, 2016a and 2016b.

5 Robot categories outside the industrial sector include service robots for professional use that are deployed in a wide range of uses, such as agriculture, professional cleaning, construction, logistics, medicine and defence, but the number of such units sold in 2015 was only about one sixth of that of industrial robots (International Federation of Robotics (IFR), 2016b). Service robots for domestic/household tasks and entertainment and leisure robots are sold in very large numbers but are of little relevance to the present discussion.

6 Sustainable Development Goal 9 aims to "Build resilient infrastructure, promote inclusive and sustainable industrialization and foster innovation" and target 9.2 to "Promote inclusive and sustainable industrialization and, by 2030, significantly raise industry's share of employment and gross domestic product, in line with national circumstances, and double its share in least developed countries". Other areas of the digital revolution have been discussed in detail in UNCTAD's *Technology and Innovation and Information Technology Reports*, as well as United Nations, 2016. For a discussion of investment-related issues in the digital revolution, see UNCTAD, 2017.

7 To understand the difference between jobs and tasks, as well as the concept of "occupations" used further below, it may be useful to recall that the ILO (2008: 11) defines a job as "a set of tasks and duties, performed, or meant to be performed, by one person, including for an employer or in self-employment" and an occupation as "a set of jobs whose main tasks and duties are characterized by a high degree of similarity".

8 The definition of different occupations results from judgements by labour experts that assign scores to different indicators that supposedly characterize these occupations. The mapping of tasks into occupations merges job task requirements from the United States Department of Labor's Dictionary of Occupational Titles to their corresponding Census occupation classifications to measure routine, abstract and manual task content by occupations (Autor and Dorn, 2013). While it is not immediately clear to what extent such a mapping based on the United States labour market is applicable to other, in particular developing, countries, these countries do not have the data required for this mapping. Contrary to the calculation of the routine-task intensity index based on responses from individual workers on the actual nature of their daily work, which is used below, this methodology does not allow for sector-specific disaggregation of routine-task intensity.

9 Two other groups of studies look at automation of occupations. One is more judgemental, views occupations rather than tasks as being threatened by automation, and arrives at alarming estimates, such as that almost half of all jobs in the United States are threatened by automation (Frey and Osborne, 2013). The other uses workers' reports on the tasks involved in their jobs from the Organisation for Economic Co-operation and Development's (OECD) Programme for the International Assessment of Adult Competencies (PIAAC) to map tasks to occupations. It emphasizes that occupations themselves are particular combinations of tasks and that many

occupations change when some of their associated tasks become automatable. As a result, relatively few occupations can be automated entirely, and jobs will be altered rather than displaced completely (Arntz et al., 2016). But contrary to Autor and Dorn (2013), these two studies do not map tasks and occupations into economic sectors.

10 This observation is often referred to as "Moore's law". While there is agreement that the price of robots has significantly declined, this will only have benefited those firms that have actually used robots. Such firm-specific factors have been discussed, for example, in the "superstar firm" literature (e.g. Autor et al., 2017) that sees the productivity performance of a sector, or even an entire economy, driven by a few firms on which sales are concentrated and which reinvest ensuing larger profits in production. This topic is beyond the scope of this chapter, not least because of the lack of firm-specific data on robot use. But such firm-specific effects may explain the apparent paradox of rapid robot use being accompanied by a deceleration of economy-wide productivity growth in many developed countries, as recently argued, for example by Haldane (2017). Such firm-specific effects may also reinforce the persistence and simultaneous presence of very different technological stages within economic sectors, and even firms, that can be widely observed across developing countries.

11 Labour compensation is also a source of income and, hence, an element of aggregate demand. This means that a decline in labour compensation will reduce demand for the goods and services produced by robots and, thus, slow down investment in automation.

12 The routine-task intensity index used here is based on data for 2011–2012 from the OECD's Programme for the International Assessment of Adult Competencies (PIAAC). The data reflect answers from 105,526 individuals from the following 20 OECD member states that participate in PIAAC and report sectorally disaggregated data: Austria, Belgium, Canada, Czechia, Denmark, Estonia, France, Germany, Ireland, Italy, Japan, Netherlands, Norway, Poland, Republic of Korea, Slovakia, Spain, Sweden, United Kingdom and United States. For further discussion of this index, see Marcolin et al., 2016.

13 Figure 3.1 indicates proximate cross-sectoral relationships between technical and economic feasibility of routine task automation, and does not reflect numerically precise estimations.

14 For recent detailed discussion of long-term industrialization experiences, see also Felipe et al., 2015; Haraguchi et al., 2017; and Wood, 2017.

15 It should be noted that the shares of world manufacturing value added accounted for by different country groups presented here significantly deviate from those reported in UNIDO's *Yearbooks of Industrial Statistics*. This is due to differences in group composition. While the table follows the standard classification of country groups used by the United Nations, UNIDO also considers a number of, according to the United Nations' classification, developing countries, as industrialized economies, including some countries in West Asia and some East Asian economies (for further discussion of the UNIDO country groups, see *Country Grouping in UNIDO Statistics* Working Paper 01/2013, available at: https://www.unido.org/fileadmin/user_media/Services/PSD/Country_Grouping_in_UNIDO_Statistics_2013.pdf).

16 This is also why the experience of Mexico may be best described as "stalled industrialization" (see *TDR 2016*).

17 One explanation for this concentration may be that larger size allows for economies of scale and higher income for a higher income elasticity of demand for manufactures, so that both these elements tend to increase the share of manufacturing in a country's gross domestic product (GDP).

18 It should be noted that all comprehensive data sets on employment are afflicted by large gaps and inconsistencies in the country and year coverage of primary sources, and are therefore necessarily based on adjustment and estimation to some extent. Differences across such databases are particularly large for China. See Wood (2017: data appendix pp. 11–12) for a discussion of this issue and what choices underlie the data reported for China in table 3.2. The discrepancies between the data reported in table 3.2 here and those in table 3.2 in *TDR 2016* are caused by the use of different databases, where the database used in this *Report* has the advantage of providing more up-to-date data as required, for example, for the calculation of the various per-employee measures used later in this chapter.

19 One explanation for this is these countries' increased specialization in less labour-intensive manufacturing (see, for example, Wood, 2017) and in the case of the United States a very strong focus on the computer and electronics industry (Baily and Bosworth, 2014).

20 One reason for this would be path-dependent technological capability, i.e. acquiring the digital capabilities required for robot use may be easier for those who already possess well-developed technological capabilities.

21 The UNCTAD secretariat is grateful to the International Federation of Robotics (IFR) for granting access to its database free of charge.

22 It is worth noting that not all countries at a mature stage of industrialization have shown rapid increases in robot use, as the data for France, Italy and the United Kingdom in table 3.3 indicate.

23 The number for robot density in China is fraught with significant uncertainty. The IFR (2016a) reports a robot density of 49 for 2015, while Wübbeke et al. (2016), report for the same year a number of 19, explaining the difference by the inclusion of migrant

workers. The figure, which reports data for 2014, reflects a still lower number of about 10 robots per 10,000 employees, based on calculations with employment data from Wood (2017), whose data appendix (available at: https://www.wider.unu.edu/sites/default/files/Publications/Working-paper/Wood-data-appendix.pdf) details the reasons for uncertainty in employment data. It should also be noted that the IFR (2016a) reports a robot density of only 36 robots per 10,000 employees for China in 2014, i.e. the year to which figure 3.5 refers.

24 The evidence in figure 3.6 is only illustrative and should not be taken as numerically exact. This holds particularly for the location of the two bubbles for electronics and electrical equipment and for rubber, plastic and chemical products for which robot and labour compensation data need to be aggregated to match the level of aggregation of the routine-task intensity index. Data for China are not included in this figure because the country does not participate in the OECD's PIAAC and because the Conference Board does not publish sector-specific compensation data for China. However, this is unlikely to bias the results shown in the figure, given that the sectoral distribution of the stock of industrial robots in China closely mirrors that of the country sample used for the calculations. According to data from IFR (2016a), almost half of the stock of robots in China is in the automotive sector with electronics and electrical equipment and rubber, plastic and chemical products accounting for the bulk of the remainder. The textiles, apparel and leather sector accounts for only about 1 per cent of the stock of robots in manufacturing in China.

25 For discussion of this special role of manufacturing see *TDR 2014* and *TDR 2016*.

26 Offshoring tends to increase productivity in developed country firms through two additional channels. One is through imports of cheaper and more varied intermediate inputs from low-wage locations that reduce production costs. The other is through offshoring of the less sophisticated and less productive tasks and specialization in the more sophisticated and more productive tasks, increasing firms' aggregate productivity in the process (see, for example, Becker and Muendler, 2015).

27 This includes both workers in manufacturing global value chains (GVCs) actually employed in the manufacturing sector and those employed in non-manufacturing sectors but delivering intermediate goods and services for the manufacturing GVCs. According to Timmer et al. (2015), the share between these two types of workers is about half with that of the latter growing. Next to the United Kingdom, the United States was also the only country in the sample of 19 developed and developing countries that lost manufacturing GVC-related jobs also in agriculture and services.

28 Arguments on the erosion of developing countries' cost advantage may be based, on the one hand, on firms finding it difficult to assure and maintain high quality levels, especially in the face of risks from long value chains in terms of supply disruptions and, on the other hand, increasing wages especially in China, where it is estimated that labour compensation in manufacturing, measured in dollar, increased almost seven-fold between 2002 and 2013 (Conference Board, 2016). While data for China and the United States are not fully comparable it is, nonetheless, interesting to note that over the same period, labour compensation in manufacturing in the United States increased by about one third. A third possible reason for eroding costs competitiveness is that lead firms in buyer-driven value chains may feel the need to incur substantial costs to ensure decent working conditions in their offshore supply firms in order to avoid potential serious damage to the reputation of their brand.

29 Some of this evidence relates to choices by United States firms to invest in the domestic economy rather than in developing countries, as provided for example by the Reshoring Institute (https://www.reshoringinstitute.org/). Locational decisions by United States firms were probably also affected by expectations of the Trans-Pacific Partnership to enter into force, whereby lower trade costs would have further weakened the case for reshoring production from countries on the Pacific Rim. There is also evidence on reshoring to Germany (http://www.economist.com/news/business/21714394-making-trainers-robots-and-3d-printers-adidass-high-tech-factory-brings-production-back) even though such episodes are unlikely to involve reshoring of mass production but to relate more to the creation of new production lines focussed on the personalization of goods for high-income consumers.

30 According to Verdoorn's law, there is a long-run positive relationship between output growth and productivity growth in manufacturing as a result of increasing returns stemming from learning-by-doing effects and market expansion, such as from increased exports.

31 It may be argued that Autor et al. (2016) underestimate the sizeable role that public investment has played in the recent innovation experience of the United States (*TDR 2014*) and that reshoring manufacturing activities attempts to reinforce and supplement the effectiveness of such public investment by a greater involvement of the private sector. Bloom et al. (2016) find a positive impact of import competition from China, as well as from other developing countries, on innovation undertaken by firms in 12 European countries from 1996 to 2007. One reason for the different outcomes for the United States and Europe may be that the shareholder paradigm as a mode of corporate governance, and

the associated greater use of profits for dividend payments rather than for reinvestment, plays a much larger role in the United States (see also *TDR 2012*: 91–92). But the greater export orientation of firms in Europe, and especially Germany, may also have allowed them to foster innovation through market expansion that spreads the fixed costs of investing in new technologies, as discussed in section D.

32 For example, Pisano and Shih (2012) argue that design cannot be separated from manufacturing in the high-end apparel industry because design/aesthetic innovation and product quality are affected by how a fabric is cut and sewn into shape. The value of co-locating design with manufacturing is therefore high.

33 The measure of the increase in robot use employed here is the average of annual robot installations divided by the average robot stock, both for the period 2005–2014, i.e. the period for which the IFR (2016a) indicates greatest data reliability. This indicator does not capture the depreciation of the operational stock of robots and therefore may overestimate the expansion of robots in countries where the level of automation was already high before 2005. However, using this indicator is preferable to using the rate of growth of the operational stock of robots. In many countries, the operational stock of robots in the initial period (2005) was close to zero and the resulting rate of growth from such a low base would be extremely large and arguably meaningless for international comparisons. Moreover, the bias in the selected indicator is small: according to the IFR (2016a), industrial robots operate for 12 years, so that robots purchased after 2005 were still in operation in 2014. Hence, the overestimation of the growth in robot use only affects the small group of countries that had a relatively large and old stock of robots in

the initial period. While Japan would be the most important of these countries, the IFR uses country-specific data that allow for a more accurate reflection of this country's robot stocks (see IFR, (2016a: 21)

34 This is not shown in the figure 3.12 in order not to blur the picture.

35 Sectorial data on robot shipments to Mexico, collected from the IFR are only available for the period 2011–2015.

36 Deploying a robot tax was discussed, for example, in May 2016 in a draft report to the European Parliament; available at: http://www.europarl.europa.eu/sides/getDoc. do?pubRef=-//EP//NONSGML%2BCOMPARL%2 BPE-582.443%2B01%2BDOC%2BPDF%2BV0// EN. Emphasizing how robots could boost inequality, the report (p. 10) proposed that there might be a "need to introduce corporate reporting requirements on the extent and proportion of the contribution of robotics and AI to the economic results of a company for the purpose of taxation and social security contributions". The public reaction to this proposal has been overwhelmingly negative, with the notable exception of Bill Gates, who endorsed it. See: https:// qz.com/911968/bill-gates-the-robot-that-takes-your-job-should-pay-taxes/.

37 Branko Milanovic, "Why 20th century tools cannot be used to address 21st century income inequality?", 12 March 2017; available at: http://glineq.blogspot. ch/2017/03/why-20th-century-tools-cannot-be-used. html.

38 Ghani and O'Connell (2014) provide an optimistic assessment, with scepticism expressed by Dani Rodrik, "Are services the new manufactures?", *Project Syndicate*, 13 October 2014; available at: https://www. project-syndicate.org/commentary/are-services-the-new-manufactures-by-dani-rodrik-2014-10.

References

Acemoglu D and Autor DH (2011). Skills, tasks and technologies: Implications for employment and earnings. In: Card D and Ashenfelter O, eds. *Handbook of Labor Economics Volume 4B*. Amsterdam and New York, North Holland: 1043–1171.

Acemoglu D and Restrepo P (2017). Robots and jobs: Evidence from US labor markets. Working Paper No. 23285, National Bureau of Economic Research, Cambridge, MA.

Arntz M, Gregory T and Zierahn U (2016). The risk of automation for jobs in OECD countries: A comparative analysis. Social, Employment and Migration Working Paper No. 189, OECD, Paris.

Autor DH (2015). Why are there still so many jobs? The history and future of workplace automation. *Journal of Economic Perspectives*, 29(3): 3–30.

Autor DH and Dorn D (2013). The growth of low-skill service jobs and the polarization of the US labor market. *American Economic Review*, 103(5): 1553–1597.

Autor DH, Dorn D, Hanson GH, Pisano G and Shu P (2016). Foreign competition and domestic innovation: Evidence from U.S. patents. Working Paper No. 22879, National Bureau of Economic Research, Cambridge, MA.

Autor DH, Dorn D, Katz LF, Patterson C and Van Reenen J (2017). The fall of the labor share and the rise of superstar firms. Working Paper No. 23396, National Bureau of Economic Research, Cambridge, MA.

Autor DH, Levy F and Murnane RJ (2003). The skill content of recent technological change: An empirical exploration. *Quarterly Journal of Economics*, 118(4): 1279–1333.

Baily MN and Bosworth BP (2014). US manufacturing: Understanding its past and its potential future. *Journal of Economic Perspectives*, 28(1): 3–26.

Becker SO and Muendler M-A (2015). Trade and tasks: An exploration over three decades in Germany. *Economic Policy*, 30(84): 589–641.

Berger T and Frey CB (2016). Structural transformation in the OECD: Digitalisation, deindustrialisation and the future of work. Social, Employment and Migration Working Paper No. 193, OECD, Paris.

Bloom N, Draca M and van Reenen J (2016). Trade induced technical change? The impact of Chinese imports on innovation, IT and productivity. *Review of Economic Studies*, 83(1): 87–117.

Brynjolfsson E and McAfee A (2014). *The Second Machine Age: Work, Progress, and Prosperity in a time of Brilliant.* New York and London, W.W. Norton & Company.

Chang J-H, Rynhart G and Huynh P (2016). ASEAN in transformation: How technology is changing jobs and enterprises. Bureau for Employers Activities Working Paper No. 9, International Labour Office, Geneva. Available at: http://www.ilo.org/public/english/dialogue/actemp/downloads/publications/2016/asean_in_transf_2016_r1_techn.pdf.

Cohen M, Cui S, Ernst R, Huchzermeier A, Kouvelis P, Lee H, Matsuo H, Steuber M and Tsay A (2016). Off-, on- or reshoring: Benchmarking of current manufacturing location decisions. The Global Supply Chain Benchmark Consortium. Available at: http://pulsar.wharton.upenn.edu/fd/resources/20160321GSCBSFinalReport.pdf.

Conference Board (2016). International comparisons of hourly compensation costs in manufacturing. Available at: https://www.conference-board.org/retrievefile.cfm?filename=ilccompensationcountrynotesApr2016.pdf&type=subsite.

De Backer K, Menon C, Desnoyers-James I and Moussiegt L (2016). Reshoring: Myth or reality? OECD Science, Technology and Industry Policy Papers No. 27, Paris. Available at: http://www.oecd-ilibrary.org/science-and-technology/reshoring-myth-or-reality_5jm56frbm38s-en.

Diao X, McMillan M and Rodrik D (2017). The recent growth boom in developing economies: A structural-change perspective. Available at: http://drodrik.scholar.harvard.edu/publications/recent-growth-boom-developing-economies-structural-change-perspective.

European Chamber of Commerce in China (2017). *China Manufacturing 2025: Putting Industrial Policy ahead of Market Forces.* Beijing. Available at: http://docs.dpaq.de/12007-european_chamber_cm2025-en.pdf.

Executive Office of the President of the United States (2016). National Network for Manufacturing Innovation Program Annual Report. Executive Office of the President National Science and Technology Council Advanced Manufacturing National Program Office, Washington, DC. Available at: https://www.manufacturingusa.com/sites/all/assets/content/2015-NNMI-Annual-Report.pdf.

Felipe J, Mehta A and Rhee C (2015). Manufacturing matters ... But it's the jobs that count. Available at: http://jesusfelipe.com/wp-content/uploads/2015/07/SSRN-id2558904.pdf.

Ford M (2015). *The Rise of the Robots: Technology and the threat Mass Unemployment.* London, Oneworld Publications.

Fratocchi L, Ancarani A, Barbieri P, Di Mauro C, Troiano A, Vignoli M and Zanoni A (2015). Manufacturing back- and near-reshoring: A comparison of European and North American evidence. In: Stentoft J, Paulraj A and Vastag G, eds. *Research in the Decision Sciences for Global Supply Chain Network Innovations.* Old Tappan, NJ, Pearson Education: 107–128.

Freeman RB (2015). Who owns the robots rules the world. IZA World of Labor. Bonn. Available at: https://wol.iza.org/articles/who-owns-the-robots-rules-the-world.

Frey CB and Osborne MA (2013). The future of employment: How susceptible are jobs to computerisation? Oxford Martin School, Oxford. Available at: http://www.oxfordmartin.ox.ac.uk/downloads/academic/The_Future_of_Employment.pdf.

Fu X, Kaplinsky R and Zhang J (2012). The impact of China on low and middle income countries' export prices in industrial-country markets. *World Development*, 40(8): 1483–1496.

Galbraith JK (2014). *The End of Normal: The Great Crisis and the Future of Growth.* New York, NY, Simon and Schuster.

Ghani E and O'Connell SD (2014). Can service be a growth escalator in low-income countries? Policy Research Working Paper No. 6971, World Bank, Washington, DC.

Goldin C and Katz LF (2008). *The Race between Education and Technology.* Cambridge, MA, Harvard University Press.

Gordon RJ (2016). *The Rise and Fall of American Growth: The U.S. Standard of Living Since the Civil War.* Princeton, NJ, Princeton University Press.

Haldane AG (2017). Productivity puzzles. Speech given at the London School of Economics, 20 March. Available at: http://www.bankofengland.co.uk/publications/Documents/speeches/2017/speech968.pdf.

Haraguchi N (2014). Patterns of structural change and manufacturing development. Working Paper No. 07/2014. Research, Statistics and Industrial Policy Branch, UNIDO, Vienna.

Haraguchi N, Cheng CFC and Smeets E (2017). The importance of manufacturing in economic development: Has this changed? *World Development*, 93: 293–315.

Hart DM, Ezell SJ and Atkinson RD (2012). Why America needs a national network for manufacturing innovation. The Information Technology & Innovation Foundation, Washington, DC. Available at: http://www2.itif.org/2012-national-network-manufacturing-innovation.pdf.

ILO (2008). International Standard Classification of Occupations: ISCO-08 – Introductory and methodological notes. International Labour Organization, Geneva. Available at: http://www.ilo.org/public/english/bureau/stat/isco/isco08/index.htm.

ILO and OECD (2015). Report prepared for the G20 Employment Working Group Antalya, Turkey, 26–27 February. International Labour Organization, Geneva and Organisation for Economic Co-operation and Development, Paris. Available at: https://www.oecd.org/g20/topics/employment-and-social-policy/The-Labour-Share-in-G20-Economies.pdf.

IMF (2017). Understanding the downward trend in labor income shares. Chapter 3. *World Economic Outlook: Gaining Momentum*, April. International Monetary Fund, Washington, DC.

IFR (2016a). *World Robotics 2016 Industrial Robots*. Frankfurt am Main, International Federation of Robotics.

IFR (2016b). *World Robotics 2016 Service Robots*. Frankfurt am Main, International Federation of Robotics.

Karabarbounis L and Neiman B (2014). The global decline of the labor share. *Quarterly Journal of Economics*, 129(1): 61–103.

Keisner CA, Raffo J and Wunsch-Vincent S (2015). Breakthrough technologies: Robotics, innovation and intellectual property. Economic Research Working Paper No. 30, World Intellectual Property Organization, Geneva.

Kozul-Wright R and Poon D (2017). Learning from China's industrial strategy. Project Syndicate, 28 April. Available at: https://www.project-syndicate.org/commentary/china-industrial-strategy-lessons-by-richard-kozul-wright-and-daniel-poon-2017-04.

Kucera D (2017). New automation technologies and job creation and destruction dynamics. Employment Policy Brief. International Labour Office, Geneva. Available at: http://www.ilo.org/wcmsp5/groups/public/---ed_emp/documents/publication/wcms_553682.pdf.

Marcolin L, Miroudot S and Squicciarini M (2016). The routine content of occupations: New cross-country measures based on PIAAC. Trade Policy Papers No. 188, OECD Publishing, Paris.

McKinsey Global Institute (2017). Harnessing automation for a future that works. Available at: http://www.mckinsey.com/global-themes/digital-disruption/harnessing-automation-for-a-future-that-works.

Mokyr J, Vickers C and Ziebarth NL (2015). The history of technological anxiety and the future of economic growth: Is this time different? *Journal of Economic Perspectives*, 29(3): 31–50.

Nübler I (2016). New technologies: A jobless future or a golden age of job creation? Research Department Working Paper No. 13. International Labour Office, Geneva.

Perez C (2016). Capitalism, technology and a green global golden age: The role of history in helping to shape the future. In: Jacobs M and Mazzucato M, eds. *Rethinking Capitalism: Economics and Policy for Sustainable and Inclusive Growth*. Chichester, Wiley.

Pisano GP and Shih WC (2012). *Producing Prosperity: Why America Needs a Manufacturing Renaissance*. Boston, MA, Harvard Business Review Press.

Stentoft J, Olhager J, Heikkilä J and Thoms L (2016). Manufacturing backshoring: A systematic literature review. *Operations Management Research*, 9(3–4): 53–61.

Timmer MP, Los B and de Vries GJ (2015). Incomes and jobs in global production of manufactures: New measures of competitiveness based on the world input-output database. In: Houseman SN and Mandel M, eds. *Factoryless Manufacturing, Global Supply Chains, and Trade in Intangibles and Data, Volume 2, Biases to Price, Output, and Productivity Statistics from Trade*. Kalamazoo, MI, WE Upjohn Institute for Employment Research: 121–164.

UNCTAD (2014). *Services: New Frontier for Sustainable Development – Exploiting the Potential of the Trade in Services for Development 2*. United Nations publication. New York and Geneva.

UNCTAD (2016a). Harnessing emerging technological breakthroughs for the 2030 Agenda for Sustainable Development. Policy Brief No. 45, UNCTAD, Geneva. Available at: http://unctad.org/en/PublicationsLibrary/presspb2016d1_en.pdf.

UNCTAD (2016b). Robots and industrialization in developing countries. Policy Brief No. 50, UNCTAD, Geneva. Available at: http://unctad.org/en/PublicationsLibrary/presspb2016d6_en.pdf.

UNCTAD (2017). *World Investment Report 2017: Investment and the Digital Economy*. United Nations publication. Sales No. E.17.II.D.3. New York and Geneva.

UNCTAD (*TDR 2010*). T*rade and Development Report, 2010: Employment, Globalization and Development*. United Nations publication. Sales No. E.10.II.D.3. New York and Geneva.

UNCTAD (*TDR 2012*). T*rade and Development Report, 2012: Policies for Inclusive and Balanced Growth*. United Nations publication. Sales No. E.12.II.D.6. New York and Geneva.

UNCTAD (*TDR 2014*). *Trade and Development Report, 2014: Global Governance and Policy Space for Development*. United Nations publication. Sales No. E.14.II.D.4. New York and Geneva.

UNCTAD (*TDR 2016*). *Trade and Development Report, 2016: Structural Transformation for inclusive and Sustained Growth*. United Nations publication. Sales No. E.16.II.D.5. New York and Geneva.

United Nations (2016). Foresight for digital development. Commission on Science and Technology for Development. United Nations Economic and Social Council. Available at: http://unctad.org/meetings/en/SessionalDocuments/ecn162016d3_en.pdf.

Wei SJ, Xie Z and Zhang X (2016). From "Made in China" to "Innovated in China": Necessity, prospect, and challenges. Working Paper No. 22854, National Bureau of Economic Research, Cambridge, MA.

WIPO (2015). *Breakthrough Innovation and Economic Growth*. World Intellectual Property Report 2015. Geneva, World Intellectual Property Organization.

Wood A (2017). Variation in structural change around the world, 1985–2015: Patterns, causes and implications. Working Paper No. 2017/34, United Nations University-World Institute for Development Economics Research (UNU-WIDER), Helsinki.

World Bank (2016). *World Development Report 2016: Digital Dividends*. Washington, DC.

World Economic Forum (2016). *The Future of Jobs: Employment, Skills and Workforce Strategy for the Fourth Industrial Revolution*. Geneva.

Wübbeke J, Meissner M, Zenglein MJ, Ives J and Conrad B (2016). *Made in China 2025: The Making of a High-Tech Superpower and Consequences for Industrial Countries*. Berlin, Mercator Institute for China Studies.

THE GENDER DYNAMICS OF INCLUSION AND EXCLUSION: A MACRO PERSPECTIVE ON EMPLOYMENT

IV

A. Introduction

As discussed in chapter II, "inclusion" has been promoted as a way to make hyperglobalization work for all. This is despite (or because of) its attendant market deregulation, attrition of the public realm, and the increasingly crowded and competitive scramble for an advantageous spot in the emerging international division of labour. It has largely followed a supply-side approach, one that overlooks the fact that individuals are already integrated into the global economy, but on exclusionary terms that stem from prevailing rules, norms and policies. The global policy narrative on women's economic empowerment, which seems to focus largely on their inclusion in markets, is an example of this limited perspective.

This chapter evaluates the employment aspects of gender inclusion from a macroeconomic perspective. It argues that increasing women's participation in the labour force, a general trend in most developing countries in recent years, is not a straightforward pathway either to faster or to more inclusive growth and development, as is too often implied. Rather, the potential for women's increasing participation in paid work, including self-employment, to substantively enhance both women's economic empowerment and gender equality is determined by prevailing socio-cultural conditions. Moreover, its wider distributional impact is fundamentally dependent on the prevailing processes of technological and structural change. Those processes in turn are affected by the global and macroeconomic conditions and policies which influence the level and structure of aggregate demand. As argued in previous chapters, the growth of inequality has dampened demand, circumscribing the expansion of high-quality jobs relative to labour supply. This has intensified competition for "good" jobs consistent with decent work. It has also resulted in gendered job rationing and the increasing exclusion

of women from better work opportunities, even as women's employment participation increases and that of men declines.

The chapter proceeds as follows. Section B provides an overview of the gender equality and growth literature. Section C discusses why gender equality in employment is an essential aspect and measure of inclusive growth. It then goes on to discuss analytical frameworks for evaluating gender in labour markets, combining perspectives on the dynamics of gender stratification and intergroup inequality with analyses of how labour markets are structurally segmented into so-called "good" jobs and "bad" jobs.[1] It highlights that in the context of the growing scarcity of high-quality work, gender is one of the ways in which economic opportunity and security are rationed. Section D presents an empirical analysis, focusing on the period since the early 1990s when systematic, gender-disaggregated data on employment by sector became available for developing countries. It argues that women's access to industrial sector jobs relative to that of men can proxy for their relative access to "good" jobs. It goes on to document both the declining availability of "good" jobs, overall, and women's increasing marginalization from them, even as their employment rate relative to men's has risen.

Section E presents a statistical analysis of women's employment concentration in the industrial sector relative to men's. It focuses on evaluating the effects of structural transformation and technological change, and the structural and policy consequences of globalization and growth. Section F evaluates how women's employment prospects affect the labour share of income, underscoring how gender inequality in the labour market is damaging for all workers, both women and men. The last section concludes.

B. The two-way causality between gender equality and economic growth

The macroeconomy is often perceived as a "gender-neutral" space; but gender matters for macroeconomic structures and outcomes. Different types of economic shocks or patterns of growth affect women and men differently, for example when labour-intensive exports increase the relative demand for women's labour, or austerity programmes have disproportionately adverse impacts on mothers and children. This causality also works the other way, in that gender relations, for example as manifested in women's low labour force participation or gender-biased access to inputs for self-employed activities, partly determine macroeconomic outcomes such as growth, trade imbalances and inflation.[2]

With respect to economic growth, the degree of gender inequality in education, health and employment has substantial adverse effects on growth.

Gender gaps in education and health are largely transmitted via their impact on labour productivity (Dollar and Gatti, 1999; Knowles et al., 2002; Klasen and Lamanna, 2009). Based on the assumption that aptitudes are equally distributed across the genders, educating more boys than girls, it is argued, causes "selection bias" and lowers the average quality of those educated. The result is an inefficient allocation of labour, with negative effects on economy-wide labour productivity and growth. On the other hand, gender equality in education has been shown to lower fertility rates and enhance children's well-being. Lower fertility rates reduce women's burden of unpaid labour and facilitate their greater participation in the labour force. Moreover, as fertility rates decline, the working age population grows at a faster rate than the overall population, thus lowering the dependency ratio and helping to boost savings and investments (including investments in children), with positive effects on per capita growth – the so-called "demographic gift".

Growth can also be stimulated by reducing gender gaps in employment, again through the "talent allocation" or selection bias channel. Narrowing the gender gap in employment also results in positive externalities. Job opportunities for women contribute to lower fertility rates, as the opportunity cost (i.e. what has to be given up) of raising children increases, and they also boost women's bargaining power in the household (Haddad et al., 1997). It has been shown that their greater bargaining power has a positive effect on investments in children's well-being, thereby contributing to long-run productivity growth. It is also important to note that equality of access to education and employment is likely to be mutually reinforcing.

While job segregation by gender can be a barrier to the efficient allocation of labour, it is also true that in some instances such segregation, coupled with wage discrimination, can be a stimulus to short-term growth under certain conditions (Blecker and Seguino, 2002). This occurs particularly if women workers are segregated into jobs in export industries. The causal mechanism is that (discriminatorily) low wages resulting from job segregation can be a stimulus to aggregate demand by increasing both export demand and investment (i.e. business spending). Gender wage inequality may also improve the balance of payments, reducing the need to rely on currency devaluation as a means to improving competitiveness, resulting in a "feminization of foreign exchange earnings" (Samarasinghe, 1998; Seguino, 2010). However, that gender inequality may, in some circumstances, contribute to aggregate growth, underscores one of the potential pitfalls of relying solely on economic efficiency arguments to promote gender equality.

The impact of growth, development and structural change on gender inequality has been much discussed since Boserup's (1970) classic work on women's roles in economic development. Early studies found a positive correlation between growth and a variety of measures of women's well-being and gender equality, including those relating to education, life expectancy, the United Nation's Gender Development Index, female labour force participation, employment segregation and the gender wage gap. But subsequent analyses have been much more mixed, suggesting that growth is no longer deemed sufficient to overcome gender inequality (Seguino, 2017).

Women's participation in work has been related to structural change through the feminization U-Curve, which describes how women's economic activity rates first decline and then increase as industrialization proceeds, in line with the disappearance of women's traditional work in agriculture and the development of new opportunities in an expanding services sector. However, while this has been true of some currently industrialized economies, it is not so clear-cut at present. Indeed, if differences in sectoral distribution of production over time are used as a proxy for structural change, there is little evidence to suggest that, in the recent period, structural change has been the driver of higher female labour force participation in developing countries (Gaddis and Klasen, 2014).

However, it is true that the feminization of the global labour force has been identified as a key trend of hyperglobalization (Standing, 1989), based on the increasing demand for women workers as well as the downward drift in the quality of men's jobs relative to those held by women. This has been related to an intensification of competition among firms in an increasingly open global economy, which has led to a search for lower cost female labour as a means to achieving export competitiveness. In general, there is considerable evidence of the positive effect of export growth on women's relative employment in labour-intensive manufacturing and services, such as tourism and call centres (Braunstein, 2006; Aguayo-Tellez, 2011; Staritz and Reis, 2013).

There has been a strong positive association between trade and women's employment in a number of labour-abundant, semi-industrialized countries. In primarily agricultural economies, by contrast, where women are concentrated in import-competing sectors such as food crop production, men are better placed to take advantage of export opportunities in cash crop production or natural resource extraction, and women tend to lose employment and income as a result of trade liberalization (Bussolo and De Hoyos, 2009; Fontana, 2009). Also, in developing economies with less competitive manufacturing sectors, particularly in Africa, tariff reductions on labour-intensive imports have resulted in higher job losses for women than for men (Seguino and Grown, 2006).

Trade liberalization can have contradictory effects on women and on gender equality (UNCTAD, 2014). In labour-intensive export industries, such as garment manufacturing, there has been a feminization of employment, but the women are often stuck in low-wage, dead-end jobs with limited opportunities for skills development. As economies move up the industrial ladder to more capital-intensive production, there is some evidence that men become the preferred source of labour supply, while women's

share in manufacturing employment declines (Tejani and Milberg, 2016). And while the expansion of the tourism sector and call centres has provided employment for women, their jobs are also more precarious and less well-paid than those of men in these sectors (Staritz and Reis, 2013).

Similarly, the narrowing of the gender gap in labour participation rates has not produced commensurate gender equality in pay and status (Razavi et al., 2012; UN Women, 2015). Instead, women's increased labour force participation has coincided with an increase in informal, unregulated and unprotected forms of work. Although jobs in export-oriented manufacturing firms (and on farms producing non-traditional agricultural exports) have benefited some women, occupational segregation by gender continues, and women face lower wages and inferior conditions of work in the industries into which they are crowded (Braunstein, 2012).

Levels and patterns of public expenditure have strong gender-related distributional effects (Agénor et al., 2010; Fontana and Natali, 2008; Seguino and Were, 2014). Public investments in physical infrastructure, by reducing the time spent in fetching water and fuel and facilitating other unpaid household maintenance activities, reduce the care burden, and consequently raise the earnings potential of both men and (especially) women. Social infrastructure spending can also relieve women's unpaid care burden through publicly funded social services, promoting gender equality in access to jobs and income (UN Women, 2015). Also, gender-related patterns of employment increase the possibilities for women to obtain jobs in social service activities or in the paid-care sector of the economy, such that public spending in this area can further narrow gender-related employment gaps. Since job multipliers for such spending are much larger than other types of public spending, including in physical infrastructure, public spending on the care sector has much greater positive effects on aggregate employment as well as on reducing gender-related employment gaps than other types of public spending (Antonopoulos et al., 2010; ITUC, 2016 and 2017; İlkkaracan et al., 2015).

Clearly, to understand the two-way causality between gender equality and economic growth, gender outcomes must be linked with the specific structures, processes and policies that underlie growth. In this chapter, this is done with a specific focus on employment, which is a critical measure of gender inclusion.

C. The employment dimension of gender-inclusive development

Remunerative employment (including self-employment) is the main mechanism by which individuals provide for themselves and their families. When combined with effective bargaining structures, it is also the most assured route to achieving a fairer distribution of income and for promoting gender equality. When women have equal access to work as men, it has positive effects on women's bargaining power within the household, improving their ability to choose how to spend their time and allocate household resources. Moreover, income in the hands of women, and reduced income and asset inequality between men and women, improve investments in children's well-being, with benefits for long-run growth (Doepke and Tertilt, 2011).

An important determinant of equality of employment is equality in education. Efforts over the past 25 years by national governments and international organizations to close the gender-based education gap (including its identification as the sole target of Millennium Development Goal (MDG) 3 – to promote gender equality and empower women) have resulted in significant progress. Figure 4.1A displays a kernel density function (akin to a histogram in that it represents a distribution of frequencies) that shows the distribution of developing countries according to the ratio of women's to men's average years of educational attainment for the population 15 years

and older, comparing 1991 and 2010. The lowest ratio is on the far left of the distribution and the highest ratio (greater gender equality) on the right. The vertical axis indicates the percentage of countries in the sample with a corresponding women's/men's educational attainment ratio, but these percentages are less important than the shapes and relative positions of the curves. Over the time period in question, the mean women's/men's ratio in developing countries rose from 71.9 to 86.1 per cent, while the dispersion between countries in educational equality substantially decreased, as illustrated by the narrowing of the distribution between 1991 and 2010. It is notable also that a much larger proportion of countries are shown as centred on a ratio of 100 (indicative of gender equality in education) in 2010 than in 1991.

However, educational equality is not sufficient to achieve gender equality in economic well-being, or even in employment. Conditions must exist to convert greater educational equality into comparable improvements in access to paid work. Yet, although employment gaps have narrowed over the past two decades, they remain significantly wider than educational gaps. In developing countries, the mean employment-to-population ratio of women to men 15 years and older rose from 57.1 per cent in 1991 to just 64.1 per cent in 2010 (figure 4.1B). The failure of educational equality to ensure employment equality

---

FIGURE 4.1 Developing-country distribution of gender equality in education and employment, 1991 and 2010

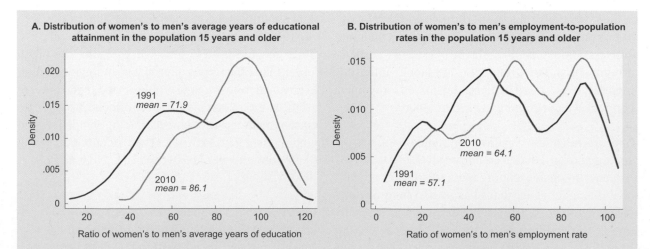

Source: UNCTAD secretariat calculations, based on Barro and Lee (2016, v. 2.1) data; and on ILO modelled employment data.
Note: Data for 1991 are interpolated from 1990 and 1995 estimates, and include 79 countries. The vertical axis indicates the percentage of countries in the sample with a corresponding women to men educational attainment ratio, hence it is referred to as a "density"; the horizontal axis gives the values for the ratio corresponding to each density.

suggests that women continue to face impediments to translating their increased education into more secure livelihoods.

Moreover, even where there are gains in access to paid work, not all forms of work are equally remunerative, stable or ultimately empowering for women. Labour markets are comprised of a hierarchy of jobs, differentiated not only by the size and regularity of the pay packet, but also by social protection, stability, working conditions, skills development and promotion prospects. Access to "good" jobs and "bad" jobs is determined by numerous factors other than education, including the structure of the economy, existing global and macroeconomic conditions, and processes of social and economic stratification that identify who is the most "deserving" of high status work, especially during challenging economic times when good jobs are scarce. Even today, women (and racially or ethnically "subordinate" groups) are more likely to be concentrated in poorly paid and informal forms of work, with little or no social or legal protection (ILO, 2015). Therefore, access to work may not be particularly empowering, especially where women continue to bear primary responsibility for unpaid care work.

Theorizing exclusion in gendered labour markets

To understand employment dynamics by gender in developing countries, in particular, how workers are allocated to various sectors and jobs, an analytical framework is needed that helps explore the determinants of intergroup inequality (sometimes known as horizontal inequality). Intergroup inequality typically reflects salient forms of stratification; that is, systems that create and reinforce social and economic hierarchies, bolstered by institutions as well as norms and stereotypes, in which some groups are identified as more deserving than others (Darity, 2005).[3] From this perspective, hierarchies based on gender are not primarily due to differences in individual characteristics such as education;[4] rather, there are systemic conditions that reproduce stratification over time, which are embedded in institutions and buttressed by social and psychological processes that construct gender roles in ways that economically advantage men as a group relative to women. For instance, widely-held gender stereotypes that suggest women are less suited for paid work due to their responsibility for unpaid care work, or their presumed lower skills, promote a set of structured advantages for men and corresponding disadvantages for women.[5]

Over time, the primary mechanisms by which gender stratification is reproduced are exploitation and exclusion. Exploitation is characterized by one group (women) being paid less than the value of what it produces, even relative to other workers. Women's unpaid work as carers, which supports the reproduction of human capacities essential to a functioning market economy, is an example. The "crowding" of women in labour-intensive export industries, where firms' greater mobility, and thus bargaining power, enables them to suppress wages, thus bolstering profits and export competitiveness, is another example (Bergmann, 1974).

The second mechanism is exclusion (or opportunity hoarding), whereby members of the dominant group monopolize valuable positions or resources. In the labour market, this may take the form of women's exclusion from access to "good" jobs that offer conditions consistent with decent work. Opportunity hoarding intensifies when "good" jobs are in short supply, leading to rationing on the basis of social forces (Smeeding, 2016). Exclusion is facilitated by norms and stereotypes concerning the suitability of different types of work for men and women, respectively, based on their gender roles. In the case of a dominant norm that women should provide the bulk of caring labour for children, the elderly and the sick, for example, women are less likely to be hired for jobs in skill- and capital-intensive industries that require on-the-job training, since firms may fear losing the "sunk costs" of their investments in training. Instead, women are seen as "secondary" wage earners, more appropriately suited to labour-intensive, low-skill or high-turnover jobs.

These mechanisms of gender stratification operate across many aspects of economic life. They provide a foundation for dual or segmented labour markets, which allocate employment in ways that reflect and perpetuate prevailing gender hierarchies both within and outside labour markets.

Theories of dual or segmented labour markets posit the existence of two technologically and institutionally distinct labour markets: the core and peripheral sectors.[6] These are distinguished by different wage-setting mechanisms and conditions of work, barriers to mobility between the labour markets and rationing of access to jobs in the privileged core sector. Dual labour markets can be viewed as having a "glass wall", with institutional practices and social norms making it difficult to move from the peripheral to the core sector (Das, 2013).

Jobs in the core sector are highly coveted. These jobs are more likely to be in the formal sector of the economy where firms offer higher wages, various benefits, greater job security, opportunities for job upgrading and better regulated working conditions. Firms in the core sector often have market power, generating rents that can be shared with workers, and they can offer higher wages relative to those in the peripheral sector. Higher profitability also enables more investment, boosting productivity and further increasing the gap between workers in the core and peripheral sectors (Gordon et al., 1982).

In contrast, jobs in the peripheral labour market are more insecure, intermittent and generally "dead-end", with fewer opportunities for on-the-job training and upward mobility. Firms in the peripheral sector tend to have little market power and thin profit margins, which inhibit the sorts of investments that raise productivity and wages.[7] The peripheral labour market in developing countries is comprised largely of informal service sector jobs, as well as agriculture and small-scale, often informal, manufacturing (Vanek et al., 2014).

The availability of, and thus access to, good jobs in the core sector depends first and foremost on the structure of an economy. The processes of development linked to industrialization, where economies of scale and scope promote more rapid productivity growth, also hold promise for expanding opportunities in core sectors. While industrial policies can facilitate structural change, macroeconomic conditions also help determine the availability of jobs in the core sector, including the level of demand and a country's trade and investment relations with the rest of the world. In recent years, patterns of stalled industrialization or premature deindustrialization have been observed in a number of developing countries, thus limiting the growth of industrial sector jobs (*TDR 2016*).

Consequently, competition for the fewer jobs available intensifies, triggering the forces of stratification that influence job access. Dominant groups tend to hoard the opportunities that remain, partly by promoting norms and stereotypes that exclude women or other workers that are not members of the dominant group. In well-paid jobs, such as in capital-intensive or information technology industries, opportunity hoarding may be facilitated by stereotypes portraying women as less technically adept than men, and therefore less qualified for such positions. In several developing countries it has been found that, paradoxically, women are less likely to be employed in certain activities (e.g. construction or agriculture) as they become more mechanised and less physically arduous (Ghosh, 2009) because of stereotypes concerning suitability for the skills required. Research also shows that this type of opportunity hoarding worsens during times of economic hardship and insecurity (Darity et al., 2006).

Employers may also perpetuate stereotypes by "crowding" women into jobs such as in labour-intensive export manufacturing, as a means of depressing women's wages and lowering export prices. For example, Elson and Pearson (1981) noted that women are ascribed as having "nimble" fingers, making them uniquely qualified for jobs in assembly operations.[8] It is more likely, however, that the desirability of women for these jobs is related to their perceived docility in a sector where labour constitutes a large proportion of total production costs.

According to conventional economic thinking, competitive markets should eliminate such gender discrimination over time, as non-discriminating profit-maximizing firms would outcompete firms that do discriminate by hiring less costly workers, thus raising their profit margins (Becker, 1957). Evidence does not support this hypothesis, however. Labour market segregation by gender is widespread and persistent in both developed and developing countries, and is a major cause of gender wage differentials (ILO, 2015; World Bank, 2012; UN Women 2015). Similarly, it was believed that trade liberalization could be a force for lowering gender-based wage discrimination in domestic labour markets, but the contrary has been found to occur when export orientation and trade liberalization have increased (Artecona and Cunningham, 2002; Berik et al., 2004; Busse and Spielmann, 2006; Braunstein and Brenner, 2007; Domínguez-Villalobos and Brown-Grossman, 2010; Menon and Van der Meulen Rodgers, 2009).

Indeed, the profit motive may induce firms to actively engage in segregating workers by race and gender, as a divided workforce would likely exhibit less solidarity and thus have weaker bargaining power. Moreover, in segregated labour markets, men are less likely to demand higher wages for fear of either losing their jobs or being relegated to peripheral labour markets that offer the kinds of low wages and poor working conditions that women endure (Hartmann, 1979). Insofar as this dynamic is occurring, there are

also likely to be negative effects on the labour share of income resulting from women's exclusion from good jobs. This depresses aggregate demand and ultimately slows economic growth.

D. Inclusion and exclusion in employment: Gender trends[9]

1. Including women, excluding men?

In most countries, women's employment rates relative to men's have been rising since 1991 (the first year for which gender-disaggregated sectoral employment data are widely available) – a positive sign in terms of gender equality. Various push and pull factors have contributed to this phenomenon. Women desire employment on its own merits, and also because earning their own incomes outside the traditional family expands their choices in a wide variety of areas. Indeed, a recent global survey found that 70 per cent of women (and 66 per cent of men) interviewed would prefer that women work at paid jobs, including a majority of the women not currently in paid employment (Gallup and ILO, 2017). To the extent that there are good jobs to be had, higher levels of education increase the opportunity cost of forgoing market work. The declining rates of fertility and increases in the productivity of unpaid work that accompany development can lessen women's time constraints and increase their ability to access the labour market. However, women may also be "pushed" into employment as a result of the impact of global stagnation and unemployment on men's earnings, economic crises, cuts in public provisioning, or simply the increasing commodification of daily life that accompanies hyperglobalization, regardless of level of development. This response by women to lower household earnings or cuts in public spending is dubbed "distress" sales of labour.

These contradictory forces can be observed in figure 4.2, which plots changes in women's employment rates relative to those of men over the period 1991 to 2014. Figure 4.2A shows this relationship by level of development, and figure 4.2B by developing region. In the majority of all these countries, women's relative employment rates rose at the same time as men's employment rates fell (the upper left quadrant in each figure), reflecting potentially conflictual gender equality in the sense that improvements for women may have been occurring at the expense of men.[10]

There are some notable differences by country grouping. Starting with the top panel, 55.9 per cent of the sample is in the gender conflictual quadrant (see upper left), with 64.7, 56.3 and 33.3 per cent of developed and developing countries and transition economies, respectively, in that quadrant. Note that gender conflictual outcomes can also occur if both women's and men's employment declines, but women's employment declines more slowly than men's. These represent over 20 per cent of cases (18 of the 85 countries) in the gender conflictual quadrant, with developed countries and transition economies accounting for two thirds of this subset. In 53.4 per cent of the transition economy group, both women and men lost employment; among those where both women's and men's employment participation declined, women's relative employment increased (i.e. women lost employment at a slower rate than men) in just under half the cases (3 out of 7 countries). This pattern was also pronounced among developed countries, but in most of these cases women's employment stayed essentially level while men's declined (5 out of the 9 developed countries where both women and men lost employment, but women lost at a slower rate than men). The widespread decline of men's employment in developed countries is linked to the lasting effects of the financial crisis, though it began even before that crisis and was exacerbated by the Great Recession.

Turning to the lower panel gives a sense of developing-country differences by region. In the Asia region, which has a large concentration of countries (44.1 per cent) in the "gender conflictive" quadrant (upper left), women gained at men's expense. The rest of the region shows a roughly even split between the upper right and lower left quadrants. Women's employment rates declined in a number of countries in the region, both among countries that started with high participation rates (China and Thailand), and those where such rates were already low by global standards (India and Turkey). In the Africa region, 55 per cent of countries are located in the gender

FIGURE 4.2 **Changes in women's to men's employment rates versus men's employment rates, 1991–2014**

(Percentage points)

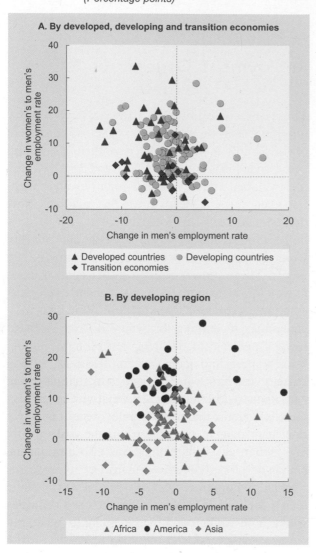

Source: UNCTAD secretariat calculations, based on ILO modelled employment rates.
Note: Employment rates refer to the proportion of the wage-earning population, aged 15 years and older. Changes are percentage point changes in 3-year average values. Also note that the axes in figure B are different from those used in figure A in order to better illustrate regional differences.

conflictive upper left quadrant, with nearly two thirds witnessing declines in men's employment. Some of these declines were quite significant (e.g. more than 5 percentage points in Kenya, Mauritius, Nigeria and South Africa). The vast majority of countries in the developing America region (77.3 per cent) are in the upper left quadrant, with increases in women's relative employment as men's employment declined; the other countries from that region are in the upper right quadrant, showing increases in both women's and men's employment rates.

While women's employment has been rising in most countries (with some notable exceptions) regardless of level of development, the associated improvement in gender equality – as measured by women's employment relative to men's – has been partly driven by substantial declines in men's employment. Given the push and pull factors driving women's labour force participation, highlighted above, it is worrying that distress sales of labour might be playing a role in what superficially appears to be greater gender equality in employment. That is, women's higher relative employment rates in a number of countries are likely to be due not to job competition between women and men, but rather, to women taking on inferior jobs in order to maintain family incomes in response to men's declining job opportunities and slow wage growth. This highlights the importance of achieving "inclusive" gender equality, in the sense of improvements for women not being at the expense of men. This partly depends on the overall state of an economy. Increasing women's employment participation without addressing demand-side constraints, or acknowledging the widespread failure of growth – when it occurs – to generate good jobs, will merely escalate labour market competition, ultimately to the detriment of both women and men.

2. Industry and "good" jobs

As noted above, gender stratification plays an important role in allocating jobs within segmented labour markets, especially as competition for core sector work intensifies. Although women's employment relative to men's has been rising in most developing countries for more than two decades, their share of "good" jobs has been falling. That is, during the past 25 years of growing global integration, women have been increasingly excluded, as compared to men, from prized jobs, even as their educational attainments and labour force participation have risen. In this chapter, jobs in the industrial sector (rather than agricultural or services sectors) are used as a proxy for "good" jobs, for reasons outlined below.

In most trajectories of productivity-enhancing structural change and development, the processes of industrialization and the shifting of resources – including labour – into higher productivity sectors support aggregate productivity growth. However, it is through the expansion of higher productivity work in the modernizing, increasingly diversified industrial sector that labour initially accesses the higher incomes that accompany industrialization and development, ultimately building domestic aggregate demand and sustaining aggregate productivity growth. (In this sense, for growth to be sustained it must also be inclusive.) When these connections fail to materialize, or weaken, stalled or premature (de)industrialization dampens the prospects for inclusive development.

Higher value-added, knowledge-intensive services, which account for a more substantial share of employment than industry in developed countries, have recently been emphasized as an alternative to the lacklustre job-generating performance of industry in developing countries. However, in developing countries, in particular, the services sector alone is not likely to provide a sufficient alternative to industry for the generation of "good" jobs, especially if it is disconnected from a dynamic industrial sector (Kucera and Roncolato, 2016; *TDR 2016*). Relative to the industrial sector, jobs in the services sector are more likely to be informal and insecure, with lower productivity and thus lower wages, especially for women. They most probably reflect the growth of low-productivity (often traditional) services rather than the beginnings of long-term dynamism – a type of disguised unemployment that ultimately reflects the failure of growth to generate enough decent work. Accounts of the links between globalization and informalization echo these problematic dynamics (Bacchetta et al., 2009). Even India, which is often cited as an exemplar of the growth of high-productivity services as a conduit for growth and development, has failed to produce many good jobs in this sector (Chandrasekhar and Ghosh, 2014).[11]

Measures of decent work, as defined by the International Labour Organization (ILO), provide a good basis for comparing the quality of employment in services and industry. Decent work is defined as work that is productive, has workplace protections, and offers social protection and prospects for individual development (such as skills upgrading). In the absence of an international dataset on decent work opportunities by sector, a measure of relative job quality can be calculated using the ratio of labour productivity in the services sector to that in the industrial sector (see table 4.1 by region). The rationale for this comparison is that higher productivity measures are associated with greater remuneration and benefits. This is not the same as saying that industrial workers are more "productive" than services sector workers. Trying to measure services sector productivity is controversial, partly because of the difficulty in

---

TABLE 4.1 Ratio of services sector to industrial sector labour productivity, 1991–2015

Region	Mean	Median
Full sample	0.89	0.87
Developed countries	1.04	1.05
Developing countries	0.79	0.75
Africa	0.83	0.75
America	0.72	0.74
Asia	0.82	0.74
Transition economies	0.83	0.75

Source: UNCTAD secretariat calculations using the World Bank, *World Development Indicators* (*WDI*) and *Penn World Tables* databases.
Note: Sectoral productivity is calculated as the value added of sectoral output relative to the number of employees in that sector; unweighted means and medians for country groups are for the period 1991–2015.

---

measuring outputs. Indeed, for the services sector at least, productivity measures can be thought of more as a consequence of wages than a cause. Hence, higher relative productivity in developed countries in this sector partly reflects higher per capita incomes. Regardless, lower productivity measures indicate lower wages. Among developing regions, to varying degrees, services sector labour productivity is lower than industrial labour productivity (with ratios less than 1). The median for all non-developed regions is close to 0.75, suggesting that average productivity is roughly 25 per cent lower in the services sector than the industrial sector.

Based on these data, for developing countries, there is a positive association between the services sector's relative productivity and the relative concentration of men in that sector. That is, the higher the aggregate labour productivity in the services sector relative to the industrial sector, the higher too is men's concentration in that sector relative to women's (with a correlation of 0.43 for the developing countries in the sample). To the extent that these measures of relative productivity mirror relative wages, this outcome is in line with the predictions about how gender stratification manifests in dual or segmented labour markets: the better the jobs, the more likely it is that members of the dominant group will "opportunity hoard", and thus the less likely it is that members of the subordinate group, in this case women, will have those jobs.

Given that jobs in the industrial sector are more likely to be part of the core labour market (that is, formal jobs with associated benefits and protections) than jobs in the agricultural or services sectors, this chapter uses relative access to industrial jobs as a proxy for gender equality.[12] Evaluating the absolute and relative trajectories of employment in this sector affords insights into whether and to what extent growth has been inclusive from a gender perspective.

3. Women's exclusion from "good" jobs

At the outset, it is important to note that the overall availability of industrial sector jobs has declined since the early 1990s, for both women and men. On average, industrial sector employment as a percentage of total employment declined in all groups of countries – developed, developing and transition economies (figure 4.3). The decline was the most pronounced in developed countries. Using three-year averages to compute changes in the share of industrial employment in total employment, developed and developing countries and transition economies experienced declines of -7.8, -3.5 and -5.2 percentage points, respectively, between 1990 and 2014.

The kernel density functions displayed in figure 4.4 provide evidence of the degree of sectoral employment segregation by gender in developing countries in 2013. This figure shows the distribution of countries according to two ratios that compare women to men: women's employment-to-population rate relative to men's, with a sample mean of 61.8 per cent; and the ratio of women's concentration in industrial employment to men's concentration, with a sample

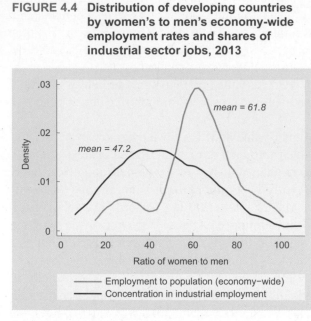

FIGURE 4.4 Distribution of developing countries by women's to men's economy-wide employment rates and shares of industrial sector jobs, 2013

Source: See figure 4.2.
Note: Women's relative concentration is calculated as three-year average of the share of women employed in the industrial sector relative to men's share. Developing country group is consistent across figures 4.4, 4.5 and 4.6, and differs from the (larger) group illustrated in figure 4.1, as the current group is limited to countries for which there is data on women's industrial share of employment across the particular years considered.

mean of 47.2 per cent. The latter measure is referred to as "women's relative concentration in industrial employment" for the remainder of the chapter, and it proxies for women's relative access to good jobs. As illustrated by the shapes of the curves in figure 4.4, women's relative concentration in industry is much more widely dispersed, and lower, on average, than women's relative employment participation overall.

This is evidenced by a decline in women's relative employment concentration in the industrial sector since 1991, from an average of 70.2 per cent in 1991 to 47.2 per cent in 2013 (figure 4.5).[13] This phenomenon occurred in all developing-country regions, with African countries showing the largest decline (table 4.2). Even in Asia, where industrialization and export-oriented manufacturing have been more substantial, a decline in women's concentration in "good" jobs in the industrial sector can be observed, although their relative share in employment rose.

Figure 4.6 contrasts the distribution of developing countries by percentage point changes between 1991 and 2013 for two measures of women's relative (to men's) employment share: in total employment and in the industrial sector. The horizontal axis displays

FIGURE 4.3 Trends in industrial employment as a share of total employment, 1990–2014

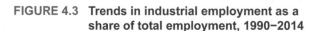
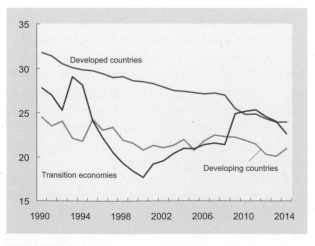

Source: See figure 4.2.
Note: Values refer to the unweighted average by year for country group, which is consistent across years.

FIGURE 4.5 **Women's relative concentration in industrial sector employment, developing countries, 1991 and 2013**

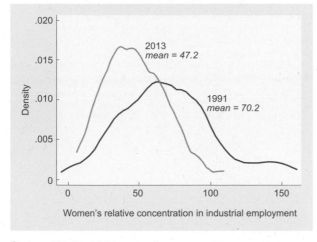

Source: See figure 4.2.

FIGURE 4.6 **Change in women's relative concentration in industrial employment and total employment in developing countries, 1991–2013**

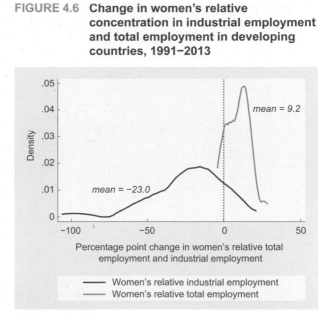

Source: See figure 4.2.

TABLE 4.2 **Employment ratios of women to men, and relative concentration of women in industrial employment, by developing region, 1991 and 2010**
(Per cent)

Developing region	Ratio of women's to men's employment rates		Relative concentration of women in industrial employment	
	1991	2010	1991	2010
Africa	53.0	57.2	91.8	47.9
America	48.0	61.1	67.9	53.1
Asia	46.3	51.0	59.3	47.2
South Asia	42.0	46.7	63.8	40.8
East Asia	62.2	73.2	75.9	33.1
West Asia	25.2	28.0	22.1	36.5
South-East Asia	62.8	66.9	87.9	66.1

Source: UNCTAD secretariat calculations, based on ILO data, extracted from the World Bank, *WDI* database (accessed 15 February 2017).

Note: The data are based on three-year averages.

values for the percentage point changes, while the vertical axis gives the corresponding incidence or percentage density of each of these values. What is important to consider is the shape of each curve, and its relative position along the horizontal axis. The ratio of women's to men's total employment increased, on average, by 9.2 percentage points, and countries are tightly grouped around that average, as illustrated by the steep curve. The curve is also centred primarily on positive values, as illustrated by its position relative to the vertical zero-intercept

line, indicating an increase in women's relative total employment in the vast majority of countries (91 per cent) over the period. Conversely, women's share in industrial employment relative to men's declined by an average of 23 percentage points, and most of the curve is situated to the left of the zero-intercept line, illustrating that the vast majority of countries (88 per cent) experienced a decline of women's share in industrial employment relative to men's.

Figure 4.7 shows the same percentage point changes in women's relative industrial employment as in figure 4.6, except that here it is by individual country, and is juxtaposed against the percentage point changes in men's concentration in industrial employment. Women's relative share in industrial jobs declined in the vast majority of countries between 1991 and 2013; in about half of these cases, men's share in industrial employment declined as well. This is indicative of both a reduction in labour demand in the industrial sector and of women's industrial employment rate falling faster than men's. These patterns provide evidence of gender-based job rationing: as industrial sector employment has declined, women's access to that employment has become more restricted.

Taken together, these figures indicate that over the past 25 years, gender stratification in labour markets has become worse, in the sense that women are increasingly excluded from good jobs, and are,

FIGURE 4.7 **Percentage point changes in women's relative and men's absolute concentration in industrial employment, selected economies, 1991–2013**

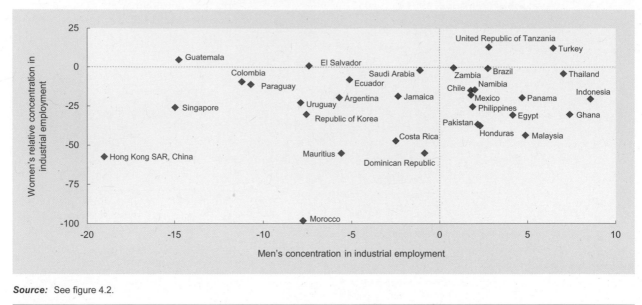

Source: See figure 4.2.

instead, crowded into work that is less remunerative and secure. Thus, contradictory forces appear to be at work in developing-country labour markets: women's increasing relative share of paid jobs, but their growing exclusion from "good jobs", suggesting the "crowding" of women in poor quality employment. This process has occurred in the context of the industrial sector's weakening role as a generator of high-quality employment, manifested as deindustrialization in developed and middle-income economies and stalled industrialization or premature deindustrialization in developing countries (*TDR 2016*).

The decline in women's relative concentration may also be due to the changing structure of the industrial sector itself, coupled with relatively rigid gender-differentiated employment in that sector. As countries upgrade to more skill- or capital-intensive production and away from labour-intensive production, where women's employment has been most notable, a falling concentration of women in the industrial sector may result. Indeed, it has been found that in the manufacturing sector, a process of defeminization of employment has been occurring since the mid-1980s (Kucera and Tejani, 2014; Tejani and Milberg, 2016).

E. Assessing gender-based exclusion in the context of structural change, globalization and growth

The previous section sketched the changing gender dynamics of employment in the industrial sector, arguing that patterns since the 1990s have been showing an increasing exclusion of women from good jobs as overall job quality has declined. This section turns to a more precise, causal investigation of this exclusion in terms that reflect some of the core issues at stake discussed in chapter II. In particular, it uses an econometric analysis of cross-country, time series data to evaluate the impacts of four sets of factors: (i) structural transformation and the inclusiveness of technological change; (ii) the structural and policy

consequences of hyperglobalization; (iii) overall growth; and (iv) changing conditions on the supply side of the labour market. It is important to note that the resulting estimated effects are averages for the sample as a whole (developing and developed countries are evaluated separately). This is both a weakness and a strength. It is a weakness because it abstracts from the specificities of particular economies, and a strength because it uncovers systemic features of the global economy – a central concern in the current era of hyperglobalization and of this *Report*.

1. The econometric model

This section describes the variables used to measure the four sets of factors noted above, all of which help explain changes in women's concentration in industrial sector employment.

Structural transformation and the gender inclusivity of technological change

To capture the dynamics of structural transformation, the model includes both industrial employment as a share of total employment and industrial value added as a share of GDP. Increases in either represent productivity-enhancing structural changes that are a key source of catch-up development (*TDR 2016*). Though the two measures may seem likely to be too highly correlated with one another to warrant separate treatment, their effects on employment are in fact likely to be contradictory, and therefore need to be assessed independently of each other. Specifically, while the growth of industrial value added suggests increased availability of good jobs (thus creating opportunities for an increase in women's relative concentration in such jobs as labour demand in this sector rises), the consequent employment generated may be insufficient to move much of the labour force into higher productivity (and paid) work. Given the stratification dynamics discussed in the chapter, this sort of employment failure would be expected to affect women more than men. Indeed, analyses of premature deindustrialization and its link with the middle-income trap suggest that it is the failure of the industrial employment channel, and not the share of industrial value added in GDP, that poses the biggest challenge to inclusive growth (Felipe et al., 2014; Rodrik, 2016; *TDR 2016*).

The model uses the capital-labour ratio as a proxy for technological sophistication; an increase represents a shift towards more capital-intensive production. As noted above, a number of studies have linked defeminization of employment in manufacturing in recent decades to processes of technological upgrading, even more so than changes in trade. Given that the model controls for women's education relative to that of men (discussed under labour supply below), a negative association between capital intensity and women's relative concentration in industrial employment would suggest a gender asymmetry in the employment costs of technological change.

Structural and policy consequences of globalization

The extent of global integration is measured by the shares of trade and foreign direct investment (FDI) in gross domestic product (GDP). In econometric studies, trade is measured in a variety of ways. Most studies simply take exports plus imports as a share of GDP, but due to the increasing import content of exports among developing countries, such measures can be misleading. As discussed in *TDR 2016*, what seems to matter more for growth and development (not to mention employment) is the value added aspect of trade. Therefore, this model uses the share of net exports of manufactures (exports less imports) in GDP as a proxy.[14] The traditional association between exports of manufactures and the feminization of industrial employment, at least when the former is more labour-intensive, is often cited as a benefit of export-led growth strategies (*TDR 2016*). Similarly, to the extent that FDI is linked with exporting labour-intensive manufactures, or more industrial activity overall, it could expand women's relative access to industrial employment.

While trade and FDI quantify the extent of an economy's global integration, they are not, in and of themselves, proxies for trade policy, as a variety of trade policies can coexist with high levels of trade or FDI. Trade policy can be restrictive even while exports are being encouraged. Trade policy stance is measured by tariffs (more precisely, applied tariffs weighted by the share of product imports), with higher values indicative of less trade liberalization.[15, 16] Clearly, the push for deregulation of global markets has been spearheaded in an important sense by the push for wholesale trade liberalization and by a narrowing of policy space for managing trade (UNCTAD, 2014). How such policies play out in terms of employment is not clear. The orthodox stance on trade policy is that less of it gives more of everything else – growth, development and high-wage employment. Discussions of global value chains (GVCs), in particular, which have come to dominate narratives on trade for developing countries, highlight the importance of importing for exporting and hence warn against the folly of taxing imports. If such trade is an important generator of industrial sector employment opportunities for women, more restrictive trade policy stances, as measured by import tariffs, may undermine gender equality.

Fiscal policy stance, measured as the share of government consumption in GDP, is included to reflect the extent of a government's involvement in economic activities. Given the prevalence of austerity in macro policy-making in most countries during the period under study, and associated efforts to limit the size of government, it is important to understand how public spending affects gender equality in employment. In many developed countries, since the public sector is a significant source of employment for women, they are likely to suffer the most from cuts in public spending (Karamessini and Rubery, 2014). However, such cuts would primarily affect women employed in the services sector, effectively increasing the share of industry in women's overall employment. On the other hand, if public spending were to be associated with either more industrial sector activity (perhaps as a result of implementing industrial policy or crowding in private industrial investment more generally) or an easing of burdens on women's unpaid care through the provision of social or physical infrastructure, one would expect a positive association between the two.

Economic growth

Per capita GDP growth is included to directly assess whether aggregate growth improves women's relative opportunities in industrial employment. A number of other model variables are also likely to be correlated with growth, but this connection is statistically weak for developing countries in the sample. Presumably, all else remaining equal, stronger growth should ease job competition and be associated with more women accessing higher quality jobs in industry. However, as discussed throughout this *Report*, the effects of growth will depend on its structure and the distribution of its benefits. "Jobless growth" or growth that generates only poor quality jobs are challenges associated with recent growth trajectories, for both developed and developing countries, which implies that growth may not alleviate gender-based job competition.

Labour supply controls

The last set of variables reflects labour supply controls. Given that industrial sector jobs tend, on average, to be more skill-intensive than other types of work, the model controls for gender differences in education, measured as the ratio of women's to men's gross secondary school enrolment rates. One would expect that, as this ratio increases, so will women's relative concentration in industrial sector

employment. The model also includes women's labour force participation relative to that of men. More women in the labour market might suggest that more of them have access to industrial sector jobs. However, if labour markets are segregated by gender, as women increase their labour force participation relative to men, these new labour market entrants may be crowded into non-industrial sectors, thus lowering women's relative share of industrial sector employment. This is particularly likely as the overall quality of jobs declines and job competition by gender intensifies. Including these controls highlights the potential for improving gender equality by targeting the supply side of the labour market –through lowering gender gaps either in education or in employment participation.

2. Main findings

Table 4.3 presents the results of the analysis for the period 1991–2014, which includes a set of three specifications each for developing and developed countries separately, as a number of the results differ significantly for the two groups (table notes include econometric details).[17] Columns (1) and (2) include all the variables discussed above, columns (3) and (4) exclude per capita GDP growth and columns (5) and (6) exclude industrial value added as a share of GDP as well. The discussion focuses on developing countries, with the developed-country results used primarily as a contrasting reference, and it takes the full model (columns (1) and (2)) as the basis for calculating the magnitude of effects.

Because the variables are taken in log-log form, coefficient estimates can be interpreted as the percentage change in women's relative concentration in industrial employment as a result of a 1 per cent change in the independent variable in question, with two exceptions: the coefficients for per capita GDP growth and net manufacturing exports as a share of GDP give the percentage change in women's relative concentration in industrial employment as a result of a 1 percentage point increase (as opposed to a 1 per cent increase) in either variable. In interpreting the relative impact of the variables, it is important to consider how much the variables actually change (i.e. a 1 percentage point increase in per capita GDP growth, which only varies by a few percentage points, is much "larger" than the same change in net manufacturing exports as a share of GDP, which varies much more). For this reason, the discussion below focuses on the

TABLE 4.3   Determinants of women's relative access to "good" jobs, developing and developed countries

Dependent variable: Women's relative concentration in industrial employment

	Developing (1)	Developed (2)	Developing (3)	Developed (4)	Developing (5)	Developed (6)
Industrial emp./total emp.	0.350* (0.180)	-0.148 (0.171)	0.350* (0.180)	-0.166 (0.168)	0.372** (0.164)	-0.012 (0.127)
Industry value-added/GDP	0.099 (0.138)	0.217 (0.143)	0.101 (0.133)	0.229 (0.138)		
Capital-labour ratio	-0.283** (0.110)	-0.198*** (0.063)	-0.284** (0.111)	-0.200*** (0.063)	-0.297*** (0.098)	-0.218*** (0.064)
Net manufacturing exports/GDP	0.006* (0.003)	-0.001 (0.002)	0.006* (0.003)	-0.001 (0.002)	0.007** (0.003)	-0.001 (0.002)
Inward FDI/GDP	-0.001 (0.024)	0.004 (0.005)	-0.001 (0.025)	0.006 (0.004)	-0.003 (0.024)	0.005 (0.005)
Weighted tariff	0.062** (0.028)	0.087*** (0.018)	0.062** (0.029)	0.087*** (0.018)	0.064** (0.028)	0.081*** (0.019)
Government consumption/GDP	0.156* (0.080)	0.045 (0.115)	0.153* (0.079)	0.003 (0.101)	0.144* (0.079)	-0.051 (0.084)
Per capita GDP growth	0.000 (0.003)	0.003 (0.002)				
Women's/men's labour force participation	-0.468 (0.334)	-0.952** (0.404)	-0.468 (0.333)	-0.984** (0.401)	-0.437 (0.335)	-0.947** (0.351)
Women's/men's secondary school enrolment	0.191 (0.295)	0.387** (0.185)	0.190 (0.293)	0.395** (0.189)	0.200 (0.268)	0.379** (0.176)
Observations	437	599	437	602	443	653
R-squared	0.267	0.728	0.267	0.728	0.277	0.742
F-stat	8.41	66.24	9.35	54.51	9.16	56.84
Number of countries	61	33	61	33	62	34

Note: All variables except for net exports of manufactures as a share of GDP and per capita GDP growth are measured in logs. All regressions are based on annual observations for the period 1991–2014, and include country fixed effects; constants are not reported. The model is of the form: $Wind_{it} = \alpha + \beta X_{it} + \mu_i + \varepsilon_{it}$, where $Wind_{it}$ is women's relative concentration for country i at time t; X is a vector of independent variables, μ is the country fixed effect, and ε is the error term. Robust standard errors, all of which are clustered by country, are shown in parentheses. All variables passed unit root tests except for employment variables, which could not be tested because of gaps in the time series; therefore the specification has been modified to include deterministic drift via the intercept term. Including time dummies for the Asian financial crisis and the most recent global financial crisis of 2008–2009 does not affect the results. Further details on data are provided in the data appendix. Statistical significance is indicated as follows: * 10 per cent; ** 5 per cent; *** 1 per cent.

economic significance of the estimates by assessing the impact of a variable's average or mean change on women's relative concentration in industrial employment. Table 4.4 shows sample mean and standard deviations; these are used in combination with the coefficient estimates to assess economic significance.

Industrial employment matters more than industrial value added

Beginning with industrial structure, industrial employment – as opposed to industrial value added – is a statistically and economically significant positive correlate of women's relative concentration in industrial employment in developing countries. This association exists across all the models, regardless of whether a control for industrial value added is included, as does the magnitude of the hypothesized effect. To get a sense of this magnitude, a one standard deviation increase from the mean in industrial employment as a share of total employment (6.7 percentage points) is associated with a roughly 11 per cent increase in women's relative industrial employment. That industrial value added is insignificant echoes the employment challenges identified in research on premature deindustrialization, and indicates that the declining job yield associated with current forms of industrialization also compromises the gender inclusiveness of growth and development. That is, job competition that results from deindustrialization disadvantages women more than men in terms of access to good jobs.

TABLE 4.4 Sample mean and standard deviations, developing and developed countries

	Developing countries		Developed countries	
	Mean	Standard deviation	Mean	Standard deviation
Relative women's/men's industrial emp.	56.85	25.92	42.50	12.80
Industrial emp./total emp.	21.72	6.65	28.06	5.79
Industry value added/GDP	32.63	11.62	29.12	5.40
Capital-labour ratio	90 796	72 191	275 771	96 748
Net exports of manufactures/GDP	-8.70	8.81	-2.03	8.58
Inward FDI/GDP	3.13	2.80	4.94	7.43
Weighted tariffs	7.85	5.05	2.44	1.73
Government consumption/GDP	13.13	3.61	19.50	2.91
Per capita GDP growth	2.74	3.56	2.21	3.39
Women's/men's labour force participation	61.01	17.19	81.88	8.30
Women's/men's secondary school enrolment	101.57	12.88	101.34	4.93

Note: See the data appendix for notes on sources.

Higher capital intensity lowers women's relative access to industrial sector jobs

The strong cross-sample results on the capital-labour ratio confirm the point, albeit at an aggregate level, that increases in capital intensity (and, by extension, improvements in average job quality) are associated with relative employment losses for women in industry in both developing and developed countries.[18] For developing countries, a one standard deviation increase in the capital-labour ratio, which almost doubles it (but is still far short of the developed-country mean), is associated with a 22.5 per cent decline in women's relative concentration in industrial employment. In response to these results, one might counter that increasing capital intensity is also associated with higher services sector productivity, which means services sector jobs are likely better, and therefore using women's relative concentration in industry as a proxy for gender exclusion from high-quality employment no longer makes sense. However, including services sector productivity relative to industrial sector productivity in the regressions (ignoring the controversies associated with measuring services sector productivity for the purposes of this discussion) does not substantially affect the estimates for developing countries; the coefficient estimate is actually positive and statistically significant in the developed-country specifications. The likely intuition is instructive: when services sector productivity is high, so is relative job quality, attracting *both* women and men to that sector. Controlling for the other factors included in the equation, men's employment shifts more than women's, suggesting once again women's concentration in lower productivity jobs, regardless of sector.

That these relationships persist despite controlling for women's education relative to that of men, suggests that it is not a question of differential skills, but rather the sorts of gender stereotypes and discriminatory access to better jobs that characterize segmented labour markets.

Net (not total) exports of manufactures help, whereas FDI does not

The results on global integration are interesting. FDI does not seem to be important in influencing women's relative access to good jobs. On the other hand, the extent of trade, as measured by net exports of manufactures, is positive and statistically and economically significant, but only for developing countries. This is in line with the trade-related links between export-oriented manufacturing and women's employment (at least when controlling for the capital intensity of production). To get a sense of magnitude, if an economy moves one standard deviation above a zero trade balance on manufactures (plus 8.8 percentage points), the associated increase in women's relative concentration in industry is 5.5 per cent. As noted above, other measures of trade (total trade, or taking imports and exports separately) are not correlated with significant changes in women's relative access to industrial employment. This casts doubt on the popularity of using participation in global value chains (GVCs) as a proxy for successful globalization, or simply targeting women's involvement in GVCs as evidence of their greater inclusion in the benefits of trade. What seems to be more important is the extent of domestic value added in trade in manufactures.

Less trade liberalization is associated with more "good" jobs for women

Regarding trade policy as measured by weighted tariffs, interestingly, this is one of the more robust positive correlates of women's relative concentration in industrial employment, for both developed and developing countries. Increasing weighted tariffs by one standard deviation from the mean (5.1 percentage points) is associated with a 4 per cent increase in women's relative concentration in industry. That a more restrictive trade policy (i.e. less trade liberalization) seems to be associated with employment gains for women is not the same as saying trade per se is not good for inclusive development. As noted above, and as evidenced by the model's results on net manufacturing exports, the extent of trade or global integration is distinct from the policy environment that manages it. Less trade liberalization, especially in developing countries, may in fact promote the expansion of domestic manufacturing (as noted in *TDR 2016*), and thereby women's industrial employment. While trade expansion has the potential to contribute to inclusive growth and development by increasing access to foreign produced goods and contributing to additional sources of demand, unfettered import competition can compromise local manufacturing and the job opportunities that go with it, with negative consequences for gender equality.

Government spending expands women's relative take-up of "good" jobs

The results show that, in developing countries, a stronger fiscal policy stance is also associated with a higher share of women's employment in industry relative to men. If the developing country with the lowest value for government consumption as a share of GDP (at 5 per cent) were to increase its government spending to reach the mean of the developing-country sample (i.e. to 13.1 per cent), the associated increase in women's relative concentration in industrial employment would be 9.7 per cent. A further increase to the developed-country mean (19.5 per cent) would give a parallel increase of another 7.6 per cent. Looking at changes in industrial employment for women versus men (i.e. running the regressions separately for the numerator and denominator), indicates that relative shifts are driven by gains for women, and not losses for men, when fiscal policy is expansive. This suggests that government spending not only encourages more demand for labour in the industrial sector, but does so in ways that reduce

job competition, and thus also opportunity hoarding for jobs in that sector. These relationships are only apparent in the developing-country sample. For developed countries, public spending is more closely associated with services sector employment, for both women and men.

The failure of growth to produce sufficient employment is also a failure for gender equality

Economic growth, on the other hand, is not a significant correlate when it is included, nor does it affect the magnitude and significance of the rest of the model's coefficients when it is dropped (as in columns (3)–(6)). Thus, growth does not appear to be an economically important factor in determining women's relative access to high-quality employment based on its record over the past couple of decades. This result indicates that the failure of growth to produce sufficient employment is also a failure for gender equality, and confirms that simply targeting growth, at least in the current global/macro context, will not, on its own, bring about inclusive development.

Increasing women's labour force participation is associated with increased segregation and crowding

Regarding the controls for labour supply, the positive coefficient signs on women's secondary school enrolment relative to men's are as predicted: women's higher education levels relative to men's result in their higher relative concentration in the skilled work associated with industrial sector jobs. However the relationship is significant only for developed countries. Perhaps more interesting and instructive are the results for relative labour force participation. The higher the ratio of women's to men's labour force participation rates, the lower is women's relative concentration in industrial sector employment. This result is consistent with the segregation and crowding hypotheses discussed above: as women's participation in the labour force increases, they tend to be crowded into services sector employment because their access to industrial sector jobs is blocked. Even though only the developed-country specification achieves statistical significance, the result for developing countries is economically significant: moving the sample average ratio of 61 per cent up by one standard deviation (plus 17.2 percentage points) is associated with a decline of 13.2 per cent in women's relative concentration in industrial employment.

This result highlights one of the problems with exclusively supply-side oriented calls for increasing women's labour force participation as a source of both growth and inclusivity. Increasing women's labour force participation on its own – without complementary policies that extend and structure aggregate demand in ways that spark the growth of good jobs – tends to compromise women's relative access to quality employment, with confounding results for gender equality in economic opportunities.

Summary

Considering the results together, the economically "largest" factors are those relating to structural change and technology. These seem to reflect a gender component to the broader literature on premature deindustrialization: as the availability of "good" industrial sector jobs declines, the consequent competition tends to be more costly for women's industrial employment than for men's. Technological change and the increasing capital intensity of production are particularly problematic for women, even after controlling for gender differences in education. An increase in employment opportunities in the industrial sector (as opposed to industrial value added) offers a gender inclusive alternative, but one that requires a sustainable expansion of demand for industrial goods. A similar point can be made with regard to globalization: higher net (not total) exports of manufactures improve industrial job prospects for women, as do public policies that provide some protection against import competition. An expansive fiscal policy also contributes to inclusion by increasing labour demand in ways that reduce job competition, thereby increasing women's industrial employment but not at the expense of men. Conversely, economic growth on its own is shown to have little impact on women's relative access to better jobs. Increasing women's labour force participation on its own – without supportive demand-side policies and structures to productively absorb these new market entrants – tends to worsen gender segregation and encourages the crowding of women into low value-added informal service sector activities. This ultimately compromises the benefits of market participation for both gender equality and development.

F. Gendered exclusion and the labour share of income

In light of the wider policy challenges around inclusiveness discussed in this *Report*, an important question is whether job segregation by gender has a negative impact on all workers as reflected in the labour share of income. Why is this important? Gender equality is a component of overall equality, and is thus an essential aspect of inclusive growth. But insofar as gender equality contributes to downward pressure on men's well-being and socio-economic status, gender-related conflict may emerge, which is troubling. Gender equality would then not only be associated with weakening the bargaining power of men vis-à-vis employers, it could also have negative externalities on wider aspects of well-being, such as increasing the incidence of household dissolution or intimate partner violence. This could have negative implications for the production of human capabilities – in the sense that poor outcomes for women compromise the overall quality of labour – and, ultimately, for long-term productivity growth.

This question of how job segregation by gender – or its obverse, job integration by gender – affects the functional distribution of income has received relatively little attention in the inequality, growth and development literature, with the exception of a handful of studies that have produced ambiguous results (Zacharias and Mahoney, 2009).

Given gender wage gaps (a universal feature in labour markets around the world), and viewed statically, an increase in women's share of employment in a sector may depress average wages in that sector.[19] This suggests that men may benefit from job segregation that excludes women from better-paid, male-dominated sectors, thus providing an economic incentive for occupational hoarding. Job segregation by gender, however, also influences labour's bargaining power overall. Jobs in the core sector, which are dominated by men, especially industrial sector jobs, are increasingly rationed, as evidenced by the falling share of industrial employment in total employment (figure 4.3). The poor working conditions associated with women's jobs in the peripheral sector demonstrate to men the "cost" of job loss if they lose their privileged positions in the core sector. This effectively weakens the fallback positions and bargaining power of men working in the industrial sector, depressing wages and making it difficult for workers to capture the benefits of any increase in productivity growth. These sorts of dynamics will exert downward pressure on the labour share of income, even though some subgroups of workers maintain privileged positions relative to others.

Building on the econometric work presented in section E, this section provides a preliminary, aggregate test of this proposition for developing countries over the period 1991–2013. It follows the panel data frameworks found in the few studies that econometrically evaluate the determinants of the labour share of income for developing countries (e.g. ILO, 2011; Jayadev, 2007; Stockhammer, 2013), but adds women's relative concentration in industrial employment as a variable that influences labour's bargaining power. The analysis also includes the ratio of women's to men's labour force participation to control for the potential wage effects of the changing structure of the labour force as women (who are systematically paid less than men) enter the labour market.

Table 4.5 presents results (with econometric details provided in the table notes), and includes two different specifications: fixed effects in column (1) and two-stage least squares in column (2), which accounts for the endogeneity of women's relative concentration in industrial employment. Because the emphasis is on the relationship between gender equality in the labour market and the labour share, the discussion is largely limited to these estimates. However, a few notes about the overall specification are warranted. In addition to the gender variables, controls include the set used above to measure structural transformation and the gender inclusivity of increasing capital intensity (industrial value added as a share of GDP, industrial employment as a share of total employment and the capital-labour ratio), as well as those used to measure the structural and policy consequences of globalization (trade and FDI as shares of GDP, weighted tariffs and government consumption as a share of GDP). Real interest rates are a standard in most specifications, and reflect the ability or willingness of governments to maintain low interest rates in the context of the liberalization of global capital flows.[20]

Because many of the regressors also determine women's relative concentration in industrial employment (as detailed in table 4.3), the results in column (2), which account for this endogeneity, are used as the basis for discussion. As with table 4.3, all the

TABLE 4.5 Determinants of labour share of income

Dependent variable: Labour share of income

	Fixed effects (1)	Two-stage least squares (2)
Women's relative concentration in industrial employment	0.080** (0.037)	0.137** (0.055)
Women's/men's labour force participation	-0.154 (0.100)	-0.091 (0.107)
Industrial emp./total emp.	-0.021 (0.051)	0.042 (0.052)
Industrial value added/GDP	-0.183* (0.092)	-0.258*** (0.086)
Capital-labour ratio	0.033 (0.064)	0.071 (0.066)
Trade/GDP	-0.037 (0.024)	-0.004 (0.004)
Inward FDI/GDP	-0.005 (0.004)	-0.025 (0.024)
Weighted tariffs	0.036** (0.016)	0.039** (0.016)
Government consumption/GDP	0.157*** (0.055)	0.173*** (0.058)
Real interest rates	0.000 (0.001)	0.000 (0.001)
Observations	469	421
R-squared	0.446	0.481
F-stat	4.9	4.7
F-stat for excluded instruments		95.07
P value, Hansen J		0.28
Number of countries	48	48

Note: All variables except for real interest rates are measured in logs; regressions are based on annual observations for the period 1991–2014, and include country fixed effects; constants are not reported. The model is of the form: $LS_{it} = \alpha + \beta X_{it} + \mu_i + \varepsilon_{it}$, where LS_{it} is the labour share of income for country i at time t, X is a vector of independent variables, μ is the country fixed effect, and ε is the error term. Robust standard errors, all of which are clustered by country, are shown in parentheses. Further details on the specifications are provided in the note for table 4.3, and on data in the data appendix. Statistical significance is indicated as follows: * 10 per cent; ** 5 per cent; *** 1 per cent.

The two-stage least squares (2SLS) estimates are also run with country fixed effects; the endogenous variable is women's relative concentration in industrial employment, and the excluded instruments used for the first stage include the lagged value for women's relative concentration and net exports of manufactures as a share of GDP. Further diagnostics for the 2SLS specification include the first stage F-statistic for excluded instruments, which is applied to the null hypothesis that the model is underidentified or weakly identified; this statistic surpasses commonly applied critical values. (Staiger and Stock (1997) propose a rule of thumb that with one endogenous regressor, an F-stat of less than 10 indicates weak instruments.) The P-value for the Hansen J test of over-identifying restrictions indicates a failure to reject the null, implying that the instruments are valid in the sense of being uncorrelated with the error term and correctly excluded from the second stage equation.

variables (except for real interest rates) are taken in logs, so that the coefficient estimates can be interpreted as the percentage change in the labour share of income that is associated with a 1 per cent increase in the independent variable in question.

In both specifications listed in table 4.5, women's relative industrial concentration (that is, increased job integration in the industrial sector) has a positive and statistically significant effect on the labour share of income. Thus, efforts to improve women's access to high-quality jobs in the industrial sector (and by extension reduce their crowding into lower quality jobs) can be a win-win for both women and men. It can thereby reduce gender conflict as women's relative employment rises. To gain a sense of magnitude, and using the estimates in column (2), between 1991 and 2013 the sample mean of women's relative concentration decreased from 70.2 to 47.2 per cent (as illustrated in figure 4.5), which was associated with a 4.7 per cent decline in the labour share. Considering that the sample mean of the labour share of income declined by about 4 per cent between the early 1990s and the late 2010s, the potential impact of changes in women's relative share of industrial employment was economically very significant by comparison.

Interestingly, the same change in the ratio of women's to men's labour force participation (which increased by about 9 percentage points between 1991 and 2013) was associated with a decline in the labour share of 1.6 per cent (which is statistically insignificant). So while there is some (weak) evidence of a negative association between women's increasing entry into the labour market and the labour share, when that entry is associated with "good" jobs, there is a net positive effect on the labour share of income.

The following are some brief comments on the other results. Among the controls for structural transformation, the only variable with a substantial and statistically significant impact on the labour share of income is the share of industrial value added in GDP, which is strongly negative. A 10 per cent increase in the share of industrial value added in GDP, (which would typically be a modest increase from say 20 per cent to 22 per cent of GDP) is associated with a 2.6 per cent decline in the labour share of income. The implication is that independently of the impact of industrialization on employment (which is one of the other controls included in the regression), industrialization on its own has not been associated with better aggregate outcomes for workers in terms of the labour share in national income. It is not enough for countries to industrialize; it has to be accompanied by good jobs in order to improve overall conditions for labour. This highlights the employment challenges associated with current processes of industrialization in developing countries, and the increasing inequality that results.

By contrast, more expansive fiscal policies along with less trade liberalization are associated with higher labour shares. And while none of the other measures of globalization appear to be significant, it is worth noting that exports as a share of GDP exert the negative correlation that appears for trade in column (1), and this persists if it is included on its own in column (2), while imports as a share of GDP show no effect. These results are in line with how one might expect global competition in export markets to manifest in terms of exerting downward pressure on labour shares.

In sum, then, this analysis indicates that occupational hoarding by gender – as reflected in women having less access to industrial sector jobs (and their crowding into lower quality jobs) – has a significant negative impact on the labour share of income. This class dynamic thus appears to be gender cooperative in the sense that what is good for women workers is also good for labour overall, including men. These findings also confirm the importance of being precise about the sorts of – and especially the context for – gender equality interventions that policy promotes, as some prescriptions can ultimately be counterproductive. In cases where access to core sector or "good" jobs is declining, increasing female labour force participation will constrain wage growth, setting in motion a low-wage growth path characterized by increasing economic insecurity and gender conflict, with poor prospects for sustainably or substantially enhancing future well-being.

G. Conclusions

This chapter illustrates how gender exclusion in the current global era follows prevailing social norms and economic structures. Singular supply-side perspectives treat women's increasing employment participation as an unqualified boost for gender equality, without accounting for how wider economic circumstances and policies determine the implications for women's well-being, as well as the impact on men. In many countries, women's employment participation is increasing as that of men declines, and what appears to be more gender equality is partly due to the exclusion of men. Because the current era of growth and globalization has failed to produce sufficient high-quality jobs, women have been increasingly integrated into the labour market only on inferior terms, with gender becoming one of the ways that economic opportunity and security are rationed. This worsens overall inequality by lowering labour's share of income, with negative consequences for aggregate demand and, ultimately, growth.

This connection reveals how inequality can breed more inequality, a point also underscored in chapter V of this *TDR*, but only from the perspective of the causes and consequences of financial crises. The expanding reach of markets, increasing global integration, and the structural changes that have accompanied them have worsened conditions for labour. And gender has become an unfortunate aspect of how inequality manifests and persists.

However, policy can play a major role in reversing this development. The employment losses associated with structural and technological change have been especially costly for women's access to the higher quality jobs associated with industrial sector work in developing countries. Combating gender stereotypes and otherwise fostering and facilitating women's access to core sector employment, especially through social infrastructure investments that better enable women to combine paid work and their responsibilities for care, are important interventions to consider. Pairing such efforts with demand-side interventions, including through more expansive fiscal stances, can increase the demand for labour and make growth more gender inclusive. This would also improve economic prospects for men. On the question of trade, more

is not necessarily better. What matters is the extent of domestic value added, at least in manufacturing. Trade policy stances involving less liberalization of imports seem to support women's relative access to industrial work in ways that preserve men's access to employment as well, suggesting that managing trade can improve the gender inclusivity of development. On its own, growth has not done much to improve gender inclusion in employment, partly because of its failure to generate sufficient employment overall.

The question of care work also needs to be addressed as it is central to growth and sustainable development. In addition, women's primary responsibility for this kind of work is an ongoing source of gender inequality. Policy dialogues on the issue have constructively progressed in terms of what economist Diane Elson first proposed as the need to "recognize, reduce and redistribute" unpaid care work.[21] However, given the employment challenges associated with structural and technological change outlined above, part of gender inclusion for growth and development must be about transforming paid care work into decent work with the wage levels, benefits and security typically associated with industrial jobs in the core sector of the labour market. This is a challenging prospect for most economists to consider, as social services (of which care work constitutes a large part) – whether provided within or outside markets, or by the public or private sectors – are treated more as consumption goods than investments in the future. Moreover, they are systematically undervalued (and underpaid) largely because they are considered to be women's work. What investing in the care sector means in economic terms is thus not well understood in relation to some of the longer term development challenges such as raising aggregate productivity, structural transformation, technological change and transforming the social relations of production. A small but powerful body of literature has begun to grapple with some of these questions,[22] but the questions themselves need to become a more standard feature of growth analytics, rather than treated as special topics on care, if gender inclusion is to be incorporated into the overall economic system rather than treated as an outcome that requires some sort of ex post facto inequality "fix". ■

Notes

1. In this chapter, jobs in the industrial sector (rather than agricultural or services sectors) are used as a proxy for "good" jobs, for reasons outlined in section D.

2. This section draws from the discussions in Seguino, 2017; and Braunstein, 2011.

3. Race/ethnicity is another type of intergroup inequality that serves to create and perpetuate economic stratification. Gender is often combined with race/ethnicity or caste to intensify intergroup inequality.

4. Indeed, stratification processes can be the cause of intergroup differences in education.

5. Evidence of the universality of such norms can be found in the *World Values Survey* (see: http://www.worldvaluessurvey.org/), although there is variation between countries in the extent to which such norms prevail (Seguino, 2011).

6. Analyses of segmented labour markets often label the core sector the "primary" sector, and the peripheral sector the "secondary" sector. Because the terms "primary" and "secondary" sectors more typically refer to the agricultural/raw materials and manufacturing sectors respectively (with "tertiary" referring to services), this chapter uses the terms "core" and "peripheral" to differentiate between the primary and secondary sectors of the labour market.

7. In important ways, this segmentation can be applied globally, with the global division of labour amidst the increasing concentration of market power among a handful of firms limiting access to core-type work for many of the world's workers.

8. Economic theory would suggest that women's "special" skill in these tasks should have resulted in a wage premium, but instead such jobs are noted for their low wages relative to those in other manufacturing activities. This form of crowding is therefore more the result of stratification designed to benefit firms and male workers than of supply conditions, such as women's labour market skills.

9. This section, particularly the emphasis on the contradiction between women's growing share in employment and rising gender segregation, especially in the industrial sector, draws from Seguino, 2016.

10. One potential problem with using men's employment rates alone (as opposed to comparing them with those of women) is that with development, one would expect men to stay in school longer and retire earlier, leading to a decline in their employment rates among the population older than 15 years. Cross-country data limitations prevent the obvious fix of restricting the sample to prime working age adults. On the basis of available data, however, limiting the sample by age does not undermine the characterization highlighted in the text.

11. To the extent that employment growth in the services sector is partly driven by the outsourcing of activities previously provided within the manufacturing sector, such as janitorial or security services, such outsourced jobs tend to offer lower pay and greater insecurity than the same jobs in industry, indicating a loss in job quality (Tregenna, 2010).

12. An important caveat here is that not all industrial sector jobs are "good", especially the ones more likely to be held by women. However, relative to most jobs in the agricultural or services sector, industrial sector jobs are likely to be "better", even when they are not that "good".

13. The shapes of the country distribution of women's relative concentration in industrial employment in 2013 differ in figures 4.4 and 4.5 due to different scales on the x- and y-axes. The underlying data are, however, the same.

14. Many other measures of trade were also tried, including total trade, exports and then imports as shares of GDP, but none were statistically or economically significant.

15. Lower income countries tend to have higher tariffs and vice versa; thus a reasonable challenge to the specification is whether coefficient estimates for tariffs are picking up per capita GDP effects (that is, differences in income levels, not tariff behaviour). The correlations here are not very strong: -0.28 for developed countries and -0.30 for developing countries. Per capita GDP is not included in the model because of its high correlation with the capital-labour ratio (0.80 for developed countries and 0.85 for developing countries). At the same time, the correlation between the capital-labour ratio and weighted tariffs is quite low, at -0.17 for developed countries and -0.19 for developing countries. If any variable is picking up the effects of income, it is the capital-labour ratio.

16. Countries also use non-tariff measures to regulate trade, but higher tariffs tend to be associated with the use of more non-tariff measures as well (UNCTAD, 2013).

17. A statistical (Chow) test of the two models confirms that the two groups should be evaluated separately. Also note that a number of years – particularly for the early 1990s – are missing for many of the countries in the developing-country group. Thus, these results need to be interpreted with caution.

18. This association remains even if per capita GDP is included.

19. Indeed, one of the stylized facts of the literature on gender wage gaps in the United States and in many other countries is that the higher the proportion of women in a sector, the lower is the average wage (Levanon et al., 2009; Lansky et al., 2016).

20. Variables used by other studies that we do not incorporate, largely because of paucity of data given the time

series, include controls for labour market institutions, financial globalization and financial liberalization. Their absence is likely taken up in the country fixed effects; however, including the Chinn-Ito index, a measure of financial openness based on the IMF's *Annual Report on Exchange Arrangements and Exchange Restrictions* gives negative but statistically

insignificant correlations with the labour share, and does not impact the other results.

21 See Elson (2017) for a recent perspective.

22 Some of this literature was reviewed in section B. For a more detailed discussion on these points, see: Braunstein, 2015; Ghosh, 2017; ITUC, 2016 and 2017; Razavi, 2007; and UN Women, 2015.

References

Agénor P-R, Canuto O and Pereira da Silva LA (2010). On gender and growth: The role of intergenerational health externalities and women's occupational constraints. Policy Research Working Paper No. 5492, World Bank, Washington, DC.

Aguayo-Tellez E (2011). The impact of trade liberalization policies and FDI on gender inequalities: A literature review. Background paper for the *World Development Report,* 2012. World Bank, Washington, DC.

Antonopoulos R, Kim K, Masterson T and Zacharias A (2010). Investing in care: A strategy for effective and equitable job creation. Working Paper No. 610, Levy Economics Institute of Bard College, Annandale-on-Hudson, NY.

Artecona R and Cunningham W (2002). Effects of Trade Liberalization on the Gender Wage Gap in Mexico. Working Paper No. 21, World Bank, Washington, DC.

Bacchetta M, Ernst E and Bustamante JP (2009). *Globalization and Informal Jobs in Developing Countries.* Geneva, International Labour Office and the World Trade Organization.

Becker GS (1957). *The Economics of Discrimination.* Chicago, The University of Chicago Press.

Bergmann B (1974). Occupational segregation, wages and profits when employers discriminate by race or sex. *Eastern Economic Journal,* 1(2): 103−110.

Berik G, van der Meulen Rodgers Y and Zveglich JE (2004). International trade and gender wage discrimination: Evidence from East Asia. *Review of Development Economics,* 8(2): 237–254.

Blecker RA and Seguino S (2002). Macroeconomic effects of reducing gender wage inequality in an export-oriented, semi-industrialized economy. *Review of Development Economics,* 6(1): 103−119.

Boserup E (1970). *Woman's Role in Economic Development.* London, George Allen & Unwin.

Braunstein E (2006). Foreign direct investment, development, and gender equity: A review of research and policy. Occasional Paper No. 12, United Nations Research Institute for Social Development, Geneva.

Braunstein E (2011). *Gender and Economic Development.* Nairobi, United Nations Human Settlements Programme (UN-HABITAT).

Braunstein E (2012). Neoliberal development macroeconomics: A consideration of its gendered employment effects. Research Paper 2012-1, United Nations Research Institute for Social Development, Geneva.

Braunstein E (2015). Economic growth and social reproduction: Gender inequality as cause and consequence. UN Women Discussion Paper No. 5, United Nations, New York.

Braunstein E and Brenner M (2007). Foreign direct investment and gendered wages in urban China. *Feminist Economics,* 13(3–4): 213–237.

Busse M and Spielmann C (2006). Gender inequality and trade. *Review of International Economics,* 14(3): 362–379.

Bussolo M and De Hoyos RE (2009). *Gender Aspects of the Trade and Poverty Nexus: A Macro-Micro Approach.* Washington, DC, Palgrave Macmillan and the World Bank.

Chandrasekhar CP and Ghosh J (2014). Growth, employment patterns and inequality in Asia: A case study of India. ILO Asia-Pacific Working Paper Series, International Labour Organization Regional Office for Asia and the Pacific, Bangkok.

Darity W, Jr. (2005). Stratification economics: The role of intergroup inequality. *Journal of Economics and Finance,* 29(2): 144–153.

Darity WA, Jr, Mason PL and Stewart JB (2006). The economics of identity: The origin and persistence of racial identity norms. *Journal of Economic Behavior and Organization,* 60(3): 283–305.

Das MB (2013). Exclusion and discrimination in the labor market. Background paper for the *World Development Report 2013.* World Bank, Washington, DC.

Doepke M and Tertilt M (2011). Does female empowerment promote economic development? IZA Discussion Paper No. 5637, Institute for the Study of Labor, Bonn.

Domínguez-Villalobos L and Brown-Grossman F (2010). Trade liberalization and gender wage inequality in Mexico. *Feminist Economics,* 16(4): 53−79.

Dollar D and Gatti R (1999). Gender inequality, income, and growth: Are good times good for women? Policy Research Report on Gender and Development, Working Paper Series, No. 1, World Bank, Washington, DC.

Elson D (2017). Recognize, reduce and redistribute unpaid care work: How to close the gender gap. *New Labor Forum,* 26(2): 52−61.

Elson D and Pearson R (1981). "Nimble fingers make cheap workers": An analysis of women's employment in

Third World export manufacturing. *Feminist Review,* 7(1): 87–107.

Felipe J, Mehta A, and Rhee C (2014). Manufacturing matters... but it's the jobs that count. Economics Working Paper Series, No. 420, Asian Development Bank, Manila.

Fontana M (2009). The gender effects of trade liberalization in developing countries: A review of the literature. In: Bussolo M and De Hoyos RE, eds. *Gender Aspects of the Trade and Poverty Nexus: A Micro-Macro Approach.* Basingstoke, Palgrave Macmillan and The World Bank: 25–50.

Fontana M and Natali L (2008). Gendered patterns of time use in Tanzania: Public investment in infrastructure can help. Paper prepared for the IFPRI Project on "Evaluating the Long-Term Impact of Gender-Focused Policy Interventions". International Food Policy Research Institute, Washington, DC.

Gaddis I and Klasen S (2014). Economic development, structural change, and women's labor force participation: A reexamination of the feminization U hypothesis. *Journal of Population Economic,* 27(3): 639–681.

Gallup and ILO (2017). *Towards a Better Future for Women and Work: Voices of Women and Men.* Geneva, International Labour Organization.

Ghosh J (2009). *Never Done and Poorly Paid: Women's Work in Globalising India.* New Delhi, Women Unlimited Press.

Ghosh J (2017). Decent work and the care economy: Recognising, rewarding, reducing and redistributing care work. Working paper, Gender, Employment and Diversity Branch, International Labour Organization, Geneva (forthcoming).

Gordon DM, Edwards R and Reich M (1982). *Segmented Work, Divided Workers: The Historical Transformation of Labor in the United States.* New York, Cambridge University Press.

Haddad L, Hoddinott J and Alderman H, eds. (1997). *Intrahousehold Resource Allocation in Developing Countries: Models, Methods, and Policy.* Baltimore, Johns Hopkins University Press.

Hartmann H (1979). Capitalism, patriarchy, and job segregation by sex. In: Eisenstein ZR, ed. *Capitalist Patriarchy, and the Case for Socialist Feminism.* New York, Monthly Review Press: 206–247.

İlkkaracan I, Kim K and Kaya T (2015). The impact of public investment in social care services on employment, gender equality and poverty: The Turkish case. Istanbul Technical University Women's Studies Center and the Levy Economics Institute, Istanbul.

ILO (2011). *World of Work Report 2011: Making Markets Work for Jobs.* Geneva, International Labour Organization.

ILO (2015). *Women at Work Trends 2016.* Geneva, International Labour Organization.

ITUC (2016). Investing in the care economy: A gender analysis of employment stimulus in seven OECD countries. The Women's Budget Group and International Trade Union Confederation, London.

ITUC (2017). Investing in the care economy: Simulating employment effects by gender in countries in emerging economies. The Women's Budget Group for the International Trade Union Confederation and UN Women, London.

Jayadev A (2007). Capital account openness and the labour share of income. *Cambridge Journal of Economics,* 31(3): 423–443.

Karamessini M and Rubery J, eds. (2014). *Women and Austerity: The Economic Crisis and the Future for Gender Equality.* Abingdon and New York, Routledge.

Kaufman RL (2002). Assessing alternative perspectives on race and sex employment segregation. *American Sociological Review,* 67(4): 547–572.

Klasen S and Lamanna F (2009). The impact of gender inequality in education and employment on economic growth: New evidence for a panel of countries. *Feminist Economics,* 15(3): 91–132.

Knowles S, Lorgelly PK and Owen PD (2002). Are educational gender gaps a brake on economic development? Some cross-country empirical evidence. *Oxford Economic Papers,* 54(1): 118–149.

Kucera D and Roncolato L (2016). The manufacturing-services dynamic in economic development. *International Labour Review,* 155(2): 171–199.

Kucera D and Tejani S (2014). Feminization, defeminization, and structural change in manufacturing. *World Development,* 64: 569–582.

Lansky M, Ghosh J, Meda D and Rani U (2016). Introduction. In: ILO, *Women, Gender and Work, Volume 2: Social Choices and Inequalities.* Geneva, International Labour Office: 3–43.

Levanon A, England P and Allison P (2009). Occupational feminization and pay: Assessing causal dynamics using 1950-2000 U.S. Census data. *Social Forces,* 88(2): 865–891.

Menon N and Van der Meulen Rodgers Y (2009). International trade and the gender wage gap: New evidence from India's manufacturing sector. *World Development,* 37(5): 965–981.

Razavi S (2007). The political and social economy of care in a development context: Conceptual issues, research questions and policy options. Gender and Development Program Paper No. 3, United Nations Research Institute for Social Development, Geneva.

Razavi S, Arza C, Braunstein E, Cook S and Goulding K (2012). Gendered impacts of globalization: Employment and social protection. Research Paper 2012–3, United Nations Research Institute for Social Development, Geneva.

Rodrik D (2016). Premature deindustrialization. *Journal of Economic Growth,* 21(1): 1–33.

Samarasinghe V (1998). The feminization of foreign currency earnings: Women's labor in Sri Lanka. *Journal of Developing Areas,* 32(3): 303–326.

Seguino S (2010). Gender, distribution, and balance of payments constrained growth in developing countries. *Review of Political Economy*, 22(3): 373–404.

Seguino S (2011). Help or hindrance? Religion's impact on gender inequality in attitudes and outcomes. *World Development,* 39(8): 1308–1321.

Seguino S (2016). Global trends in gender equality. *Journal of African Development,* 18(1): 1–30.

Seguino S (2017). Engendering macroeconomic theory and policy. Working Paper, World Bank, Washington, DC (forthcoming).

Seguino S and Grown C (2006). Gender equity and globalization: Macroeconomic policy for developing countries. *Journal of International Development,* 18(8): 1081–1114.

Seguino S and Were M (2014). Gender, development, and economic growth in sub-Saharan Africa. *Journal of African Economies,* 23 (supplement 1): i18–i61.

Smeeding TM (2016). Multiple barriers to economic opportunity for the "truly" disadvantaged and vulnerable. *The Russell Sage Foundation Journal of the Social Sciences,* 2(2): 98–122.

Staiger D and Stock JH (1997). Instrumental variables regression with weak instruments. *Econometrica,* 65(3): 557–586.

Standing G (1989). Global feminization through flexible labor. *World Development,* 17(7): 1077–1095.

Staritz C and Reis JG, eds. (2013). *Global Value Chains, Economic Upgrading, and Gender. Case Studies of Horticulture, Tourism, and Call Center Industries.* Washington, DC, World Bank.

Stockhammer E (2013). Why have wage shares fallen? A panel analysis of the determinants of functional income distribution. Conditions of Work and Employment Series No. 35, International Labour Office, Geneva.

Tejani S and Milberg W (2016). Global defeminization? Industrial upgrading and manufacturing employment in developing countries. *Feminist Economics,* 22(2): 24–54.

Tregenna F (2010) How significant is intersectoral outsourcing of employment in South Africa? *Industrial and Corporate Change,* 19(5): 1427–1457.

UNCTAD (2013). Non-tariff measures to trade: Economic and policy issues for developing countries. Developing Countries in International Trade Studies, United Nations publication, New York and Geneva.

UNCTAD (2014). Looking at trade policy through a "gender lens": Summary of seven country case studies conducted by UNCTAD. United Nations publication, Geneva.

UNCTAD (*TDR 2016*). *Trade and Development Report*: *Structural Transformation for Inclusive and Sustained Growth.* United Nations publication. Sales No. E.16. II.D.5. New York and Geneva.

UN Women (2015). *Progress of the World's Women 2015-2016: Transforming Economies, Realizing Rights.* New York, UN Women.

Vanek J, Chen MA, Carré F, Heintz J and Hussmanns R (2014). Statistics on the informal economy: Definitions, regional estimates & challenges. Working Paper (Statistics) No. 2, Women in Informal Employment: Globalizing and Organizing (WIEGO), Cambridge, MA.

World Bank (2012). *World Development Report 2012: Gender Equality and Development.* Washington, DC, World Bank.

Zacharias A and Mahoney M (2009). Do gender disparities in employment increase profitability? Evidence from the United States. *Feminist Economics,* 15(3): 133–161.

Data appendix

Variable	Explanation	Source
Relative women's/men's industrial emp.	Women's relative concentration in industrial employment, which equals (women's industrial employment/women's total employment)/(men's industrial employment/men's total employment)	Calculation based on data from World Bank, *World Development Indicators* (*WDI*) database and ILO modelled estimates
Industrial emp./total emp.	Industrial employment as a share of total employment (per cent)	Calculation based on data from *WDI* database
Industry value-added/GDP	Industry value added as a share of GDP (per cent)	*WDI* database
Capital-labour ratio	Capital stock at constant 2011 national prices (in 2011 dollars) divided by total employment	Calculated based on data from *Penn World Tables* 9.0
Per capita GDP growth	Annual per capita GDP growth based on real local currency (per cent)	*WDI* database
Net manufacturing exports/GDP	Manufacturing exports less manufacturing imports as a share of GDP (per cent)	Calculation based on data from UN *Comtrade* and *WDI* databases
Weighted tariffs	Weighted mean of applied tariff rate, all products (per cent), taken at the 2-digit HS level	Calculated based on the UNCTAD *Trade Analysis Information System* (*TRAINS*) database
Inward FDI/GDP	Net FDI inflows as a share of GDP (per cent)	*WDI* database
Government consumption/GDP	General government final consumption expenditure as a share of GDP (per cent)	*WDI* database
Women's/men's labour force participation	Ratio of women's to men's labour force participation rates, in the population aged 15–64 years (per cent)	Calculation based on data from *WDI* database and modelled ILO estimates
Women's/men's secondary school enrolment	Ratio of women's to men's gross secondary school enrolment rates (per cent)	Calculation based on data from *WDI* database
Labour share of income	Share of labour compensation, including estimates for the self-employed, in national income	*Penn World Tables* 9.0
Real interest rate	Real interest rate (per cent)	*WDI* database

Note: World Bank, *WDI* database (accessed December 2016).

INEQUALITY AND FINANCIAL INSTABILITY: STRUCTURAL LIMITS TO INCLUSIVE GROWTH

V

A. Introduction

The illusion that unregulated financial markets could combine limitless prosperity with durable stability disappeared with the 2008–2009 global financial crisis. In addition, it is now recognized that a prolonged period of rising inequality preceded the financial crisis, and the rise was particularly marked in countries at the epicentre of that crisis. Some observers see a clear and direct association between huge inequalities in income distribution and financial crises (Milanovic, 2010), while others consider the search for a "one-note narrative" too simplistic (Galbraith, 2014).

What is certain is that little has been done since the crisis to tackle the problems of skewed wealth and income distribution. Indeed, efforts to revive the "Great Moderation" of the two decades prior to the crisis, marked by low inflation, fast growth and confidence in self-equilibrating market forces, appear to be based on a view of the crisis as an unfortunate accident stemming from the complexity of modern financial systems. On that view, growing inequality is deemed a temporary deviation from the historical norm, likely to be corrected as recovery takes hold.

This chapter challenges that view: it discusses, from a macroeconomic perspective, how increased financial instability, culminating in a financial crisis, may be related to growing inequality. The next section begins by examining the concept of "financialization" and how this contributes to both inequality and instability, followed by some stylized facts about the rise of financialization in developed and developing countries. Section C presents an empirical approach for uncovering linkages between rising income inequality and financial crises. It first examines the economic, financial, policy and international channels through which rising inequality intensifies the build-up of financial vulnerabilities. It goes on to show how financial and economic adjustment mechanisms, changes in external conditions and policy reactions in the aftermath of financial crises affect the distribution of income and wealth. The final section draws conclusions, and proposes how growth and financial stability may be pursued along with significant improvements in income distribution.

B. The finance-inequality nexus

There is a large body of empirical evidence which shows that a rising proportion of income in most countries is being captured by the financial sector. Indeed, in many cases, this sector is also exerting a growing influence on the wider economy and on policy.[1] Many such policy regimes that are driven by finance, and which have also supported fiscal austerity and allowed a continuing decline of labour income shares, are coming under growing scrutiny (Boyer, 2009; Stiglitz, 2012).

Studies critical of finance-driven regimes adopt a wide spectrum of approaches. One strand stresses that unregulated market forces that tend to foster growing market concentration, will generate excess savings and productive capacity, whereby the search for profits will shift from productive investment to financial investment, leading eventually to economic stagnation. This can occur because of insufficient demand for the goods that investment produces, or because less successful industries, along with smaller enterprises that are outcompeted by the larger conglomerates, adopt high-risk investment strategies in an effort to service high levels of debt.[2] Another strand acknowledges that unregulated markets are prone to financial speculation and boom-bust cycles that constrain growth and stability, and suggests that improved incentives and information flows, along with appropriate regulations, could correct the problem.[3] While there are significant differences between these two lines of thinking, it is possible to adopt a schematic approach drawing from both, which recognizes the interrelations between inequality and financial instability.

1. Revisiting the links between financialization, inequality and instability

A common entry point in the search for linkages between financialization, inequality and instability can be provided by an analysis of the three main aggregate components of global demand. The first two − private consumption and investment derived from wages and profits or credit − contribute directly to spending flows. Conversely, income not spent can leak into various forms of acquisition of financial assets (net financial savings). The third component − government expenditure out of tax revenues or deficit-financing − plays a critical macroeconomic role in sustaining aggregate demand, particularly in situations of sluggish private expenditure. (This implies that fiscal austerity in a weak economic environment can exacerbate deflationary tendencies.) Total net world exports are zero by definition (hence not a component of global demand), but from the perspective of individual countries, net exports can be a source of demand, provided that equivalent net imports and financial inflows occur elsewhere in the global system.

Households, whose income depends on a mixture of wages and revenues generated from assets, are a major source of consumption. However, the propensity to save is higher for rentiers and high-income groups than it is for working families. Thus, greater inequality or declining labour income shares tend to reduce consumption, but it can stabilize, or even rise, to the extent that consumer credit compensates for falling wages. By contrast, investment is essentially driven by profit expectations, which are influenced by economic and financial processes and by assumptions made by entrepreneurs and speculators, including about wages, sales and asset prices. These varying expectations can have very different implications for the nature and sustainability of private debt, as well as for investment and economic growth.

Therefore, income distribution influences the composition of aggregate demand. Low levels of consumption relative to income (thus higher savings) may be consistent with high levels of investment, *if* all such savings are utilized. One of Keynes's main observations was that in modern economies there is a tendency for consumption to fall because of a general pattern of uneven distribution of income and wealth, while the greater productivity of newly installed capacity, together with "animal spirits", higher savings from increased profits and easier monetary policy, can stimulate the urge to invest. However, when there is uncertainty about future revenue streams from investment and a growing predominance of speculative activity, there is the danger of investment becoming part of a casino economy (Keynes, 1936: 159). In the medium to long term, in order to ensure a steady pace of private investment and stable economic growth under full employment, it is necessary that real wages increase at the same rate as real labour productivity (Kalecki, 1965; Pasinetti, 1974). Failing to ensure this distributional prerequisite will lead to savings-investment paths that are unstable and below full employment.

Hyperglobalization, which has been associated with generally declining wage shares, has also exposed countries to new sources of external vulnerability, including sequences of global imbalances, price shocks and boom-bust cycles of capital flows. As anticipated by Minsky (1963, 1975 and 1986), the dependence of profits on physical investment has been greatly reduced in many countries, while financial innovation has expanded at a more rapid pace than countervailing regulations.[4] Over time, speculative finance takes hold, feeding into a "normal" evolution of an economy based on the development of instruments and markets that enable ever higher levels of financial activity. While rising profits under these conditions can lead to a more widely shared sense of prosperity, the resulting apparent tranquillity accelerates the pace of financial innovation and encourages even more reckless investment decisions, leaving the system increasingly vulnerable to shocks: stability thus feeds instability.

Financialization − a process by which financial institutions and markets increase in size and influence − has been a growing trend under hyperglobalization, and is widely documented (Epstein, 2005; Duménil and Lévy, 2004; Brown et al., 2015; *TDR 2015*). Its features include, inter alia, the rise of shareholder corporate governance, a proclivity to undertake short-term financial operations, unprecedented political power of large financial institutions and weak regulation of financial markets (Stockhammer, 2004; Epstein, 2005; Vasudevan, 2016). Turner (2016b: 89) notes that financial players have generated huge amounts of money, managing assets and trading on their own account, and he stresses that, "in addition to the financial system doing more units of activity vis-à-vis the real economy, it does phenomenally more units of activity with *itself*".[5] The huge profits reaped by financiers in the years preceding the global financial crisis, and the losses that had to be absorbed by the rest of the economy in its aftermath, have led some observers to characterize this process not as financial innovation, but rather as "fraud" and "counterfeit" (Galbraith, 2014).

At the international level, Polanyi Levitt (2013: 86) refers to a "Great Financialization" taking place, involving an explosion of unfettered "movements of cross-border capital and trading in foreign currencies … greatly exceeding the requirements of trading in goods and services". She adds, "Finance-driven globalization, associated with excessive promotion of financial profits and speculation, has greatly increased the interconnections within the financial sector, with consequences for vulnerability and instability that were all too evident during the great financial crisis (GFC), and are becoming apparent once again". It has diverted resources needed for long-term investment, while increasing developing countries' vulnerability to external shocks (UNCTAD, 2011; *TDR 2015*; Akyüz 2011 and 2013), including shocks resulting from the disruption from trade (Cornford, 2012). The reverse causation also holds: globalization of trade and investment increases the scale and complexity of cross-border connections between financial institutions, thereby increasing the potential for cross-border financial contagion.

The financial liberalization processes that took place in various Latin American countries during the 1970s and 1980s, and especially the policy interventions in the aftermath of financial crises, characterized by nationalization of the huge losses incurred by private investors, are testimony to the role of governments in supporting capital accumulation and financial instability (Diaz-Alejandro, 1985; *TDR 2015*, chap. II). Indeed, States have been serving the interests of financial markets, both in opening up and absorbing losses, through the East Asian financial crisis in 1997–1998 and subsequently, exposing at the same time the heightened threat of contagion in an increasingly interconnected world economy (Baker, 2003; Sheng, 2009). Moreover, the global financial crisis of 2008–2009 exposed the gap between too-big-to-fail financial institutions, whose income derived from a mixture of service fees and asset management, and the majority of (wage-earning) households. This gap was, in part, engineered by pervasive "regulatory capture", which enabled these institutions to shape policy decisions in their favour (Claessens and Perotti, 2007; Johnson and Kwak, 2011). The aftermath of the global crisis continues to show just how powerful financial institutions have become, not only requiring unprecedentedly large interventions by central banks, but also, de facto, acquiring an effective veto over various government policies (Polanyi Levitt, 2013).[6] The adjustments imposed on other sectors of the economy, and the negative spillovers of such actions to other countries, have been huge.[7]

It follows that the dynamics of profit accumulation under financialization are associated with worsening income and wealth distribution, as well as recurrent financial crises. Also, when crises occur and governments and central banks react, policy space is likely to become even more constrained, with the risk of exacerbating income inequalities even further. The nature of each crisis undoubtedly varies depending on initial institutional conditions, the factor(s) triggering the crisis and the policy responses (Kregel, 1998 and 2014; Taylor, 1993). But a few common traits can be discerned. Foreign inflows dry up and capital flight occurs. Exchange rate depreciations sometimes follow, with an impact on domestic inflation as well as on the cost of external debt. In addition, investment is adversely affected (regardless of whether the interest rate is raised in an attempt to attract or retain capital, or if it falls as a result of monetary policy) because investors deleverage and do not expect consumption to rise in the medium term. Financial bailouts that rescue investors, both domestic and international, are not generally concerned with alleviating the strain on public finances caused by a crisis, or with providing relief to households who pay a heavy price through employment and income losses. This is compounded by a scaling down of social protection and services, and privatization of public transport and utilities. Negative multiplier effects cause further deterioration in the labour market in the form of even lower levels of employment, depressed wages and greater tendencies to informalization. At the same time, policies attempting to reignite investment and financial activity, especially through measures such as direct transfers, tax rebates and asset repurchases, tend to help those at the top of the income ladder.

The following stylized economic cycle emerges under hyperglobalization:

- Profit-makers with increasingly complex financial commitments tend to limit the growth of labour costs, and the resultant downward pressure on wages limits effective demand, thereby leading to excess capacity.

- The need to generate new sources of profits prompts financial innovations, which in turn provide expanding opportunities for profit accumulation in speculative activities.

- The pace of such financial innovations exceeds that of regulation.

- However, governments seeking rapid growth tend to support and incentivize profit-taking opportunities, thereby exacerbating inequality and reducing their capacity to avert future crises.

- These dynamics induce efforts to expand to other markets, often facilitated by the power and influence of the industrial and financial conglomerates of the major economies, given their larger size and more advanced techniques.

- Global integration offers new channels for capital accumulation through rents from financial operations, including in equity, bonds and foreign exchange markets, pushing up asset prices and allowing households to sustain credit-driven expenditure.

- The result is a pattern of "Ponzi finance" at the international level, causing massive vulnerabilities in the global financial system.

- When crises occur, the macro-financial dislocations, one-sided reliance on monetary policy, and consequent protracted weakness of aggregate demand and employment tend to worsen income distribution and exacerbate tendencies towards instability.

- Finally, under crisis situations, the burden is almost always borne by the public sector and transmitted to the domestic economy, as international investors exercise pressure to be served first.

2. Financialization in practice

This subsection considers various dimensions of the financialization process by examining three variables that can be measured using standard statistical methodologies. First, the size of the financial sector is proxied by the value of the assets of financial institutions – including "depository corporations" and "other financial corporations" – relative to GDP, as compiled by the International Monetary Fund (IMF) for its *International Financial Statistics* (IFS) database.[8,9]

Second, the magnitude of external financial operations is estimated by calculating the values of cross-border assets and liabilities captured in the International Investment Position (IIP) tables of the IMF's *Balance of Payment Statistics* (BoPS) database.[10] These measures are also calculated relative to GDP. Taken together, they highlight the degree of internationalization of financial activities. By using stocks, rather than flows, these variables identify the size of inherited positions at each point in time. While the rise of external assets and liabilities, together, suggest greater exposure of a country to events beyond its control, the risk of financial vulnerability arising from high levels of liabilities tends to be higher for countries that do not issue currency traded in the major foreign exchange markets. Third, financial concentration and power are approximated using a variable that measures the assets of the top five banks relative to GDP, so as to combine the notions of bank concentration and their systemic importance. This can indicate how critical such banks are for the functioning of an economy. The consolidated balance sheets of financial institutions are used here (as opposed to unconsolidated balance sheets, which can vary considerably, especially for international banks), because even if a bank fails as a result of its cross-border financial operations, the most traumatic impact of its failure is felt by the economy of its headquarters.[11] This indicator can also implicitly suggest how much political power is wielded by the largest banks headquartered in a country.

The "financialization" variables described above are shown in figures 5.1 and 5.2 for selected OECD countries and developing economies. A general observation for all countries is the dramatic acceleration of all indicators of financialization since the 1990s. As noted in previous *TDR*s, OECD countries show a considerably greater degree of financialization on the three measures than developing countries.[12] While the financial crisis of 2008–2009 triggered some deceleration or even weakening of financialization in some OECD countries, no such tendency is evident in developing countries.

The degree of global integration of the financial sector of selected OECD countries economies, measured

FIGURE 5.1 Degree of financialization in selected OECD countries, 1975–2015
(Per cent of GDP)

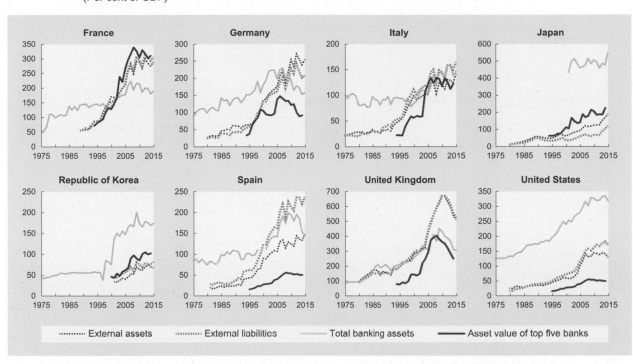

Source: UNCTAD secretariat calculations, based on IMF, *IFS* database for total banking assets; IMF, *BoPS* database for external assets and liabilities; Bankscope and WorldScope for assets of the top banks; *UNCTADstat* for GDP figures.

Note: Various categories of banking institutions and reported assets are provided in the IMF, *IFS* database. The series of banking assets shown are the most comprehensive, providing the longest series available. Thus, they may differ from country to country. The total assets of the top five banks are calculated by ranking banks, excluding central banks and development banks, from the two mentioned sources using the common methodology of consolidated balance sheets (i.e. encompassing all domestic and international activities of banks headquartered in each country).

by their external assets and liabilities, is striking. For example, the combined external assets and liabilities represented about 13 times the GDP of the United Kingdom just before the global crisis; and they accounted for between three and six times the GDP of the other developed countries by the time of the crisis, while in Japan they rose to that level after the crisis. The dramatic growth of external liabilities relative to assets in Spain (and to a lesser extent in Italy) point to the growing vulnerability of those economies over the past decade.

Large bank conglomerates are the main vehicles for integration into global financial markets and for expansion into foreign portfolio markets. Other than Spain and the United States, the value of the assets of the top five banks (consolidated) was greater than GDP in the selected OECD countries.[13] In France and the United Kingdom, the asset values of the top banks were between three-and-a-half and four times their GDP at the time of the 2008–2009 global crisis, while in Germany, Italy and Japan they were between one-and-a-half and two times their GDP. Most asset

values (except loans in domestic currency) are typically handled by trading desks in these large banks, and are valued at market prices that can fluctuate rapidly (especially foreign exchange positions, equities and bonds, and practically all financial derivatives). Indeed, most of the falls observed in the immediate post-crisis period reflect the sharp valuation effects triggered by the crisis.

The total assets of these countries' banks relative to GDP have more than doubled since the 1990s, reaching more than 200 per cent of GDP prior to the global crisis, with only Italian banks' assets below that mark, while those of Japan and the United Kingdom were more than 400 per cent of GDP. Even if banks' asset values have been considerably lower than those of total external assets and liabilities, it illustrates the asymmetric expansion of financial operations compared with other economic activities. And it is reasonable to infer that institutions conducting these financial operations exert a significant influence on macroeconomic performance as well as political decision-making in many countries.

FIGURE 5.2 Degree of financialization in selected developing and transition economies, 1990–2015
(Per cent of GDP)

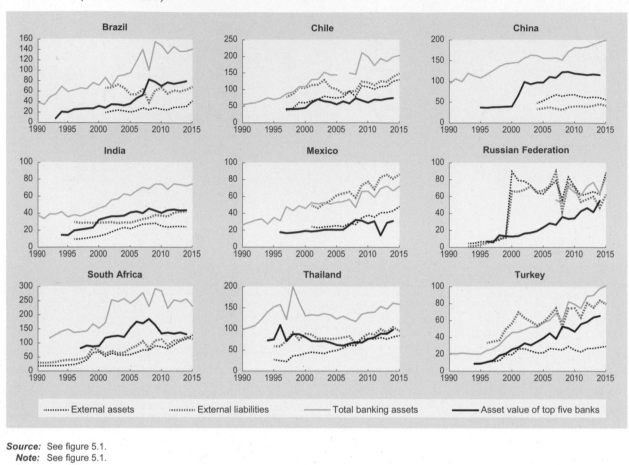

Source: See figure 5.1.
Note: See figure 5.1.

Compared with the OECD countries, the picture for the selected developing and transition economies (figure 5.2) differs only in degree. Although the available data series for some of the latter countries are shorter, all of them have experienced rapid financialization since the mid-1990s. Their international investment positions, as measured by total assets and liabilities combined, have been large, ranging from about 100 per cent of GDP for Brazil, China and Turkey, to 250 per cent of GDP for Chile and South Africa. The only exception among the selected countries is India, at around 65 per cent of GDP, but even this represents a doubling over two decades. Particularly for the countries for which the foreign liability position has risen dramatically, this indicates a considerable rise in external vulnerability, made worse by the fact that most of their external debts are not denominated in domestic currencies.[14]

Except for India and Mexico, the values of the assets of the top five banking institutions headquartered in the selected developing countries are at present within the range of 65 per cent (Turkey) and 130 per cent of GDP (South Africa);[15] and in the Russian Federation the assets increased from under 20 per cent in the mid-1990s to nearly 60 per cent of GDP in 2015. In all the countries there has been an increasing trend.

Evidence from the countries presented underlines the growing importance of financial activity vis-à-vis the real economy. It highlights the asymmetric expansion of international positions involving markets that are beyond the control of domestic public authorities, as well as greater banking concentration and the large size of their balance sheets relative to domestic income.

3. Weak financial regulation as a major enabling factor

One major reason for the processes noted above is that, even after the 2008–2009 crisis, financial regulation has remained focused primarily on prudential regulations rather than structural controls. The Basel I (1988) and Basel II (2004) prudential norms for banks were designed to equalize conditions for cross-border competition. They sought to level the international playing field among banks by harmonizing rules on capital requirements, risk management and transparency of individual banks, while ignoring systemic challenges related to bank size and their interrelations within an expanding and mutating financial sector. These shortcomings partly led to the creation of the Financial Stability Board (FSB) soon after the global financial crisis in April 2009, which was tasked with making recommendations to address the challenges arising from systemically important financial institutions.

Similarly, Basel III (2011) emphasized capital requirements at the expense of other regulatory measures, and made only limited progress in addressing systemic risks. Whether or not the new capital requirements are high enough (Admati and Hellwig, 2013), there is widespread agreement that the continued reliance on bank self-regulation, which is at the core of the Basel Accords, is not appropriate. More precisely, by maintaining the premise that banks are best placed to assess their own risk-taking, and that they should therefore themselves attribute risk-weights to the assets they use for fulfilling imposed capital requirements, the Basel Committee on Banking Supervision (BCBS) has ignored a key lesson that should have been learned from the global financial crisis. Only after observing the continued gaming of risk-weighted assets for the purpose of reducing regulatory capital requirements, have international standard setters seriously grappled with the problem of designing more stringent rules for the measurement of credit risk, and this in the teeth of fierce opposition from banks and regulators.

In any case, higher capital requirements only imperfectly address systemic risk arising from the rapid contagion and emergence of intensified liquidity risk. As observed amidst cascading fire sales during the global and other financial crises, the procyclicality and uniformity of existing accounting rules structurally reinforce herd behaviour, which adds to systemic risk.

There is widespread belief that the application of fair-value accounting by financial and non-financial institutions can aggravate financial instability and the procyclical behaviour of banks.[16] In the absence of market prices, fair value is estimated by valuation models. According to the Financial Stability Forum (FSF, 2009: 26), fair-value accounting has

> [E]ncouraged market practices that contributed to excessive risk-taking or risk-shedding activity in response to observed changes in asset prices… When the markets for many credit risk exposures became illiquid over 2007-08, credit spreads widened substantially as liquidity premia grew… Wider spreads drove down mark-to-market valuations on a range of assets… The extensive use of fair value accounting meant that, across the financial system, these declines translated into lower earnings or accumulated unrealized losses… Mark-to-market losses eroded banks' core capital, causing balance sheet leverage to rise. Banks sold assets in an attempt to offset this rise in balance sheet leverage and to address liquidity issues, but such sales only pushed credit spreads wider, causing more mark-to-market losses.

Such observations led the FSF and the BCBS to recommend modifications to this form of accounting practice. However, these modifications have not been included in the International Financial Reporting Standards – IFRS 9 – which are the accounting rules for the valuation of financial instruments adopted by the International Accounting Standards Board in 2014. As a result, accounting and regulatory rules in this area can diverge. This could further reduce the transparency of reporting by banks, and complicate the work of regulators and accountants, especially in developing countries.

The recommendations of the FSF and BCBS amount to decentralized delegation of standard-setting to local regulators. But the perception that even the revised regulatory rules for controlling credit risk are inadequate, has led to more detailed alternative proposals. For example, Persaud (2015) has proposed "mark-to-funding" accounting, which would value assets not based on real-time market fluctuations, but on principles that would take into account the maturity of the sources of funding for financing liabilities. This would contribute to reducing liquidity risks which remain significant even under the Liquidity Coverage Ratio and Net Stable Funding Ratio measures introduced under Basel III. Such risks are likely to keep growing as herd behaviour among human and computerized operators intensifies as a consequence of increasingly homogeneous information sources, algorithms and regulations.

Notwithstanding the Basel and FSB recommendations, a growing number of large and complex banks have become too large to supervise, not just for external regulators, but even internally. The necessity for restructuring the financial sector has been persuasively demonstrated after rigorous examination of the overall costs of correcting miscalculations of risks by a large and deregulated financial system (Felkerson, 2012). To avoid further costs to taxpayers, most regulators tend to converge on proposing measures for simplifying the structure of banks by separating and redistributing their various activities, including ring-fencing their retail operations. Simplifying the structure of banks' operations could also entail breaking down synthetic financial products into more transparent instruments tradable on financial markets, while subjecting more opaque and less liquid instruments traded over the counter to higher capital requirements. Regulatory approaches should allow regulators to manage the capital account in ways that are consistent with specific country needs (Reddy, 2013; *TDR 2015*). A Tobin tax has also been suggested as a measure for mitigating risks by absorbing a substantial share of the profits of short-term trading into a global fund (Shirreff, 2016).

Various experts and some regulatory insiders have also suggested breaking up big universal banks, not only because the stress experienced by such large institutions has potentially systemic implications, but also because financial concentration wields political power and breeds a culture of entitlement that lauds rent extraction and extravagant remuneration (Galbraith, 2014; Johnson and Kwak, 2011; Shirreff, 2016).

Finally, the proliferation of financial crises and the implied costs to the public have led to calls for reinstating the essential role of the public sector in ensuring the proper functioning of the financial system. A more permanent participation by governments in financial institutions, especially depository banks, could improve information flows between banks and regulators, contribute to subordinating profit motives to social objectives, and leverage financial intermediation with the aim of mobilizing technical and scientific talents for a less financialized, more equitable and sustained development process (Chandrasekhar, 2010).

C. Probing deeper into the inequality-instability nexus

It is common to trace episodes of financial crises and rising inequality within relatively separate paradigms.[17] The analysis proposed below departs from this approach in order to highlight the feedback mechanisms between worsening inequality, financial instability and non-inclusive growth.

To start with, it should be noted that financialization can worsen inequality in a variety of ways, regardless of whether a financial crisis eventually occurs. For instance, the financialization of a range of goods and services, which is often linked to privatization or inadequate delivery of public utilities and basic social services, has been an important means of extracting profits from households. Medical insurance and debts incurred because of medical expenditures, including hospitalization, provide one such example. A striking recent tendency in many countries is the explosion of student loans (discussed in chapter I), which reflects the financialization of tertiary education (Eaton et al., 2016; Messer-Davidow, 2017). This process has been described as "the takeover of social policy by financialization" (Lavinas, 2017). The expansion of digital (non-cash) modes of transaction that

involve fees for transactions imposed by banks and financial technology (fintech) companies, such as e-wallet providers, represents an extreme version of financialization which affects money as the means of exchange (Ghosh et al., 2017). All of these add to inequality because they involve payments from the general population to banks and to other financial agents that make profits from these processes. While recognizing this, the discussion that follows focuses on the relationship between financial crises and inequality.

An empirical examination of inequality and financial crises can be approached in different ways. This chapter considers systemic banking crises as defined by Laeven and Valencia (2008 and 2012).[18] Such crises are closely linked to risky behaviour by private sector financial institutions and corporations as well as households. And, as noted above, they can trigger responses such as capital flight or forced socialization of private debts, and thus exacerbate external or public sector imbalances. Banking crises frequently occur with, or predate, currency crises or sovereign debt crises, and, in extreme cases, both.

FIGURE 5.3 Inequality before and after financial crises, 1970–2015

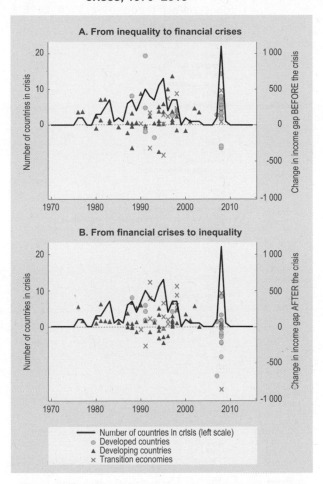

Source: UNCTAD secretariat calculations, based on Laeven and Valencia, 2012; and the *GCIP* database.

Note: Change in monthly income gap is estimated in 2005 purchasing power parity (PPP) dollars by measuring the absolute change between t-2 and t-6 (panel A) and t+6 and t+2 (panel B) – t being the year of the crisis – of the 3-year moving-average income gap between the top 10 per cent and the bottom 40 per cent.

With respect to inequality, the empirical analysis that follows focuses on personal income inequality, estimated in net terms,[19] based on survey data[20] collected in the *Global Consumption and Income Project* database (GCIP, version March 2016) (see Lahoti et al., 2014). A global analysis of within-country inequality is a complex undertaking due to the diversity of economic and social class structures across developing and developed countries. A feasible way to deal with this diversity is to look at a set of population cohorts, such as the top 10 per cent, middle 50 per cent and bottom 40 per cent income segments. A universally valid observation is that the top income segment is also the "asset-wealthiest" (Davies et al., 2011; Piketty, 2014). However, wealth data are more scarce than income data, making an empirical investigation

combining both across many countries impossible. The middle segment can be "asset-rich" to a limited extent, while the bottom segment is unequivocally "asset-poor" or "asset-deprived" across both developed and developing countries. Palma (2011) has argued that inequality is best understood by looking at the tails of the distribution, which is confirmed by cross-country research that has found relative stability in the share of the middle 50 per cent over the past few decades (Cobham et al., 2015). Accordingly, this chapter uses the Palma ratio, which captures changes in the income shares of the top 10 per cent of the population relative to the bottom 40 per cent, as well as income gaps between these two groups as indicators of inequality.[21]

Figure 5.3 shows a systematic pattern of rising inequality across a sample of 91 crisis episodes,[22] both before (5.3A) and after (5.3B) the crises. On the left-hand vertical axis in both panels, the line shows the number of financial crises each year since 1970. On the right-hand vertical axis, the position of the various symbols indicates whether the income gap between the top 10 per cent and bottom 40 per cent increased or decreased (above or below the zero line) in the run-up to financial crises (5.3A) and in their aftermath (5.3B). In the run-up to financial crises, the income gap rose in 81 per cent of the cases, and in their aftermath, it rose in 66 per cent of the cases.[23]

Developing countries in the 1980s and 1990s, transition economies in the 1990s and, most recently, developed countries, all experienced rapidly widening income gaps in the run-up to financial crises, irrespective of their initial level of inequality. However, patterns have differed across country groups in the wake of financial turmoil. Among developing economies, countries with higher levels of inequality were more likely to record declining income gaps, while among developed economies, this was more likely to occur in the most egalitarian countries. Among transition economies, most of which still featured low levels of inequality in the 1990s, financial crises erupted in the singular context of the political and economic dislocations resulting from the break-up of the former Eastern bloc.[24]

Admittedly, financial crises can have multiple causes and consequences, and rising inequality may not always be one of them, especially in smaller countries that are more vulnerable to changes in external conditions, as illustrated by a minority of cases in figure 5.3. However, beyond special cases, the stylized facts captured in that figure underscore the plausibility of feedback mechanisms between inequality and instability before and after financial crises, as discussed in more detail below.

1. Disentangling inequality in the run-up to financial crises

Figure 5.4 decomposes widening income gaps in the run-up to financial crises (i.e. those mapped in the upper half of figure 5.3A). In 85 per cent of observed cases, both top and bottom incomes increased, though very asymmetrically. Income gaps were driven by the "great escape" of the top 10 per cent, outpacing modest increases in the average income of the bottom 40 per cent, which in a few cases masked declining incomes for the lowest decile.

A supply-side narrative linking inequality and financial instability (Kumhof et al., 2015; Coibion et al., 2016), suggests that a permanent increase in the share of top incomes in national income allows more savings to be channelled to the financial sector. The subsequent expansion of credit supply to poorer households means that debt and leverage increase, leading eventually to a financial crisis. This narrative posits a simplistic role for the financial sector as a passive intermediator of savings through credit supply. It ignores the creation of private liquidity through banking leverage and the broader process of financialization described above, thus overlooking the potential for instability that arises out of risky financial innovations in response to demand from asset-wealthy product classes (e.g. asset-backed securities or structured derivative products). As a corollary, this narrative further overstates the role of low-income households in causing the crisis (Lysandrou, 2011a and 2011b).[25]

However, as alluded to in Laeven and Valencia's description of systemic banking crises, it is the financial strategies of corporations and financial institutions that constitute the critical mechanism underlying financial instability. While destabilizing financial processes are always country- and crisis-specific, they are very often rooted in the quest for higher financial yields from asset-wealthy classes; this was the case in the 2008–2009 financial crisis in the United States (Goda and Lysandrou, 2014). In countries hit by the Asian financial crisis in 1997–1998, speculative practices by large domestic and foreign investors similarly played a key role. In

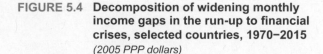

FIGURE 5.4 Decomposition of widening monthly income gaps in the run-up to financial crises, selected countries, 1970–2015
(2005 PPP dollars)

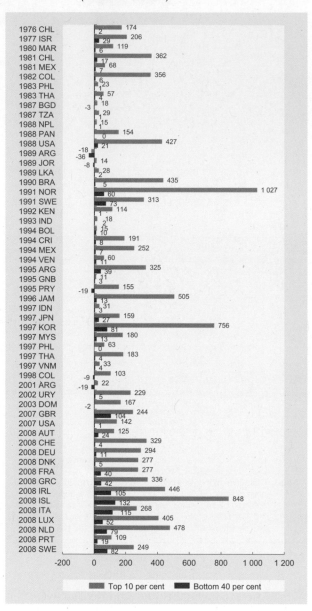

Source: UNCTAD secretariat calculations, based on Laeven and Valencia, 2012; and the *GCIP* database.
Note: Changes are measured as the difference between the 3-year centred moving average at t-2 and t-6, t being the year of the crisis. Crises are presented in chronological order with abbreviations for the selected countries based on the ISO Alpha-3 country codes, and the years refer to the year of crisis in the respective countries.

the Republic of Korea, for example, the volume of private debt barely increased in the run-up to the crisis (figure 5.5). Yet creeping financialization in this country enabled the rise of short-term operations of large industrial and financial conglomerates to finance long-term activities, thus putting the entire economy at risk (Lee, 2011). Cross-border speculative

FIGURE 5.5 Private debt and inequality in the run-up to financial crises, 1970–2015

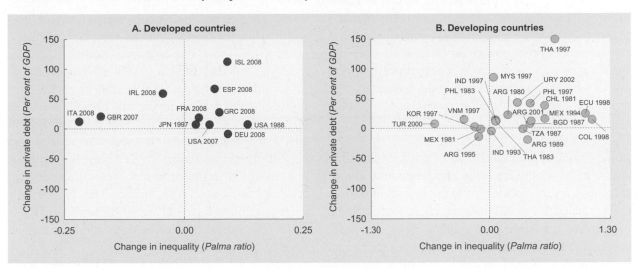

Source: UNCTAD secretariat calculations, based on Laeven and Valencia, 2012; the *GCIP* database; and the United Nations *Global Policy Model* (*GPM*)
database (https://www.un.org/development/desa/dpad/publication/united-nations-global-policy-model/).
Note: See note to figure 5.4.

operations that exacerbated currency and maturity mismatches also played a destabilizing role in other Asian countries (Chandrasekhar and Ghosh, 2013). But the spectacular rise of private debt in countries such as Thailand (Phongpaichit and Baker, 2007) and Malaysia (Jomo, 2007) may be traced back to external as well as domestic financial liberalization in a context of growing inequality. Meanwhile, Mexico suffered from excessive private debt build-up in the decade preceding its 1994 financial crisis (Gil-Diaz, 1998; Griffith-Jones, 2001), which then exploded as a balance-of-payments crisis (Kregel, 1998).

The main factor at work in all of these cases was the ability of the financial sector to engineer innovations aimed at exploiting weak regulations and loopholes to increase the profitability of financial operations on a global scale, irrespective of the robustness of domestic demand in the real sector or the viability of public sector finances. Furthermore, the political balance of power between different social classes and economic interests (e.g. trade unions, industrialists, bankers and exporters) is central to determining the direction of public policies, including for social protection, corporate taxation, financial, trade and other regulations. Political power also influences which incomes and sources of demand will be strengthened and the financial vulnerabilities that are exposed as a consequence. Outcomes are further influenced by incentives provided by the global trade and financial systems and a country's position, and strategies

within it, as well as by the general inclination for countries to pursue debt-led and export-led growth (Stockhammer, 2011; Goda et al., 2014). These accumulation regimes pose significant threats to equity and financial stability, and they also generate international coordination challenges which existing domestic political coalitions and international governance arrangements have failed to address.

As is widely acknowledged, financial cycles and crises are closely linked to private leverage (Borio, 2012; Schularick and Taylor, 2012). Moreover, changes in private debt as a share of GDP are positively correlated with increases in income inequality (figure 5.5 northeastern quadrants).[26] A variety of cases help explain the postulated correlation in developed countries.

In Ireland, Italy and the United Kingdom, relative inequality may have declined, but the income gap rose and household indebtedness increased considerably, so that the resulting vulnerability became a major trigger of the financial crisis. Only Germany experienced a simultaneous rise in inequality (in relative and absolute terms) and a decline in private debt prior to the crash of many of its banks in 2008. This outcome may have resulted from its export-led growth regime, which sustained employment creation through the compression of unit labour costs relative to trading partners in the euro zone and elsewhere. Whether the limitations of this regime lie in unsustainable asymmetries of competitiveness and inflation within a common currency area (Flassbeck and Lapavitsas, 2013; Flassbeck, 2007), or in a continuing weakening of regional aggregate demand (Storm, 2016), the evidence is consistent with a co-movement of inequality and financial instability for the euro zone as a whole. These processes were induced by policy choices within the broader institutional architecture of the euro zone (Goodhart, 2007; Eatwell, 2012; Irvin and Izurieta, 2011).

Policy-induced inequalities and the macro-financial structures resulting from the compression of labour incomes were also at the root of the global imbalances that preceded the global financial crisis. In the context of growing financialization and openness (figures 5.1 and 5.2), inequality that depressed domestic demand led to an unsustainable combination of debt-led and export-driven growth strategies feeding one another in a polarizing and destabilizing process. At one end, surplus countries pursuing export-led growth compressed wage incomes to gain a competitive edge in international markets, thus increasing industrial profits and accumulation at the top. At the other end, the recycling of these profits abroad stimulated domestic asset inflation in deficit countries as well as financial rents accruing to asset-rich classes in surplus and deficit countries alike, which in turn fed into more financial engineering and instability (Akyüz, 2012; Cripps et al., 2011; Patnaik, 2010).

The impact of policy choices is also marked in developing countries, which showed a similar common pattern of private debt rising along with inequality (figure 5.5B), despite apparent differences across countries, regions and time periods. This resulted in diverse processes of financial destabilization. In the early 1980s, when the global drive for financial liberalization and openness was just beginning, financial excesses in the run-up to crises in Latin American countries such as Argentina, Chile, Colombia and Mexico were generally characterized by smaller increases in private debt levels compared to later crises in the same region in the 1990s and 2000s. In Asia, a number of countries also experienced financial instability in earlier decades, but the most significant private debt increases occurred in countries such as Malaysia, the Philippines and Thailand prior to the Asian financial crisis in 1997, which propagated contagious destabilization across the region and beyond (Delhaise and Beckerling, 1998).

By contrast, the tight control of the Chinese Government over its financial sector throughout the 1990s reduced the scope for rapid increases in private debt.[27] A decade later, with export-led growth in full throttle, record profits and current account surpluses were being registered. Unlike German surpluses, however, Chinese surpluses recycled abroad were mostly invested in safe United States Treasury bonds rather than in speculative financial products. This limited the financial spillover effects of the subprime crisis on the Chinese economy. However, subsequent attempts to foster growth have been associated with very dramatic increases in debt levels of all the major players in the economy, generating some of the risks associated with financialization despite a more controlled financial sector (figure 5.2). This is evident in the speculation in domestic housing and asset markets (Galbraith, 2012).

2. Disentangling inequality in the aftermath of financial crises

As noted above, income gaps between the top 10 per cent and the bottom 40 per cent widened in two out of every three observed financial crisis episodes. Decomposing such income gaps (i.e. those mapped in the upper half of figure 5.3B), reveals that they were driven by rising incomes for the top earners, though to a much lesser extent than in the run-up to a crisis (figure 5.6). More importantly, in many instances incomes for those at the bottom of the income ladder fell or stagnated. However, during post-crisis periods, characterized by rising unemployment and weak demand, such stagnation generally masked an income decline for the first and second income deciles that encompass the poorest segments of society. Furthermore, bottom incomes also declined in the overwhelming majority of crisis episodes that were also characterized by sharp falls in top incomes.

Even when income inequality does not worsen, the lowest income earners bear the brunt of painful market adjustments and economic policies adopted in response to financial crises. Financial instability and subsequent economic disruptions tend to have regressive distributional consequences that are compounded by the magnitude of the aggregate cost imposed on the economy. Figure 5.7 shows a "dynamic" GDP gap between its actual rate each year after a financial crisis and the trend growth prevailing before the crisis. Among more financialized developed economies all, without exception, endured lasting losses in GDP dynamism following financial

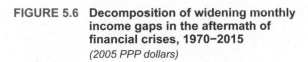

FIGURE 5.6 **Decomposition of widening monthly income gaps in the aftermath of financial crises, 1970–2015**

(2005 PPP dollars)

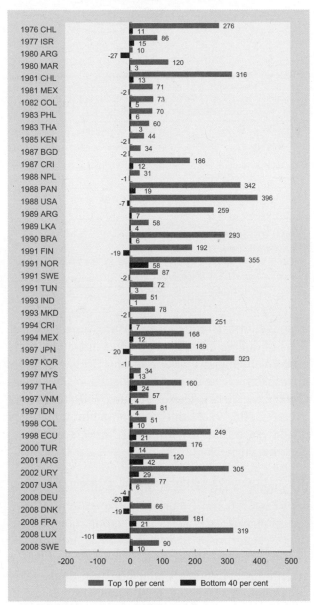

Source: UNCTAD secretariat calculations, based on Laeven and Valencia, 2012; and the *GCIP* database.

Note: Changes are measured as the difference between the 3-year centred moving-average at t+6 and t+2, t being the year of the crisis. Regarding countries and years listed, see note to figure 5.4.

This made it even harder for economies individually to export their way out of recession, as only a few "winners" with favourable initial conditions could succeed. Most countries seeking export-led recovery aimed to improve competitiveness and attract foreign capital by means of labour market flexibilization and protracted austerity measures. In these countries, wage compression and fiscal restraint mostly led to income losses among those at the bottom of the ladder without corresponding net export gains, resulting in declining GDP and employment. For example, Greece, Ireland and Spain ended up permanently losing around 30 per cent or more of their trend GDP growth as inequality worsened noticeably.

Among the selected developing countries, about half recorded large cumulative losses following the financial crises that erupted over the course of the last 40 years (figure 5.7). In Asia, countries such as Indonesia, Malaysia, the Republic of Korea and Thailand experienced the sharpest GDP losses in the decade following the Asian financial crisis. China, the Philippines and Viet Nam fared better and recovered within less than a decade, largely owing to more successful export-led strategies, and, in the cases of China and Viet Nam, a more effective government response, particularly in maintaining and influencing investment (Abbot and Tarp, 2011). However, in most countries, deleterious changes in patterns of economic growth, including rising savings and declining private investment and public expenditure had negative effects on employment, poverty and inequality (Chandrasekhar, 2007; Patnaik, 2007).

In Latin America, market adjustments and economic policies induced by crisis episodes in the early 1980s in countries such as Chile, Colombia, Ecuador, Mexico and Uruguay unfolded in the challenging international context of high interest rates and sharp depreciations of national currencies. Governments responded by absorbing private sector liabilities denominated in foreign currency. The consequent severe deterioration of public finances led to steep falls in government spending (Diaz-Alejandro, 1985; Younger, 1993). All in all, the adjustments were costlier than for most subsequent crisis episodes in the region.

crises; and none were able to return to their pre-crisis trend even a decade later. As most of these crisis episodes occurred during the global financial crisis, the sluggishness of economic recovery was exacerbated by simultaneous declines in GDP in the largest developed economies. Thus, negative feedback loops between major developed economies (e.g. France, Germany, the United Kingdom and the United States) and the rest of the world, created a deflationary bias.

Of 37 crisis episodes examined using the United Nations *Global Policy Model* database, only two resulted in no apparent GDP loss: India in 1993 and Brazil in 1994. In both countries, drastic adjustments created conditions conducive to growth recovery,

FIGURE 5.7 GDP gap following financial crises in selected countries, 1970–2015

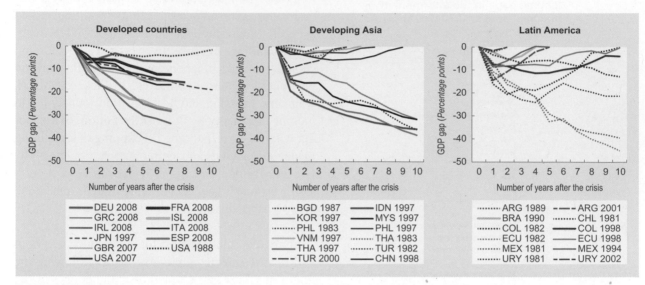

Source: UNCTAD secretariat calculations, based on Laeven and Valencia, 2012; and the United Nations *GPM* database.
Note: The pre-crisis trend is defined as the average growth rate of GDP over the 10 years preceding a crisis. Regarding countries and years listed, see note to figure 5.4.

but with increases in the Palma ratio in India, and worsening conditions for the middle-class in Brazil because of falling employment in the public sector and in small and medium-sized enterprises (SMEs).

The aggregate costs of financial crises in terms of GDP result partly from inevitable dislocation and a rupture with unsustainable growth patterns which preceded the crises, but also from discretionary decisions that reflect the political balance of power across all relevant institutions, including central banks. Particularly in economies with relatively developed financial sectors and high levels of speculative activity, sharp asset deflation is a common outcome that policy makers need to address. In other economies with less sophisticated portfolio markets, large firms, and at times governments, have assumed unsustainable burdens of (mostly external) debt. Balance sheet failures present policymakers with a further dilemma: allowing insolvencies could exacerbate the negative effects on employment and stability.[28]

In most past episodes of crisis, central banks actively sought to ensure the continued access to liquidity of privileged actors, including banks and other financial institutions, in addition to providing direct bailouts and recapitalization. Typically, private debts ended up being nationalized, leaving the richest segment of the population relatively untouched (*TDR 2015*). Policy reactions in the wake of the global financial crisis followed a similar pattern (Wray, 2012), with

unconventional monetary measures injecting trillions of dollars of public resources into supposedly efficient financial markets in an effort to reignite growth through an artificial reinflation of asset prices (Felkerson, 2012). These measures left the issue of excessive financial concentration and rents largely unaddressed, thereby allowing financialization to continue unchecked.

In general, apart from some measures adopted to avoid widespread financial collapse, few, if any, pressures were exerted on the favoured institutions (banks, enterprises and well-to-do households) to re-engage in the real economy by extending credit, generating employment and boosting demand. In addition, in many cases, public finances were over-stretched, because of either direct bailout programmes and rising public debt-servicing or the negative shock to tax revenues. This forced widespread cuts in public spending, particularly in areas that tend to have greater multiplier effects, such as social welfare programmes and infrastructure development.

Few governments have been able to avoid the pressures for fiscal austerity or resist its proponents' assurances that large capital inflows into the economy would follow. However, those assurances run against growing evidence that the stagnation resulting from such fiscal stringency discourages more investment. Indeed, only a few countries resorted to expansionary fiscal policies to counter the recessionary effects

FIGURE 5.8 Public expenditure gap and inequality following financial crises, 1970–2015

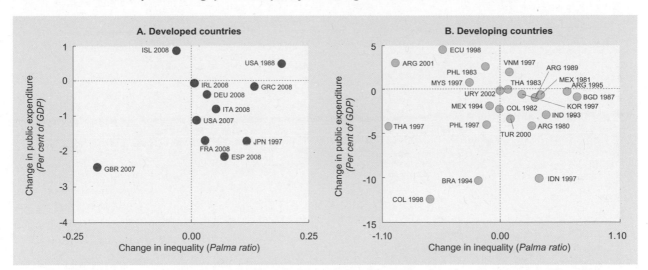

Source: UNCTAD secretariat calculations, based on Laeven and Valencia, 2012; the *GCIP* database; and the United Nations *GPM* database.
Note: The change in government expenditure (GE) is measured as the difference between the 10-year average of GE before crises and the 7-year average of GE after crises (data runs up to 2015, the 7-year horizon is chosen to include recent crisis episodes in developed countries). The change in the Palma ratio is measured as the difference between the 3-year centred moving-average at t+6 and t+2, t being the year of the crisis. Regarding countries and years shown, see note to figure 5.4.

of financial turmoil (figure 5.8). One example is Argentina, which introduced fiscal and redistributive policies in support of employment creation following its financial crisis of 2001.[29] Similarly, policymakers in Iceland restricted capital outflows, and ensured that the banks under government control helped to sustain the real economy, while the cuts in public expenditure required for accession to the European Union were postponed.

Following the global financial crisis, most developed countries (figure 5.8A) which, earlier, had opted for limited fiscal stimulus, reverted to severe austerity programmes to restore financial credibility. But cuts in social protection and public sector jobs only exacerbated deflationary effects, restricting employment generation and contributing to worsening inequality in most countries (south-eastern quadrant of the figure).[30] Despite claims to the contrary, the outcome has been further financialization, a continuing concentration and power of "too-big-to-fail" financial institutions, even more vulnerable households and financially stressed public sector balances weakened by sluggish revenue.

Employment declined in the hardest-hit euro-zone countries, such as Greece, Ireland and Spain, which were unable to devalue their currency or adopt an expansionary fiscal stance (figure 5.9). The United States in 1988 and Germany in 2008 were the only

FIGURE 5.9 Employment gaps following financial crises, developed countries,1970–2015

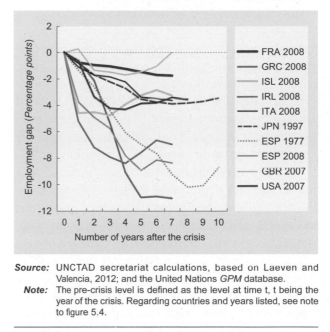

Source: UNCTAD secretariat calculations, based on Laeven and Valencia, 2012; and the United Nations *GPM* database.
Note: The pre-crisis level is defined as the level at time t, t being the year of the crisis. Regarding countries and years listed, see note to figure 5.4.

countries that avoided severe declines in employment. In the United States, the continued entry of women into the labour force in a context of rising income inequality and easing credit conditions for consumers helped to sustain employment. In the case of Germany, programmes to retain most of the labour force, even if only in part-time employment,

FIGURE 5.10 Private debt and inequality following financial crises, 1970–2015

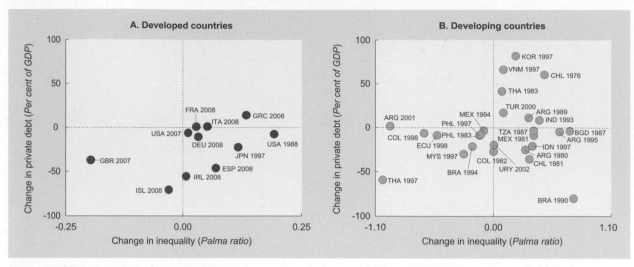

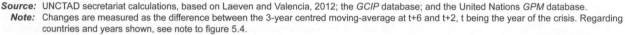

Source: UNCTAD secretariat calculations, based on Laeven and Valencia, 2012; the *GCIP* database; and the United Nations *GPM* database.
Note: Changes are measured as the difference between the 3-year centred moving-average at t+6 and t+2, t being the year of the crisis. Regarding countries and years shown, see note to figure 5.4.

combined with export-promotion measures, allowed a rapid recovery, albeit at the expense of economic activity and employment in other euro-zone countries (Flassbeck and Lapavitsas, 2013). In both countries, however, inequality continued to rise.

Among developing countries (figure 5.8B), the pattern of changes in public expenditure and inequality varied much more. Even so, as in developed countries, most developing countries contained or reduced public expenditure and sold State assets following their respective crises. For the most part, financially constrained governments opted for cutting public expenditure, given the threat of capital flight and continuing currency depreciation pressures. Privatization did not necessarily improve budgetary positions, however, and in many countries the receipts were used to pay external creditors. The combined impact of fiscal austerity and privatization hurt the most vulnerable groups (Stiglitz, 2003; ILO, 2014), which explains the observed rising inequality in most cases (south-eastern quadrant). In Indonesia, which experienced the largest GDP loss in the wake of the 1997–1998 Asian financial crisis, monetary and fiscal tightening recommended by the IMF precipitated a devastating liquidity crisis and sharpened economic contraction. Forced to rescue large corporate and financial groups and nationalize their debt to prevent systemic collapse, the Government let public debt rise, from $54 billion in 1997 to $134 billion in 2001, including $74 billion paid to international creditors.

In 2002, debt servicing was more than three times as large as the salaries of the entire civil service and military personnel, while the Government opted to increase taxes, fuel and electricity prices, thus hurting the poor disproportionally (Ramli and Nuryadin, 2007). In post-1997 Republic of Korea, the adjustments of large export firms and banks led to massive worker layoffs and a lasting deterioration in working conditions, in breach of the prevailing "developmental" social compact; this was soon followed by rising poverty and inequality (Kyung-Sup, 2007).

Excessively tight monetary policies imposed by the IMF on several crisis-hit countries through the conditionalities attached to its lending held back economic recovery and polarized income distribution even further. This was the case in the early 1980s in countries such as Chile, Mexico and the Philippines (*TDRs* 1986 and 1993).

The factors that trigger a financial crisis in the first place, as well as the policy responses to the crisis, determine when and to what extent private sector debt rises again. A general pattern can be discerned from figure 5.10. Most developed countries in the sample (figure 5.10A) experienced crises after a period of excessive or rising household debt. But their policy response mainly supported financial institutions and large corporations (and indirectly the asset-wealthy households owning them), with little regard for the needs of the middle class and the more vulnerable elements of society who would have benefited from debt restructuring. The expectation that the recovery of banks and portfolio markets would reignite household spending based on credit expansion proved unfounded, as household deleveraging in many of these countries continued and private investors in productive sectors maintained a wait-and-see attitude.[31] If the experience of Japan from the 1990s onwards is any indication, there are significant risks ahead for other developed countries with respect to the unresolved problems of income distribution and weak aggregate demand.

The picture for developing countries (figure 5.10B) reflects different combinations of private sector behaviour and policies. In some countries (e.g. Chile in 1976 and Argentina in 1989), where private

sector debt continued to increase after financial crises, policies supporting debt-driven expenditure contributed to triggering new financial crises a few years later (in 1981 and 1995, respectively). In other countries (figure 5.10B, north-eastern quadrant), currency devaluation led to a rise in the value of debts denominated in foreign currency, in many instances accompanied by policies aimed at gaining competitiveness to support export-led strategies. In a few other countries, rising private debt may simply have reflected the inability to meet debt repayment schedules, necessitating rescheduling. The majority of developing countries, lacking a successful export model, displayed a pattern of private sector deleveraging, in many cases accompanied by increasing inequality along a path of weakened economic growth (south-eastern quadrant).[32]

D. Conclusion: Taming finance

The theoretical insights and empirical examination of financialization processes, financial crises and inequality reveal a complex and varied picture. However, a few clear lessons emerge.

First, the dynamics of hyperglobalization tend to enlarge the financial sector, stimulate financial innovations and cross-border operations.

Second, such expansion of finance, within each economy and across the global economy, adversely influences income distribution. Growth through such expansion tends to be polarizing in a cumulative manner, with versatile asset management and exuberant wealth creation at the top of the distribution scale, but oppressive debt burdens and restricted employment, income generation and social development at the bottom.

Third, financial innovations tend to develop at a faster pace than regulations, particularly where the latter depend on resource-constrained public agencies.[33] Further, since successful financial innovations depend heavily on making markets, which in turn requires volume,[34] they tend to be most lucrative when implemented by larger actors. This adds to concentration tendencies in the financial sector.

Fourth, the greater concentration into larger institutions and the weight of the largest operators, in turn,

threaten wider economic stability. The threat of collapse, together with its contagion across a broad swath of economic activities, provides finance with a unique influence over policymakers. The ability of finance to constrain policy space grows commensurately with its size relative to that of the real economy, as well as to the size of the top financial institutions relative to the rest.

Fifth, the influence of major financial institutions on government institutions is enhanced by their ability to expand beyond national borders. At the same time, attempts to regulate finance at the global level are limited by two factors. First, national regulators and standard setters need sufficient autonomy in order to take into account country-specific conditions. However, this entails the risk that the regulations considered will not be able to keep pace with financial innovators operating internationally. Second, global regulations are expected to conform to the conventional thinking of how finance works and what kinds of discipline should be imposed on it. Unfortunately, despite the wake-up call from the most recent financial crisis, the recognition that finance is inherently unstable is still not a globally accepted idea. As a result, international financial regulations continue to be subject to the flawed concepts of modern financial theory and behavioural finance which postulate that asset price arbitrage and utility maximization should guide adjustments in a world of free capital movements. Indeed, the influence of this ideology reaches beyond the financial sector, for example in the design of new accounting standards for small enterprises or governments (e.g. International Public Sector Accounting Standards or IPSAS), as if it were natural, and even desirable, for the accounting practices of all economic organizations in a country to give priority to meeting the information needs of financial investors (Baud and Chiapello, 2017; Chiapello, 2016).

Sixth, the *prima facie* expectation that financial crises may serve to contain the power of finance and help to reverse the underlying tendency to inequality does not stand scrutiny. Although some instances of wealth losses and therefore falls in asset values relative to aggregate income can be observed, and despite concerns about unregulated finance among experts and the public, what eventually seems to prevail is the intent to return the financial system to its pre-crisis modus operandi. Thus, policy actions are tending to contribute to greater concentration, and to reinforcing the overarching role of finance. As a result, governments have become more constrained than in the preceding booms. The real economy is not being served by finance; quite the opposite. Employment and wages are being negatively affected, often in a permanent manner. The poor are bearing the greatest brunt of market adjustments and regressive economic policies; cumulative causation is taking effect, and recovery for those at the bottom of the income ladder is generally not as fast as for those at the top. The result is worsening inequality.

Seventh, empirical evidence suggests that when there is a rising trend in income inequality, financial crises become more frequent and widespread. This is because of the relative insufficiency of demand that results from incomes of those at the bottom of the ladder (and in much of the middle) lagging behind aggregate income growth. As a result, profit-makers tend to divert investment into financial innovation that seeks new forms of rent extraction. Regressive income distribution promoted by neoliberal policies therefore exercises a perverse incentive to undertake more financial risk, and risk-taking ventures tend to spread across the global economy. Thus, feedbacks from financial instability in one part of the world frequently transmit to other parts.

These conclusions broadly capture the current state of the global financial system. A continuation of financialization processes, along with deepening inequality, increases the likelihood of financial crises recurring. For these trends to change in a more inclusive and sustainable direction, policy action is required on various fronts.

Some essential directions of the policies needed to effect change are sketched here, while more comprehensive policy recommendations are drawn in the last chapter of this *Report*.

- Policies need to influence primary income distribution in order to contain the rising share of profits in national income and its translation into unequal financial wealth. This can be done through proactive labour and employment policies, including the introduction of minimum wages tied to acceptable living standards, along with aggregate wage increases linked to average productivity growth.[35] Government action should contribute to employment, and should support social and infrastructure spending.

- Redistributive policies should include progressive taxes and transfers (Kohler, 2015). The net effect of both rising government tax revenue and social spending can have strong multiplier effects on aggregate demand, employment and technical progress.

- The economic and political power of finance needs to be contained. The financial system should be smaller and less leveraged, and it should focus more on meeting the credit needs of the real economy (Bair, 2014; Wolf, 2015). Institutions that are "too big to fail" and "too big to prosecute" pose a threat to stable and inclusive societies. Therefore policymakers need to consider breaking up the banks and imposing unlimited liability on partners in investment banks (Shirreff, 2016). More generally, smarter regulations are needed (Persaud, 2015).

- Publicly owned banks can help to subordinate profit motives to social motives and encourage credit for employment creation and investment. They can also help improve information flows that are needed to advance regulations that keep pace with innovations.

- Capital controls (*TDR 2015*; Reddy, 2013) need to be considered where required at the national level. But these should be combined with other reforms to influence the structure, size and governance of banks operating internationally. ◼

Notes

1   See Duménil and Lévy, 2001; Crotty, 2003; Epstein, 2005; Krippner, 2005; and this *TDR*, chapter VI.

2   Examples of this approach include Crotty, 2003; Foster and McChesney, 2012; Lapavitsas, 2013; Patnaik, 2003; Smith, 2011.

3   Examples of this approach include, Galbraith, 2012 and 2014; Kindleberger, 2000; Plender, 2015; Turner, 2016a and 2016b; Smith, 2011; Stiglitz, 2012; Taylor, 2010.

4   Although Minsky considered regulation and institutional strength to be essential for controlling financial instability, he was a cautious observer of psychological motives and institutional constraints (see also Galbraith (Sr.), 1994; Shiller, 2005; Turner 2016a). According to Minsky (1986: 220), one of the factors for the excessively rapid pace of financial inventions is the fact that "successful innovators are rewarded by fortunes and flattered by imitators". Investors innovate to circumvent regulations and expand their profit opportunities, assuming ever greater risks and expecting to be bailed out if they fail.

5   Some experts (Turner, 2016a; D'Arista, 2009) have observed that large financial profits are to a great extent the result of "alchemy" and of developments such as cross-subsidies between trading operations and retail banking, high leverage, public sector support and deposit warranties (see also Bair, 2014; Haldane, 2014; Kay, 2015; King, 2016).

6   Sheila Bair, Chair of the Federal Deposit Insurance Corporation of the United States from 2006 to 2011, when asked at a panel discussion on financial regulation whether banks were, in effect, driving the reform process, agreed that they indeed seemed to be doing so (Bair, 2014: 133). See also Johnson and Kwak, 2011; Plender, 2015; Shirreff, 2016; Smith, 2011; House of Commons Treasury Committee, 2010.

7   See UNCTAD (2012) for a succinct analysis of the global spillovers from the quantitative easing experiments undertaken by major central banks in the aftermath of the 2008–2009 crisis. These affected market conditions (correlation across asset classes) and portfolio behaviour (risk-on/risk-off, herd behaviour), and further limited the effectiveness of domestic policies.

8   Results for different countries are not necessarily comparable because data availability is not uniform (see, for example, IMF, 2008 and 2016).

9   Some authors have instead used the value added of financial enterprises, usually presented in the institutional accounts that are part of the standards of national accounting. However, those authors nevertheless note some limitations of this as a comprehensive indicator of financialization (for example, Turner, 2016b; Polanyi-Levitt, 2013). Haldane (2010) provides a comprehensive discussion about the limitations of using value added of financial corporations to measure the size of the financial sector. Others have emphasized the increasing "financialization of the non-financial corporate sector" (Milberg and Winkler, 2010), as well as the pervasive propagation of financialization to broader sectors of government, society and the environment (Brown et al., 2015).

10   Complementary, additional information is drawn from the locational banking statistics produced by the Bank for International Settlements.

11   According to Charles Goodhart (House of Commons Treasury Committee, 2010: Ev.2), what makes large financial institutions "too important to fail" is the fact that while they are "international in life they become national in death".

12   Data availability for most developed countries is more complete than for developing countries, which makes comparisons difficult. For example, most developing countries do not provide all components for "other financial corporations", and only a few of them provide all components for the "depository corporations" or report "claims on non-bank financial institutions". On the other hand, for countries in the euro area, there are breaks in the series for "reserves in the central bank" and for "foreign assets" due to institutional changes that accompanied the creation of the euro. But none of these differences can account for the great disparity in levels between the two groups of economies.

13   Non-banking financial institutions and shadow banking institutions are not included in the ranking of the top five banks. However, in countries such as the United States, the largest financial institutions are not necessarily banks, as illustrated by the rise of BlackRock, a hedge fund that had $5 trillion of total assets under management in 2017, exceeding those of the largest American banks (see, for example, Schatzker, 2017).

14   Most of the developing economies' banks have had large exposure to liabilities incurred in foreign currency, at around 90 per cent of the total, on average, and this has not changed significantly in the past few years (see BIS, *Locational Banking Statistics* database).

15   Low figures in some developing countries, such as India, can be attributed to the continued existence of many informal financial operations (Ghosh et al., 2012).

16   Fair value in its basic form is defined as the amount for which an asset can be exchanged or a liability settled between knowledgeable, willing partners in an arm's-length transaction. Fair value accounting applies to assets and liabilities other than those, such as simple debt instruments, held solely for the

purpose of collecting contractual cash flows (which are measured at amortized cost).

17 See Kumhof et al. (2015) for a review of mainstream literature, and section C (introductory paragraph) and C.1 (above) for a discussion of authors who link both phenomena.

18 According to Laeven and Valencia (2008), "In a systemic banking crisis, a country's corporate and financial sectors experience a large number of defaults and financial institutions and corporations face great difficulties repaying contracts on time. As a result, non-performing loans increase sharply and most of the aggregate banking system capital is exhausted. This situation may be accompanied by depressed asset prices (such as equity and real estate prices) on the heels of run-ups before the crisis, sharp increases in real interest rates, and a slowdown or reversal in capital flows. In some cases, the crisis is triggered by depositor runs on banks, though in most cases it is a general realization that systemically important financial institutions are in distress."

19 *Net (or disposable) income* is measured after direct taxes on income (from labour or capital) and direct transfers (such as social protection), which are generally intended to reduce *market (or gross) income* inequality. Policy measures, such as indirect subsidies (e.g. for green energy) or indirect taxes (e.g. regressive value-added taxes on consumption, a progressive Tobin tax on financial transactions) influence *post-fiscal income*, while in-kind transfers (e.g. public services for education or health) determine *final income* (Kohler, 2015).

20 Personal income inequality can be estimated using two different sources of information, though both have limitations. *Survey-based income inequality data* are available for a large number of countries, and provide estimates of net incomes (after tax and redistribution) or household consumption. They tend to underestimate inequality because top incomes are underrepresented in samples and top-coded in surveys; that is, instead of reporting the precise level of top incomes, surveys tend to assign them to a single top category of, for example, more than $1 million (Alvaredo, 2010). Non-truncated *fiscal data* from the *World Wealth and Income Database* (http://wid.world) are available for a more limited number of developed and developing countries, but that database does not yet include any transition economy. It provides a more accurate picture of income distribution at the top (before tax), but has not been able to tackle the problem of underreporting of income to tax authorities and tax evasion, which has grown rapidly over the past few decades (Palan et al., 2009; Zucman, 2013; Alstadsaeter et al., 2017). Consequently, most available data tend to underestimate the real extent of income and wealth inequality.

21 Relative measures such as the Palma ratio or income gaps between top and bottom average incomes offer the advantage of highlighting changes among the income groups that historically fluctuate the most and exacerbate income disparities, whereas Gini indices are more synthetic and do not provide such information.

22 Among the 147 episodes identified by Laeven and Valencia (2012), 56 were not backed by sufficient original sources for income inequality estimates in the *GCIP* database (Lahoti et al., 2014). Despite attempts to improve the quality and comparability of income distribution data (e.g. Conceição and Galbraith, 2000; Solt, 2009; Lahoti et al., 2014), a fundamental limitation is that many developing countries started to conduct income surveys only in the 1980s, or even later. Consequently, changes in inequality cannot be investigated around all financial crises since the 1970s.

23 Inequality between income segments can be measured in absolute terms (income gap in monetary terms) or in relative terms (the ratios between income shares, such as the Palma ratio). The former option is used in figure 5.3. Using the latter leads to a slightly lower proportion of episodes of rising inequality in the run-up to financial crises (75 per cent instead of 85 per cent), because the income gap may increase even if the ratio of income shares decreases, depending on initial income levels. However, the share remains unchanged in the aftermath of financial crises (65 per cent).

24 Owing to the prevalence of singular political circumstances and unusually deep economic recession affecting all income segments in the transition economies during their transformation to market-driven models, along with data limitations (see footnote 20), financial crisis episodes in these economies are not considered in the rest of the empirical analysis.

25 Labelling the recent global financial crisis as a subprime crisis misleadingly shifts the blame for the crisis to the demands of asset-poor households in the United States for basic financial intermediation to match their expenditure patterns (such as house mortgages backed by stagnating or declining future income).

26 In charts produced using data from the United Nations *GPM* database, which is limited to 40 countries, the sample of crisis episodes is reduced further compared to charts based on data from Laeven and Valencia, 2012 and the GCIP, 2016.

27 Besides China, declining private debt is only observed in a few peculiar cases in the run-up to financial crises. Brazil in 1994 and Argentina in 1995 were just exiting a previous financial crisis (in 1990 and 1989, respectively), and Argentina in 1989 had just gone through several economic recessions, which explains why these countries experienced private deleveraging.

28 See Cornford (2016) for a critical review of approaches to assessing macroeconomic costs of financial crises, especially the most recent approaches proposed by the BIS.

29 In post-2001 Argentina, the Program for Unemployed Male and Female Heads of Households (Plan Jefes y Jefas de Hogar Desocupados) represents a clear example of a successful public intervention in an expansionary direction (Kostzer, 2008). By contrast, Ecuador post-1999, which is also an outlier in the north-west quadrant of figure 5.8, did not adopt a fiscally expansionary redistributive policy. There was a significant increase in public sector investment relative to the previous 10 years of financial instability and weak economic performance, but that increase was mostly driven by windfall gains in the oil-exporting sector. And while inequality measured by the Palma ratio decreased, the income gap actually increased (see figure 5.6).

30 Recalling footnotes 19 and 20, in the United Kingdom, the observed decline in net income inequality can be explained by a rise in the income tax threshold by 1,000 to 11,000 pounds sterling in early 2010, which reduced direct taxes on poorer households, as reflected in the measure of inequality used in figure 5.8. By contrast, austerity measures implemented subsequently, especially the reduction of in-kind transfers, are only imperfectly reflected in this measure. Importantly, wealth inequality remains above its pre-crisis level.

31 Greece may be considered a weak exception to this general pattern, partly because its crisis was not primarily triggered by private domestic debt, and partly because the slow pace of recovery of private sector incomes under a protracted recession has induced greater borrowing in order to maintain spending.

32 Argentina (2001) was an exception to this pattern, as the policies to support employment and household income helped to significantly reduce inequality without having to resort to increases in private sector debt (Galbraith, 2012). Other developing countries, such as Malaysia, the Philippines and Thailand also displayed declining inequality following the Asian financial crisis. However, this assessment is based on truncated survey data (see footnote 20) and is contradicted by whatever fiscal data are available, as in the case of Malaysia, where the top 1 per cent income share increased by about 1 percentage point after 1997.

33 Plender (2015) provides a detailed account of the thousands of pages of intricate regulations proposed by many of the large regulatory bodies.

34 See, for example, Duhon (2012), and Golin and Delhaise (2013), who describe how credit markets expand and banks' trading floors work.

35 As discussed in earlier *TDR*s (e.g. 2013 and 2016), the usual objection to protecting minimum wages and allowing growth of labour income at par with productivity is that profits tend to be squeezed, thus discouraging investment. However, if both social and infrastructure policies work in tandem with distribution policies, technical progress, rather than wage repression, becomes the main driver of profit gains (see also Galbraith, 2012).

References

Abbott P and Tarp F (2011). Globalization crises, trade, and development in Vietnam. Working Paper No. 2011/20, United Nations University-World Institute for Development Economics Research (UNU-WIDER), Helsinki.

Admati AR and Hellwig M (2013). *The Bankers' New Clothes: What's Wrong with Banking and What to Do about It*. Princeton, NJ, Princeton University Press.

Akyüz Y (2011). *The Management of Capital Flows in Asia*. Penang, Third World Network.

Akyüz Y (2012). *Financial Crisis and Global Imbalances: A Development Perspective*. Geneva, South Centre.

Akyüz Y (2013). Developing countries after the financial crisis: Waving or drowning? *Economic and Political Weekly,* 48(37): 36–44.

Alstadsaeter A, Johannesen N and Zucman G (2017). Tax evasion and inequality. Available at: https://gabriel-zucman.eu/files/AJZ2017.pdf.

Alvaredo F (2010). A note on the relationship between top income shares and the Gini coefficient. Discussion Paper No. 8071, Center for Economic Policy and Research, London.

Bair S (2014). Everything the IMF wanted to know about financial regulation and wasn't afraid to ask. In: Akerlof GA, Blanchard O, Romer D and Stiglitz JE, eds. *What Have We Learned? Macroeconomic Policy After the Crisis*. Cambridge, MA, MIT Press: 129–134.

Baker C (2003). Opportunity and danger: Globalization, states and politics in 1990s' Asia. In: Ghosh J, and Chandrasekhar CP, eds. *Work and Well-Being in the Age of Finance*. New Delhi, Tulika Books: 561–578.

Baud C and Chiapello E (2017). Understanding the disciplinary aspects of neoliberal regulations: The case of credit-risk regulation under the Basel Accords. *Critical Perspectives on Accounting*, 46: 3–23.

Borio C (2012). The financial cycle and macroeconomics: What have we learnt? BIS Working Papers No 395, Bank for International Settlements, Basel.

Boyer R (2009). Feu le régime d'accumulation tiré par la finance: La crise des subprimes en perspective historique. *Revue de la Régulation,* 5(1): 2–34.

Brown A, Veronese Passarella M and Spencer D (2015). The nature and variegation of financialisation: A cross-country comparison. Working Paper Series No. 127, Financialisation, Economy, Society and Sustainable Development (FESSUD), Leeds.

Chandrasekhar CP (2007). Continuity or change? Finance capital in developing countries a decade after the Asian Crisis. *Economic and Political Weekly*, 42(50): 36–44.

Chandrasekhar CP (2010). Learning from the crisis: Is there a model for global banking? In: Jomo KS, ed. *Reforming the International Financial System for Development*. New York, NY, Columbia University Press: 271–295.

Chandrasekhar CP and Ghosh J (2013). The Asian financial crisis, financial restructuring and the problem of contagion. In: Wolfson MH and Epstein GA, eds. *The Handbook of the Political Economy of Financial Crises*. Oxford and New York, Oxford University Press: 311–325.

Chiapello E (2016). How IFRS contribute to the financialization of capitalism. In: Bensadon D and Praquin N, eds. *IFRS in a Global World: International and Critical Perspectives on Accounting*. Cham, Springer International Publishing Switzerland: 71–84.

Claessens S and Perotti E (2007). Finance and inequality: Channels and evidence. *Journal of Comparative Economics*, 35(4): 748–773.

Cobham A, Schlogl L and Sumner A (2015). Inequality and the tails: The Palma proposition and ratio revisited. Working Paper No. 143, United Nations, Department of Economics and Social Affairs (UN DESA), New York, NY.

Coibion O, Gorodnichenko Y, Kudlyak M and Mondragon J (2016). Does greater inequality lead to more household borrowing? New evidence from household data. Working Paper No. 2016-20, Federal Reserve Bank of San Francisco, San Francisco, CA.

Conceição P and Galbraith JK (2000). Constructing long and dense time-series of inequality using the Theil Index. *Eastern Economic Journal*, 26(1): 61–74.

Cornford A (2012). Notes on GATS rules for international trade in banking services. Presentation at a public forum at the World Trade Organization, Geneva, 26 September.

Cornford A (2016). New in-house estimates of the impact of the Basel Capital Framework. IDEAs. Available at: http://www.networkideas.org/featured-articles/2016/12/new-in-house-estimates-of-the-impact-of-the-basel-capital-framework/ (accessed on 24 April 2017).

Cripps F, Izurieta A and Singh A (2011). Global imbalances, under-consumption and over-borrowing: The state of the world economy and future policies. *Development and Change,* 42(1): 228–261.

Crotty J (2003). Structural contradictions of current capitalism: A Keynes-Marx-Schumpeter analysis. In: Ghosh J and Chandrasekhar CP, eds. *Work and Well-Being in the Age of Finance*. New Delhi, Tulika Books: 24–51.

D'Arista J (2009). Setting an agenda for monetary reform. Working Papers No. 190, Political Economy Research Institute (PERI), University of Massachusetts, Amherst, MA.

Davies JB, Sandström S, Shorrocks A and Wolff EN (2011). The level and distribution of global household wealth. *The Economic Journal,* 121(551): 223–254.

Delhaise P and Beckerling L (1998). *Asia in Crisis: The Implosion of the Banking and Finance Systems*. Sussex, John Wiley & Sons Inc.

Diaz-Alejandro C (1985). Good-bye financial repression, hello financial crash. *Journal of Development Economics*, 19(1-2): 1–24.

Duhon T (2012). *How the Trading Floor Really Works*. Sussex, John Wiley & Sons.

Duménil G and Lévy D (2001). Costs and benefits of neoliberalism: A class analysis. *Review of International Political Economy,* 8(4): 578–607.

Duménil G and Lévy D (2004). *Capital Resurgent: Roots of the Neoliberal Revolution*. Cambridge, MA, Harvard University Press.

Eaton C, Habinek J, Goldstein A, Dioun C, García Santibáñez Godoy D and Osley-Thomas R (2016). The financialization of US higher education. *Socio-Economic Review*, 14(3): 507–535.

Eatwell J (2012). The transformation of international financial markets and the future of the eurozone. AUGUR Project, final report. Available at: http://www.augurproject.eu/IMG/pdf/Financial_markets-2.pdf (accessed 22 May 2017).

Epstein GA (2005). *Financialization and the World Economy*. Cheltenham, Edward Elgar Publishing.

Felkerson JA (2012). A detailed look at the Fed's crisis response by funding facility and recipient. Public Policy Brief No. 123, Levy Economics Institute of Bard College, Annandale-on-Hudson, NY.

Flassbeck H (2007). Wage divergences in Euroland: Explosive in the making. In: Bibow J, and Terzi A, eds. *Euroland and the World Economy: Global Player or Global Drag?* London, Palgrave Macmillan: 43–52.

Flassbeck H and Lapavitsas C (2013). The systemic crisis of the euro – true causes and effective therapies. Available at: http://www.rosalux.de/publication/39478/the-systemic-crisis-of-the-euro-true-causes-and-effective-therapies.html (accessed 25 May 2016).

Foster JB and McChesney RW (2012). *The Endless Crisis. How Monopoly Finance Capital Produces Stagnation and Upheaval from the US to China*. New York, NY, Monthly Review Press.

FSF (2009). Report of the Financial Stability Forum on Addressing Procyclicality in the Financial System, April. Available at: http://www.fsb.org/wp-content/uploads/r_0904a.pdf.

Galbraith JK (Sr.) (1994). *A Short History of Financial Euphoria*. New York, NY. Penguin.

Galbraith JK (2012). Inequality and Instability: A Study of the World Economy Just Before the Great Crisis. Oxford and New York, Oxford University Press.

Galbraith JK (2014). The End of Normal: The Great Crisis and the Future of Growth. New York, NY, Simon and Schuster.

Ghosh J, Chandrasekhar CP and Patnaik P (2017). *Demonetisation Decoded: A Critique of India's Currency Experiment*. New York, NY, Routledge Taylor and Francis.

Ghosh S, Gonzalez del Mazo I and Ötker-Robe İ (2012). Chasing the shadows: How significant is shadow banking in emerging markets? World Bank, *Economic Premise* (88): 1–7.

Gil-Diaz F (1998). The origin of Mexico's 1994 financial crisis. *Cato Journal*, 17(3): 303–313.

Goda T and Lysandrou P (2014). The contribution of wealth concentration to the subprime crisis: A quantitative estimation. *Cambridge Journal of Economics*, 38(2): 301–327.

Goda T, Onaran Ö and Stockhammer E (2014). A case for redistribution? Income inequality and wealth concentration in the recent crisis. CIEF Working Paper No. 14-17, EAFIT University, Medellin.

Golin J and Delhaise P (2013). *The Bank Credit Analysis Handbook: A Guide for Analysts, Bankers and Investors* (2nd edition). Singapore, John Wiley & Sons.

Goodhart CAE (2007). Replacing the Stability and Growth Pact? In: Bibow J, and Terzi A, eds. *Euroland and the World Economy: Global Player or Global Drag?* London, Palgrave Macmillan: 135–153.

Griffith-Jones S (2001). Causes and lessons of the Mexican peso crisis. In: Griffith-Jones S, Montes MF, and Nasution A, eds. *Short-Term Capital Flows and Economic Crises*. Oxford and New York, Oxford University Press: 144–172.

Haldane AG (2010). The contribution of the financial sector: Miracle or mirage? Speech at The Future of Finance Conference, Bank of England, London, 14 July. Available at: http://www.bis.org/review/r100716g.pdf.

Haldane AG (2014). On being the right size. *The Journal of Financial Perspectives*, 2(1): 13–25.

House of Commons Treasury Committee (2010). *Too Important to Fail - Too Important to Ignore*. Ninth Report of session 2009-10, vol. 2: Oral and written evidence. London, The Stationery Office.

ILO (2014). *World Social Protection Report 2014-15*. Geneva, International Labour Office.

IMF (2008). *Monetary and Financial Statistics: Compilation Guide*. Washington, DC, International Monetary Fund.

IMF (2016). *Monetary and Financial Statistics Manual and Compilation Guide*. Washington, DC, International Monetary Fund.

Irvin G and Izurieta A (2011) Fundamental flaws in the European Project. *Economic and Political Weekly*, 46(32): 14–16.

Johnson S and Kwak J (2011). *13 Bankers: The Wall Street Takeover and the Next Financial Meltdown*. New York, NY, Vintage.

Jomo KS (2007). Financial liberalisation, crises and the role of capital controls: The Malaysian case. *Economic and Political Weekly*, 42(50): 73–78.

Kalecki M (1965). *Theory of Economic Dynamics: An Essay on Cyclical and Long-Run Changes in Capitalist Economy*. New York and London, Modern Reader Paperbacks.

Kay J (2015). *Other People's Money: Masters of the Universe or Servants of the People?* London, Profile Books.

Keynes JM ([1936], 1997). *The General Theory of Employment, Interest, and Money*. New York, NY, Prometheus Books.

Kindleberger CP (2000). *Manias, Panics and Crashes: A History of Financial Crises* (4th edition). New York, NY, John Wiley & Sons.

King M (2016). *The End of Alchemy: Money, Banking and the Future of the Global Economy*. New York, NY, W.W. Norton & Company.

Kohler P (2015). Redistributive policies for sustainable development: Looking at the role of assets and equity. Working Paper No. 139, United Nations, Department of Economics and Social Affairs, New York, NY.

Kostzer D (2008). Argentina: A case study on the *Plan Jefes y Jefas de Hogar Desocupados*, or the Employment Road to Economic Recovery. Working Paper No. 534, Levy Economics Institute of College, Annandale-on-Hudson, NY.

Kregel JA (1998). East Asia is not Mexico: The difference between balance of payments crises and debt deflations. In: Jomo KS, ed. *Tigers in Trouble: Financial Governance, Liberalization and Crises in East Asia*. London, Zed Books: 44–62.

Kregel JA (2014). *Economic Development and Financial Instability: Selected Essays*. London and New York, Anthem Press.

Krippner GR (2005). The financialization of the American economy. *Socio-Economic Review*, 3(2): 173–208.

Kumhof M, Rancière R and Winant P (2015). Inequality, leverage, and crises. *American Economic Review*, 105(3): 1217–1245.

Kyung-Sup C (2007). The end of developmental citizenship? Restructuring and social displacement in post-crisis South Korea. *Economic and Political Weekly*, 42(50): 67–72.

Laeven L and Valencia F (2008). Systemic banking crises: A new database. Working Paper No. 08/224, International Monetary Fund, Washington, DC.

Laeven L and Valencia F (2012). Systemic banking crises database: An update. Working Paper No. 12/163, International Monetary Fund, Washington, DC.

Lahoti R, Jayadev A and Reddy SG (2014). The Global Consumption and Income Project (GCIP): An overview. Working Paper No. 02/2014, New School for Social Research, New York, NY.

Lapavitsas C (2013). *Profiting Without Producing. How Finance Exploits Us All*. London and New York, Verso.

Lavinas L (2017). *The Takeover of Social Policy by Financialization: The Brazilian Paradox*. London, Palgrave Macmillan.

Lee KS (2011). *The Korean Financial Crisis of 1997: Onset, Turnaround, and Thereafter*. Washington, DC, World Bank and the Korea Development Institute.

Lysandrou P (2011a). Global inequality as one of the root causes of the financial crisis: A suggested explanation. *Economy and Society*, 40(3): 323–344.

Lysandrou P (2011b). The primacy of hedge funds in the subprime crisis. *Journal of Post Keynesian Economics*, 34(2): 225–254.

Messer-Davidow E (2017). Investing in college education: Debtors, bettors, lenders, brokers. *Humanities, Special Issue,* 6(2): 20.

Milberg W and Winkler D (2010). Financialisation and the dynamics of offshoring in the USA. *Cambridge Journal of Economics,* 34(2): 275–293.

Minsky HP (1963). *Can "It" Happen Again? Essays on Instability and Finance* (reprinted 1982). Armonk, NY, Routledge.

Minsky HP ([1975], 2008). *John Maynard Keynes*. New York, NY, McGraw-Hill Education.

Minsky HP (1986). *Stabilizing an Unstable Economy*. New Haven, CT, Yale University Press.

Milanovic B (2010). *The Haves and the Have-Nots: A Brief and Idiosyncratic History of Global Inequality*. Philadephia, PA, Basic Books.

Palan R, Murphy R and Chavagneux C (2009). *Tax Havens: How Globalization Really Works*. Ithaca, NY, Cornell University Press.

Palma JG (2011). Homogeneous middles vs. heterogeneous tails, and the end of the "Inverted-U": The share of the rich is what it's all about. Working Papers in Economics No. 1111. Cambridge, University of Cambridge.

Pasinetti LL ([1974], 1979). *Growth and Income Distribution: Essays in Economic Theory*. Cambridge, Cambridge University Press.

Patnaik P (2003). *The Retreat to Unfreedom. Essays on the Emerging World Order*. New Delhi, Tulika Books.

Patnaik P (2007). Financial crises, reserve accumulation and capital flows. *Economic and Political Weekly*, 42(50): 45–51.

Patnaik P (2010). The diffusion of activities. *Economic and Political Weekly,* 45(10): 40–45.

Persaud A (2015). *Reinventing Financial Regulation. A Blueprint for Overcoming Systemic Risk*. New York, NY, Apress.

Phongpaichit P and Baker C (2007). Thai capital after the Asian crisis. *Economic and Political Weekly*, 42(50): 58–66.

Piketty T (2014). *Capital in the Twenty-First Century*. Cambridge, MA, Harvard University Press.

Plender J (2015). *Capitalism: Money, Morals and Markets*. London, Biteback Publishing.

Polanyi Levitt K (2013). *From the Great Transformation to the Great Financialization: On Karl Polanyi and Other Essays*. London, Zed Books.

Ramli R and Nuryadin P (2007). Ten years after: Impact of monetarist and neoliberal solutions in Indonesia. *Economic and Political Weekly*, 42(50): 79–88.

Reddy YV (2013). *Economic Policies and India's Reform Agenda: New Thinking*. New Delhi, Orient BlackSwan.

Schatzker E (2017). Can a man responsible for $5 trillion convince you he's not powerful? Bloomberg. Available at: https://www.bloomberg.com/features/2017-blackrock-larry-fink-interview/ (accessed 30 May 2017).

Schularick M and Taylor AM (2012). Credit booms gone bust: Monetary policy, leverage cycles, and financial crises, 1870–2008. *American Economic Review*, 102(2): 1029–1061.

Shiller RJ (2005). *Irrational Exuberance*. Princeton, NJ, Princeton University Press.

Sheng A (2009). *From Asian to Global Financial Crisis: An Asian Regulator's View of Unfettered Finance in the 1990s and 2000s*. Cambridge, Cambridge University Press.

Shirreff D (2016). *Break up the Banks! A Practical Guide to Stopping the Next Global Financial Meltdown*. Brooklyn and London, Melville House Publishing.

Smith Y (2011). *ECONned: How Unenlightened Self Interest Undermined Democracy and Corrupted Capitalism*. New York, NY, St. Martin's Griffin.

Solt F (2009). Standardizing the World Income Inequality Database. *Social Science Quarterly,* 90(2): 231–242.

Stiglitz JE (2003). *Globalization and Its Discontents*. New York, NY, W.W. Norton & Company.

Stiglitz JE (2012). *The Price of Inequality: How Today's Divided Society Endangers Our Future*. New York, NY, W.W. Norton & Company.

Stockhammer E (2004). Financialisation and the slowdown of accumulation. *Cambridge Journal of Economics*, 28(5): 719–741.

Stockhammer E (2011). Neoliberalism, income distribution and the causes of the crisis. In: Arestis P, Sobreira R and Oreiro JL, eds. *The Financial Crisis: Origins and Implications*. London, Palgrave Macmillan: 234–258.

Storm S (2016). What is missing in Flassbeck & Lapavitsas. Available at: https://www.ineteconomics.org/perspectives/blog/what-is-missing-in-flassbeck-lapavitsas (accessed 28 April 2017).

Taylor L (1993). *The Rocky Road to Reform: Adjustment, Income Distribution, and Growth in the Developing World*. Cambridge, MA, MIT Press.

Taylor L (2010). *Maynard's Revenge: The Collapse of Free Market Macroeconomics*. Cambridge, MA, and London, Harvard University Press.

Turner A (2016a). *Between Debt and the Devil: Money, Credit, and Fixing Global Finance*. Princeton, NJ, Princeton University Press.

Turner A (2016b). Economies and the banks. In: Skidelsky R and Craig N, eds. *Who Runs the Economy? The Role of Power in Economics*. London, Springer Nature: 87–100.

UNCTAD (2011). *Development-led Globalization: Towards Sustainable and Inclusive Development Paths*. Report of the Secretary-General of UNCTAD to UNCTAD XIII. United Nations. New York and Geneva.

UNCTAD (2012). Background note: The rising sea of global financial markets. Contribution to the G20 Framework Working Group for the Discussion on Spillovers. Available at: http://unctad.org/en/Docs/webgds2013_g20d04_en.pdf.

UNCTAD (*TDR 1986*). *Trade and Development Report, 1986*. United Nations publication. Sales No. E.86.II.D.5. New York and Geneva.

UNCTAD (*TDR 1993*). *Trade and Development Report, 1993*. United Nations publication. Sales No. E.93.II.D.10. New York and Geneva.

UNCTAD (*TDR 2013*). *Trade and Development Report 2013: Adjusting to the changing dynamics of the world economy*. United Nations publication. Sales No. E.13.II.D.3. New York and Geneva.

UNCTAD (*TDR 2015*). *Trade and Development Report 2015: Making the International Financial Architecture Work for Development*. United Nations publication. Sales No. E.15.II.D.4. New York and Geneva.

UNCTAD (*TDR 2016*). *Trade and Development Report 2016: Structural Transformation for Inclusive and Sustained Growth*. United Nations publication. Sales No. E.16.II.D.5. New York and Geneva.

Vasudevan R (2016). Financialization, distribution and accumulation: A circuit of capital model with a managerial class. *Metroeconomica*, 67(2): 397–428.

Wolf M (2015). The case for keeping US interest rates low. *Financial Times*, 8 September.

Wray LR (2012). Global financial crisis: A Minskyan interpretation of the causes, the Fed's bailout, and the future. Working Paper No. 711, Levy Economics Institute of Bard College, Annandale-on-Hudson, NY.

Younger SD (1993). The economic impact of a foreign debt bail-out for private firms in Ecuador. *Journal of Development Studies,* 29(3): 484–503.

Zucman G (2013). The missing wealth of nations: Are Europe and the U.S. net debtors or net creditors? *The Quarterly Journal of Economics,* 128(3): 1321–1364.

MARKET POWER AND INEQUALITY: THE REVENGE OF THE RENTIERS

VI

A. Introduction

The changing international division of labour, economic policy choices, political decisions and new technologies all help to explain persistently rising patterns of asset and income inequality under hyperglobalization since the early 1980s. However, achieving a more inclusive growth performance at the global level also requires an explicit understanding of how these inequalities have been nurtured by growing imbalances of economic power. The previous chapter has looked at such imbalances in relation to financialization dynamics; this chapter examines some systemic shifts in power relations between core economic actors in the non-financial corporate sector. It is based on the understanding that "institutions matter, a lot" (*The Economist*, 2013), and that "rebalancing power" (Atkinson, 2015: 99) is essential for achieving sustainable and inclusive prosperity at both national and international levels. In particular, it examines how the continuous deregulation of labour, product and financial markets has given rise to structural shifts in power relations between labour and capital in developed economies, and between States and large corporations at the global level.

Concerns that economic analysis has not paid much attention to power relations, and specific concerns about the structural effects of the growing market domination and lobbying powers of large corporations, are not new. Raúl Prebisch, UNCTAD's first Secretary-General, argued that such effects had hampered catching up in the South after the end of the Second World War, and had systemically tilted the gains from international trade and investment in favour of the North.[1] As Prebisch noted in 1986,

> To the siphoning-off of income from the enterprises producing and exporting primary goods and importing manufactures, prior to industrialization, as well as from the public utility enterprises, was added the drainage of income through the transnational corporations, as they came to play a more and more active part in industrialization, often sheltering behind an exaggerated degree of protection. I do not, of course, exclude banking and financial corporations. Thus a change took place in the composition of the dominant peripheral groups linked up with the centres and a web of relations favourable to their economic, political and strategic interests was woven (Prebisch, 1986: 198).

These concerns have been largely ignored in the single-minded pursuit of hyperglobalization, but they are now resurfacing. A focus on "the science of taming powerful firms" was evident in 2014, when the Swedish Central Bank Prize in Economic Sciences in Memory of Alfred Nobel was awarded to the French economist Jean Tirole "for his analysis of market power and regulation", and his role in addressing concerns that highly concentrated markets, if "left unregulated ... often produce socially undesirable results – prices higher than those motivated by costs, or unproductive firms that survive by blocking the entry of new and more productive ones."[2] What is new in this debate is not so much a preoccupation with "bad apples" or the use of potentially abusive practices by individual firms in isolation; rather, it is the concern that increasing market concentration in leading sectors of the global economy and the growing market and lobbying powers of dominant corporations are creating a new form of global rentier capitalism to the detriment of balanced and inclusive growth for the many.[3]

This chapter takes a closer look at these concerns. Section B discusses the intellectual and historical roots of contemporary debates about rents, rentiers and rentier capitalism. It highlights the fact that rents and rentier behaviour are not limited to the owners of financial assets and to financialized investment strategies;

they also extend to non-financial corporations that use their growing market domination and lobbying powers to engage in regulatory capture. This section also estimates the growth of non-financial rents in the form of "surplus" or "excess" profits since 1995. For this purpose, UNCTAD has constructed a database of consolidated financial statements of listed non-financial companies in 56 developed and developing countries (*CFS* database). Section C provides empirical evidence on trends in market power and concentration in non-financial corporations. Section D explores some core mechanisms that underlie corporate rentierism, such as the strategic use of intellectual property rights (IPRs), tax evasion and the proliferation of public subsidies to large corporations, as well as stock market manipulation to boost compensation for firms' chief executive officers (CEOs) and top management. Section E concludes with a brief discussion of the mechanisms that facilitate and reinforce the emergence of global rentier capitalism.

B. Rentier capitalism revisited

1. From the landlord to the corporate raider: The origins and impacts of economic rents

Broadly speaking, rents refer to income derived solely from the ownership and control of assets, rather than from innovative entrepreneurial activity and the productive use of labour. The origin of rents and their impact on wider economic performance have been the subject of some debate.

One source of economic rents is the natural scarcity of some economic assets or resources. The obvious example is land. Even though the application of technology to boost agricultural yields or to facilitate the extraction of mineral deposits will increase the market value of land, it is ultimately in fixed supply. This allows its owners to command rental income from its use by others. The argument for rents arising from the scarcity of an asset or economic resource is less convincing when these are reproducible. In this case, specific talents and skills may be temporarily scarce in specific locations and for specific markets, but there is no intrinsic scarcity to justify rental incomes. It is for this reason that Keynes characterized the modern financial rentier as a "functionless investor" who "presumably can obtain interest because capital is scarce, just as the owner of land can obtain rent because land is scarce. But whilst there may be intrinsic reasons for the scarcity of land, there are no intrinsic reasons for the scarcity of capital" (Keynes, 1936: 376).

In Keynes' observation, rents derived from the ownership of capital are thus the result of artificial scarcity, imposed by "rules of the game" (i.e. property rights, regulations, institutional arrangements and power relations between stakeholders), which determine who generates an income from privileged access to, and control of, specific assets, and who will have to make a living through traditional entrepreneurial activity or the provision of labour. More generally, "a person gets a rent if he or she earns an income higher than the minimum that person would have accepted, the minimum usually being defined as income in his or her next-best opportunity" (Khan and Jomo, 2000: 21). Standard economic textbooks define this "minimum" in terms of a zero-rent model of perfectly competitive markets in which there are no rents because there is neither market power nor political power. Other approaches, such as in classical and Keynesian economics, question the utility of such an abstract (zero-rent) model. Rents have existed throughout history, but their predominant forms and their weight relative to productive behaviour have changed over time alongside structural economic and socio-institutional change. The relevant benchmark is therefore not some fictitious notion of a world without rents or power, but earlier institutional and economic settings characterized by specific types of rents. In this view, the public face of the rentier has varied over the course of economic history, including landowners and landlords, shareholders, financiers and, eventually, top managers and CEOs of large corporations (box 6.1).

Economists mostly agree that, by and large, rents are unproductive. The exception is Schumpeterian rents (box 6.1), since these do not result from regulatory protection, and are, by definition, temporary. From a neoclassical point of view, other rents are unproductive, since they result from distortions to perfectly competitive, efficient markets. Monopolists, for example, are seen as not contributing to the growth of the pie, but grabbing a larger share of it, in the process often also destroying wealth, for example through monopolistic restrictions on production (Stiglitz, 2016a). Moreover, the very act of seeking rents imposes additional costs on society in the form of the efforts and resources spent by rent-seekers on gaining access to the rents (Krueger, 1974).

Keynes famously advocated "the euthanasia of the rentier, and consequently, the euthanasia of the cumulative oppressive power of the capitalist to exploit the scarcity-value of capital" (Keynes, 1936: 376). He put his faith in a monetary policy of low long-term interest rates that, in combination with "a somewhat comprehensive socialisation of investment" (Keynes, 1936: 378), would create a large enough capital stock to make rental income from capital non-viable, as well as ensure full employment. Many of Keynes' ideas to rein in financial rentierism were anticipated in the New Deal policies of the 1930s in the United States (discussed in the next chapter). Similar measures, covering regulations of the banking system, the stock market, labour relations as well as antitrust legislation, were adopted in most Western European economies in the period leading up to, during and after the Second World War. The result was a period of unprecedented growth (averaging almost 5 per cent annually) in these economies between 1960 and 1980, low – and often falling – inequality, and the virtual absence of financial crises. While there are a number of reasons for the strong performance of that period, the repression of rentierism was one of them.

The renewed rise of financial rentierism since then (*TDR*s 1997 and 2015) has been widely blamed on the reversal of regulations relating to the banking and financial sectors, such as the repeal of the Glass-Steagall Act in the United States in 1999. Until recently, less attention was paid to the pervasiveness of predatory rentier behaviour beyond the financial sector and financialized corporate investment strategies. A widely recognized consequence of these strategies has been the systematic favouring of short-term financial returns to institutional shareholders, which has biased investment patterns towards sectors and activities that promise quick returns at the expense of long-term commitments of financial resources to productive activities (*TDR 2016,* chap. V). In addition, these strategies have facilitated the expansion of market power and domination by allowing firms to leverage short-term financial success and high market valuation to engage, for example, in aggressive mergers and acquisitions

(M&As) (Lazonick, 2016). While financial rentierism undoubtedly continues to play a central role, the growing market power of large corporations more generally has led to a proliferation of non-financial corporate rent strategies and to the emergence of a new generation of rentiers (e.g. Standing, 2016; Baker, 2015).[4]

Fast-rising market power and concentration (discussed further in section C) is at least partly another result of the reversal of New Deal-type measures, such as antitrust policies, financial regulations and fiscal policies that were designed to achieve full employment and strengthen labour's countervailing bargaining powers. New non-financial rent strategies, flourishing on and reinforcing vast market power, include the excessive and strategic use of IPRs to boost profits (see section D.1), as well as what Baumol (1990: 915) referred to as "unproductive entrepreneurship [that] takes many forms. Rent-seeking, often via activities such as litigation and takeovers, and tax evasion and avoidance efforts seem now to constitute the prime threat to productive entrepreneurship". In addition, abuse of privatization schemes, excessive public subsidies for large private corporations, and the systematic use or abuse of management control over investment strategies to boost senior management remuneration schemes have also been mentioned in the literature (e.g. Lazonick, 2016; Philippon and Reshef, 2009) (section D.2). Furthermore, it has been noted that ground rent is making a significant comeback in the context of housing policies and the expansive debt-financing of mortgages, which have driven up land values and facilitated real asset price inflation (Ryan-Collins, 2017).

Two final observations about debates on rents deserve brief mention, since they have important policy implications. From a neoclassical perspective, rents are mostly the direct or indirect result of State intervention in perfectly competitive markets. On this view, monopolists can only behave as such because States create the rules that allow them to restrict production or increase prices. From an institutional perspective, however, governments are only one of several actors in an economy. Rents result from the power relations between economic interest groups and governments, which determine whether States are able to regulate and negotiate those interests. Market power and lobbying power are therefore as much drivers of rents and rent-seeking as is State intervention. What matters is not that States intervene and regulate, but

---

BOX 6.1   A brief history of rentier capitalism

The French and British classical economists of the eighteenth and nineteenth centuries considered rent to be a share of the economic surplus product (defined as total or national income in excess of costs of production, including labour costs), alongside profits, interest payments and taxes (see, for example, Fratini, 2016). In the early stages of the Industrial Revolution in Europe, rents and rentiers were primarily associated with incomes derived from the historical ownership of land and mines – a legacy of feudal times. The French Physiocrats of the eighteenth century saw ground rent as income attributable only to the size and location of land – not its produce – and argued that it should be the main source of taxation, since changes to the locational value of land were the result of societal developments, rather than the efforts of individual landowners – a proposition also advocated by John Stuart Mill ([1848] 1884). The political economists of the early nineteenth century, most prominently David Ricardo, took into account the emergence of capitalist farming. Tenant farmers could obtain "differential rents" arising from natural differences in the fertility of farmed land, which nevertheless still represented unearned income, rather than entrepreneurial effort. But with wages assumed to be subsistence wages, it was contractual and institutional arrangements that determined which part of the differential rent went to the tenant farmer and which to the landowner (Ricardo, [1817] 1962: 67–92). At the height of the European Industrial Revolution, Karl Marx argued that agriculture had become commercialized to the extent of largely being subject to the same competitive pressures experienced in other sectors of the economy. Usually, competitive pressures ensure that any surplus or excess profits of individual firms in a sector are eventually eliminated, along with underperforming firms. But when competition is impeded through institutional obstacles or market power, temporary surplus profits can turn into lasting rents, and underperforming firms can carve out a parasitic existence.

Later, Schumpeter pointed out that temporary surplus profits, or rents, could play an important role in facilitating technical progress by compensating innovative entrepreneurs (as opposed to imitators) for risk-taking and initiative. Importantly, these entrepreneurial rents – now generally referred to as Schumpeterian rents – do not require protective regulation such as, for example, IPRs. They are the result of "thinking ahead of the curve". According to Schumpeter (1942: 84–85), since imitators would eventually catch up, such rents or surplus profits would be only temporary.

Gradually, rents from land and mineral deposits that owed their existence to feudal legacies became less important, while rents resulting from conflicting interests between the main emerging stakeholders in modern market societies – workers, the growing middle classes, financiers and industrialists – became more significant. Whether or not temporary surplus profits would turn into lasting redistributive rents depended primarily on the ability of modern nation States and their elected governments to regulate and negotiate conflicting group interests in the wider public interest, so as to ensure that no particular interest group could prevail for long in its quest for rental incomes.

A pressing concern in the final phases of the European Industrial Revolution was the rise of market concentration and monopoly power as a source of rents – a danger Adam Smith had warned against much earlier. According to Smith ([1776] 1981: 267):

> To widen the market and to narrow the competition is always the interest of the dealers. To widen the market may frequently be agreeable to the interest of the public; but to narrow the competition must always be against it, and can serve only to enable the dealers, by raising their profits above what they naturally would be, to levy, for their own benefit, an absurd tax on the rest of their fellow citizens. The proposal of any new law or regulation of commerce which comes from this order ought always to be listened to with great precaution, and ought never to be adopted till after having been long and carefully examined, not only with the most scrupulous, but with the most suspicious attention. It comes from an

---

how they regulate, as well as the extent to which their regulation is captured by particular interests.

Moreover, whether or not rents are productive also depends on the wider institutional and macroeconomic setting in which they operate. For example, from a development perspective, temporary learning rents for emerging industrialists to facilitate late development (Khan and Jomo, 2000) essentially mimic Schumpeterian rents, in that they are based on the recognition that entrepreneurial and technological learning in developing countries require State intervention to enable the emergence of an entrepreneurial class that can eventually compete with developed-country

order of men whose interest is never exactly the same with that of the public, who have generally an interest to deceive and even to oppress the public, and who accordingly have, upon many occasions, both deceived and oppressed it.

These concerns were exemplified a century later by the political battle around the modern shareholding corporation and its defining legal characteristic, namely corporate limited liability.[a] Corporate limited liability is seen today as an indispensable requirement for the financing of private investment in the presence of risk (e.g. Hansmann and Kraakman, 2001). At the time, however, the shifting of risk (liabilities) away from shareholders to creditors, employees and society at large was greeted with scorn and widespread opposition. Its adoption in the United Kingdom was driven not by industrialists and large companies, but by rising middle-class rentiers and wealthy investors, who wanted their share of fast-growing industrial and financial wealth without having to shoulder the burdens of entrepreneurship (Ireland, 2010). Opponents like John Stuart Mill and Alfred Marshall shared the public fear that corporate limited liability would come at a high cost to society by making credit provision more difficult, but above all, by facilitating fraudulent investment schemes and generally encouraging excessive speculation. Anthony Trollope's *The Way We Live Now* (1873) is a portrayal of corporate fraud brought on by limited liability and insufficient financial disclosure. Economic scholars' ex post justification of corporate limited liability as an efficiency-enhancing device to facilitate raising capital for large-scale industrial development is certainly not borne out by history. As Deakin (2005) has stressed, the Industrial Revolution in the United Kingdom took place with only very few companies taking advantage of corporate limited liability. Similarly, in Europe and the United States, the use of incorporation and limited liability only became widespread during the very late phase of industrialization.

The rise of the modern corporation leading up to the turn of the twentieth century occurred alongside the vast expansion and deepening of developed countries' financial sectors. Money markets (credit and other financial companies) expanded rapidly, while older financial instruments, such as financiering (the debt-financed acquisition of securities) and call money (money lent to stockbrokers by banks "on call" to finance holdings of stock portfolios in expectation of asset price inflation) were refined (Kindleberger and Aliber, 2011) and new ones invented.[b] This period also saw numerous severe financial crises in leading economies (e.g. in France in 1866 and 1882, in the United Kingdom in 1893 and 1896, and in the United States in 1907), culminating in the Great Crash of 1929 and the ensuing Great Depression. Rentiers became identified with the owners of financial assets and receivers of interest, and rentier capitalism with financial rentierism. This understanding of rentier capitalism was given a new lease of life with the growth of financialization under hyperglobalization and the global financial crisis of 2008–2009 (see, for example, Palma, 2009).

---

[a] The legal concept of limited liability governs restrictions on the extent to which owners of economic resources can be held financially liable for damage caused to third parties through the use of these resources. Modern corporate limited liability is based on the legal doctrine of "separate corporate personality", according to which a company constitutes a separate legal entity from its owner-shareholders. If the company fails and/or causes harm, the liability of its owner-shareholders is limited to the nominal value of their shares. The legal principle of "separate personality" has also been extended to the relationship between parent and subsidiary companies, and the protection of limited liability is granted to parent companies with respect to claims against their subsidiaries, independently of the degree to which parent companies own and/or control subsidiary companies.

[b] One example is the famous binder cut that established the sellable right to buy land at a stated price in Florida, thereby fuelling the Florida real estate boom that is often considered as having tipped the balance in the run-up to the Great Crash of 1929 (Galbraith, 1954).

---

rivals. Interventions that create such rents, such as import-substituting or export-promoting policies, were adopted at one time or another in most developing countries, including the successful East Asian economies during their phase of rapid industrialization. Whether or not such temporary State-created rents turn into unproductive distributive rents largely depends on the ability of the State to rein in demands from interest groups to make such rents permanent (*TDR 2016*, chap. VI). From this perspective, if the corporate rent strategies described above are widely seen as unproductive, an important reason is that these result primarily from corporate regulatory capture in the wake of growing market power.

2. Size matters: How big is non-financial corporate rentier capitalism?

Growing concerns over the renewed rise of rentier capitalism have inspired various attempts to assess the size of such rentier income. In examining trends and cycles in rentier income in some OECD countries, Epstein and Power (2003) approximated such rentier income as deriving primarily from financial intermediation plus interest income for all non-financial non-government resident institutional units. They found that rentier income, thus defined, rose steadily in those countries between the end of the 1970s and 2000. Seccareccia and Lavoie (2016: 207) defined rentier income more narrowly as "the interest return to government long-term bond holders". Tracing such income from the mid-1920s to 2011 in Canada and the United States, they found that this rose sharply from the late 1970s, followed by a pronounced decline in the second half of the 1990s, and then an upward trend until the global financial crisis of 2008–2009. Phillippon and Reshef (2009) looked at the rise of a financial managerial class in the United States. Analysing the dramatic rise of relative wages in that country's financial sector from the mid-1980s, they argued that pay at the top end of the "salaried" class, earned mostly by financial managers, is rentier income that results more from dubious remuneration policies and management practices than from education or ability.

These contributions shed some light on increases in rentierism over recent decades, but their focus is essentially on financial rentier incomes (variously defined) in a few developed countries. While this largely reflects problems of data availability, it fails to capture a defining feature of hyperglobalization, namely the proliferation of rent-seeking strategies in the non-financial corporate sector.[5] This chapter's estimate of the size of rentier income in recent years, and its evolution, therefore focuses on the non-financial dimension of rentier capitalism, with a view to complementing, rather than replacing, existing estimates of financial rentierism. It also widens geographical coverage to include both developed and developing countries.

The conceptual approach is simple, building on the general approach in economics to define rents relative to some benchmark. Theoretical limitations aside, the zero-benchmark model of perfectly competitive markets is unsuitable for an empirical analysis of contemporary real-world markets, since these markets are typically characterized by the presence of some degree of market power. Assuming a hypothetical zero-rent benchmark that does not exist in reality would heavily overstate the presence of rents. A more realistic alternative, then, is to define a benchmark that captures typical firm performance in given market conditions. The idea is to measure the gap between actually observed profits on the one hand, and typical or benchmark profits on the other. A positive gap between these two variables means that some firms are able to accumulate surplus or "excess" profits. If this gap persists and grows over time, the measure provides an indication of forces at work that may facilitate the transformation of temporary surplus profits into rents.[6]

Specifically, the analysis here uses the *CFS* database (mentioned in section A above),[7] which covers non-financial companies listed in 56 developed, transition and developing economies[8] that provided annual company balance sheet data for the period 1995–2015. The relevant variable for our purpose is non-financial firms' operating profits.

To establish a benchmark for typical profitability, we use the median value of firms' rate of return on assets (ROA), or the ratio of their operating profits ("profits" hereafter) to their total assets – a widely used accounting measure of profitability. Since this can depend on sectoral factors, such as sector-specific technologies, the benchmark ROA is defined separately for each sector, rather than for the total universe of firms in the database. In addition, since ROAs can be affected by macroeconomic shocks, the benchmark ROA is calculated separately for three sub-periods within the overall period of observation – 1995–2000, 2001–2008 and 2009–2015 – as these periods are separated by two major financial crises: the dotcom bubble of 2000–2001, and the global financial crisis of 2008–2009.[9]

Typical profits have been estimated for each year by applying the relevant sector- and period- specific benchmark ROA to each firm in the database in that year. Summing these firm-level typical profits provides the total of typical profits by year. These are the profits that would have resulted if all firms in the sample had recorded the benchmark ROA in that year. Surplus profits are the difference between this estimate of total typical profits and the total of actually observed profits of all firms in the sample in that year.

As figure 6.1 shows, the share of surplus profits in total profits grew significantly for all firms in the databasc until thc global financial crisis, from 4 per cent during the period 1995–2000 to 19 per cent in 2001–2008. It increased again to 23 per cent in the subsequent period, but the increase was much more muted, suggesting that many firms' ability to generate surplus profits may have been dented by the global financial crisis. The top 100 firms, ranked by market capitalization,[10] also saw the growth of their surplus profits decelerate somewhat after 2008, but even so, by the latest period, 40 per cent of total profits in this group were surplus profits, and these firms had widened their lead over all other firms. This suggests an ongoing process of bipolarization in the distribution of firms in the database into a few high-performing firms and a growing number of low-performing firms, which is confirmed by our analysis of market concentration and productivity trends in section C below.

Clearly, these results need to be interpreted with caution. More important than the absolute size of surplus profits for firms in the database in any given sub-period, is their increase over time, in particular the surplus profits of the top 100 firms. Of course, not all surplus profits may be attributable to corporate rent-seeking strategies in these non-financial sectors,

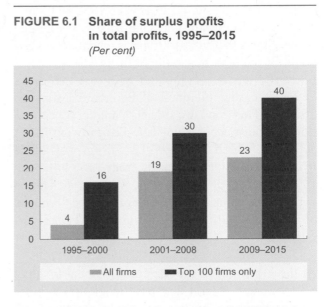

FIGURE 6.1 Share of surplus profits in total profits, 1995–2015
(Per cent)

Source: UNCTAD secretariat calculations, based on *CFS* database, derived from Thomson Reuters *Worldscope Database*.

rather than, for example, "Schumpeterian" innovative firm performance. One way of gaining added insight into this question is by looking more closely at market concentration trends and their core drivers.

C. "The winner takes most": Market concentration on the rise

1. General trends in non-financial sectors

Growing market concentration has attracted renewed attention in recent years. Most studies focus on the United States economy, where many of the largest corporations operating worldwide are based and relevant data are more readily available. Foster et al. (2011) show that the proportion of manufacturing industries in which the four largest firms accounted for 50 per cent or more of the total shipment value of their industries increased significantly, from below 20 per cent in 1980 to over 35 per cent in 2007. In retail, the top four firms operating in general merchandise saw their share in total sales increase from 47 per cent to 73 per cent between 1992 and 2007. Similarly high increases were recorded for information goods. The Economic Innovation Group (EIG) reports that market concentration in terms of revenues increased in two thirds of United States industries between 1997 and 2012. In nearly half of all industries (manufacturing and other), the four largest firms accounted for at least 25 per cent of all industry revenues by 2012,

and in 14 per cent of all industries, the four largest firms captured over 50 per cent of the total revenues (EIG, 2017: 25). Grullon et al. (2017) find that 75 per cent of United States industries experienced greater concentration over the past two decades, and firms in industries with the largest increases in product market concentration also showed higher profit margins, abnormally high returns on stocks and more profitable M&A deals. Furthermore, the increased profit margins were mainly driven by higher operating margins, rather than by increases in operational efficiency, which suggests that market power is becoming an important source of value for companies.

In many instances, large corporations operate across several industries, resulting in the formation of big conglomerates,[11] which necessitates the measurement of aggregate concentration. Foster et al. (2011: 6) show that the top 200 United States companies increased their share of total business revenue in the country from 21 per cent in 1950 to 30 per cent in 2008, and their share of total business profits from

13 per cent to 30 per cent between 1950 and 2007. A study of listed non-financial firms in the United States shows that in 2014, returns on capital investment for the 90th percentile of firms were over five times the median, compared with just two times 25 years earlier (Council of Economic Advisers, 2016: 5). This trend towards high market concentration has been accompanied by fast-growing M&A activities, which reached $4.3 trillion worldwide in 2015 (Dealogic, 2017), up from $156 billion in 1992 (Nolan, 2002: 133). And since 2008, United States firms alone have gone through several rounds of mergers totalling $10 trillion (*The Economist*, 2016: 25).

At the global level, the McKinsey Global Institute (2015), using a large database of 28,000 companies, each with annual revenues of more than $200 million,[12] found that firms with annual revenues of $1 billion or more accounted for nearly 60 per cent of global corporate revenues in 2013, while only 10 per cent of the world's publicly listed companies accounted for 80 per cent of total profits.

Since the early 2000s, corporations from emerging economies have benefited from fast-growing home markets and associated economies of scale. As a result, several of them feature among the world's largest firms. In 2013, emerging market firms accounted for 26 per cent of the Fortune Global 500, with Chinese firms alone accounting for 20 per cent (McKinsey Global Institute, 2015: 41). The 50 largest emerging market firms significantly expanded their share of revenues from overseas, from 19 per cent in 2000 to 40 per cent in 2013. Meanwhile, global firms headquartered in the United States and Western Europe saw their share in the Fortune Global 500 decline from 76 per cent in 1980 to 54 per cent in 2013 (McKinsey Global Institute 2015:10, 14). Nevertheless, developed-country firms remain the dominant global players in industries that have the highest profit margins, such as pharmaceuticals, media and information technologies (ITs). Their profit margins are bolstered by patents, brands and copyrights, as well as by size, with the most profitable firms also being the larger ones.[13] In contrast, the focus of emerging market corporations has been less on returns on capital and more on revenue growth and scale. Moreover, they have grown rapidly, and have gained substantial market shares in commodity-based, capital-intensive industries, such as minerals, steel and chemicals, where profit margins have been squeezed since the early 2000s as a result of a rapid expansion

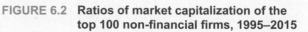

FIGURE 6.2 Ratios of market capitalization of the top 100 non-financial firms, 1995–2015

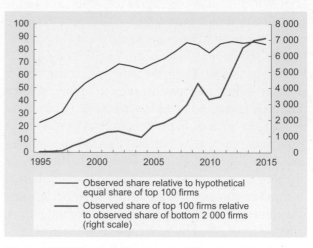

Observed share relative to hypothetical equal share of top 100 firms

Observed share of top 100 firms relative to observed share of bottom 2 000 firms (right scale)

Source: UNCTAD secretariat calculations, based on *CFS* database, derived from Thomson Reuters *Worldscope Database*.

of supply. Thus, while the corporate landscape has changed in recent years, multinational enterprises (MNEs) from developed countries still account for most of the transfer of profits across borders. That said, a growing number of emerging market companies are now expanding internationally through M&As by targeting higher technology firms, with the goal of acquiring capabilities, brands and technologies (McKinsey Global Institute, 2015: 6–10, 56).

An analysis of the *CFS* database yields results consistent with these observations, confirming a sharp increase in market concentration of the top 100 non-financial firms in that database in each year. Figure 6.2 presents market concentration in terms of firms' market capitalization between 1995 and 2015. The red line shows the actual share of the top 100 firms in the database relative to their hypothetical equal share, assuming that total market capitalization was distributed equally over all firms. The blue line shows the observed share of the top 100 firms relative to the observed share of the bottom 2,000 firms in the sample.[14]

Both measures in figure 6.2 indicate that the market power of the top companies, as measured by their (relative) shares in market capitalization, increased substantially over the period 1995–2015. For example, in 1995, the combined share of market capitalization of the top 100 firms in the database was 23 times higher than the share these firms would have held had market capitalization been distributed equally across all firms. By 2015, this gap had increased nearly fourfold, to 84 times. This overall upward surge in concentration, measured by market capitalization since 1995, experienced brief interruptions in 2002–2003 after the bursting of the dotcom bubble, and in 2009–2010 in the aftermath of the global financial crisis, and it stabilized at high levels thereafter.

This trend highlights the growing domination of stock market valuation by a few leading firms. While there were many more publicly listed non-financial firms on global markets in 2015 than in 1995, the relative weight and ability of the bottom firms to pose a credible competitive threat to the top 100 firms, as measured by market capitalization, seems to have waned over time. While the market capitalization of the top 100 firms amounted to around 31 times that of the bottom 2,000 firms in 1995, by 2015 the "winner-takes-most" firms were worth 7,000 times more than their smaller rivals. The two main episodes of financial turmoil during the observation period (the dotcom bubble and the global financial crisis) also seem to have accelerated this trend of a growing "market power" gap between the top and the bottom firms.[15]

Figure 6.3 breaks down the analysis of market concentration by looking at different aspects of company performance, such as revenues, physical assets, other assets and employment performance, with firms ranked by market capitalization year by year.[16] Revenues refer to firms' net income in an accounting period, or their "bottom line" (after deducting all operating and non-operating income and expenses, reserves, income taxes, minority interests and extraordinary items). Physical assets refer to net property, plant and equipment; other assets represent total assets minus physical assets, such as financial and other intangible assets, and employment refers to the total number of employees (excluding seasonal or emergency employees). As in figure 6.2 (red line), these concentration indices are simple ratios that measure the observed firms' shares for these variables relative to their (hypothetical) equal shares. For example, the concentration index for revenues is the ratio of the observed revenue shares of the top 100 firms relative to their equal shares had total revenues been distributed equally among all firms. An increase in this ratio (and equivalent ratios for other variables) signals an increase in market concentration.

It is evident that over the two decades, 1995 to 2015, market concentration increased steeply in terms of revenues, physical assets and other assets. At their peaks in around 2011, observed shares reached 67, 72

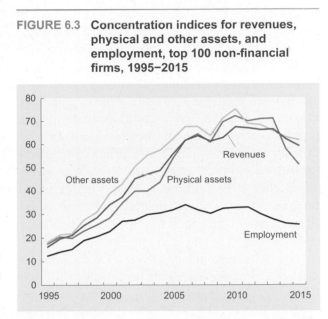

FIGURE 6.3 Concentration indices for revenues, physical and other assets, and employment, top 100 non-financial firms, 1995–2015

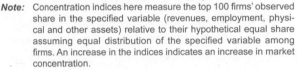

Source: UNCTAD secretariat calculations based on *CFS* database, derived from Thomson Reuters *Worldscope Database*.

Note: Concentration indices here measure the top 100 firms' observed share in the specified variable (revenues, employment, physical and other assets) relative to their hypothetical equal share assuming equal distribution of the specified variable among firms. An increase in the indices indicates an increase in market concentration.

and 75 times the respective equal shares, assuming equal distribution of revenues, physical assets and other assets respectively.[17] In contrast, while market concentration also rose in terms of employment, this increase was much less pronounced, flattening considerably following the dotcom bubble of the early 2000s. This widening gap between indicators of market concentration in terms of revenues and assets, on the one hand, and employment on the other, highlights the wider distributional impacts of market concentration. It supports the view that the era of hyperglobalization is one of "profits without prosperity" (Lazonick, 2013; *TDR 2016*, chap. V), and that rising market power and concentration are strong contributory factors to the long-term trend of falling labour shares in global incomes (Autor et al., 2017a; Barkai, 2016).

2. Drivers of rising market power and concentration

The degree of competition (or market power) in any one industry largely depends on the barriers to entry for new arrivals, rather than on the incumbent firm's size per se (Sylos-Labini, 1969). Two basic types of barriers to entry are those that arise from the intrinsic features of the dominant technology in a sector or industry, and those that arise from institutional factors. A simple example of the first type of barrier is the existence of sizeable economies of scale, typical of almost all modern technology. Contrary to the standard textbook model of perfectly competitive markets, this means that the costs of production do not rise proportionally to the quantities produced. Instead, firms investing in, say, information and communication technology (ICT) or in pharmaceuticals, initially experience high sunk costs (for example in the form of expenditures on research and development (R&D)), after which the variable costs of producing additional units of output are negligible. Since sunk (fixed) costs arise independently of the number of sales by a firm: the higher the firm's sales, the lower its average per unit production costs. Thus, the firm's expansion becomes increasingly profitable. This typically does not lead to pure monopolies, but either to oligopolies (i.e. a few large firms) or monopolistically competitive markets (i.e. a larger number of firms each of which has some degree of market power). The main reason is that a firm's expansion does not take place in a static environment. As firms produce and create jobs, demand for their products changes, both in quantity as well as in terms of specific quality specifications, thus widening existing markets and opening up new related markets. Similarly, their investment activity can have positive learning and network spillover effects to the wider industry, from which potentially new entrants can benefit.[18] The second category of barriers to entry that creates market power is of an organizational, institutional and political nature. This includes firms' control structures, regulatory measures (or the lack thereof) that affect an industry, as well as wider socioeconomic dynamics, such as shifts in the relative bargaining and lobbying powers of core stakeholders in the economy.

A recent example of a technology-driven analysis of rising market power and concentration is the so-called "superstar firm" model (Autor et al., 2017a and 2017b). In contrast to the "trade-cum-technology" explanation of a falling share of labour income in functional income distribution (see chapter II of this *Report*), Autor et al. attribute this trend to a rise in market concentration, enabling a "winner takes most" outcome, "where one firm (or a small number of firms) can gain a very large share of the market" (Autor et al., 2017b: 2). Higher sales concentrations in the industries in their sample were associated with higher productivity performance as well as lower labour shares. They suggest that

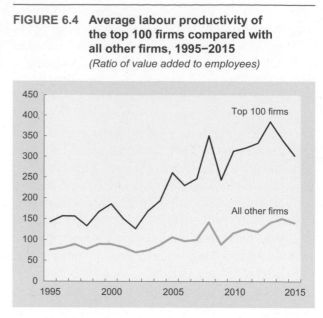

FIGURE 6.4 Average labour productivity of the top 100 firms compared with all other firms, 1995–2015
(Ratio of value added to employees)

Source: UNCTAD secretariat calculations, based on *CFS* database, derived from Thomson Reuters *Worldscope Database*.
Note: A significant number of firms included in the CFS database do not reveal their labour (staff) costs, and have therefore been excluded from calculations for this figure. This is particularly the case for firms in the top 100 category, including new entrants from the health and technology sectors.

the emergence of such superstar firms is due more to their technological nature than to institutional or regulatory factors. Indeed, high-productivity superstar firms are mostly located in high-technology industries (Autor et al., 2017a: 23), suggesting that large economies of scale (for example in online services and software platforms) and large network effects of information-intensive goods and services (e.g. high switching-over costs for consumers between service providers, the accumulation of large user databases, and thus informational advantages) make it difficult for newcomers to compete with few and fast-growing incumbents (Autor et al., 2017b: 2; Council of Economic Advisers, 2016). On this basis, the decline in the overall labour share in the United States is explained by sectoral shifts towards a few, more capital-intensive superstar firms, and away from a larger number of firms with higher labour shares, rather than firm-level substitutions of capital for labour.

Figure 6.4 provides some support for the idea that the emergence of high-productivity superstar firms, combined with technological barriers to entry, may have played a role in rising market concentration. In particular, after 2002, the productivity performance (here measured by the ratio of value added to number of employees)[19] of the top 100 non-financial firms was much higher than that of all other firms in the sample, which experienced largely stagnating productivity performance. While the number of software and IT firms in the top 100 firms more than doubled between 1995 and 2015, from 5 to 11,[20] reflecting both the dynamism of this sector and its high degree of market concentration, superstar firms are not limited to this sector.[21]

It would, however, be premature to attribute market concentration or the "winner takes most" feature of high-tech markets solely to technological developments and related barriers to entry that produce "natural monopolies" (Katz and Shapiro, 1999). In reality, both types of barriers to entry described above – technological and institutional – interact over time. Large firms can use patent protection (both through in-house research and by acquisition) to raise barriers to entry in an industry and bolster their own market power. Thus, superstar firms benefiting from erecting initial technological barriers to entry can use this advantage to further expand their market power in other ways, for example through pricing strategies that make new entrants non-viable, by systematically buying start-ups with new ideas, and by using their growing lobbying power to prevent regulatory authorities from intervening (see box 6.2). More generally, technological progress can facilitate institutional and organizational changes that enhance firms' market power, such as with advances in ICTs as well as transportation technologies that have facilitated the emergence of global value chains (GVCs) and the formation of global control networks.[22] Both of these have become core mechanisms that have weakened the regulatory powers of nation States and caused the workplace to become more "fissured" (Weil, 2014), along with an erosion of the bargaining power of labour in the era of hyperglobalization. Conversely, regulatory measures (or their absence) and macroeconomic policies can affect the way firms make use of technical progress to reinforce their market power. For example, extensive labour market deregulation in developed countries has facilitated the use of new technologies to "casualize" and monitor labour input, thereby further weakening labour's bargaining power (Glyn, 2006: 104). In the case of superstar firms, there is, in principle, nothing to stop regulatory authorities from using antitrust legislation and competition policy tools to rein in such "natural monopolies" in the interest of a more balanced and inclusive evolution of high-tech markets, and in the process facilitating faster technological diffusion. The failure to devise and implement such comprehensive

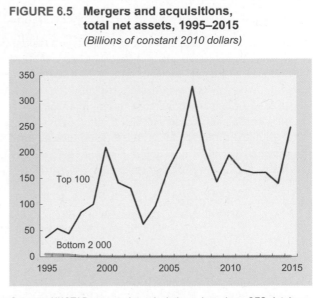

FIGURE 6.5 Mergers and acquisitions, total net assets, 1995–2015
(Billions of constant 2010 dollars)

Source: UNCTAD secretariat calculations, based on *CFS* database, derived from Thomson Reuters *Worldscope Database*.

regulation constitutes as much of an institutional or political barrier to entry, as does regulation designed to increase protection for industry.

Many commentators (e.g. Kwoka, 2015) have pointed to the weakness of antitrust legislation in the United States and, with some minor differences, in the European Union (EU) since the early 1980s, as a major institutional factor facilitating the accumulation of market power in the hands of a few large firms. The post-1982 approach to antitrust legislation in the United States, inspired by the so-called "Chicago School of antitrust", essentially limits regulatory challenges to M&A activities, and to instances of increased market power in which it can be proven, on a case-by-case basis, that such activities will unequivocally harm consumer welfare, primarily through higher prices (Stiglitz, 2016a). This has effectively opened the floodgates to heightened M&A activity, but confines such activity to the largest firms (figure 6.5).

Thus, while some of the observed steep increase in market concentration in recent years can be attributed to technical progress and concomitant technological or structural barriers to entry, institutional, political and strategic factors have played a significant role in enhancing lead firms' market powers, and consequent lobbying powers. This has further tilted the balance of power in their favour, and helped to turn what might appear to be temporary surplus profits driving innovation into rents.

BOX 6.2   The drivers of market concentration in software and IT services

Software and IT services are considered the powerhouse of economic growth, generating large spillover effects on other manufacturing and high-skill service industries. It is, however, also one of the most concentrated industries. Indeed, concentration in this sector increased sharply over the two decades from 1995 to 2015, in terms of revenues and assets (figure 6.B2.1), in line with results for all sectors (see figure 6.3 above). The much lower relative increase in employment concentration also confirms the general trend. Contrary to the all-sample analysis depicted in figure 6.3, this gap between market concentration indices in terms of market capitalization, revenues and assets, on the one hand, and employment on the other, has continued to widen since 2013, indicating support for the hypothesis of a growing predominance of "winner takes most" superstar firms, particularly in this sector.

FIGURE 6.B2.1 **Concentration indices of market capitalization, revenues, physical and other assets, and employment, top 30 software and IT firms, 1995–2015**

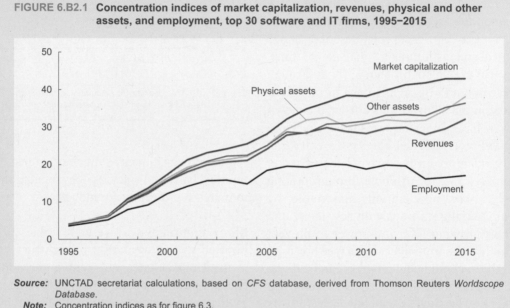

Source: UNCTAD secretariat calculations, based on *CFS* database, derived from Thomson Reuters *Worldscope Database*.
Note: Concentration indices as for figure 6.3.

Apart from primarily technological barriers to entry such as economies of scale, the growing market power of superstar firms has also been driven by institutional or regulatory factors. For example, "other assets" include IPRs, which are an institutional barrier to entry crucial to this information- and knowledge-intensive sector. Furthermore, at least since 2010, the high pace of market concentration in this sector has been driven as much by M&As as by organic corporate growth (see figure 6.B2.2).

This wave of M&As has targeted promising new technology start-ups operating in areas such as cloud computing, open source software and artificial intelligence (Cusumano, 2010). It has also aimed at tightening industry leaders' grip on online retailing and consumer data. The acquisition by Amazon of the United States chain, Whole Foods Markets, in June 2017 for $13.7 billion is the most recent example of a superstar firm's bid to consolidate its already far-reaching domination of online markets and delivery, as well as its access to consumer data (Khan, 2017). There are also acquisitions of new technological developments, such as cloud computing, by only a few lead companies – Amazon's Web Service, Microsoft's Azure and Alphabet (Google's parent company). "Clouds" or server networks increasingly provide the technological and informational infrastructure essential for the delivery of public services (Mahdawi, 2017).

FIGURE 6.B2.2 Number of mergers and acquisitions in the software and IT industry, 2007–2016

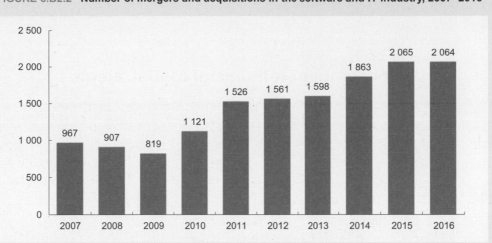

Source: Compilation from Berkery Noyes, Mergers and Acquisitions (several trend reports).

Such domination by very few private companies dealing in data and technological gateways poses obvious dangers to the future provision of both public services and a growing number of private services, with online retailing being only the start. Yet antitrust laws in the EU[a] and the United States have proved too weak to curb such unprecedented market power. In addition to a general shift in the focus of antitrust legislation since the 1970s – from an integrated view of the various dimensions and impacts of market power on the wider economy and society, to a relatively stunted policy tool to keep prices low for consumers – antitrust authorities have been inclined to adopt a lenient "wait-and-see" approach, particularly with respect to the software and IT services sector. Regulators appear to have assumed that Schumpeterian dynamics of creative destruction would do their job for them. Their hope is that market power, which is initially required to compensate high-risk innovators for their large R&D outlays, will eventually be eroded by later imitators flooding standardized markets (e.g. Barnett, 2008).[b] While the fast pace of technological developments in the sector undoubtedly poses a challenge to regulators, "Big Tech" has not hesitated in using its growing market powers to lobby lawmakers. The Internet and electronics industry is now one of the largest corporate lobbyists in the United States, in addition to funding an array of non-governmental organizations with differing agendas to help argue their case, or at least not oppose it (Foroohar, 2017). The overall lax enforcement of antitrust legislation stands in stark contrast to the stringent implementation of intellectual property laws (Walsh, 2013).

---

[a] This is notwithstanding EU regulators' imposition of a record €2.4 billion fine on Google in June 2017 for abusing its dominant position as a search engine to promote its own comparison shopping over that of competitors.

[b] For example, Barnett (2008: 1200), the then Assistant Attorney General for the United States Department of Justice Antitrust Division, argued that "since dynamic efficiency is crucial, preserving innovation incentives is one of the most important concerns of U.S. antitrust law. This can mean bringing an action to prevent conduct that reduces innovation or it can mean declining to act where overly aggressive antitrust enforcement risks chilling the type of vigorous, innovative competition that brings long-term benefits to consumers. In this regard, we recognize that when innovation leads to dynamic efficiency improvements and a period of market power, it is not a departure from competition, but it is a particular type of competition, and one that we should be careful not to mistake for a violation of the antitrust laws."

However, lax antitrust legislation is far from the only, or even the main, source of such rentierism in non-financial firms. Subsequent sections take a closer look at other major institutional and regulatory mechanisms that have fuelled the rise of rent strategies in non-financial private investment activities.

D. Corporate non-financial rent strategies

1. Making knowledge scarce: Strategic use of patent rights[23]

There is evidence in evolving IPR frameworks of a growing bias towards the excessive protection of private investor interests, often at the expense of wider public interests. The use (and abuse) of IPRs (patents, copyrights and trademarks) has become one of the main means of enhancing market power, and thereby generating and appropriating more and higher rents. The practices, policies and regulations relating to the granting of IPRs have become the subject of intense scrutiny and debate in recent years (Standing, 2016; Patterson, 2012). This debate touches upon the fundamental question of whether, in the context of the growing importance of knowledge- and information-intensive production and exchange, "the knowledge factor" continues to provide the basis for the granting of IPRs, particularly patents.

(a) Intellectual property right rents and the abuse of market power

It is now widely known that substantial lobbying by the patent community has been a primary force in the steady privatization of IPR rents since the 1990s.[24] Some authors (e.g. Drahos, 2003; Bessen and Meurer, 2008) have gone so far as to argue that IPRs have become subject to regulatory capture by large companies dominating the knowledge-intensive industries with a view to raising institutional barriers to entry, and thus defending or expanding their market power. Two regulatory developments in the area of IPRs have played an important role in promoting this trend towards their strategic, rather than productive, use: the excessive strengthening of patent protection (i.e. broadening the scope of patents, allowing discoveries to be patented and extending the lives of patents), and the expansion of intellectual property (IP) protection to cover newer areas (Patterson, 2012). Obvious examples of the first development are "evergreening" strategies adopted by global pharmaceutical firms, which seek to lengthen the patent lives of drugs on questionable economic grounds.[25] Examples of the expansion of IP protection to new areas include the rise of financial and business method patents (box 6.3), as well as patents on life forms and on developments in software (Lerner et al., 2015).

As a result of reforms favouring IPRs in these new areas, patent filings that stood at one million in 1995 had more than doubled by 2011, with applications for utility models (see box 6.3) increasing more than fourfold, and industrial design and trademark applications more than doubling (Fink, 2013: 41, based on data from the World Intellectual Property Organization). Globally, around 10 million patents were in force in 2014, worth (on one estimate) around $15 trillion (Standing, 2016: 52). But since global R&D productivity has been declining over the same period (Fink, 2013), these trends suggest that IPRs, particularly patents, are being used disproportionately to benefit incumbent firms in core and secondary markets (Bessen and Meurer, 2014). According to the OECD (2015a: 32), the "average technological and economic value of inventions protected by patents has eroded over time", and the legal right to exclude others has become broad and susceptible to abuse (Drexl, 2008).

Two particular practices are worth highlighting in this context: patent thickets (the acquisition of overlapping patents to cover a wide area of economic activity and potential downstream inventions) and patent fencing (excessive patenting with the intention of cordoning off areas of future research). Both of these lead to expanded patent protection over entire technological domains, and guarantee continuing economic advantages to incumbent firms in technology sectors. In a well-known case, Google bought Motorola solely for its patent portfolio. Although it incurred a hefty loss from the resale of parts of the Motorola business, Google clearly thought that a cost of an estimated $2.5 billion–$3.5 billion for Motorola's collection of patents was a worthwhile investment (OECD, 2015a: 30). As noted by one observer, "The vast bulk of patents are not only useless, they don't represent innovation at all. They are

---

BOX 6.3   Changing standards of patentability and the rise of financial and business method patents

Financial and business method patents loosely refer to utility models[a] granted to inventors in finance, e-commerce, marketing and the computer sciences industry (Locke and Schmidt, 2008). They concern methods that are not tied to any particular technological product or process, but involve steps to process data and information purely in the electronic medium.

Since 1998, when the United States patent regime opened IPR protection to financial and business services, there has been a remarkable surge in the patenting of financial innovation. Studies estimate that over 600 patents in this category have been successfully filed annually in the United States since 2000 (Locke and Schmidt, 2008). While the main beneficiaries of a financial or business patent are financial institutions, insurance companies and e-commerce, such patents are increasingly popular in the wider service and marketing industries and distribution networks.

Business and financial method patents are not clearly defined and cover a broad range of firms' organizational activities, including: financial processes (i.e. credit and loan processing, point-of-sales systems, billing, funds transfer, banking clearing houses, tax processing and investment planning); financial instruments and techniques (derivatives, valuation, index-linking); marketing (advertising management, cataloguing systems, incentive programmes, including coupon redemption); information acquisition, human resource management, accounting and inventory monitoring; e-commerce tools and infrastructure (i.e. user interface arrangements, auctions, electronic shopping carts, transactions, and affiliate programs); and voting systems, games, gambling, education and training (Hall, 2009).

The rise of these kinds of patents has spurred a number of outcomes of doubtful public interest. An infamous example is Amazon's 1-click checkout patent, granted in 1997 by the United States Patent and Trademark Office and due to expire soon, but recently refused by the European Patent Convention authorities on the grounds that patents for business methods are not permissible unless an innovative technological component is clearly identifiable. Financial sector firms have added in-house patenting offices, and United States financial patents have increased their licensing revenues from overseas markets (Hunt, 2007). Most of the largest global financial institutions, including commercial banks, investment banks, insurance companies and financial exchanges, are the main beneficiaries of financial/business method patents. Banks were the last to jump on the bandwagon, starting only in 2008, but the Bank of America, for instance, filed for 235 patents in 2011, putting it in the list of the top 300 companies granted patents in 2012 in the United States (Cumming, 2015).

Several countries, including Australia and Japan, now allow some forms of financial and business method patents.

---

[a]   Utility models are similar to patents, but grant a more limited exclusive right. They are sometimes referred to as "short-term patents", "utility innovations" or "innovation patents".

---

part of an arms race" (Boldrin and Levine, 2012, quoted in Standing, 2016: 57). Given the obvious economic advantages of owning patent portfolios, patent trolling (i.e. the buying up of unexploited or undervalued patents by non-innovator firms for their anticipated value) has also been on the rise, and there is evidence linking increased litigation in software and chemical sectors in the United States to the presence of patent trolls (Miller, 2013). In another well-known case, Qualcomm Inc., a firm in the wireless telephony sector, is defending itself in a United States Federal Trade Commission (FTC) antitrust suit against claims that it leveraged its position as the owner of essential patents for wireless phones and related electronic devices to impose unfair licensing terms on customers and drive out

competing manufacturers. The ongoing case provides a glimpse into the potential for abuse through trolling in the United States market. It also underscores how such anti-competitive effects can be devastating when firms enjoy similar IPR privileges in many countries: Qualcomm was already fined $853 million by the Korean Fair Trade Commission in 2017, and complaints against the company are pending in China and Taiwan Province of China (Fildes, 2017).

These concerns about the growing strategic use of IPRs also extend to the superstar firms discussed in section C. Doubts have been raised about the nature of the "blockbuster" inventions to which these firms often owe their reputation. This would suggests that, rather than representing genuine technological breakthroughs, these inventions may only turn into "blockbusters" because they cover broad and patent-protected technological uses on which other firms depend to survive and invent in core and secondary markets (Lemley, 2015).

(b) Patent power at work in developing countries

The aggressive expansion of patent rights by multinational enterprises (MNEs) to fend off rivals abroad and establish market shares has been facilitated by the proliferation of free trade agreements (FTAs). A range of regulatory reforms are often contained in these agreements, which aim to bring the patent regimes of signatory countries broadly in line with United States standards in terms of scope and coverage, including IPRs, investment regulations and rules regarding the digital economy (Gehl Sampath and Roffe, forthcoming).[26] While some of these treaties incorporate exceptions on grounds of public interest and innovation, often these are not clearly specified and are difficult to utilize in practice.

One way of gaining a broad insight into the role played by patent reforms in developing countries is to look at their impact on the economic performance of MNEs in developing- country markets. If patents confer an unfair market advantage, the effects can normally be captured by examining growth in sales, rates of return, or other such variables at the firm level, after controlling for country- and sector-level effects. A study undertaken for this *Report* used data for United States MNEs and their foreign affiliates in Brazil, China and India covering three sectors (ICT, chemicals and pharmaceuticals) that are perceived to be both patent-intensive and highly concentrated.[27] The results show that in the United States market (including United States MNEs and foreign affiliates operating in United States markets), a growing concentration of patent ownership (rather than the number of patents per se) contributed significantly to product market concentration. In Brazil, China and India, the study reveals that increasing patent protection was associated with increases in sales per worker in United States MNE affiliates,[28] but not in listed local companies (box 6.4).

Econometric analysis shows that the ROA (here calculated as net income to total assets) of United States MNE affiliates operating in these markets responded strongly to the strengthening of patent rights:[29] a 1-per cent increase in the index of patent protection across sectors and countries was associated with a 1.14-per cent overall increase in the ROA of these MNE affiliates. The increase in those affiliates' profitability rose to 2.1 per cent after controlling for firm-level labour productivity effects, but it did not significantly affect their R&D expenditure in the local markets. This suggests that patent protection for these firms may be excessive; a decrease in patent protection would lower the profitability of the affiliates but would have no effect on their R&D activity in local markets (see also *TDR 2005*).

In the absence of data on market concentration for these three countries, the analysis used market ratio as a proxy, calculated as the total sales of United States MNE affiliates relative to the total sales of local publicly listed companies in that sector. This market ratio helps to measure the slice of the local market captured by the MNE affiliates relative to local firms. The larger the ratio, the more dominant are the affiliates in the local market. The study finds that in all the three sectors of interest, profitability rises with relative market size. The net impact of a firm's relative market size on its rate of return is positive and highest for the chemicals sector and lowest for the pharmaceutical sector, as the MNE affiliates face greater competition from the local drug industries of China and India, and to a lesser extent, Brazil.

This provides evidence of the interplay between incumbent advantages for United States MNE affiliates in terms of relative market share, and their profitability increases due to greater patent protection.

The effect of a 1-per cent increase in IPR protection on MNE affiliates' ROAs is highest in the Indian ICT market, where it leads to a 2.1-per cent increase in the rate of return. This shows that in the software sector, despite the short technology cycles, patents help to cement the incumbent advantages that the MNE affiliates would not otherwise have enjoyed in the context of relatively strong local competition. A strengthening of patent rights also has a positive effect on those affiliates' ROAs in the chemicals industry, but the response is less elastic, and once again highest in India, with a 1.1-per cent rate of return. In the pharmaceuticals industry, patent rights had the lowest effect in Brazil, where MNE affiliates have had long-term leads over increasingly weakened local competitors. In contrast, in China and India, where there is competition from local firms, a rise in patent protection has clearly been more instrumental in protecting the returns of the United States MNE affiliates.

BOX 6.4 **Patent reforms and sales per worker of United States MNE affiliates and listed local companies in the chemical and pharmaceutical sectors in Brazil, China and India**

Brazil, China and India have well-established local production in the chemical and pharmaceutical sectors, which therefore serve as good examples of the impact of patent protection on the relative performance of local and foreign firms. Figures 6.B4.1A–C show the sales per worker of United States MNE foreign affiliates and companies with local headquarters that are listed in the BEA database.[a] It is evident that sales per worker of United States MNE affiliates (hereafter referred to as MNE affiliates) showed a clear overall increase following greater patent protection in all three countries, as measured by the Park index.[b] This was not the case for listed local companies: in both Brazil and India, sales per worker in these companies were lower in 2016 than in 1996, and in China initial increases petered out after 2012.

In Brazil, the two domestic IPR reforms of 1997 and 2001 are captured in the patent index measured on the axis of figure A. Following these reforms, sales per worker of the MNE affiliates outperformed those of local companies, where sales per worker declined with stronger IPR protection, and remained flat thereafter.

India had a strong industrial policy stance and had limited IPRs for process patents (rather than product patents) in the pharmaceutical sector, and these only for seven years, until 2005. However, even before the full implementation of the provisions of the WTO Agreement on Trade-related Aspects of Intellectual Property Rights (TRIPS) in 2005, the sales of MNEs' affiliates grew rapidly from 1998, largely due to the TRIPS "mailbox" provision.[c] After 2005, when product patents for drugs were introduced, sales per worker of the MNE affiliates more than doubled, whereas sales per worker in local companies were stagnant throughout the period, and declined after 2010, despite a resilient local pharmaceutical sector.

In China, increases in the median sales per worker of MNE affiliates in the chemical and pharmaceutical sector clearly followed the strengthening of the country's patent regime. There was greater volatility in sales per worker for these affiliates after 2012, when the sales per worker of local firms also stagnated.

a   Given the relatively small number of United States pharmaceutical companies' affiliates in developing countries, pharmaceutical firms were pooled with non-pharmaceutical chemical firms. These broad trends in local company performance are confirmed by other studies on Brazil (Caliari and Ruiz, 2014), China (Deloitte, 2011) and India (Joseph, 2015).

b   Patent reforms were captured using an updated version of the comprehensive patent rights index detailed in Park (2008). This patent index is the unweighted sum of five separate scores for: coverage (inventions that are patentable), membership in international treaties, duration of protection, enforcement mechanisms and restrictions (e.g. compulsory licensing in the event that a patented invention is not sufficiently exploited).

c   This refers to the provision in the TRIPS Agreement that allows firms to file for patents in developing countries that have not already implemented patent protection for pharmaceutical product inventions that are "in the pipeline"; those patents are to be granted by the country when it becomes fully TRIPS-compliant. The least developed countries (LDCs) can now benefit from the transition period until 2033 without providing mailbox provisions (Least Developed Country Members – Obligations under Art. 70(8) and Art. 70(9) of the TRIPS Agreement with respect to Pharmaceutical Products, Decision of 30 November 2015, General Council Document WT/L/971).

FIGURE 6.B4.1 **Patent reforms and sales growth of United States MNE affiliates and listed local companies, 1996–2016**
(Median company sales per employee)

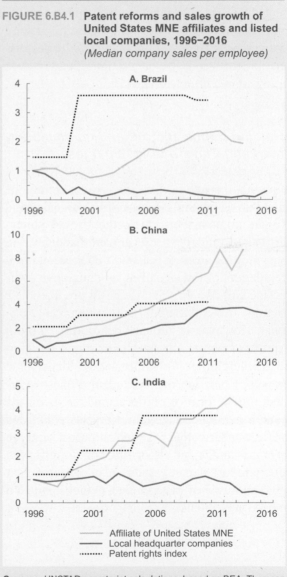

Source: UNCTAD secretariat calculations, based on BEA, Thomson Reuters Eikon (TRE) databases; and Park, 2008.
Note: Sales are median sales per worker in real 2009 dollars. The sales per worker series are normalized, setting these to a value of one for the initial year of the period of observation computed for each host country and industry pair. The local companies considered here are only the publicly listed companies in the TRE database.

Overall, changes in patent protection regimes have had a positive impact on the affiliates' relative sales and profitability performance in these emerging markets. It is not just patent activity that matters, since local companies in Brazil, China and India have also increased patenting across the three sectors surveyed in recent years. What also matters is the concentration of patent ownership in the hands of MNE affiliates, as shown by the analysis using the example of United States MNE affiliates. This, above all, helps to raise their profitability by strengthening incumbent advantages. Therefore, the case for curbing patent reach and scope cannot be emphasized enough. In all three countries – Brazil, China and India – despite relatively competitive markets, patent grants have cemented the affiliates' incumbent advantages in different ways, depending on country-specific factors. In less competitive developing countries or sectors, future outcomes could be devastating if these trends are allowed to continue unchecked.

2. Raiding public sectors and manipulating markets: The "looting" business

In a seminal paper on "Looting" in the context of financial crises in the 1980s, and in particular, the Savings and Loan episode in the United States, Akerlof and Romer (1993: 2) argued that deliberate "bankruptcy for profit will occur if poor accounting, lax regulation, or low penalties for abuse give owners an incentive to pay themselves more than their firms are worth and then default on their debt obligations". However, under such conditions, "looting can spread symbiotically to other markets, bringing to life a whole economic underworld with perverse incentives" (ibid: 3). A core concern of those arguing that a new form of rentier capitalism is on the rise under hyperglobalization is precisely that this "economic underworld" has been allowed not only to creep to the surface, but also to drain public resources directly – rather than only indirectly – by relying on the guarantor role of governments to pick up the tab from bad investments.

(a) Privatization and subsidies

Privatization, or the transfer of State-owned enterprises (SOEs) to private ownership, gained prominence with the United Kingdom's privatization programmes of the early 1980s, and soon after it was widely adopted throughout the world, including in many developing and transition economies. Strongly encouraged by

many international organizations, privatization was expected to improve management practices, increase efficiency and break monopolies, thereby generating net welfare gains. However, instead, many privatization programmes became highly effective vehicles to boost corporate monopoly rents. In some cases, the privatization of SOEs in monopoly industries such as oil, gas and public utilities was preceded by corporate debt restructuring and cost-cutting, and involved strong undervaluation of the assets put up for sale in order to attract buyers (Harvey, 2005). Initially, many such privatization schemes produced new industry players and reduced market concentration by breaking up large State monopolies (Rocha and Kupfer, 2002). However, the widespread lack of a concomitant strengthening of industry oversight enabled the newly privatized companies to retain and grow monopoly power, at times generating exorbitant rents for their new owners. In some cases, this contributed to the growing internationalization of corporate ownership, with foreign investors taking control of major local beneficiary companies of privatization (Ferraz and Hamaguchi, 2002) and transferring rents back home. A well-known example is the privatization in 1990 of the Mexican telecommunications company, Telmex. In addition to tax benefits, Telmex was granted a six-year exclusivity contract over the entire sector. It took more than five years for a regulatory framework and watchdog to be established in Mexico. Meanwhile, monopoly rents secured in the Mexican market allowed the new private owner to finance the expansion of its telecommunications group, America Movil, to an extent that it is now the largest provider of wireless communication services in Latin America (MarketLine, 2016) and the largest non-financial Latin American MNE (Perez-Ludeña, 2016). However, this process has brought few benefits to Mexico, whose consumers were estimated by the OECD to have been overcharged $25.8 billion annually between 2005 and 2009, equivalent to 1.8 per cent of Mexico's average annual GDP during this period (Stryszowska, 2012).

Privatization, broadly defined, may take other forms than the full transfer of ownership from the State to private actors, such as contractual and intermediate forms of public-private partnerships (PPPs),[30] including private finance initiatives (PFI), whereby the private sector provides the capital for investment in a given project and then manages it (Titolo, 2013). Cash-strapped governments, in both developed and developing countries, have promoted such initiatives, rather than trying to increase tax revenues to finance public capital expenditure. Across the world, PFIs now cover a wide range of social service delivery, such as health facilities and schools. However, the consequence has been the creation of streams of annual rental charges that imply future increases in public expenditure, which might weaken the State's capacity to provide social welfare in the future (*TDR 2014*; Shapiro, 2017). Other forms of PPPs, such as leases and concessions, have been employed primarily in the context of a de facto privatization of physical infrastructure. In the case of lease agreements, contract arrangements generally include compensation clauses, or non-compete and adverse action clauses, committing governments to pay up in the case of unexpected events, and prohibiting them from investing in competing infrastructure projects. In addition, such clauses give contractors the right to oppose any government policy that may affect their profitability (Titolo, 2013).

Benefits for the wider public in terms of efficiency from such arrangements have been scarce. A recent study of the water industry in the United Kingdom (Bayliss and Hall, 2017), for example, found that end-users of water and sewage services were paying around 2.3 billion pounds sterling more a year to the private owners of water companies than they would have, had the companies been under State ownership. Similarly, in France, it was estimated that in 2004, the price of water provided through PPPs was 16.6 per cent higher than that provided to communities by public municipalities (Chong et al., 2006). And there is evidence that PPPs engaged in road projects across Europe are, on average, 24 per cent more expensive than similar projects run by public agencies (Blanc-Brude et al., 2006).

Beyond privatization programmes, large corporations have also increasingly benefited from various forms of public subsidies, such as selective tax rates, tax breaks of various kinds, bailouts and direct subsidies, without obvious benefits for taxpayers. Direct subsidies to support specific sectors in difficulty or to promote specific types of activities can end up being extremely regressive transfers. For example, agricultural subsidies are one of the largest per capita transfer programmes in the United States. It has been estimated that around 75 per cent of total subsidies go to 10 per cent of farming companies, including Riceland Foods Inc., Tyler Farms and Pilgrims' Pride

Corp., as well as to MNEs such as Archer Daniels Midland, Cargill and Monsanto (*The Week*, 2013), and just the top three recipients (all agribusiness companies) received more than $1 billion in United States government subsidies between 1995 and 2014.[31] Similarly, almost all of the subsidies still paid to the United Kingdom under the EU's Common Agricultural Policy – around 3.6 billion pounds sterling annually – go to the 10 per cent richest farmers (Standing, 2016: 104).

As the case of the United States oil and gas industry illustrates, such subsidies have a habit of persisting beyond their original purpose. Most subsidies in this sector originated in the early twentieth century, when they were designed to attract capital to a sector with high risks of technological failures and accidents. But they have persisted to the present, long after technology has greatly reduced such risks (Hsu, 2015). G-20 countries spent, on average, $70 billion annually in subsidies for fossil fuel production in 2013 and 2014, with the United States being the biggest spender, at around $20 billion (Bast et al., 2015). Despite clear evidence that the elimination of tax subsidies in this sector in the United States would have only a negligible, if any, impact on fossil fuel production (Allaire and Brown, 2009), those subsidies remain intact thanks to lobbying efforts and campaign contributions by corporate stakeholders.

There is a long list of recent subsidy deals for large corporations across a large number of sectors and developed countries, without obvious benefit to taxpayers (Young, 2016). In addition, tax breaks reduce companies' tax bills for certain types of spending, and are equivalent to direct transfers, but are less visible than increases in public spending. In practice, these tax breaks are often captured by powerful corporations, but have not induced significant changes in investment. For example, in 2010, tax breaks in the United States reduced the statutory corporate tax rate of 35 per cent to an average effective rate of 12.6 per cent, allowing corporations to capture more than $180 billion annually (United States Government Accountability Office, 2013). This needs to be seen against the background of steadily falling corporate tax rates under hyperglobalization, from roughly 40 per cent in 1980 to below 25 per cent in 2013 (IMF, 2014), even as investment rates have declined (*TDR 2016*, chap. V).

(b) Tax avoidance: Base erosion and profit shifting (BEPS) practices

Another example of the misuse of corporate power, while not strictly classified as rent-seeking, also shows how large companies can slip through regulatory cracks and exploit differences in national laws to deny resources to public authorities, and thereby to citizens. The growing ability of MNEs to avoid taxation (as opposed to outright tax evasion, which would be illegal) has been a public concern for some time. BEPS practices include profit shifting – primarily through transfer pricing – along global production chains controlled by MNEs, and the exploitation of gaps and mismatches in national tax rules and regulations (*TDR 2014*, chap. VI; OECD, 2015b). There are no precise and comprehensive global estimates of the extent of BEPS practices, in part because MNEs as well as many governments, particularly in developed countries, have successfully resisted attempts to make country-by-country reporting (CBCR) of core financial company data, including taxes paid, publicly available (Cobham and Jansky, 2017). In the absence of adequate CBCR data that would enable comparisons across countries, and thus allow systematic detection of mismatches, establishing a global baseline for the extent of profit misalignment and tax avoidance is not possible.

Nevertheless, rough estimates of revenue losses due to BEPS practices can be attempted. One recent study suggests that, globally, such losses amounted to 4–10 per cent of corporate income tax revenues (OECD, 2015b: 136–181), corresponding to an accumulated revenue loss of $0.9–$2.1 trillion between 2005 and 2014. Of these, about two thirds are estimated to have been due to profit shifting, and the remaining third to mismatches between tax systems and preferential tax treatment. Crivelli et al. (2015) suggest that global revenue losses due to profit shifting by MNEs may have amounted to around $600 billion in 2013 alone, taking account of the fact that the impact of profit-shifting on public revenues may be felt only with some delay. Zucman (2014) found that the proportion of the profits made by United States firms domestically and abroad that were held in tax havens rose tenfold between the early 1980s and 2013. UNCTAD (2015) has estimated that developing countries are losing $100 billion annually in tax revenues owed by MNEs, solely from their use of offshore hubs as an investment conduit. Given developing countries' greater reliance on corporate tax revenues, as well as their weaker enforcement capabilities, it is likely that their loss of public revenues from such practices is proportionately larger than that of developed countries.[32]

(c) The value-extracting CEO

With market concentration levels as high as described above, CEOs and top managers of large corporations have considerable power over the allocation of economic resources. Misuse of this power, for example to artificially drive up shareholder value in the short term through stock market speculation, rather than to promote productive longer term investment, can have adverse consequences for the economy as a whole (*TDR 2016*, chap. V). It has been argued that such stock market manipulation for rent-seeking purposes increasingly serves to line the pockets of not only rentier shareholders, but also, above all, of the "value-extracting CEOs" themselves (Lazonick, 2016) The main vehicle of this form of managerial rentierism is the practice of stock buybacks that boost the compensation packages of CEOs (a large part of which is usually in the form of stock options and awards), but do little or nothing to improve innovation and, more generally, companies' productivity. Using the Standard & Poor's Executive Compensation database, Lazonick found that highly paid corporate executives from financial as well as non-financial sectors were "very well represented" among the top 0.1 per cent of United States income receivers, with an average income of $7.5 million in 2012. Of this, 64 per cent consisted of realized gains from stock-based compensation (Lazonick, 2016: 22). Other research also shows that such exorbitant rents, and their steep growth over time, were unrelated to talent or to the expansion of a company's production and market shares, thus contributing to growing income inequalities (Keller and Olney, 2017).

As Lazonick (2016: 15–16) points out, this turn to (managerial) rentierism is anything but insignificant: "Over the years 2006–2015, the 459 companies in the S&P 500 Index in January 2016 that were publicly listed over the ten-year period expended $3.9 trillion on stock buybacks, representing 53.6 percent of net income, plus another 36.7 percent of net income on dividends. Much of the remaining 9.7 percent of profits was held abroad, sheltered from U.S. taxes."

The explosion of share buy-backs as the core strategy to boost a company's market valuation (as opposed to financing productive investment from retained earnings and paying dividends to shareholders), particularly in the United States, has pernicious effects, in addition to the impact of absurdly high CEO compensation, on overall income distribution. The short-term financial success of companies engaging in this strategy often forces firms that began with a more productive approach to investment planning, to follow suit in order to compete on the stock markets. It also strongly reinforces more general financialized investment strategies by which companies distribute more than their total income to shareholders, and use debt and the sale of assets to refinance their investments (Lazonick, 2016).[33]

E. Conclusions

This chapter has highlighted the emergence of a new form of rentier capitalism as a result of some recent trends: highly pronounced increases in market concentration and the consequent market power of large global corporations, the inadequacy and waning reach of the regulatory powers of nation States, and the growing influence of corporate lobbying to defend unproductive rents (Drutman, 2015; George, 2015). These factors are closely related, creating a vicious cycle of underregulation and regulatory capture, on the one hand, and further rampant growth of corporate market power on the other. Panic (2011) has described this self-reinforcing dynamic of the interplay between lobbying and market power as one between the institutionally determined integration of the global economy and its spontaneous integration. Institutional integration has been led by nation States advocating and adopting both national and international policy frameworks to govern the global economy and economic integration. Spontaneous integration refers to the international division of labour "achieved mainly through the actions of multinational corporations in pursuit of their corporate interests and objectives" (ibid: 4). As spontaneous integration progresses, its main protagonists begin to shape institutional integration to further their own interests and objectives. As the chapter argues, once institutional countervailing powers – such as those of nation States, civil society and labour organizations – have been weakened, corporate rentierism has flourished. More generally, this raises the possibility of a "Medici vicious circle, where money is used to get political power and political power is used to make money" (Zingales, 2017).

A major arena in which the rising tension between the powers of corporations and nation States is being played out, is in bilateral and regional trade and investment agreements. In the absence of decisive multilateral action to redress the growing economic and power imbalances at the heart of the global economy, supranational regulatory frameworks covering a wide range of economic policies – IPR regimes, industrial policy and public procurement policies foremost amongst these – are being shaped by corporate rentier interests, rather than by considerations of wider public interests.

In a context in which the "revolving doors" of economic and political power keep turning frantically (LaPira et al., 2017), it will not be easy to rein in corporate rentierism and cut through regulatory capture in order to promote inclusive growth. As a general starting point, there is growing recognition that both knowledge and competition are public goods (Stiglitz, 2016b), and that policies designed for their use need to take into account distributional objectives and impacts.[34] But, as discussed in the next chapter, it will require the countervailing power of a well-functioning intergovernmental machinery to eradicate the "economic underworld" of global corporate rent-seeking.

Notes

1   For a more detailed discussion of Prebisch's contribution, see Toye and Toye, 2004.

2   Royal Swedish Academy of Sciences, The Science of Taming Powerful Firms, 13 October 2014 (see: http://www.nobelprize.org/nobel_prizes/economic-sciences/laureates/2014/press.html).

3   See, for example, Baker 2015; *The Economist,* 2016; Standing 2016; Stiglitz, 2016a; Zingales, 2017.

4   Thus, Piketty, for example, suggests that we may have gone from a "society of rentiers", by which he means the Keynesian financial rentier, to a "society of managers" (i.e. highly paid top managers and CEOs of large corporations) (Piketty, 2014: 276).

5   A recent exception is Keller and Olney (2017), who examined executive pay in firms in the United States between 1993 and 2013 and found that globalization had enhanced their ability (particularly that of the larger firms) to capture rents.

6   For a detailed technical discussion of the construction of this measure and comparisons with alternative measures using company level data, see the online annex to this chapter at: http://unctad.org/tdr2017/Annex.

7   The data are extracted from Thomson Reuters *Worldscope Database* that takes into consideration a variety of accounting conventions, and is designed to facilitate comparisons between companies and industries, within and across national boundaries. The recorded number of quoted companies increased from 5,600 in 1995 to 30,100 in 2015. The scope of the analysis is restricted to publicly listed companies. These represent a homogeneous and coherent group to the extent that they are generally large corporations operating across national borders; they face similar opportunities and constraints with regard to financing, and their profitability relies less on national contexts than on the state of the world economy (Artus, 2007). We assume that the weight of non-publicly quoted multinational enterprises (MNEs) is not important enough to significantly alter our results for the top of the distribution.

8   *Developed economies (30)*: Australia, Austria, Belgium, Bulgaria, Canada, Cyprus, Czechia, Denmark, Estonia, Finland, France, Germany, Greece, Iceland, Ireland, Italy, Japan, Latvia, Lithuania, Luxembourg, the Netherlands, New Zealand, Norway, Poland, Portugal, Spain, Sweden, Switzerland, the United Kingdom and the United States.
    Developing and transition economies (26): Argentina, Bahrain, Brazil, Chile, China, Colombia, Hong Kong (China), India, Indonesia, Jordan, Kuwait, Lebanon, Malaysia, Mexico, Oman, the Philippines, Qatar, the Russian Federation, Singapore, South Africa, the Republic of Korea, Taiwan Province of China, Thailand, Turkey, the United Arab Emirates and Viet Nam.

9   The historical series for sector-adjusted benchmark ROAs were in fact stable for the entire period of observation (1995 to 2015), with the exception of breaks during the two major financial crises mentioned.

10 Market capitalization refers to the total market value of publicly listed firms, calculated as the year-end share price times the number of shares outstanding.

11 It should be noted, nonetheless, that a strategy of vertical disintegration to refocus on core business was pursued in the 1980s and 1990s partly in response to demands for increased shareholder value in the short term. This somewhat slowed down the expansion of large conglomerates, in some instances even reversing the process (*TDR 2016*, chap. V).

12 The database includes 17,000 publicly listed firms and 11,400 privately held firms from 42 countries (McKinsey Global Institute, 2015).

13 According to McKinsey Global Institute (2015: 6), the most profitable firms operating in industries such as pharmaceuticals, medical devices and IT are between 40 and 110 per cent larger than their median-sized counterparts. See also Starrs (2014), who arrives at a similar result using the Forbes Global 2000 annual list of the world's top publicly traded companies.

14 Results using either the top 200 firms and/or the bottom 1,000 firms show very similar trends. More generally, adjustment of this concentration index, by referencing this to the hypothetical equal share of market capitalization of the top 100 firms (assuming an equal distribution of market shares) as well as to the observed share of the bottom 2,000 firms, ensures that the trend analysis remains meaningful despite absolute changes in the denominator of these ratios, with the total number of publicly listed non-financial firms in the database rising from 5,600 in 1995 to 30,100 in 2015. What is measured is evolving market capitalization concentration, or its trend, rather than absolute magnitudes.

15 Decker et al. (2016) ascribe this trend to declining business dynamics and entrepreneurship in the case of the United States.

16 The general advantage of a unique ranking criterion is that it allows a direct comparison of these various concentration measures. Market capitalization is the most comprehensive of such ranking criteria, behaving like a summary index of revenues and assets, since it is closely correlated with these two variables. For this reason, using any of the above criteria for ranking a firm's performance yields the same trend results. Market capitalization, however, best captures interrelated aspects of a firm's performance: a high stock price facilitates acquisitions, and conversely, protects against (hostile) takeovers. It also helps raise capital in the capital markets and may, in addition,

bring diverse, less tangible benefits through reputational effects and lobbying powers.

17 The subsequent slight decline, especially in the ratio of the observed share of the top 100 firms in physical assets relative to their hypothetical equal shares, largely reflects a shift in the composition of those firms after 2013 and following the oil price slump since 2014. This shift was away from energy firms with extensive ownership of physical assets, to firms in the health-care and technology sectors that have higher market capitalization but much lower levels of ownership of physical assets. The number of energy firms in the top 100 fell from 18 in 2013 to only 8 by 2015. Even so, the average ratio of physical assets to market capitalization for energy firms was 1.4, compared to 0.6 for other industries.

18 The first type of economies of scale (sunk fixed costs) are often also referred to as static returns to scale, whereas the latter type of economies of scale – the gradual widening and differentiation of markets and positive (learning and network) spillover effects on industry supply – are generally referred to as dynamic returns to scale.

19 Note that while Autor et al. (2017b) measure productivity in a number of ways, including value added per worker, output per worker, patents per worker and total factor productivity, no significant changes to their results are observed.

20 The scope of the software and IT services industry is based on Thomson Reuters Business Classification.

21 The decline in the productivity performance of the top 100 firms after 2013 mirrors that of market concentration indicators in figure 6.3 above; that is the exit of many firms in the energy sector in the wake of the price slump in 2014, and to a lesser extent, also of firms in the telecommunication services sector, in favour of the health-care and technology sectors.

22 Global control networks are loose alliances between firms operating in the same industry, held together primarily through common ownership stakes by a few large institutional investors in the firms constituting these networks (Vitali et al., 2011). These institutional investors therefore wield substantial control over the strategic decision-making by network firms, including their strategies for expansion through pricing policies and the use of barriers to entry, such as network effects, information asymmetries, patents, branding and access to new markets. Global value chains are usually described as the fragmentation of the production process into discrete activities – the transformation of primary products, the supply of intermediate products and services, technological design, branding, advertising and delivery – that are spread across different geographical locations (e.g. Davis et al., 2017). A variety of business models combining horizontal with vertical integration and direct ownership with arm's-length control of outsourced and subcontracted suppliers give lead firms a high degree of overall control over the rules and conditions of participation in these production chains, and thus also considerable market power.

23 The statistical analysis of firm level data on United States multinational enterprises and their foreign affiliates was conducted at the Bureau of Economic Analysis (BEA), United States Department of Commerce, under arrangements that maintain legal confidentiality requirements. Views expressed in this report do not necessarily reflect those of the United States Department of Commerce.

24 Buckman (2005: 94), for instance, quotes an interview with a Chief Executive of Pfizer, who stated: "Our combined strength allowed us to establish a global private sector/ government network to lay the ground for what became TRIPS."

25 Glasgow (2001) identifies five evergreening strategies: (i) using legislative provisions and loopholes to apply for a patent extension; (ii) suing generic manufacturers for patent infringement; (iii) merging with direct competitors as patent rights expire in an effort to continue the monopoly; (iv) recombining drugs in slightly different ways to secure new patents, and layering several patents on different aspects of the drug to secure perennial monopoly rights; and (v) using advertising and brand name development to increase the barrier to entry of generic drug manufacturers.

26 The WTO Marrakesh Agreement included no so-called regulatory issues with the exception of IP protection, the inclusion of which was hotly debated at the time. In contrast, the first generation of FTAs covered investment as well as a wider range of provisions that stipulated, at least in part, stronger IPRs (i.e. TRIPS plus). With the second generation of FTAs, such as the Free Trade Agreement between the United States and the Republic of Korea , there is a full blown expansion of regulatory issues, attempts to promote sector-specific harmonization of such issues(e.g. for the pharmaceutical sector), as well as the inclusion of new areas such as ecommerce.

27 For full details of the empirical analysis, see the online annex to this chapter, available at: http://unctad.org/tdr2017/Annex.

28 Sales per worker was used as the relevant variable rather than total sales, because of disclosure constraints in the BEA database.

29 Comparable data to assess the impact of patent rights protection on rates of return in these sectors are available only for the listed companies in the database.

30 In most cases, public accounting rules allow PPPs to be recorded off-balance sheet (EPEC, 2015), a practice long criticized by the IMF (IMF, 2004).

31 UNCTAD secretariat calculations, based on the Farm Subsidy database of the Environmental Working Group (available at: http://www.ewg.org/agmag/2010/06/farm-subsidy-database#.WXRrc4pLfUp).

32 OECD (2015b), corroborated for example by Johannesen et al. (2016). Monkam (2012) also suggests that

transfer pricing is the most damaging corporate tax avoidance strategy for developing countries.

33 In some industries, the interaction with other strategies to assist rent extraction is particularly obvious. For example, pharmaceutical companies in the United States have allocated the profits generated from high drug prices resulting from patent monopolies, to massive repurchases or buy-backs of their own corporate stock for the sole purpose of giving manipulative boosts to their stock prices (Lazonick et al., 2017).

34 For example, the EU's competition watchdog has recently sought to strengthen antitrust policies (Toplensky, 2017).

References

Akerlof GA and Romer PM (1993). Looting: The economic underworld of bankruptcy for profit. *Brookings Papers on Economic Activity* (2): 1–73.

Allaire M and Brown S (2009). Eliminating subsidies for fossil fuel production: Implications for U.S. oil and natural gas markets. Issue Brief No. 09-10, Resources for the Future, Washington, DC.

Artus P (2007). Profitabilité: Sociétés cotées et ensemble des entreprises. *Flash Économie*, No. 355, Natixis, 28 September.

Atkinson AB (2015). *Inequality: What can be Done?* Cambridge, MA, Harvard University Press.

Autor D, Dorn D, Katz LF, Patterson C and Van Reenen J (2017a). Concentrating on the fall of labor share. Working Paper No. 23108, National Bureau of Economic Research, Cambridge, MA.

Autor D, Dorn D, Katz LF, Patterson C and Van Reenen J (2017b). The fall of the labor share and the rise of superstar firms. Discussion Paper No. 1482, Centre for Economic Performance, London School of Economics, London.

Baker D (2015). The upward redistribution of income: Are rents the story? Working paper, Center for Economic and Policy Research, Washington, DC.

Barkai S (2016). Declining labor and capital shares. Working Paper, University of Chicago, Chicago, IL.

Barnett TO (2008). Maximizing welfare through technological innovation. *George Mason Law Review,* 15(5): 1191–1204.

Bast E, Doukas A, Pickard S, Van Der Burg L and Whitley S (2015). Empty promises: G20 subsidies to oil, gas and coal production. Overseas Development Institute and Oil Change International, London and Washington, DC.

Baumol WJ (1990). Entrepreneurship: Productive, unproductive and destructive. *Journal of Political Economy,* 98 (5, Part 1): 893–921.

Bayliss K and Hall D (2017). Bringing water into public ownership: Costs and benefits. Working paper, School of African and Oriental Studies and University of Greenwich, London.

Bessen J and Meurer MJ (2008). *Patent Failure: How Judges, Bureaucrats and Lawyers put Innovators at Risk.* Princeton, NJ and Oxford, Princeton University Press.

Bessen J and Meurer MJ (2014). The direct costs from NPE disputes. *Cornell Law Review*, 99(2): 387–424.

Blanc-Brude F, Goldsmith H and Valila T (2006). Ex ante construction costs in the European road sector: A comparison of public-private partnerships and traditional public procurement. Economic and Finance Report No. 2006/1, European Investment Bank, Luxembourg.

Buckman G (2005). *Global Trade: Past Mistakes, Future Choices.* London, Zed Books.

Caliari T and Ruiz RM (2014). Brazilian pharmaceutical industry and generic drugs policy: Impacts on structure and innovation and recent developments. *Science and Public Policy,* 41(2): 245–256.

Chong E, Huet F, Saussier S and Steiner F (2006). Public-private partnerships and prices: Evidence from water distribution in France. *Review of Industrial Organization*, 29 (1–2): 149–169.

Cobham A and Jansky P (2017). Global distribution of revenue loss from tax avoidance: Re-estimation and country results. Working Paper No. 2017/55, United Nations University-World Institute for Development Economics Research (UNU-WIDER), Helsinki.

Council of Economic Advisers (2016). Benefits of competition and indicators of market power. April, Issue Brief, Washington, DC.

Crivelli E, De Mooij R and Keen M (2015). Base erosion, profit shifting and developing countries. Working Paper No. 15/118, International Monetary Fund; Working Paper No. 15/09, Oxford University Centre for Business Taxation, Oxford.

Cumming C (2015). What's behind the huge increase in bank patent filings? *American Banker*, 2 July. Available at: http://www.law.edu/res/docs/2015-0702-AmericanBankerArticle.pdf.

Cusumano MA (2010). *Staying Power: Six Enduring Principles for Managing Strategy and Innovation in an Uncertain World.* Oxford, Oxford University Press.

Davis D, Kaplinsky R and Morris M (2017). Rents, power and governance in global value chains. Working Paper Series No. 2, PRISM School of Economics, University of Cape Town, Cape Town.

Deakin S (2005). The coming transformation of shareholder value. *Corporate Governance: An International Review,* 13(1): 11–18.

Dealogic (2017). Investment banking scorecard. Available at: http://graphics.wsj.com/investment-banking-scorecard/ (accessed 13 March 2017).

Decker RA, Haltiwanger J, Jarmin RS and Miranda J (2016). Where has all the skewness gone? The decline in high-growth (young) firms in the US. *European Economic Review* (86): 4–23.

Deloitte (2011). The next phase: Opportunities in China's pharmaceutical market. Deloitte Touche Tohmatsu, Hong Kong.

Drahos P (2003). When the weak bargain with the strong: Negotiations in the World Trade Organization. *International Negotiation*, 8(1): 79–109.

Drexl J (2008). Is there a 'more economic approach' to intellectual property and competition law? In: Drexl J, ed. *Research Handbook on Intellectual Property and Competition Law*. Cheltenham, Edward Elgar Publishing: 27–53.

Drutman L (2015). *The Business of America is Lobbying: How Corporations Became Politicized and Politics Became More Corporate*. Oxford, Oxford University Press.

EIG (2017). Dynamism in retreat: Consequences for regions, markets, and workers. Economic Innovation Group, Washington, DC.

EPEC (2015). Debt and deficit treatment of PPPs according to Eurostat. European PPP Expertise Centre. Available at: http://www.eib.org/epec/g2g/i-project-identification/12/125/index.htm.

Epstein G and Power D (2003). Rentier incomes and financial crises: An empirical examination of trends and cycles in some OECD countries. Working Paper Series No. 57, Political Economy Research Institute (PERI), University of Massachusetts, Amherst, MA.

Ferraz JC and Hamaguchi N (2002). Introduction: M&A and privatization in developing countries: Changing ownership structure and its impact on economic performance. *The Developing Economies*, 40(4): 383–399.

Fildes N (2017). What is at stake in the Apple-Qualcomm dispute? *Financial Times*. 28 April.

Fink C (2013). Intellectual property activity worldwide: Key trends, facts and figures. In: Abbott FM, Correa CM and Drahos P, eds. *Emerging Markets and the World Patent Order*. Cheltenham, Edward Elgar Publishing: 37–45.

Foroohar R (2017). Release Big Tech's grip on power. *Financial Times*. 18 June.

Foster JB, McChesney RW and Jonna RJ (2011). Monopoly and competition in twenty-first century capitalism. *Monthly Review*, 62(11): 1–39.

Fratini SM (2016). Rent as a share of product and Sraffa's price equations. *Cambridge Journal of Economics*, 40(2): 599–613.

Galbraith JK (1954). *The Great Crash 1929*. London and New York, Penguin Books.

Gehl Sampath P and Roffe P (forthcoming). The untimely death of the Transpacific Partnership Agreement: Where do we go next? CEIPI-ICTSD Series on Trade and Intellectual Property, Strasbourg and Geneva.

George S (2015). *Shadow Sovereigns: How Global Corporations are Seizing Power*. Cambridge, Polity Press.

Glasgow LJ (2001). Stretching the limits of intellectual property rights: Has the pharmaceutical industry gone too far? *IDEA, The Journal of Law and Technology* 41(2): 227–258.

Glyn A (2006). *Capitalism Unleashed: Finance, Globalization and Welfare*. Oxford, Oxford University Press.

Grullon G, Larkin Y and Michaely R (2017). Are US industries becoming more concentrated? Available at: https://ssrn.com/abstract=2612047 or http://dx.doi.org/10.2139/ssrn.2612047.

Hall BH (2009). Business and financial method patents, innovation and policy. *Scottish Journal of Political Economy*, 56(4): 443–473.

Hansmann H and Kraakman R (2001). The end of history for corporate law. *Georgetown Law Journal*, 89(2): 439–468.

Harvey D (2005). *A Brief History of Neoliberalism*. Oxford, Oxford University Press.

Hsu S-L (2015). The rise and rise of the one percent: Considering legal causes of wealth inequality. *Emory Law Journal Online*, 64: 2043–2072. Available at: http://law.emory.edu/elj/elj-online/volume-64/essays/considering-legal-causes-wealth-inequality.html.

Hunt RM (2010). Business method patents in U.S. financial services. *Contemporary Economic Policy*, 28(3): 322–352.

IMF (2004). Public-private partnerships. International Monetary Fund, Washington, DC.

IMF (2014). Spillovers in international corporate taxation. Policy paper. International Monetary Fund, Washington DC.

Ireland P (2010). Limited liability, shareholder rights and the problem of corporate irresponsibility. *Cambridge Journal of Economics*, 34(5): 837–868.

Joseph RK (2015). *Pharmaceutical Industry and Public Policy in Post-Reform India*. London, Routledge Taylor and Francis.

Johannesen N, Tørsløv T and Wier L (2016). Are less developed countries more exposed to multinational tax avoidance? Method and evidence from micro-data. Working Paper No. 2016/10, United Nations University-World Institute for Development Economics Research (UNU-WIDER), Helsinki.

Katz ML, and Shapiro C (1999). Antitrust in software markets. In: Eisenach JA and Lenard TM, eds. *Competition, Innovation and the Microsoft Monopoly: Antitrust in the Digital Marketplace*. New York, NY, Springer Science and Business Media: 29–81.

Keller W and Olney WW (2017). Globalization and executive compensation. Working Paper No. 23384,

National Bureau of Economic Research, Cambridge, MA.

Keynes JM ([1936] 1973). *The Collected Writings of John Maynard Keynes: The General Theory of Employment, Interest and Money*, vol. VII. London, Macmillan.

Khan LM (2017). Amazon bites off even more monopoly power. *New York Times*, 21 June.

Khan MK and Jomo KS, eds. (2000). *Rents, Rent-Seeking and Economic Development: Theory and Evidence in Asia*. Cambridge, Cambridge University Press.

Kindleberger CP and Aliber RZ (2011). *Manias, Panics and Crashes: A History of Financial Crises*. London, Palgrave Macmillan.

Krueger AO (1974). The political economy of the rent-seeking society. *American Economic Review*, 64(3): 291–303.

Kwoka J (2015). The changing nature of efficiencies in mergers and in merger analysis. *The Antitrust Bulletin*, 60(3): 231–249.

LaPira TM and Thomas HF (2017). *Revolving Door Lobbying: Public Service, Private Influence, and the Unequal Representation of Interests*. Lawrence, KS, University Press of Kansas.

Lazonick W (2016). The value-extracting CEO: How executive stock-based pay undermines investment in productive capabilities. Working Paper No. 54, Institute for New Economic Thinking (INET), Oxford.

Lazonick W (2013). The financialization of the U.S. corporation: What has been lost, and how it can be regained. *Seattle University Law Review*, 36(2): 857–909.

Lazonick W, Hopkins M, Jacobson K, Sakinç ME and Tulum Ö (2017). US pharma's financialized business model. Working Paper No. 60, Institute for New Economic Thinking (INET), Oxford.

Lemley MA (2015). Faith-based intellectual property. *UCLA Law Review*, 62: 1328–1346.

Lerner J, Baker J, Speen A and Leamon A (2015). Financial patent quality: Finance patents after state street. Working Paper No. 16-068, Harvard Business School, Cambridge, MA.

Locke SD and Schmidt WD (2008). Business method patents: The challenge of coping with an ever-changing standard of patentability. *Fordham Intellectual Property, Media and Law Journal*, 18(5): 1079–1094.

Mahdawi A (2017). It's not just Amazon coming for Whole Foods – Silicon Valley is eating the world. *The Guardian*. 20 June.

MarketLine (2016). Company Profile: America Movil, SAB de CV (AMX). Available at: https://www.marketresearch.com/ (accessed 19 June 2017).

McKinsey Global Institute (2015). Playing to win: The new global competition for corporate profits. Available at: http://www.mckinsey.com/mgi/overview/in-the-news/playing-to-win-the-new-global-competition-for-corporate-profits.

Mill JS ([1848] 1884). *Principles of Political Economy*. New York, NY, D. Appleton.

Miller SP (2013). Where's the innovation: An analysis on the quantity and quality of anticipated and obvious patents. *Virginia Journal of Law and Technology*, 18(1): 2–55.

Monkam N (2012). ATAF regional studies on reform priorities of African tax administrations: Africa-wide Report. Johannesburg, African Tax Administration Forum. Available at: http://ataftax-dev.co.za/images/atrn_documents/15617%20-%20ATAF_AFRICA-WIDE%20REPORT_ENG_v8.pdf (accessed 26 July 2017).

Nolan P (2002). China and the global business revolution. *Cambridge Journal of Economics*, 26(1): 119–137.

OECD (2015a). *Enquiries into Intellectual Property's Economic Impact*. Paris, OECD Publishing.

OECD (2015b). *Measuring and Monitoring BEPS, Action 11 – 2015, Final Report*. OECD/G20 Base Erosion and Profit Shifting Project, Paris, OECD Publishing.

Palma JG (2009). The revenge of the market on the rentiers: Why neo-liberal reports of the end of history turned out to be premature. *Cambridge Journal of Economics,* 33(4): 829–869.

Panic M (2011). Globalization in the age of transnationals: The claims and the reality. In: Panic M, ed. *Globalization: A threat to International Cooperation and Peace?* (2nd edition). London, Palgrave Macmillan: 3–56.

Park WG (2008). International patent protection: 1960–2005. *Research Policy*, 37: 761–766.

Patterson MR (2012). Leveraging information about patents: Settlements, portfolios, and holdups. *Houston Law Review*, 50(2): 483–522.

Perez Ludeña M (2016). Multinational enterprises from Latin America: Investment strategies and limits to growth and diversification. *Transnational Corporations Review*, 8(1): 41–49.

Philippon T and Reshef A (2009). Wages and human capital in the U.S. financial industry: 1909-2006. Working Paper No. 14644, National Bureau of Economic Research, Cambridge, MA.

Piketty T (2014). *Capital in the Twenty-First Century*. Cambridge, MA, Belknap Press of Harvard University Press.

Prebisch R (1986). Address delivered at the twenty-first session of ECLAC, Mexico City, 24 April. *CEPAL Review*, 29: 13–16.

Ricardo D ([1817] 1962). On the principles of political economy and taxation. In: Sraffa P, ed. *The Works and Correspondence of David Ricardo, Vol. 1*. Cambridge, Cambridge University Press.

Rivera E (2006). Modelos de privatización y desarrollo de la competencia en las telecomunicaciones de Centroamérica y México. *Estudios y Perspectivas,*

No. 66. Economic Commission for Latin America and the Caribbean (ECLAC), México, DF.

Rocha F and D. Kupfer (2002). Structural changes and specialization in Brazilian industry: The evolution of leading companies and the M&A process. *Developing Economies*, 40(4): 497–521.

Ryan-Collins J (2017). How land disappeared from economic theory. *Evonomics*, 4 April. Available at: http://evonomics.com/josh-ryan-collins-land-economic-theory/.

Schumpeter JA (1942). *Capitalism, Socialism and Democracy*. New York, NY, Harper Torchbooks.

Seccareccia M and Lavoie M (2016). Income distribution, rentiers and their role in a capitalist economy. *International Journal of Political Economy,* 45(3): 200–223.

Shapiro N (2017). The hidden cost of privatization (blog). Institute for New Economic Thinking. Available at: https://www.ineteconomics.org/perspectives/blog/the-business-of-government.

Smith A ([1776] 1981). An Inquiry into the Nature and Causes of the Wealth of Nations. In: Campbell RK and Skinner AS, eds. *The Glasgow Edition of the Works and Correspondence of Adam Smith*, vol. II. Indianapolis, IN, Liberty Fund.

Standing G (2016). *The Corruption of Capitalism: Why Rentiers Thrive and Work Does not Pay*. London, Biteback Publishing.

Starrs S (2014). The chimera of global convergence. *New Left Review,* 87: 81–96.

Stiglitz J (2016a). Inequality and economic growth. In: Mazzucato M and Jacobs M, eds. *Rethinking Capitalism: Economics and Policy for Sustainable and Inclusive Growth*. Hoboken, NJ, Wiley Blackwell: 134–155.

Stiglitz J (2016b). Towards a broader view of competition policy. Lecture presented at the 4th BRICS International Competition Conference in Durban, November 2015.

Stryszowska M (2012). Estimation of loss in consumer surplus resulting from excessive pricing of telecommunication services in Mexico. Digital Economy Papers No. 191, OECD Publishing, Paris.

Sylos-Labini P (1969). *Oligopoly and Technical Progress* (revised edition). Cambridge, MA, Harvard University Press.

The Economist (2013). Institutions matter, a lot. 6 March.

The Economist (2016). Too much of a good thing. 26 March.

The Week (2013). Farm subsidies: A welfare program for agribusiness, 10 August. Available at: http://theweek.com/articles/461227/farm-subsidies-welfare-program-agribusiness.

Tirole J (2015). Market failures and public policy. *American Economic Review,* 105(6): 1665–1682.

Titolo M (2013). Leasing sovereignty: On State infrastructure contracts. *University of Richmond Law Review*, 47(2): 631–693.

Toplensky R (2017). EU considers tougher competition powers. *Financial Times*. 2 July.

Toye J and Toye R (2004). *The UN and Global Political Economy: Trade, Finance, and Development*. Bloomington, IN, Indiana University Press.

UNCTAD (2015) *World Investment Report 2015: Reforming International Investment Governance*. United Nations publications. Sales No. E.15.II.D.5. New York and Geneva.

UNCTAD *(TDR 1997)*. *Trade and Development Report, 1997*. United Nations publication. Sales No. E.97.II.D.8. New York and Geneva.

UNCTAD *(TDR 2014)*. *Trade and Development Report, 2014: Global Governance and Policy Space for Development*. United Nations publication. Sales No. E.14.II.D.4. New York and Geneva.

UNCTAD *(TDR 2015)*. *Trade and Development Report, 2015: Making the International Financial Architecture Work for Development*. United Nations publication. Sales No. E .15.II.D.4. New York and Geneva.

UNCTAD *(TDR 2016)*. *Trade and Development Report, 2016: Structural Transformation for Inclusive and Sustained Growth*. United Nations publication. Sales No. E.16.II.D.5. New York and Geneva.

United States Government Accountability Office (2013). Corporate tax expenditures: Evaluations of tax deferrals and graduated tax rates. GAO 13-789, Washington, DC.

Vitali S, Glattfelder J and Battiston S (2011). The network of global corporate control. *PLoS ONE,* 6(10): e25995. Available at: https://doi.org/10.1371/journal.pone.0025995.

Walsh JS (2013). The future of the small software firm: A case for the proper balance of laws protecting software and competition (doctoral dissertation). University of Leicester, Leicester.

Weil D (2014). *The Fissured Workplace: Why Work Became so Bad for so Many and What can be Done to Improve it*. Cambridge, MA, Harvard University Press.

Young A (2016). Taxpayer-funded capitalism: Here are the biggest corporate subsidy deals of 2016. *Salon,* December 27. Available at: http://www.salon.com/2016/12/27/taxpayer-funded-capitalism-here-are-the-biggest-corporate-subsidy-deals-of-2016/.

Zingales L (2017). Towards a political theory of the firm. New Working Paper Series No. 10, Stigler Center for the Study of the Economy and the State, University of Chicago, Chicago, IL.

Zucman G (2014). Taxing across borders: Tracking personal wealth and corporate profits. *Journal of Economic Perspectives*, 28(4): 121–148.

TOWARDS A GLOBAL NEW DEAL

VII

A. Introduction

Much will have to change if the "inclusive economy" is to become a working reality, as argued in previous chapters of this *Report*. Today's hyperglobalized world economy is delivering unfair and inequitable outcomes for far too many people in too many places. Economic and financial crises, like that of 2008–2009, are only the most visible manifestations of a world economy that has become increasingly unbalanced in ways that are not only exclusionary, but also destabilizing and dangerous for the future political, social and environmental health of the planet.

Previous chapters in this *Report* have indicated that these imbalances cannot be considered simply as collateral damage from technological changes or the spread of global market forces, but rather result from policy decisions and omissions, along with the rollback of regulations and the decay of representative institutions. Above all, shifts in power relations and bargaining appear to have had a particularly pernicious bearing on the kinds of outcomes witnessed in recent decades. The imbalances, and the challenges they pose, can be found in both developed and developing economies, but even with the periodic growth spurts that have emerged under hyperglobalization, they are often accentuated in poorer countries by the traditional obstacles to sustained and shared growth associated with resource constraints, informal employment conditions and technological deficits.

United Nations initiatives such as the Sustainable Development Goals (SDGs) and the Paris Climate Agreement suggest a more hopeful future. But what is still needed is a supportive policy narrative to correct the imbalances that generate exclusionary outcomes, so that social inclusion goes hand in hand with economic prosperity, shared technological progress and a healthy environment. Unlocking the creative impulses of markets will be central to this task, but

controlling their more destructive tendencies is just as important. The notion that markets, left to their own devices, can deliver socially and economically optimal outcomes is a fallacy and should be dropped. The experiences of recent years – as during other major crises of the last century – are a powerful reminder that the State can and must reform and adapt markets at all levels to create an environment that can deliver growth and development for the population as a whole (UNCTAD, 2015a: 22).

This calls for more engaged States that are also more accountable. Across today's increasingly interdependent world, the nation State still remains the basic unit of legitimacy and leadership, and one that citizens ultimately turn to for economic security, political loyalties and social cohesion. However, the capacities needed by the State to deliver these conditions have been eroded in many countries, thanks in part to the heightened power of mobile capital and the policy overreach of market fundamentalists. The subordination of political leadership to the management, accounting practices and narrow profit orientation of private business interests is raising fears that the public sector too often shoulders the risks while the private sector grabs the gains. There is potential to enhance the developmental impact of cooperation between the public and private sectors, but achieving this will require a clear distinction between private interests and the broader public good, and addressing the tensions that inevitably arise between the two.

If not, the difficult trade-offs and distributional choices that should be the subject of democratic debate and compromise are effectively ceded to unregulated or underregulated market processes and to the interests that benefit too frequently, leading to outcomes that are unfair, perverse and far from socially optimal.

These outcomes would not have been supported by the earliest proponents of market economies, such as the influential Adam Smith, who always insisted that the benefits of markets depended upon having true competition alongside a strong State (Smith, 1776), as well as strong ethical underpinnings (Smith, 1759). Today's development is troubling for not only undermining representative politics, but in the longer run threatening to undermine the legitimacy of the market itself by increasing the risks of a destabilizing backlash from those who consider themselves neglected by their elected leaders in favour of supposedly impersonal forces of market competition.

Much can still be achieved at the level of the nation State, as discussed later in this chapter, and typically that is the main locus of transformative development strategies (*TDR 2016*). But the integrated nature of the world economy inevitably places limits on national policies and their effectiveness. Many of the sources of exclusion and stratification can be traced to the international level, as hyperglobalization reproduces the same global patterns of growth as those observed within countries. At the same time, a number of tools needed for a more inclusive economy are constrained (and in some cases forbidden) by international rules and agreements. A balanced global economy cannot emerge if countries lack the policy space to leverage the potential benefits and mitigate the costs of international competition.

This makes greater international coordination an urgent requirement of any global new deal. It is essential for strengthening and revamping genuine multilateralism that is geared towards proactively promoting more and better quality employment, reinstating the regulations that previously afforded protection against speculative and misdirected finance, and making social welfare a universal right provided by governments, rather than being treated as just another commodity to be sold in the market. Thus, international coordination will need to be the underlying principle of any comprehensive and consistent policy agenda, so that national policy efforts can be supported, beggar-thy-neighbour approaches avoided, and the benefits of more inclusive growth shared fairly among all countries.

This may seem a tall order in the current geopolitical climate, especially after three decades of excessively unregulated and overly market-oriented economic and social policies. Indeed, it will clearly be a huge challenge for the international community. But encouragement can be drawn from previous episodes in history when dramatic policy changes and coordination were undertaken, often very quickly and in ways that had not been anticipated even a short time earlier. The last century provides many instances of visionary leaders and practical policymakers successfully forging forward-looking paths when the world faced seemingly intractable challenges to the prevailing economic and social order. This chapter draws on such lessons from the mid-twentieth century: the New Deal of the 1930s, the Marshall Plan and the lesser known United Nations Conference on Trade and Employment which culminated in the Havana Charter for an International Trade Organization, both launched in 1947. Unlike the more limited rescue and repair efforts of this century, these initiatives profoundly shook up conventional thinking, and negotiated bold and generous schemes that both addressed the immediate problems at hand and planted seeds for longer term economic and social transformation.

In many ways, the current conjuncture is just as propitious for introducing an equally transformative agenda. The established order is under attack from both ends of the ideological spectrum, and its legitimacy has significantly diminished, as reflected in growing protests by the general public. In many parts of the world there is widespread anxiety that the current system is not delivering the results needed, and even fear that things may get worse. On the positive side, political momentum for change has been created by the SDGs – a negotiated agreement by all United Nations member countries for what is essentially the largest investment push in history. It is no longer an option to wait until the next crisis in order to mobilize the requisite political will and coordination; the goal now must be to harness this moment of consensus for delivering the required combination of resources, policies and reforms necessary for a more inclusive process and outcomes at both global and national levels.

This chapter draws on the lessons of the past to help sketch a new policy agenda that can help create more inclusive societies and economies. It argues that it is possible, and even necessary, to construct a global new deal that fosters proactive fiscal policies in different countries, along with coordinated strategies that address the triple challenges of large inequalities, demographic change and environmental problems. Section B focuses on some of the broad policy principles that emerged from earlier efforts to meet the rebalancing challenge. Section C offers proposals for some policy elements of a global new deal, picking up on the issues raised in previous chapters.

A final section raises some fundamental institutional issues that will need to be addressed to achieve more inclusive and sustainable development in the future.

B. Back to the future? Some lessons from a not too distant past

The original New Deal proposed by President Franklin Roosevelt to the United States electorate in the 1930s[1] represented a concerted effort to repair and rebalance the United States economy and society in the aftermath of the Great Depression. Famously, Roosevelt offered a positive alternative to a fearful society, making job creation and social security the pillars of a more hopeful strategy. He abandoned the austerity policies that had promised a recovery through tax increases and cuts in government programmes, and offered instead recovery through enhanced government spending and targeted support for different regions and sectors (beginning with agriculture). This was to be made sustainable through strengthened regulation of markets, beginning with taming financial markets but more generally by managing competition. In addition, it was expected to deliver more inclusive outcomes through redistributive measures beginning with labour market reforms to protect workers, followed by progressive fiscal measures and welfare programmes. Recovery, regulation and redistribution became the bases of the New Deal.

As economic historians have pointed out, Roosevelt's break with austerity policies was initially short-lived, with a reversal in 1936; it was fully completed only with the surge of war-related expenditures from the end of the 1930s. But the degree of State intervention embedded in multiple programmes and institutions marked a fundamental change from the past – a vision of government, according to a leading New Deal architect, "equipped to fight and overcome the forces of economic disintegration ... to the realization of our vast social and economic possibilities" (Katznelson, 2013: 232). New Deal legislations and reforms not only made the State a more active agent in the economy, but also empowered and mobilized a wide range of interest groups that would counter the influence of traditional elites, support a mixed economy and underpin a new social contract.

While the New Deal represented a retreat from the idea of a self-regulating, automatic and impersonal international economic framework based on adherence to the international gold standard and free trade, it would be misleading to portray it as a retreat into isolationism. Rather, efforts to manage competition at home had their international analogue in managed trade abroad. Indeed, while attempts throughout the second half of the 1930s to internationalize the New Deal were somewhat ad hoc, the urgency, ambition and voice that underpinned its domestic agenda were extended to the discussions of a new international economic and security order that led to the negotiations at Bretton Woods and Dumbarton Oaks. They also acquired a strong regional accent with the Marshall Plan, which remains one of most successful aid programmes in modern history. Its influence, albeit more contested, extended to the negotiations at the United Nations Conference on Trade and Employment which sought to promote openness by managing trade, and fostering full employment in the North and industrial development in the South.

Without going into the details of these domestic and international programmes, a number of common principles can be gleaned from these experiences, which are relevant to any contemporary discussion of a global new deal.

1. Speed, scale and generosity

One important lesson from these efforts is that, to be effective, policy changes should be rapid and of sufficient scale and generosity; slow and small incremental increases are likely to be less inspiring or transformative. The New Deal, for example, was driven by the urgent and pressing need to get large numbers of people rapidly into paid work, and to repair the United States' shattered economy. The Public Works Administration's $3.3 billion spending programme in 1933 exceeded total private sector investment for that year (Patel, 2016: 79), and, along with the Works Progress Administration (a work programme for the unemployed), marked an abrupt reversal of the policy status quo of limited monetary and fiscal actions that had prevailed during the decade leading up to the

Great Depression (Kregel, 2017). Within just the first month alone, for example, 4 million jobs were created (around 10 per cent of the total labour force of the time), and by 1934 more than 20 million United States citizens (more than one in six) were receiving some form of benefit (Kelber, 2008). In fact "bold, persistent experimentation" was the hallmark of the New Deal, even when the extreme sense of emergency began to ebb and the Roosevelt Administration moved to consolidate the gains, thereby redefining the boundaries between the public and private realms to achieve more inclusive outcomes. This also meant reinventing State institutions, with 10 new federal agencies established between 1933 and 1939, compared with just 4 between 1940 and 1960 (Patel, 2016: 279). These operated on a changed relationship between State and citizen, with a greater emphasis on the State's obligations to meet citizens' rights.

The Marshall Plan, otherwise known as the European Recovery Programme, launched by the United States Government in 1947 to revive employment and economic recovery in post-war Europe, was also very quick to get started, and similarly generous in its scope and scale. As with the New Deal, at the core of the Marshall Plan was the idea that government direction was needed to help a reluctant (and in this case shattered) private sector back to the business of productive investment and job creation. The Plan was put together in weeks and implemented with impressive speed. By the end of five years, the United States had provided Western Europe with some $12.4 billion, largely in the form of grants, amounting to slightly over 1 per cent of the United States' GDP and over 2 per cent of its recipients' GDP. Like their New Deal counterparts, the Marshall planners understood that large-scale public expenditure was needed to crowd in private investment, and they quickly put into place new institutions (the Organisation for European Economic Co-operation and the European Payments Union) as well as a framework of organizing principles intended to encourage policymakers to forge a new kind of social contract that would be radically different from the deflationary and divisive actions of the inter-war period (Mazower, 1998: 299).

2. Voice and counterbalancing power

It is important to point out that these major initiatives occurred through extended processes of negotiation and contested politics, which recognized existing power imbalances and sought to redress them. The

scale, speed and success of the New Deal does not mean that its path was easy. Each step involved a political compromise – the outcome of negotiations and trade-offs between the demands of workers' organizations, businesses and agricultural groups, as well as the great mass of dispossessed poor.[2] Finance had been at the centre of the Great Depression, and its reorganization was key to the success of the New Deal. The measures introduced to tame finance marked a concerted attempt by the Roosevelt Administration to break with the "outworn tradition" of self-correcting markets, and it was the clearest demonstration that the State would employ a visible hand to counter the interests that had supported that tradition. They included initiatives aimed at weakening the strength of financial rentierism, such as the Glass-Steagall Act and the Securities Act (both of 1933), as well as the establishment of the United States Securities and Exchange Commission (SEC) the following year, to regulate the stock market and prevent abusive practices, along with the strengthening of antitrust laws.

In addition to measures to rein in powerful interests, legislative actions of the New Deal included government support to weaker groups in society by allowing them to negotiate better deals in a marketplace that was otherwise left substantially intact. Some commentators, such as JK Galbraith (1952), believed these institutional reforms that aimed to create social and economic balance were the most important aspect of the entire programme. This was most obviously the case with regard to legislation such as the National Labour Relations Act (1935) in support of collective bargaining rights for workers and trade union organizations (Levy and Temin, 2007). But equally important were laws that provided support to small farmers, consumers and citizens, such as the Social Security Act 1935, which granted universal retirement pensions and unemployment insurance. This process created a new middle class, and simultaneously encouraged middle-class taxpayers to identify with the less fortunate majority. At the same time, less developed areas of the country that had received the least government support in the past were included in national projects, such as the Tennessee Valley Authority (Rauchway, 2008). The combination of economic, regulatory and political actions was critical to the speed, scale and success of the programme.

Similar processes of balancing between various economic interest groups played out in the formulation of the Marshall Plan. Because of the damage to

European productive capacities and the great dispar-ity of economic strength between the United States and war-torn Europe, the Plan placed a moratorium on foreign investment until European recovery was in full swing (Kindleberger, 1989). This was at least partly to prevent United States corporations from buying up German businesses, which would not have contributed to winning over the "hearts and souls" of future allies and trade partners (Kozul-Wright and Rayment, 2007). It also avoided a rapid and sym-metric liberalization of trade and payments, based on the fear that a one-way flow of trade would provoke balance-of-payments crises in European countries. Instead, it allowed a gradual dismantling of the wide range of direct and indirect controls on trade over a period of eight years. This gave European produc-ers some protection against competition from the United States. At the same time, the United States agreed to a more rapid opening up of its own markets to European products – a policy of generous and asymmetric liberalization that favoured the weaker partner even as it kick-started growing markets for United States exports. Addressing the international interdependence of national economies was a priority for both Roosevelt and the Marshall Planners, more so than it seems today, even though economies are now more deeply integrated and interdependent.

More generally, individual countries were expected to design their own policies and strategies for indus-trial regeneration, respecting the fact that recipient countries were better informed about their situation than outsiders. This fed into subsequent approaches to multilateralism. Thus, not only was the Bretton Woods Agreement designed to provide the policy space and international stability needed to pursue New Deal-type agendas, but those negotiations were heavily shaped by negotiators and initiatives with New Deal roots (*TDR 2014*; Helleiner, 2013).

3. Cooperation and coordination

None of these initiatives would have been successful without significant cooperation and coordination at different levels between governments and other actors. The New Deal was an integrated agenda that required considerable coordination across programmes and institutions at both local and national levels of the United States. This was exemplified by the Tennessee Valley Authority, which combined economic, social and environmental goals and brought in different agencies to work together to revitalize a previously

neglected part of the South. A similar approach was adopted in programmes of the Agricultural Adjustment Administration, the National Recovery Administration and the Resettlement Administration, albeit with vary-ing degrees of success.

This focus on integrating different policies through cooperation also transposed to the international level. The Marshall Plan, from the outset, recognized that delivery on its economic and political goals would depend on regional cooperation and unity. Such a framework was essential when transboundary issues were involved, in order to avoid failure that could stem from externalities, economies of scale and the chal-lenges of merging different national systems such as interregional transport and energy. A special regional body was created to coordinate the plan. Peer review of national programmes gave national policymakers a regional perspective that would otherwise have been lacking, while also encouraging a culture of regular contact and cooperation among national bureaucracies within the region (Kozul-Wright and Rayment, 2007).

The United Nations Conference on Trade and Employ-ment, like the Marshall Plan that started at more or less the same time, drew on the New Deal's prem-ise that boosting aggregate demand to support full employment was central to achieving a stable and inclusive world economy, and that, given the degree of interdependence, policy coordination and sharing (e.g. of financial, technical assistance and manage-rial skills) across countries was essential. Since it included a large number of developing countries, it was more focused on the challenge of structural transformation than on reconstruction. The Havana Charter[3] that it negotiated represented an ambitious effort to create a multilateral trade organization that was envisaged to be the third leg to the Bretton Woods institutions of the World Bank and IMF (Graz, 2016). However, interest in the Charter eventually dropped, as the United States Congress was already moving away from the more activist ambitions of the New Deal. Nonetheless, it remains instructive as an example of a coherent and cooperative approach to address concerns that are remarkably similar to those of today, including structural constraints on job crea-tion, crisis-related unemployment, low investment and weak aggregate demand. Specifically, the attempt to establish a mutually compatible set of policies blending closer trade relations with recognition of the need for State intervention in both the domestic sphere and in sectoral aspects of international trade provides many important lessons for our times.

C. Elements of a global new deal

These historical examples emphasize the importance of ambition and the need for a coordinated approach, which, together, can work to transform both economy and society in the face of what seem like insuperable odds. A high level of international ambition is already evident in the very formulation of the SDGs, but what is required now is a programmatic understanding of how these goals are to be achieved, along with clear fiscal and regulatory commitments that encompass both the national and international levels. Just as in the past, today's global new deal will have to face the challenge of reclaiming and renewing the public sphere in ways that offer an alternative to the short-term, predatory and, at times, destructive behaviour of deregulated markets that is increasingly provoking a popular backlash. Achieving this will require a more proactive State, but it will also mean empowering non-State actors to better mobilize and direct productive resources, and to establish levels of cooperation and coordination to match the ambition required.

Three interconnected elements – recovery, regulation and redistribution – remain at the heart of any attempt to forge more inclusive and sustainable growth and development paths. This section elaborates on each of these elements, bearing in mind both the lessons from successful initiatives of the past and the insights into technology, labour markets, financial markets and the nature of corporate power provided in earlier chapters.

1. Recovery: Ending austerity and the significance of increased public spending

The growth and productivity slowdown in developed economies has intensified existing inequalities, raised the threat of further shocks and crises, and dragged down future growth prospects in those economies. It has also begun to damage growth prospects in the South. Part of the problem is that recent recovery strategies in the North have been based almost exclusively on loose monetary policies, which in turn have spilled into asset booms (and busts) in developing countries, even as they have failed to boost capital formation and generate sustained growth in the developed countries. Indeed, as chapter I indicates, expansionary monetary policies have been accompanied in many cases by tighter fiscal policies, based on the premise that fiscal austerity is inherently desirable even in countries that are not facing public debt or balance-of-payments problems, or inflationary pressures. This attitude has also permeated policymaking in developing countries, causing governments to tighten their spending more than is warranted by their specific conditions.

Since the global slowdown has a significant demand-side dimension, policies that favour reducing labour costs and public spending will, in fact, make matters worse. They will also prove inadequate to deal with the multiple challenges of inequality and lack of sustainability generated by current economic patterns. Ending austerity therefore remains a basic prerequisite for building sustainable and inclusive growth paths. This means that there should be a greater willingness in both developed and developing countries to use proactive fiscal policy to manage demand conditions and aim at full employment as one of the central goals of macroeconomic policy. This is necessary to move countries out of what some perceive as "secular stagnation", but which, in reality, is more a collective failure of policy leadership and imagination (Wren-Lewis, 2017).

This shift necessarily requires more public spending to address five interconnected imbalances: inadequate and insecure employment; increased inequalities and income polarization; uneven development, including the failure to uplift backward regions along with the emergence of newly depressed regions; demographic pressures relating to ageing and young societies; and environmental stresses, due not only to climate change but also to pollution, degradation and over-exploitation of natural resources.

(a) Full and decent employment

An explicit focus on generating good-quality employment is necessary for economic recovery, redistribution and future social sustainability of the growth trajectory. In both developed and developing economies, a high level of employment is clearly one of the most important ways of mitigating inequality and alleviating poverty, as it raises wage incomes, boosts aggregate demand and counters deflationary pressures. In addition, decent work, which has social, civic and creative implications, is an essential plank of an inclusive society. Also in the context of insufficient global aggregate demand, a full-employment agenda is necessary for revitalizing and rebalancing world trade and fending off protectionist threats (*TDR 2016*). In the case of developing countries, UNCTAD has consistently argued that strengthening domestic demand should be given as much attention as boosting exports when building a balanced development strategy.

All this provides justification for reviving the idea of the State as "employer of last resort" (Minsky, 2013). This is urgent, given current levels of unemployment and underemployment throughout the world,[4] and the informal and precarious nature of much of existing employment. With too many people chasing too few good jobs (as discussed in chapter IV), not only is it taking longer than ever for job-seekers to find work, but the kinds of jobs they eventually find do not seem likely to support more stable and inclusive communities. Even where unemployment rates have declined, good jobs are in short supply, long-term unemployment, disability and drop-out rates remain stubbornly high compared with pre-crisis levels, and youth unemployment is a persistent problem (Blanchflower, 2015; ILO, 2017). As discussed in chapters III and IV, this is related not so much to technological change, per se, as to macroeconomic strategies that hamper more rapid employment generation in other activities.

In addition to direct employment, considerable indirect impacts on employment and output can be achieved through public spending more generally, which has much stronger multiplier effects than other forms of stimulus such as tax cuts (Mineshima et al., 2014). Spending (as opposed to tax cuts) was an important contributory factor in the fiscal expansion in the United States associated with the New Deal, as also in countries that were beneficiaries of the Marshall Plan. In the current context of weak demand in most individual economies and the global economy as a whole, this should become the single most important ingredient in public policy for employment creation.

However, the type of public spending matters, not only for its welfare implications but also for its macroeconomic impact. Government spending on social services, in particular in care activities that are typically underprovided by the State in most countries, generates much higher multiplier effects on employment: on average it generates three times the number of jobs than investment in construction in developed countries (ITUC, 2016), and nearly double the jobs in developing countries (Women's Budget Group, 2017) for the same amount of investment. It also has the important effect of improving the quality of life of citizens, especially when the goals are the universal provision of good-quality public services and the creation of both social cohesion and buy-in of the population whose tax payments would help fund such expenditure. It can also be crucial in reducing inequalities, not just across income groups but also across gender and other social categories (see chapter IV).

In addition to a general increase in government spending on physical and social infrastructure, specific public employment schemes can be very effective, especially in low-income countries, where much of the workforce is engaged in informal and self-employed activities. In recent years, some countries, such as Argentina, India, Sierra Leone and South Africa, have introduced public employment schemes based on the concept of "employer of last resort".[5] Although limited in scope, these have served as important countercyclical buffers and macroeconomic stabilizers, in addition to their obvious anti-poverty effects. The multiplier effects of such spending are also generally high, since the wage earnings from such work are typically spent on consumption, so that they generate even more indirect employment.

In order to maximize the "bubbling up" benefits of such spending and boost aggregate demand relatively quickly, public expenditure on job creation is best directed to the regions, places and activities where unemployed persons and poor households can best benefit (Minsky, 1965; 2013). This would suggest taking "workers as they are" and providing jobs tailored to their current skills and abilities, while including training and retraining as part of the programmes, instead of only providing training for jobs that might subsequently become available (Minsky, 1965). This may be particularly well-suited to some work programmes where training can be provided relatively fast (e.g. pollution clean-up, infrastructure repair, reforestation and care-related activities). The added advantage is that such an approach is likely to benefit from popular support. Meanwhile, multilateral initiatives should at the least ensure that there are no impediments to national governments expanding public employment or procurement. This is particularly important in the context of the explicit or implicit constraints on such employment promotion in international trade and investment agreements.

Ending austerity and boosting employment should help to begin rebalancing the unequal division of national income between capital and labour. In one way or another that still depends on ensuring that workers have an effective voice and representation. However, it is also important to foster institutions and processes that can encourage cooperation between workers, employers and governments, so that productivity growth translates into commensurate increases in earnings (*TDR 2010*: 137). A more ambitious agenda could include incomes policies that help boost demand and create outlets for private investment, while also having positive impacts on labour productivity. Since increased levels of activity and employment are known to foster productivity, this can create a virtuous circle of demand and supply expansion that provides the basis for future sustained, non-inflationary growth (*TDR 2013*, chap. I).

Treating employment as a top priority immediately changes the way policymakers consider other policies that also have a bearing on inclusiveness in economic development. Instead of premature financial liberalization, a heavy reliance on interest rates and very low inflation targets to manage capital inflows and the balance of payments, a judicious combination of fiscal policy, capital controls and exchange rate management can help attract the right kind of productive external finance, while also encouraging domestic investment. In addition, central banks can and should do more than just maintain price stability or competitive exchange rates to support development. This raises the issue of just how "independent" central banks should be (*Economist*, 2016; Munchau, 2016). For instance, they could use credit allocation and interest rate policies to facilitate industrial upgrading and provide strong support to development banks and fiscal policy, as has been done by central banks in many of the rapidly industrializing economies. In any case, the important point that should now be clear from a cross-country analysis covering the past few years is that monetary policy alone is not enough; a broad menu of proactive fiscal and industrial policies is essential for generating the structures and conditions that support the expansion of aggregate demand and domestic productivity growth. As long as loose monetary policy remains a major component of the policy toolkit, it should be increasingly directed towards boosting public expenditure rather than being directed to improving the balance sheets of commercial banks.

(b) Infrastructure spending for regional regeneration

A spatial dimension to economic inequality has also emerged (or intensified) in recent years. This refers not only to differences across national boundaries, but also – and sometimes even more importantly – within countries. The resultant problems have been well known in developing countries for some time, particularly with respect to their neglected agricultural and mining regions. But, increasingly, it has become evident that there are also significant regional differences in developed economies as well, often because of neglected or distressed regions where earlier forms of employment are no longer viable, such as in the hollowed out rust-belt and coal-mining communities of the United Kingdom and the United States, that consequently have become hotbeds of political discontent (Meyerson, 2017; Hazeldine, 2017).

Clearly a combination of measures – macroeconomic, industrial and social – is needed to overcome this problem, but increased public spending in such regions should be a major component of any coordinated effort. One of the less discussed but particularly effective elements of Roosevelt's New Deal was its investment in public works in deprived regions. At that time it was specifically designed to lift the economies of the southern and western regions of the United States closer to the national norm. Similarly, in China over the past two decades, a substantial push for public infrastructure and other spending in the hitherto neglected western and central provinces played a crucial role in reducing regional disparities in levels of development and per capita income (Huang, 2012; Salidjanova, 2013).

(c) Turning the demographic challenge into an opportunity

Because of rising life expectancy, the world as a whole faces the prospect of many more people living much longer. At the same time, some developing regions have burgeoning youth populations for whom employment prospects are limited. This demographic pattern highlights the growing importance of care activities not only as socially necessary, but also as a likely future source of employment of people of working age (caring for the young as well as the elderly). Moreover, women's increasing labour force participation further raises the demand for paid care services which are mainly undertaken by women.

An important feature of care work is that, because of its relational nature and the associated flexibilities required of workers, even in its most "unskilled" form, it is never likely to be "routine", and will generally require cognitive inputs and responses. For this reason, technology can never replace human engagement completely, even if it can assist in reducing the drudgery of some care activities and facilitate others. Precisely because of its continuing relational and interactive nature, the care economy is likely to expand at a faster rate than many other economic activities. However, only part of this expansion would be automatically delivered by market processes, and there is little likelihood that such employment would be of good quality. Therefore, expanding public investment in care is necessary, particularly in ways that enhance the quality and conditions of paid care work.

It would likely yield larger multiplier effects in terms of aggregate employment increases, and create the foundations for a more sustainable growth process over time.[6] Such spending could also contribute to other positive outcomes, such as reducing gender inequality and relieving urbanization pressures, as well as responding to other social changes, including the erosion of extended families that makes formal provision of child care and elderly care a necessity.

This is a global issue as well as a national one, because many developed countries depend on care service providers from developing countries. Moreover, the working conditions of these migrant workers often tend to be precarious, unregulated and exploitative. A good start to forging a more inclusive economy would be to formalize this work, and include globally portable insurance and pension schemes that give migrant or expatriate workers similar social assurance coverage as the people for whom they are caring.

(d) Tackling environmental problems

Climate change mitigation and adaptation will require massive investments across energy, transport and food systems. While innovative sources of finance have been considered, private investment alone will not be sufficient; ambitious and urgent public action will also be needed (United Nations, 2009). Restructuring State energy subsidies – estimated at over five trillion dollars worldwide – away from fossil fuels and in favour of renewables would be an obvious place to start (IMF, 2015). Apart from

subsidies and various other incentives offered to private investment, more directly effective would be public investment in ways that reduce carbon emissions. Research concerning the United States (Pollin et al., 2014) and several developing countries (Pollin et al., 2015) has shown how "green" investments can lead to large-scale increases in job opportunities, as well as new opportunities for alternative ownership forms, including various combinations of smaller scale forms of public, private and cooperative ownership. In many developing countries (as well as developed ones), people are already being affected by the impacts of climate change, but the available infrastructure for coping with them, or the investments required to build resilience and the avenues for alternative livelihood generation in the face of such changes, are woefully inadequate. Thus there is clearly a need for significant public spending in a range of related areas.

Climate change is only one of the environmental challenges facing countries, especially developing countries, and in many of them the pressures of pollution and environmental degradation are currently enormous. Patterns of expansion in some of the fastest growing economies, such as China and India, have created massive problems of atmospheric and water pollution that are already adversely affecting living conditions, morbidity and mortality. In addition, rapid urbanization in developing countries is associated with inadequate urban planning and poor provision of basic amenities, and the associated unsustainable patterns of production and consumption are giving rise to even more environmental concerns for the future. All this requires not just greater regulation, but, even more importantly, more public investment to mitigate the worst effects of pollution and reduce such damage in the future.

2. Expanding fiscal space

Advocating substantially greater public spending is obviously irresponsible without considering how it is to be financed. Therefore, strengthening government revenues is key to a global new deal. Fiscal space is both a cause and an effect of economic growth and structural change. Higher average income levels and an expansion of the modern sectors of the economy not only bring more of the informal economy into formal regulatory structures; they also broaden the tax base and strengthen governments' capacities to mobilize fiscal revenues. This in turn enables higher

---

BOX 7.1   **Financing a global new deal**

How could a coordinated global stimulus, or a version of the Marshall Plan on a global scale, involving large public expenditures that crowd in private investment be financed? While borrowing is an option in many countries that have sufficient fiscal headroom, that option alone may not be adequate. In any case, in a world dominated by finance, debt-financed public expenditures would face considerable opposition.

However, greater public borrowing (though not to be shunned in specific circumstances) is not the only or principal option. Given the evidence-based consensus that the last few decades have seen a substantial increase in inequality, even while taxation rates have fallen and tax exemptions have risen, resource mobilization through additional taxation of the top income earners is an obvious possibility. In this sense inequality is as much an opportunity as it is a challenge.

To estimate how much could be collected by taxing the richest segments of the population, one can estimate the incomes that accrue to the relevant fraction of that population (top 1, 5 or 10 per cent), and then estimate the effect of an average additional tax on their incomes. It could include assuming that, even within the relevant range, some progressivity is maintained, especially in countries where the threshold income for the specified range is not very high. Thus, for example, an average tax on the top 5 per cent could be distributed such that the top 1 per cent pays a higher rate than those in the fifth percentile.

Taking data for 43 countries that either belong to the high-income OECD countries or those that are not OECD members but are part of the G20, the GCIP database (referred to in chapter V of this *TDR*) provides information on the share of the top income quantiles (Lahoti et al., 2016). Combining this with the GDP data in United States dollars for 2015, it emerges that the total income of the top 10 per cent in each of these 43 countries in 2015 was $19.7 trillion.[a] Adding an additional average tax of just 5 percentage points in that group of countries alone would yield around $0.98 trillion. This compares with $130–$135 billion (in 2015 prices)[b] spent on the Marshall Plan for Western Europe in the mid-twentieth century.

Such a proposed 5 per cent additional tax on the richest 10 per cent in this set of countries has to be seen in the light of major direct tax reductions offered in most countries during the hyperglobalization era. From 1971 to 2008, the highest marginal tax rate fell from 70 per cent to 35 per cent in the United States, from 53 per cent to 45 per cent in Germany, and from 61.2 per cent to 53 per cent in France. As Atkinson (2016) has shown, there is a very strong relationship between the amount top earners retain from every extra dollar they earn and levels of income inequality. Reversing this even partially could substantially help finance a global new deal.

There are other options as well. In some countries, wealth and inheritance taxes have been substantially reduced or even eliminated altogether: inheritance taxes or estate duties have been abolished in Australia, Austria, Canada, India, Norway, Sweden, Mexico and Portugal, for example. Even a relatively small tax of this kind could be a significant source of revenue in the context of the growing amounts of inherited wealth.

In sum, as this simple exercise illustrates, financial constraints need not be an obstacle to a global new deal.

---

[a] GDP data are from https://www.un.org/development/desa/dpad/publication/united-nations-global-policy-model.

[b] Estimated using the figure of more than $12 billion spent on the Marshall Plan (Office of the Historian, United States Department of State, available at: https://history.state.gov/milestones/1945-1952/marshall-plan) and the official consumer price indices of the United States for 1947 and 2015 (see: https://www.minneapolisfed.org/community/teaching-aids/cpi-calculator-information/consumer-price-index-and-inflation-rates-1913).

---

growth-enhancing public spending, both on the supply side, through investment in infrastructure, research and development, and health and education, and on the demand side, through universal provision of good-quality public services and social transfers.

At present, much of the strategy for augmenting State revenues relies heavily on indirect taxation, which is inherently regressive and can exacerbate inequality if the poor and less well-off are not compensated through public spending that enhances their access to goods and services. However, it is possible for governments to widen their fiscal base through domestic efforts, including higher taxes on property and other forms of rents, and, equally importantly, in progressive ways that do not increase inequalities

(*TDR 2014*). Indeed, relatively small changes to the income tax structure for the top earners could generate fiscal revenues on the kind of scale needed to finance the investment push required by a global new deal (box 7.1). However, corporate tax rates have been on the decline in developed and developing countries alike, often accompanied by subsidies or exemptions to attract or retain foreign investment. Yet there is little evidence to suggest that this has been good for capital formation or for economic growth (see, for example, Ljungqvist and Smolyansky, 2014). While reversing this trend may well be appropriate, it may not be necessary to increase tax rates if strong and effective measures are taken to reduce exemptions and remove loopholes that allow corporations and rich individuals to avoid or evade tax. It is possible to legislate for the adoption of a general anti-avoidance rule so that "aggressive" schemes which exploit loopholes in the existing law can be declared illegal when challenged in courts (UNCTAD, 2014).

Other innovative measures have been proposed that could boost fiscal revenues and help redistribute wealth or income. These include an annual wealth tax (Atkinson, 2016), a "social dividend" or "sovereign wealth" fund based on taxing the returns to capital (as opposed to the returns to labour), taxing the rents from intellectual property rights (IPRs), or acquiring shares in publicly supported companies or from initial public offerings in key sectors. All of these could help rebalance the distribution of benefits between businesses and the wider society, and would reflect society's investment in those businesses (Atkinson, 2016; Varoufakis, 2017).

A major challenge is that hyperglobalization has weakened the ability of governments to mobilize domestic revenues as a result of the lowering of tariffs, the increased mobility of capital, illicit capital flows and the greater use of fiscal havens (*TDR 2014*). On the other hand, it is likely that governments have overestimated the need to offer incentives to attract and retain investment (Keen and Mansour, 2009; *TDR 2014*, chap. VII). It is also encouraging that there have been a number of recent initiatives aimed at improving transparency and exchange of information for tax purposes. Further efforts, such as a global financial register that would record the owners of financial assets throughout the world, and the adoption of public registers of the beneficial ownerships of companies, would be an important step forward (Zucman, 2015). Reporting on the country-wise distribution of core financial company data, including taxes paid, would also be important,

since it would enable cross-country comparisons and the detection of mismatches (Murphy, 2012).

While these initiatives would be steps in the right direction, they would only be effective if they are efficiently implemented and enforced. This is particularly so with regard to abuses relating to transfer pricing that are extremely harmful for developing countries, and where international companies have been well ahead of regulators. Genuine and coordinated efforts to reduce base-shifting and transfer mispricing by global corporations should be strengthened, as these practices account for billions of dollars worth of foregone fiscal revenues that could otherwise be directed towards productive investment in public goods and services (Leite, 2012). Advance price agreements are another area of growing interest, since these allow tax authorities to review a firm's transfer pricing in advance rather than through costly ex-post audits. However, since developing countries seriously lack capabilities in this and similar areas, more systematic cooperation and information-sharing between developed and developing countries' tax authorities are necessary.

More generally, because policy and best practice initiatives are mostly led by developed economies – which are still the most significant home countries of multinational corporations, and remain among the leading secrecy jurisdictions, despite recent initiatives to tighten controls and improve transparency – there needs to be a more balanced inclusion of the voices and needs of developing and transition economies in international discussions and initiatives. At the same time, the influence of sophisticated lobbyists and interest groups on national and international policymaking needs to be more explicitly recognized, and countermeasures adopted. In pursuing this agenda at the international level, it will be important to give a more prominent role to monitoring institutions such as the United Nations Committee of Experts on International Cooperation in Tax Matters, but also to adopt a fully multilateral convention against tax avoidance and evasion.

3. Regulating rentier capitalism

(a) Taming finance capital[7]

It is not only financing for public spending that requires a stronger push; significantly higher levels of productive investment are also needed in most developing countries in order to enable a sustained recovery with more inclusive employment. Yet recent investment rates are well below expectations in some developing countries, and have even been falling; they are also falling in most developed countries. This points to one of the main paradoxes of hyperglobalization, that despite a singular emphasis on establishing an investment-friendly business environment, very few countries have been able to increase their rates of capital formation; and in those that have succeeded in doing so, market forces on their own have not been relied on to generate the required financial resources, nor to direct them in the most productive manner.

In a healthy investment climate, a large proportion of capital accumulation is typically financed from retained profits, often in a symbiotic relationship with long-term bank lending. A worrying feature of hyperglobalization is the breakdown of the nexus between profit, credit and investment. This has been particularly pronounced in the most financialized developed economies, but increasingly it is also apparent in emerging economies (*TDR 2016*). The extent to which the rich save and invest their incomes in productive assets can, of course, vary considerably among countries, depending on how profits are generated and how much of these are retained and spent productively. If profits are siphoned off into luxury consumption or financial assets, as witnessed in recent years, the investment linkages required for inclusive development will be weak or missing.

Despite the primacy of finance in the era of hyperglobalization, private financial institutions have often failed to provide credit on a sufficient scale or on appropriate terms or, indeed, to the kinds of investors that would create productive and job-generating enterprises as opposed to investing in real estate or speculation. Far-reaching reforms have been proposed from many quarters since the financial crisis, but have met with strong, and largely successful, resistance from the banking and finance lobbies. Ongoing efforts to strengthen prudential regulations by raising capital and liquidity requirements are welcome, but not sufficient; also needed are structural reforms that focus both on financial stability and on developmental and social objectives. These include regulations defining which activities different kinds of banks are allowed to perform. Meanwhile, the Basel regulations remain too dependent on self-assessment by large banks, and their framework was not conceived with the particular needs of developing countries in mind. They aim to harmonize national regulations and avoid regulatory arbitrage across countries hosting large and complex, internationally active financial institutions, but they do not focus on the challenge of encouraging the kinds of lending practices that may be required for industrialization and financial inclusion. In addition, much more concerted efforts will be needed to regulate the financial industry's use of the kinds of "toxic" financial products that have been a persistent source of financial instability. This will mean addressing the highly concentrated market for credit rating and the potential conflicts of interest between the agencies that dominate that market and the shadow banking institutions that have allowed toxic products to flourish. As noted in chapter V, capital controls are required at the national level in specific circumstances, but these need to be combined with other measures to regulate the structure, size and governance of banks and other financial institutions operating internationally.

A financial system that accords a more significant role to public banks of various kinds and to smaller private banks with limited political influence and stronger regulatory oversight is less likely to generate speculative excesses, boom and bust cycles and austerity. It is also more likely to provide security for people's savings, mobilize resources for productive investment and extend credit for employment creation. In addition, it should help improve the information flows needed to formulate regulations that keep pace with innovations (Chandrasekhar, 2008). Development banks can play a potentially prominent role in supporting the profit–investment nexus in developing countries by filling financing gaps in the form of credit provision at near-commercial rates on a general basis and on more favourable terms for selective sectors, as well as providing other investment support services (*TDR 2016*).

Multilateral institutions' financial resources should be increased in line with the growth of cross-border transactions, bringing them to a level sufficient to enable them to undertake effective countercyclical financing and to deal with payments difficulties that might emerge on a country's capital account. The recent tripling of IMF funding marks progress in this direction, but, as discussed in previous *TDR*s, it is also necessary to move towards more reliable and less politicized ways of creating international liquidity.

Multilateral development banks, both old and new, should support greater infrastructure lending as well as ensuring the provision of trade finance, particularly during crises. In addition, they can play a constructive role in the development of local bond markets, and devise more innovative mechanisms to combine public and private resources in support of developmental and socially inclusive goals (Griffith-Jones et al., 2008). Existing institutions with a strong regional focus might be complemented by more specialist financing agencies in areas such as agricultural development or climate finance (UNCTAD, 2016). These institutions should also have the capacity to take initiatives in financing projects that are developmental, rather than following the choices made by commercial banks. For example, development banks could favour projects with greater employment-generating potential, or seek positive opportunities for public procurement in major infrastructure projects. Funding for these institutions could come from increased national tax revenue (as discussed in box 7.1), a dedicated international tax (such as a financial transaction tax) or an international bond issue (Varoufakis, 2017).

Because stable, affordable and long-term finance remains a constraint on sustainable and inclusive growth in many developing countries, particularly the least developed countries (LDCs), upgrading the development cooperation agenda in line with the ambitions of the SDGs will necessitate not only meeting the 0.7 per cent target for official development assistance (ODA), but also refocusing aid programmes in ways that enable recipients to mobilize their own resources for development as quickly as possible (UNCTAD, 2006). Moreover, ODA should not be diverted from core development purposes to fund additional and broader areas of concern, such as combating climate change, which should be funded by other sources (UNCTAD, 2016).

A global new deal will need to tackle the economic and political threats that have accompanied the massive accumulation of sovereign debt during the era of hyperglobalization. Currently, the system of sovereign debt restructuring is based on ad hoc arrangements, and is thus highly fragmented. Recent efforts to improve the legal underpinnings of debt contracts are welcome, but a more balanced approach to sovereign debt restructuring is needed. This should include principles to better guide and coordinate the restructuring process as a stepping stone to an international bankruptcy process which would prevent the economic and social damage caused by a default. It should involve establishing a set of statutory procedures that facilitate relief restructuring and recovery in the best interests of both creditors and debtors.

(b) Contesting corporate power

Efforts to clamp down on corporate rent-seeking behaviour are necessary, both to bring about more inclusive outcomes and to create a healthier investment climate. At the national level, competition and antitrust policies have been watered down considerably. The result (as noted in chapter VI) has been an unprecedented growth in corporate market and lobbying powers, which now threatens economic stability and the future of economic globalization, and is dubbed by the Chicago economist, Luigi Zingales (2017) as the "Medici vicious circle". Corporations have gained rights at least equivalent to those of citizens, but have avoided charges of criminalization of activities that would be deemed illegal when pursued by citizens (Eisinger, 2017). Consequently, competition policy, and, more generally, measures aimed at curtailing restrictive business practices, should be designed with an explicit distributional objective.

Much of the regulatory structure dismantled under hyperglobalization needs to be restored and updated. A starting point might be the Set of Multilaterally Agreed Equitable Principles and Rules for the Control of Restrictive Business Practices adopted by the United Nations General Assembly in 1980. These paid particular attention to the interests of developing countries with respect to price fixing, collusion, transfer pricing, and the more generally predatory behaviour towards competitors and abuses of dominant position (Muchlinski, 2007). Since then, increasing concentration at the top end of global value chains and heightened competition at the bottom end have further intensified, and may require a new institution, such as a global competition observatory, to monitor trends in international markets (*TDR 2016*). There are encouraging signs that some developed-country governments may be rethinking their approach to competition issues and policies. For instance, European Union regulators slapped a record fine on Google in June 2017 for abuse of its dominant position as a search engine, and the European Commission is considering a generally more proactive stance to curb market power and corporate abuses (Toplensky, 2017).

Another policy essential for supporting the development of inclusive economies is to revisit bilaterally and regionally negotiated restrictions on the sharing of knowledge and IPRs that are more onerous and constraining than multilateral agreements such as those negotiated under the aegis of the World Trade

Organization (WTO). Some of these agreements contain many more provisions on IPR issues (83 in the Trans Pacific Partnership Agreement compared with 21 in the North American Free Trade Agreement), including extending IP protection to new uses of known products and new methods of using a known product. Many of them deal with a broad range of areas, such as public procurement, new investment issues and disputes between corporations and States, while some of them also extend regulatory coverage to new areas, such as e-commerce, harmonization in the pharmaceutical sector and digitalization (Gehl Sampath and Roffe, forthcoming).

Corporate influence in shaping rules and policies is nothing new, but it has increased markedly over time.[8] It is particularly problematic when trade negotiations take place in an opaque or secretive manner. These power asymmetries are especially evident in investor-State dispute settlement processes, which are now included in thousands of bilateral investment treaties, and which allow foreign investors to challenge national laws and policies but do not grant the same right to national firms or citizens. This is increasingly recognized in the broad discussions led by the OECD, UNCTAD and, more recently, also the G20, which emphasize the need for a more balanced approach to the right to regulate at national levels and to the kind of FDI that should be encouraged to promote sustainable development. Numerous reform proposals are currently under consideration, including improved investment principles that foster sustainable development (UNCTAD, 2015b), the creation of a more independent (and legally sound) investment tribunal along with an appeals mechanism (European Commission, 2015), and a greater reliance on national laws (UNCTAD, 2014).

4. The redistribution challenge and transformational social policy

This *Report* has suggested that piecemeal approaches are unlikely to meet the SDG on reducing inequality, nor indeed in responding to the dissatisfaction and anger of many people and communities across the world. Comparing the present situation with that of the 1930s, what is notable is the extent to which today's high-income earners have preserved, or improved, their position. Indeed, hollowing out of the middle and polarization of the tails appear to be systemic features of hyperglobalization, whether at the macro and micro levels, or the national and international levels. These concerns with rising inequality could be addressed through policies, regulations and institutional reforms that focus on some key areas such as employment, market concentration and wage determination.

Labour market interventions, including minimum wage legislation, are crucial, for achieving not only social policy goals (i.e. reducing poverty and gender discrimination), but also macroeconomic goals such as higher employment levels and reduced income inequality. This is scarcely surprising given the additional employment resulting from the income multiplier effects of the higher demand generated by such wage increases.

However, creating more inclusive economies and societies also requires directly tackling various forms of discrimination, including by gender and other social categories, by means of proactive social policies. Hyperglobalization, to the extent that it has contributed to a slowdown in productivity growth, greater inequality and the erosion of national fiscal space, has placed added pressures on the provision of welfare. However, these pressures are not qualitatively different from the past, and the fundamental problems remain the lack of political will and support, collective solidarity and policy ambition (Glyn, 2006; Atkinson, 2016).

Under hyperglobalization, the main objective of social policy has been narrowly conceived as the provision of support and protection targeted at the chronically poor and most vulnerable, or, more recently, as a matter of social risk management in the face of unforeseen shocks.[9] Various market-friendly measures have been undertaken along these lines, mainly by a growing number of non-governmental or not-for-profit organizations. The influence of market forces on the provision of public services, including through cash transfers, can become especially unbalanced if the services are financialized. For example, privatization can dilute the social priorities of utility companies through the imposition of fees (e.g. for sanitation) or other restrictions on use (e.g. relating to health-care services or water supply), or it can subject the providers to the vagaries of the stock market and the threat of takeover, with the attendant pressures for subcontracting, downsizing, break-up, investment cutbacks, or deterioration of standards of service in order to enhance short-term profitability. The new emphasis on cash transfers, as opposed to public spending on public goods and services, has also encouraged households to seek private sector alternatives, even as both the quality and quantity of State provision have been reduced. This reinforces the dynamic towards the commercialization of such services on the basis of loans made available to ever wider strata of society (Lavinas, 2013).

For social policy to be transformational, however, it must go beyond offering simply a residual category of safety nets or floors designed to pick up (or stop falling) those left behind; equally importantly, it needs to address the economic structures, processes and norms of social and economic exclusion by giving greater attention to economic production, reproduction, redistribution and social solidarity. The mere fact of providing some degree of social protection or welfare to those in greatest need does not make society more "inclusive"; indeed, quite the opposite: evidence suggests that social policies which are designed and targeted to help the poorest or the most needy are typically less inclusive than those that are universal and that seek to overcome problems of both unwarranted exclusion and unjustified inclusion (Mkandawire, 2005; Le Grand, 2006; Atkinson and Stiglitz, 1980). Social and economic outcomes tend to be more equitable in societies that pursue universal policies than in those that rely on means-testing and other forms of selectivity (Korpi and Palme, 1998; Huber and Stephens, 2012; Standing and Orton, 2017). Moreover, against a backdrop of rapid structural change, social policies are often part of a more integrated policy package aimed at managing such change. And in some of the most successful cases of economic catch-up, they have been instrumental in fostering technological upgrading and productivity gains (Ringen et al., 2011; Ove and Wallerstein, 2006).

In countries that have already built State capacities in support of development, the administrative infrastructure required to manage universal social programmes is likely to be in place, or can be set up relatively quickly. In other countries, universal social policies and programmes can be rolled out gradually (e.g. by providing one product or service at a time), or in selected regions, making them relatively simple and cost-effective. Even with the provision of universal coverage, it is possible to incorporate several advantages of narrowly targeted programmes through "smart targeting", so that they are available to all and at the same time de facto targeted, because each project or initiative will affect distinct social groups differently. These welfare programmes should not be optional extras; they should be essential components of an inclusive development strategy, because they will support productivity growth, skills development, and the growth and stabilization of demand as the economy is transformed through rapid economic development.

As with the other public spending proposals discussed here, financing remains the main challenge for universal programmes that offer good-quality public services, particularly in developing countries. It is evident that, even with the more progressive tax measures suggested above, such programmes will ultimately need to be funded by the mass of wage and salary earners. For this reason, raising both the growth rate and national share of wages from their current levels is essential for inclusive and universal welfare provision. To ensure they remain politically sustainable, it is also important to maintain a sufficiently high quality of public services so that most taxpayers will wish to use them.

Recently, there has been a revival of interest in basic income schemes – a regular and unconditional cash grant paid to every citizen – on the grounds that they have desirable administrative, egalitarian and transformational qualities (box 7.2). In developed economies, that revival is partly a response to the technological threat of a jobless world. However, even if this threat appears less imminent than is often suggested (as discussed in chapter III), the idea of a universal or even targeted basic income merits further discussion as part of an effective welfare system, and as a means of "conquering poverty".[10] However, such schemes should not be treated as *substitutes* for the provision of universal good-quality public services, but as *additions* to them. This consideration is crucial, though often somewhat disguised in debates about such schemes, because if the basic income is seen as a replacement or substitute for other provisions, the wider macroeconomic, growth and income distributional benefits are likely to be lost.

BOX 7.2   The basics of basic income

A "basic income" is an old idea harking back to Thomas More's Utopia published over 500 years ago, and it has resurfaced at relatively regular intervals over the past century (Atkinson, 2003). On some interpretations, it is even enshrined in Article 25 of the Universal Declaration of Human Rights (Bregman, 2017).

A universal basic income (UBI) programme requires the State to pay an amount of cash to every adult (and potentially a smaller amount to a child) on a regular basis, and as an economic right. Unlike unemployment or social benefits that are withdrawn once the person gets a job or if their personal situation changes in some way, a UBI is not contingent on particular circumstances, nor can it be withdrawn. However, it may be limited to legal citizens or legal residents of a country, or in some cases, provided on a smaller scale at the level of geographical regions or even cities.

The idea is unusual in that it has had a surprising capacity to garner political support from opposite ends of the political spectrum. On the right, from Milton Friedman's negative "income tax proposal" to high-tech libertarian support for a "start-up culture" (Schneider, 2015), it is linked to views of "economic freedom" associated with reducing the welfare and regulatory roles of the State. On the liberal left, support for the idea has come from Friedman's nemesis, John Kenneth Galbraith, and from contemporary utopian thinkers anticipating a post-work world (Bregman, 2017). These thinkers associate it with notions of redistributive justice and social solidarity, which also extends to the feminist call for State payment for household work (James, 2012).

Much of the current discussion focuses on developed economies, where it is linked to anticipated changes in employment resulting from technological advances, which in turn are seen as upending the post-war welfare State built around traditional work relations (Standing, 2016). However, the idea has found expression in several developing countries as well. In China, there is already a *dibao*, or minimum livelihood guarantee (set at different levels in urban and rural areas) that supplements the incomes of those categorized as poor, to allow them to reach a certain defined minimum income level. In several other countries, there are pilot projects or ongoing policy debates about the usefulness and practicability of a basic income scheme (Standing and Orton, 2017).

From a new deal perspective, however, a basic income alone is insufficient and can even be damaging. According to Rogers (2017: 15), it can "only be part of the solution to economic and social inequalities – we also need a revamped public sector and a new and different collective bargaining system. Indeed, without such broader reforms, a basic income could do more harm than good". In a similar vein, Glyn (2006) and Galbraith (2014) see a basic income as one element in rebalancing economies away from a singular focus on growth to a greater focus on more egalitarian development. Other proponents of a basic income view it, along with other forms of social spending, as a macroeconomic stabilizer in response to financial and other economic shocks (Standing and Orton, 2017).

There are several concerns about the practical aspects of a UBI. First, an initial consensus on its desirability often falls apart over the level of payment envisaged, what tax level might be required to finance it, and how it would fit within the broader social welfare framework (Varoufakis, 2017). Even its proponents in the developed economies accept that, at least initially, it would probably have to be at a "relatively austere level" (Glyn, 2006: 183). In developing countries especially, the amounts involved must be high enough to positively affect real incomes, and they should be directed to a large enough segment of the population to have a significant impact overall. In the absence of reforms to expand the fiscal base in a more progressive direction, even small payments could prove to be unaffordable in these countries.

Second, governments providing a UBI may have to reduce other crucial social expenditures, which would effectively result in the State making cuts in its delivery of essential public services. This is clearly problematic, given that public provision of good-quality social services is necessary for many reasons (including reducing inequalities of income and gender), as highlighted in this chapter. It could also lead to privatization of many activities that, for reasons of asymmetric information and imperfect market functioning, are still best left to the public sector, though that sector should be made more accountable for their functioning.

Third, and most significantly, depending on how the prices of food and other necessities change, a UBI could even end up reducing the real incomes of the supposed beneficiaries, as argued by Minsky (2013) when he critiqued Friedman's "negative income tax". He noted that if such transfers caused inflation, as might happen if they increased aggregate purchasing power without ensuring concomitant supply increases, this could result in the scheme delivering less in real terms than promised to the poor, and reducing the real incomes of the not-poor, but not very well-off, population. Such a possibility is supported by the recent inflationary experience of the Islamic Republic of Iran, which in 2010 stopped its fuel subsidy and liberalized energy prices, but at the same time, granted households a regular cash grant to compensate for the increased costs of food and energy (Meskoub, 2015).

Although there has been some tentative talk in the European Parliament of a Europe-wide basic income, scaling it up to a global dimension would seem far-fetched. Indeed, insofar as an inclusive economy is the goal, a universal employment programme at a minimum wage would contribute more directly to poverty alleviation and to improving distribution in most developing countries, because such a programme would tend to exercise upward pressure on wages. Moreover, an employment guarantee that recognizes that paid work is both a source of income and of dignity is transformational, in that it not only shifts power relations between workers and employers, but also has a tendency to force structural changes in a way that raises productivity.

D. Conclusions

It has been a decade since the public sector was mobilized to save hyperglobalization through a slew of policies, including quantitative easing, the absorption of bad debts, guarantees and, in some cases, expansionary public investment and expenditure policies. The idea of a self-regulating market has not survived intact, but nor have the social and economic imbalances that led to the crisis been addressed. In the interregnum, as growth has stagnated in developed economies and sharply slowed in emerging economies, resentful nationalism and xenophobic fantasies have made an all too predictable return. The international community has provided an alternative and hopeful agenda with a series of goals and targets that could secure an inclusive and sustainable future. What is still needed, however, is a compelling and persuasive narrative that could move from ambitious decision-making to decisive policy action.

Building the institutional structures and flexibilities in support of inclusive growth and development has become more challenging as the world has become more interdependent. Institutions for consultation, discussion and participation remain essential for generating the popular support needed to challenge the entrenched interests that have formed under hyperglobalization. To the extent that those interests are linked to global markets and firms, global rules and regulations are an urgent necessity. They are also needed in order to provide and manage global public goods that markets are unable or loath to deal with, including emerging threats and dangers related to a changing climate. However, given existing gaps, asymmetries and interests, designing appropriate rules and flexibilities at the global level is likely to be an even greater challenge than at the national or regional levels. Moreover, if a government, at any stage of development, is to agree to cede some degree of influence to international bodies, those bodies will need to be much more transparent and democratic than they are at present.

In recent years, attempts to improve representation and accountability in the Bretton Woods institutions have been only tentative at best. The G-20 process has helped to broaden participation in global decision-making beyond the traditional powers. However, there remain significant gaps in its architecture, and the voice of most developing countries remains either weak or absent. In response, several developing countries have struck out on their own, forming regional institutions, funds and banks that are effectively providing regional public goods and meeting many countries' needs. However, such initiatives can go only so far, and can never be sufficiently large or well-resourced to meet systemic crises or fulfil all needs at the same time. A global new deal would have to accelerate the reform process so as to achieve more effective approaches to global problems. There have been intermittent calls for modernizing the structures established at the end of the Second World War, including pruning back overlapping mandates and finding better ways to coordinate their actions and policy advice. But despite the recognition that the growth of global interdependence poses greater problems today, the mechanisms and institutions that have existed for the past three decades have not been up to the challenge of ensuring coherence, complementarity and coordination in global economic policymaking. Proposals for making globalization more inclusive in the current context should start with an attempt to address these problems, inter alia through the appropriate organs of the United Nations system.

Beyond that, each country should be able to decide where the boundaries are drawn between the State, private and social sectors; and developing countries seeking to catch up with those higher up the development ladder, should be free to choose their own pattern of development, whether it be following in the footsteps of countries such as the United States or Denmark or China. Such freedoms of choice have been sidelined or abandoned altogether over the past 30 years under the dominance of a one-size-fits-all policy agenda, to which no alternative has been considered viable or acceptable. Indeed, even as these positions have softened, and the capture of policymaking by narrow interests challenged, one of the lingering features of hyperglobalization has been the application of business methods to social problems, which "exaggerate what technology can do, ignore the complexities of social and institutional constraints, often waste sums that would have been better spent more carefully, and wreak havoc with the existing fabric of society in places they know very little about" (Mazower, 2014: 417). Such business methods can have far-reaching exclusionary consequences, whether due to adverse selection or cherry-picking of the most profitable activities, leaving the chronic or expensive responsibilities to the State. This is an effective denial of representative politics, which is essentially about weighing various alternatives and choosing between them, managing the trade-offs that such a choice necessarily entails, and confronting the various interests that inevitably come into play.

Strong multilateral institutions are just as necessary for fostering sustainable and inclusive growth paths as strong and representative national governments. Indeed, it is difficult to see one working without the other. However, in the search for stronger multilateralism, there is an obvious tension between its association with a rules-based system and the kind of flexibility needed by national policymakers to deal with the complexities and radical uncertainties that characterize today's interdependent world. On one level, rules lend themselves to a degree of predictability and transparency; on another, and as discussed in the previous chapter, rules are not simply the product of technocratic expertise but also of political influence. Rules designed to help boost profits at the expense of the public – a toxic feature of hyperglobalization over the past 30 years – appear to have weakened multilateralism and exposed it to capture by a narrow set of private interests (*TDR 2014*). This is likely to be a persistent source of political tensions in a more open global economy. Addressing these institutional challenges will be central to a more inclusive global new deal for the twenty-first century. ■

Notes

1　The "new deal" idea was first introduced, in passing, by President Roosevelt in his acceptance speech as a Democratic candidate for the Presidency of the United States, but it was only made a central campaign promise by subsequent reporting by the press. For useful accounts, see Leuchtenburg, 2009; and Hiltzik, 2012.

2　Political horse-trading, for example, meant that policies destined for the United States South did not include black households; more generally, employment programmes were slow to include women, immigrants and black workers, and even when they did, the conditions were different, restricted by quotas and with lower wages (see Katznelson, 2013).

3　United Nations Conference on Trade and Employment, Havana, Cuba, Final Act and Related Documents. Interim Commission for the International Trade Organization, Lake Success, New York, April 1948.

4　According to the ILO (2017), the number of people defined as "unemployed" are estimated to reach a record of more than 204 million by 2018; of these, 163 million are likely to be in emerging and developing countries and 38 million in developed economies. The fact of being employed is in itself no guarantee of inclusion – as many as an estimated 28 million people are identified as the "working poor", and just under half of total employment worldwide is defined as "vulnerable employment". Vulnerability has been particularly prevalent in developing countries, accounting for four out of five workers.

5　On the success of India's Mahatma Gandhi National Rural Employment Guarantee Scheme, see Ghosh, 2014.

6　A study of six developing countries (among them, Brazil, China, India and Indonesia) found that increases in health spending, even of only 2 per cent of GDP, would lead to increases in overall employment by 1.2 per cent to 3.2 per cent, depending on the country (Women's Budget Group, 2017).

7　These issues have been extensively discussed in previous *Reports*, most recently in *TDR 2015*.

8　See *TDR 2015* for a discussion on the role of lobbyists in financial markets and in the drafting of financial regulations.

9　A World Bank study on social inclusion is fairly typical of this approach, with its focus on the marginalized or excluded in society. The study described the problems of exclusion of "indigenous people, new immigrants, people with disabilities, people with different skin tones, people who spoke the official language imperfectly…" (World Bank, 2013: 1), and advocates education as a critical solution.

10　The economist, James Tobin, wrote an article in the *New York Times* 50 years ago entitled Conquering Poverty in America, which called for a guaranteed basic income, and the following year he wrote an open letter to the United States Congress co-signed by 1,200 fellow economists, including Kenneth Galbraith and Paul Samuelson. The United States House of Representatives passed legislation in support of such a move beginning in 1970, but it was rejected several times by the United States Senate, and the idea was finally abandoned in 1978 (Bregman, 2017).

References

Atkinson AB (2003). *Public Economics in Action: The Basic Income/Flat Tax Proposal*. Oxford and New York, NY, Oxford University Press.

Atkinson AB (2016). *Inequality: What Can be Done?* Cambridge, MA, Harvard University Press.

Atkinson AB and Stiglitz JE (1980). *Lectures on Public Economics*. New York, NY, McGraw-Hill International Editions.

Blanchflower D (2015). Britain's hidden army of underemployed. *The Independent*, 29 April.

Bregman R (2017). *Utopia for Realists, and How We Can Get There*. London, Bloomsbury.

Chandrasekhar CP (2008). Financial policies. In: *National Development Strategies: Policy Notes*. United Nations, Department of Economic and Social Affairs, New York, NY, United Nations.

Economist (2016). Rethinking central bank independence. 17 November.

Eisinger J (2017). *The Chickenshit Club: Why the Justice Department Fails to Prosecute Executives*. New York, NY, Simon and Schuster.

European Commission (2015). Investment in TTIP and beyond: The path for reform. Concept paper, 12 May. Available at: https://www.transnational-dispute-management.com/legal-and-regulatory-detail.asp?key=13949.

Galbraith John K (1952). *American Capitalism: The Concept of Counterveiling Power*. Boston, Houghton Mifflin.

Galbraith James K (2014). *The End of Normal: The Great Crisis and the Future of Growth*. New York, NY, Simon and Schuster.

Gehl Sampath P and Roffe P (forthcoming). The untimely death of the Trans-Pacific Partnership Agreement: Where do we go next? CEIPI-ICTSD Series on Trade and Intellectual Property, Strasbourg and Geneva.

Ghosh J (2014). Can employment schemes work? The case of the rural employment guarantee in India. In: Papadimitriou DB, ed. *Contributions to Economic Theory, Policy, Development and Finance: Essays in Honour of Jan A. Kregel*. London, Palgrave Macmillan: 145–171.

Glyn A (2006). *Capitalism Unleashed: Finance, Globalization, and Welfare*. Oxford, Oxford University Press.

Graz J-C (2016). The Havana Charter: When State and market shake hands. In: Reinert ES, Ghosh J and Kattel R, eds. *Handbook of Alternative Theories of Economic Development*. Cheltenham, Edward Elgar Publishing: 281–290.

Griffith-Jones S, Griffith-Jones D and Hertova D (2008). Enhancing the role of regional development banks. G-24 Discussion Paper Series No. 50, UNCTAD, Geneva.

Hazeldine T (2017). Revolt of the rustbelt. *New Left Review*, 105: 51–79.

Helleiner E (2013). Back to the future? The social protection floor of Bretton Woods. *Global Social Policy*, 14(3): 298–318.

Hiltzik M (2012). *The New Deal: A Modern History*. New York, NY, Free Press.

Huang PCC (2012). Profit-making State firms and China's development experience: "State Capitalism" or "Socialist Market Economy"? *Modern China*, 38(6): 591–629.

Huber E and Stephens JD (2012). *Democracy and the Left: Social Policy and Inequality in Latin America*. Chicago, IL, University of Chicago Press.

ILO (2017). *World Employment and Social Outlook: Trends for Women 2017*. Geneva, International Labour Organization.

IMF (2015). How large are global energy subsidies? Working Paper No.15/105, International Monetary Fund, Washington, DC.

ITUC (2016). Investing in the care economy: A gender analysis of employment stimulus in seven OECD countries. International Trade Union Confederation, Brussels.

James S (2012). *Sex, Race, and Class – The Perspective of Winning: A Selection of Writings, 1952–2011*. Oakland, CA, PM Press.

Katznelson I (2013). *Fear Itself: The New Deal and the Origins of Our Time*. New York, NY, W.W. Norton and Company.

Keen M and Mansour M (2009). Revenue mobilization in Sub-Saharan Africa: Challenges from globalization. Working Paper No. 09/157, International Monetary Fund, Washington, DC.

Kelber H (2008). How the New Deal created millions of jobs to lift the American people from Depression. *The Labour Educator*. Available at: http://www.laboureducator.org/newdeal2.htm.

Kindleberger CP (1989). *The German Economy, 1945–1947: Charles P. Kindleberger's letters from the field*. Westport, CT, Meckler.

Korpi W and Palme J (1998). The paradox of redistribution and strategies of equality: Welfare State institutions, inequality and poverty in the Western countries. *American Sociological Review*, 63(5): 661–687.

Kozul-Wright R and Rayment P (2007). *The Resistible Rise of Market Fundamentalism: Rethinking Development Policy in an Unbalanced World*. London, Zed Books.

Kregel J (2017). The concert of interests in the age of Trump. Policy Note No. 2, Levy Economics Institute of Bard College, Annandale-on-Hudson, NY.

Lahoti R, Jayadev A and Reddy SG (2016). The global consumption and income project (GCIP): An overview. Working paper (27 March version). Data available at: www.gcip.info.

Lavinas L (2013). 21st century welfare. *New Left Review* (84): 5–40.

Le Grand J (2006). *Motivation, Agency, and Public Policy: Of Knights and Knaves, Pawns and Queens*. Oxford, Oxford University Press.

Leite CA (2012). The role of transfer pricing in illicit financial flows. In: Reuter P, ed. *Draining Development? Controlling Flows of Illicit Funds from Developing Countries*. Washington, DC, World Bank: 235–264

Leuchtenburg WE (2009). *Franklin D. Roosevelt and the New Deal: 1932-1940*. New York, NY, Harper Perennial.

Levy F and Temin P (2007). Inequality and institutions in 20th century America. Working Paper No. 13106, National Bureau of Economic Research, Cambridge, MA.

Ljungqvist A and Smolyansky M (2014).To cut or not to cut? The impact of corporate taxes on employment and income. Working Paper No. 20753, National Bureau of Economic Research, Cambridge, MA.

Mazower M (1998). *Dark Continent: Europe's Twentieth Century*. London, Penguin Books.

Mazower M (2014). *Governing the World: The History of an Idea*. London, Penguin Books.

Meskoub M (2015). Cash transfer as a social policy instrument or a tool of adjustment policy: From indirect subsidies (to energy and utilities) to cash subsidies in Iran, 2010–2014. Working Paper No. 610, International Institute of Social Studies, Erasmus University, Rotterdam.

Meyerson H (2017). Place matters. *The American Prospect,* 22 June.

Mineshima A, Poplawski-Ribeiro M and Weber A (2014). Size of Fiscal multipliers. In: Cottarelli C, Gerson P and Senhadji A, eds. *Post-Crisis Fiscal Policy*. Cambridge, MA, MIT Press: 315–372.

Minsky HP (2013). *Ending Poverty: Jobs, Not Welfare* (edited by Papadimitriou DB, Wray LR and Kregel J). Annandale-on-Hudson, NY, Levy Economics Institute of Bard College.

Minsky HP (1965). The role of employment policy. Hyman P Minsky Archive Paper No. 270. Available at: http://digitalcommons.bard.edu/hm_archive/270.

Mkandawire T (2005). Targeting and universalism in poverty reduction. Social Policy and Development Programme Paper, No. 23, United Nations Research Institute for Social Development, Geneva.

Muchlinski PT (2007). *Multinational Enterprises & the Law*. Oxford, The Oxford International Law Library.

Munchau W (2016). The end of the era of central bank independence. *Financial Times*, 13 November. Available at: https://www.ft.com/content/8d52615e-a82a-11e6-8898-79a99e2a4de6 .

Murphy R (2012). How companies avoid tax – a quick summary in 8,000 words. Available at: http://www.taxresearch.org.uk/Blog/2012/01/06/how-companies-avoid-tax-a-quick-summary-in-8000-words/.

Oye Moene K and Wallerstein M (2006). Social democracy as a development strategy. In: Bardhan P, Bowles S and Wallerstein M, eds. *Globalization and Egalitarian Redistribution*. Princeton, NJ, Princeton University Press: 148–168.

Patel KK (2016). *The New Deal: A Global History*. Princeton, NJ, Princeton University Press.

Pollin R, Garrett-Peltier H, Heintz J and Hendricks B (2014). Green growth: A U.S. program for controlling climate change and expanding job opportunities. Center for American Progress. Available at: https://cdn.americanprogress.org/wp-content/uploads/2014/09/ PERI.pdf.

Pollin R, Garrett-Peltier H, Heintz J and Chakraborty S (2015). *Global Green Growth: Clean Energy Industrial Investments and Expanding Job Opportunities (Vol. I and Vol. II)*. Vienna and Seoul, United Nations Industrial Development Organization and Global Green Growth Institute.

Rauchway E (2008). *The Great Depression and the New Deal: A Very Short Introduction*. Oxford, Oxford University Press.

Ringen S. Kwon H-J, Yi I, Kim T and Lee J (2011). *The Korean State and Social Policy: How South Korea Lifted Itself from Poverty and Dictatorship to Affluence and Democracy*. Oxford, Oxford University Press.

Rogers B (2017). Basic income in a just society. *Boston Review,* 15 May. Available at: http://bostonreview.net/forum/brishen-rogers-basic-income-just-society.

Salidjanova N (2013). China's new income inequality reform plan and implications for rebalancing. U.S.-China Economic and Security Review Commission, Washington, DC.

Schneider M (2015). Why the tech elite is getting behind universal basic income. *Vice*, 6 January. Available at: https://www.vice.com/en_us/article/mv5d3y/something-for-everyone-0000546-v22n1.

Smith A ([1759] 2002). *The Theory of Moral Sentiments*. Reprinted in series: *Cambridge Texts in the History of Philosophy*. Cambridge, Cambridge University Press.

Smith A ([1776] 2008). *An Inquiry into the Nature and Causes of the Wealth of Nations*. Oxford, Oxford University Press.

Standing G (2016). *The Corruption of Capitalism: Why Rentiers Thrive and Work Does Not Pay*. London, Biteback Publishing.

Standing G and Orton I (2017). Development and basic income: An emerging economic model. Background paper prepared for UNCTAD, Geneva. Unpublished.

Toplensky R (2017). EU considers tougher competition powers. *Financial Times*, 2 July.

UNCTAD (2006). *Economic Development in Africa Report 2006: Doubling Aid –Making the "Big Push" Work*. United Nations publication. Sales No. E.06. II.D.10. New York and Geneva.

UNCTAD (2014). *World Investment Report 2014: Investing in the SDGs – an Action Plan*. United Nations publication. Sales No. E.14.II.D.1. New York and Geneva.

UNCTAD (2015a). *From Decisions to Actions*. Report of the Secretary-General of UNCTAD to UNCTAD XIV. United Nations publication. Geneva, UNCTAD.

UNCTAD (2015b). *World Investment Report 2015: Reforming International Investment Governance*. United Nations publication. Sales No. E.15.II.D.5. New York and Geneva.

UNCTAD (2016). The Role of Development Banks in Promoting Growth and Sustainable Development in the South. United Nations publication. New York and Geneva.

UNCTAD (*TDR 2010*). *Trade and Development Report 2010: Employment, Globalization and Development*. United Nations publication. Sales No. E.10.II.D3. New York and Geneva.

UNCTAD (*TDR 2013*). *Trade and Development Report 2013: Adjusting to the Changing Dynamics of the World Economy*. United Nations publication. Sales No. E.13.II.D3. New York and Geneva.

UNCTAD (*TDR 2014*). *Trade and Development Report 2014: Global Governance and Policy Space for Development*. United Nations publication. Sales No. E.14.II.D3. New York and Geneva.

UNCTAD (*TDR 2015*). *Trade and Development Report 2015: Making the International Financial Architecture Work for Development*. United Nations publication. Sales No. E.15.II.D3. New York and Geneva.

UNCTAD (*TDR 2016*). *Trade and Development Report 2016: Structural Transformation for Inclusive and Sustained Growth*. United Nations publication. Sales No. E.16.II.D3. New York and Geneva.

United Nations (2009). *World Economic and Social Survey 2009*. United Nations publication. Sales No. E.09. II.C.1. New York.

Varoufakis Y (2017). The universal right to capital income. Project Syndicate, 31 October. Available at: https://www.project-syndicate.org/commentary/basic-income-funded-by-capital-income-by-yanis-varoufakis-2016-10?barrier=accessreg.

Women's Budget Group (2017). Investing in the care economy: Simulating employment effects by gender in countries in emerging economies. International Trade Union Confederation and United Nations Women, Brussels.

World Bank (2013). *Inclusion Matters: The Foundation for Shared Prosperity*. Washington, DC.

Wren-Lewis S (2017). Underestimating the impact of austerity. *Mainly Macro*, 7 May.

Zingales L (2017). Towards a political theory of the firm. New Working Paper Series No. 10, University of Chicago Booth School of Business, Chicago, IL.

Zucman G (2015). *The Hidden Wealth of Nations: The Scourge of Tax Havens*. Chicago, IL, Chicago University Press.

TRADE AND DEVELOPMENT REPORT
Past issues